CIMA EXAMINATION TEXT

Intermediate Level
Paper 7a

Financial Reporting
UK Accounting Standards

ISBN 184390 247 8

British Library Cataloguing-in-Publication data

A catalogue record for this book is available from the British Library.

We are grateful to the Chartered Institute of Management Accountants for permission to reproduce past examination questions. The solutions have been prepared by The Financial Training Company.

Published by

The Financial Training Company
22J Wincombe Business Park
Shaftesbury
Dorset
SP7 9QJ

Contents

	Page
How to use this examination text	v
Syllabus	vii
Mathematical tables	xi
Meaning of CIMA's examination requirements	xiv
Examinable documents covered in this text	xv
Objective test questions	xvii

Chapter

Group financial statements

1	The consolidated balance sheet: basic principles	1
2	The consolidated balance sheet: further issues	19
3	The consolidated balance sheet: associates and joint ventures	35
4	The consolidated profit and loss account	45
5	Fair values in acquisition accounting	63
6	Accounting for mergers	69
7	Group accounts: complex structures	81
8	Group accounts: piecemeal acquisitions	101
9	Foreign currency: direct transactions	113
10	Foreign currency: indirect transactions	123
11	Group accounts: disposals	143
12	Group accounts: cash flow statements	161
13	Capital reconstruction schemes	183

The measurement of income and capital

14	Conceptual framework	195
15	Reporting financial performance	205
16	Price level accounting	231
17	Accounting for tangible fixed assets	247
18	Intangibles	257
19	Tax	271
20	Pensions	283
21	Reporting the substance of transactions	291
22	Financial instruments	299
23	Leasing	313

Developments in financial reporting

24	International issues	327
25	Environmental and social reporting	339

The analysis of financial statements

26	Ratio analysis	347
27	Earnings per share	367
28	Segmental reporting	375
29	Solutions to practice questions	379
Index		475

How to use this examination text

Objective

The aim of this Examination Text is a simple one: to give you the best possible chance of achieving the pass mark when you attempt the CIMA Financial Reporting – UK Accounting Standards examination. To do this, we follow three main principles:

♦ The text covers **all** areas of the syllabus with sufficient depth to ensure that you are fully prepared. However, we use our knowledge and experience to home in on the key syllabus areas and give these areas extra attention.

♦ We use our extensive experience of teaching CIMA students to assess how much the majority of students can assimilate. We do not make the mistake of overloading you with material that you will find worthless in the examination room.

♦ We believe that the best way to prepare for an examination is by practice. We intersperse explanatory text with frequent examples for you to try your hand at. Full solutions are provided in all cases.

Using the Examination Text

Each chapter begins with a section headed 'Exam focus'. This reflects our key objective: we are interested above all in your examination success.

We set out CIMA's own Learning Outcomes and the main structural divisions into which the chapter is organised. This gives you a clear picture of what you should be aiming to achieve as you work through the text, and guidance on the steps to follow on the way.

The main body of each chapter consists of very full explanation of all syllabus areas. We concentrate on clear explanations of what really matters. We emphasise drills — standardised approaches that you can follow for typical questions. Never again need you ask: 'Where do I begin?'

Most chapters include several practice questions. These are graded: earlier questions involve material from the earlier sections of the chapter, while in later questions we progress to include more complex examples, including exam-standard questions. To get the best from the text you should make a serious attempt to tackle all the practice questions. Only then should you refer to our suggested solutions, which are contained in the final chapter of the text.

Each chapter ends by summarising the main points that you should have digested as you worked your way through.

Key features

The text is written in an interactive style:

- ◆ key terms and concepts are clearly defined

- ◆ 'pitfalls' and 'examination tips' help you avoid commonly made mistakes and help you focus on what is required to perform well in your examination

- ◆ frequent practice examples throughout the chapters ensure that what you have learnt is regularly reinforced

Icons

Throughout the text we use symbols to highlight the elements referred to above.

 Key facts

 Examination tips and techniques

 Pitfalls

 Practice questions

Syllabus

Syllabus overview

This syllabus is an advanced study of financial accounting. It concerns the financial statements of groups of companies in an international context prepared in accordance with UK Generally Accepted Accounting Practice (GAAP). Students elect to answer in terms of Financial Reporting Standards (FRSs), Statements of Standard Accounting Practice (SSAPs) and UK company legislation but they should also be familiar in general terms with major differences of practice between UK GAAP, International Accounting Standards (IASs) and USA GAAP. A detailed knowledge of individual IASs or USA accounting standards will not be required. It should also be noted that certain concepts utilise terms seen in the wider accounting literature and not just those found in FRSs and SSAPs.

This syllabus will draw upon all of the accounting standards seen in the earlier paper, Financial Accounting. However, the following earlier standards seen in that syllabus will be particularly relevant to questions asked in this paper: SSAPs 21, 25 and FRSs 1, 3, 4, 5, 10, 11, 12, 14, 15, 18 and 19. It should be noted that some of these standards are shown again within this syllabus where their content is relevant to group situations.

Aims

This syllabus aims to test the student's ability to:

♦ prepare financial statements for groups of companies, for publication in accordance with UK accounting standards;

♦ evaluate accounting practice with particular reference to capital maintenance theory, asset valuation and disclosure and the expression of economic substance over legal form;

♦ evaluate recent developments under discussion to improve the regulation of financial reporting;

♦ analyse and interpret financial statements in an international context.

Assessment

There will be a written paper of three hours. There will be three sections: section A will be compulsory as 10 multiple choice questions for 20% of the marks; section B will be a compulsory question on consolidated accounts for 30% of the marks; and section C will offer a choice of two from four questions for 50% of the marks.

Learning outcomes and syllabus content

	Chapter where covered in this textbook

7a(i)   Group financial statements – 45%

Learning outcomes

On completion of their studies students should be able to:

♦ Explain the conditions required for an undertaking to be a subsidiary or an associate of a group	1, 3
♦ Explain and apply the rules for the exclusion of subsidiaries from consolidation	1
♦ Prepare a consolidated profit and loss account and a consolidated balance sheet for a group of companies	1, 2, 4, 7
♦ Prepare a group cash flow statement with appropriate notes	12
♦ Explain and apply the concept of fair value at the point of acquisition	5
♦ Prepare financial statements when a subsidiary is acquired or disposed of part way through an accounting period; to include the effective date of acquisition and dividends out of pre-acquisition profits	2, 11
♦ Prepare consolidated financial statements where the shareholdings, or control, are acquired in stages	8
♦ Explain the concept of an associate and a joint venture	3
♦ Prepare consolidated financial statements to include an associate or joint venture within the group	3, 4
♦ Explain the merger method of consolidation	6
♦ Prepare consolidated financial statements under the merger method	6
♦ Compare and contrast merger, acquisition and equity methods of accounting	6
♦ Prepare accounts for a capital reconstruction scheme or a demerger	11, 13
♦ Explain and apply foreign currency translation principles	9
♦ Explain the difference between the closing rate/net investment method and the temporal method	10
♦ Explain the correct treatment for foreign loans financing foreign equity investments	9

Syllabus content

♦ Relationships between investors and investees and the exclusion of subsidiaries from consolidation with reference to dominant influence, participating interest, managed on a unified basis and significant influence	1-8
♦ The preparation of consolidated financial statements (to include the group cash flow statement) involving one or more subsidiaries, sub-subsidiaries and associates, under the acquisition and merger methods (FRS 1 + 2 + 6 + 10)	1-8, 12
♦ The treatment in consolidated accounts of minority interests, pre- and post-acquisition reserves, goodwill, fair value adjustments (FRS 7), intra-group transactions and dividends, piece-meal and mid-year acquisitions, and disposals to include sub-subsidiaries and mixed groups	1-8
♦ The accounting treatment of joint ventures and associates (FRS 9) using the equity method and proportional consolidation method	3, 4

	Chapter where covered in this textbook

♦ The accounting entries for mergers, demergers and capital reconstruction schemes — 11, 13

♦ Foreign currency translation (SSAP 20) to include overseas transactions and investments in overseas subsidiaries — 9, 10

7a(ii)   The measurement of income and capital – 20%

Learning outcomes

On completion of their studies students should be able to:

♦ Explain the problems of profit measurement and alternative approaches to asset valuations — 16, 17, 18

♦ Explain measures to reduce distortion in financial statements when price levels change — 16

♦ Discuss the principle of Substance over Form to a range of transactions — 21

♦ Explain the difference between liabilities and shareholders' funds, and allocate finance costs appropriately — 22

♦ Explain the recognition and valuation issues concerned with pension schemes and the treatment of actuarial deficits and surpluses — 20

Syllabus content

♦ The problems of profit measurement and the effect of alternative approaches to asset valuation; current cost and current purchasing power bases and the real terms system; accounting for hyper inflation (UITF abstract 9) — 16, 17, 18

♦ The principle of Substance over Form (FRS 5) and its application to transactions including debt factoring, securitised assets, loan transfers and the Private Finance Initiative (PFI) — 21

♦ The accounting treatment of goodwill, intangible and tangible assets (FRS 10 + 15) — 17, 18

♦ Impairment of fixed assets, brands and goodwill (FRS 11) — 18

♦ Capitalisation of interest (FRS 15), and discounting — 17, 18

♦ Provisions and contingent liabilities and contingent assets (FRS 12) — 15

♦ Capital instruments classified as liabilities or shareholders funds and the allocation of finance costs over the term of the borrowing (FRS 4) — 22

♦ The measurement and disclosure of financial instruments (FRS 13) — 22

♦ Retirement benefits, including pension schemes – defined benefit schemes and defined contribution schemes, actuarial deficits and surpluses (FRS 17) — 20

7a(iii)   Developments in financial reporting – 15%

Learning outcomes

On completion of their studies students should be able to:

♦ Explain how financial information concerning the interaction of a business with the natural environment can be communicated in the published accounts — 25

♦ Identify those environmental issues which should be disclosed — 25

♦ Explain the process of measuring, recording and disclosing the effect of exchanges between a business and its sociological environment – human resource accounting — 25

♦ Identify the influences on financial reporting of cultural differences across the world — 24

	Chapter where covered in this textbook

- ◆ Identify major differences between UK GAAP, IASs and US GAAP — 24
- ◆ Discuss emerging developments in financial reporting evidenced by discussion and exposure drafts issued by regulatory bodies — 14, 19, 20

Syllabus content

- ◆ Environmental and social accounting issues; differentiating between environmental measures and environmental losses, and explain the capitalisation of environmental expenditure, and the recognition of future environmental costs by means of provisions — 25
- ◆ Human resource accounting — 25
- ◆ The influence of different cultures on financial reporting — 24
- ◆ Major differences between UK GAAP, US GAAP and IASs — 24
- ◆ Emerging issues and exposure drafts issued by the regulators — 14, 19, 20

7a(iv)   The analysis of financial statements – 20%

Learning outcomes

On completion of their studies students should be able to:

- ◆ Evaluate financial statements and prepare a concise report on the results of the analysis — 26, 27, 28
- ◆ Identify the limitations of analysis based on financial statements — 26
- ◆ Explain the weaknesses of the financial report which reduce its effectiveness in communicating meaningful information to users — 26
- ◆ Prepare and interpret segmental analysis, inter-firm and international comparisons — 24, 26, 28

Syllabus content

- ◆ Advanced aspects of the interpretation of financial statements via the analysis of corporate reports — 26, 27, 28
- ◆ The identification of information required to assess financial performance and the extent to which financial statements fail to provide such information — 26
- ◆ Ratios in the areas of performance, profitability, financial adaptability, liquidity, activity and gearing of business — 26
- ◆ Segmental analysis; inter-firm and international comparison (SSAP 25) — 28

MATHEMATICAL TABLES

PRESENT VALUE TABLE

Present value of £1 ie $(1 + r)^{-n}$ where r = interest rate, n = number of periods until payment or receipt.

Periods (n)	Interest rates (r)																			
	1%	2%	3%	4%	5%	6%	7%	8%	9%	10%	11%	12%	13%	14%	15%	16%	17%	18%	19%	20%
1	.990	.980	.971	.962	.952	.943	.935	.926	.917	.909	.901	.893	.885	.877	.870	.862	.855	.847	.840	.833
2	.980	.961	.943	.925	.907	.890	.873	.857	.842	.826	.812	.797	.783	.769	.756	.743	.731	.718	.706	.694
3	.971	.942	.915	.889	.864	.840	.816	.794	.772	.751	.731	.712	.693	.675	.658	.641	.624	.609	.593	.579
4	.961	.924	.888	.855	.823	.792	.763	.735	.708	.683	.659	.636	.613	.592	.572	.552	.534	.516	.499	.482
5	.951	.906	.863	.822	.784	.747	.713	.681	.650	.621	.593	.567	.543	.519	.497	.476	.456	.437	.419	.402
6	.942	.888	.837	.790	.746	.705	.666	.630	.596	.564	.535	.507	.480	.456	.432	.410	.390	.370	.352	.335
7	.933	.871	.813	.760	.711	.665	.623	.583	.547	.513	.482	.452	.425	.400	.376	.354	.333	.314	.296	.279
8	.923	.853	.789	.731	.677	.627	.582	.540	.502	.467	.434	.404	.376	.351	.327	.305	.285	.266	.249	.233
9	.914	.837	.766	.703	.645	.592	.544	.500	.460	.424	.391	.361	.333	.308	.284	.263	.243	.225	.209	.194
10	.905	.820	.744	.676	.614	.558	.508	.463	.422	.386	.352	.322	.295	.270	.247	.227	.208	.191	.176	.162
11	.896	.804	.722	.650	.585	.527	.475	.429	.388	.350	.317	.287	.261	.237	.215	.195	.178	.162	.148	.135
12	.887	.788	.701	.625	.557	.497	.444	.397	.356	.319	.286	.257	.231	.208	.187	.168	.152	.137	.124	.112
13	.879	.773	.681	.601	.530	.469	.415	.368	.326	.290	.258	.229	.204	.182	.163	.145	.130	.116	.104	.093
14	.870	.758	.661	.577	.505	.442	.388	.340	.299	.263	.232	.205	.181	.160	.141	.125	.111	.099	.088	.078
15	.861	.743	.642	.555	.481	.417	.362	.315	.275	.239	.209	.183	.160	.140	.123	.108	.095	.084	.074	.065
16	.853	.728	.623	.534	.458	.394	.339	.292	.252	.218	.188	.163	.141	.123	.107	.093	.081	.071	.062	.054
17	.844	.714	.605	.513	.436	.371	.317	.270	.231	.198	.170	.146	.125	.108	.093	.080	.069	.060	.052	.045
18	.836	.700	.587	.494	.416	.350	.296	.250	.212	.180	.153	.130	.111	.095	.081	.069	.059	.051	.044	.038
19	.828	.686	.570	.475	.396	.331	.277	.232	.194	.164	.138	.116	.098	.083	.070	.060	.051	.043	.037	.031
20	.820	.673	.554	.456	.377	.312	.258	.215	.178	.149	.124	.104	.087	.073	.061	.051	.043	.037	.031	.026

CUMULATIVE PRESENT VALUE OF £1

This table shows the Present Value of £1 per annum, receivable or payable at the end of each year for *n* years $\dfrac{1-(1+r)^{-n}}{r}$.

Periods (n)	\multicolumn{20}{c}{Interest rates (r)}																		
	1%	2%	3%	4%	5%	6%	7%	8%	9%	10%	11%	12%	13%	14%	15%	16%	17%	18%	19%	20%
1	.990	.980	.971	.962	.952	.943	.935	.926	.917	.909	.901	.893	.885	.877	.870	.862	.855	.847	.840	.833
2	1.970	1.942	1.913	1.886	1.859	1.833	1.808	1.783	1.759	1.736	1.713	1.690	1.668	1.647	1.626	1.605	1.585	1.566	1.547	1.528
3	2.941	2.884	2.829	2.775	2.723	2.673	2.624	2.577	2.531	2.487	2.444	2.402	2.361	2.322	2.283	2.246	2.210	2.174	2.140	2.106
4	3.902	3.808	3.717	3.630	3.546	3.465	3.387	3.312	3.240	3.170	3.102	3.037	2.974	2.914	2.855	2.798	2.743	2.690	2.639	2.589
5	4.853	4.713	4.580	4.452	4.329	4.212	4.100	3.993	3.890	3.791	3.696	3.605	3.517	3.433	3.352	3.274	3.199	3.127	3.058	2.991
6	5.795	5.601	5.417	5.242	5.076	4.917	4.767	4.623	4.486	4.355	4.231	4.111	3.998	3.889	3.784	3.685	3.589	3.498	3.410	3.326
7	6.728	6.472	6.230	6.002	5.786	5.582	5.389	5.206	5.033	4.868	4.712	4.564	4.423	4.288	4.160	4.039	3.922	3.812	3.706	3.605
8	7.652	7.325	7.020	6.733	6.463	6.210	5.971	5.747	5.535	5.335	5.146	4.968	4.799	4.639	4.487	4.344	4.207	4.078	3.954	3.837
9	8.566	8.162	7.786	7.435	7.108	6.802	6.515	6.247	5.995	5.759	5.537	5.328	5.132	4.946	4.772	4.607	4.451	4.303	4.163	4.031
10	9.471	8.983	8.530	8.111	7.722	7.360	7.024	6.710	6.418	6.145	5.889	5.650	5.426	5.216	5.019	4.833	4.659	4.494	4.339	4.192
11	10.368	9.787	9.253	8.760	8.306	7.887	7.499	7.139	6.805	6.495	6.207	5.938	5.687	5.453	5.234	5.029	4.836	4.656	4.486	4.327
12	11.255	10.575	9.954	9.385	8.863	8.384	7.943	7.536	7.161	6.814	6.492	6.194	5.918	5.660	5.421	5.197	4.988	4.793	4.611	4.439
13	12.134	11.348	10.635	9.986	9.394	8.853	8.358	7.904	7.487	7.103	6.750	6.424	6.122	5.842	5.583	5.342	5.118	4.910	4.715	4.533
14	13.004	12.106	11.296	10.563	9.899	9.295	8.745	8.244	7.786	7.367	6.982	6.628	6.302	6.002	5.724	5.468	5.229	5.008	4.802	4.611
15	13.865	12.849	11.938	11.118	10.380	9.712	9.108	8.559	8.061	7.606	7.191	6.811	6.462	6.142	5.847	5.575	5.324	5.092	4.876	4.675
16	14.718	13.578	12.561	11.652	10.838	10.106	9.447	8.851	8.313	7.824	7.379	6.974	6.604	6.265	5.954	5.668	5.405	5.162	4.938	4.730
17	15.562	14.292	13.166	12.166	11.274	10.477	9.763	9.122	8.544	8.022	7.549	7.120	6.729	6.373	6.047	5.749	5.475	5.222	4.990	4.775
18	16.398	14.992	13.754	12.659	11.690	10.828	10.059	9.372	8.756	8.201	7.702	7.250	6.840	6.467	6.128	5.818	5.534	5.273	5.033	4.812
19	17.226	15.679	14.324	13.134	12.085	11.158	10.336	9.604	8.950	8.365	7.839	7.366	6.938	6.550	6.198	5.877	5.584	5.316	5.070	4.843
20	18.046	16.351	14.878	13.590	12.462	11.470	10.594	9.818	9.129	8.514	7.963	7.469	7.025	6.623	6.259	5.929	5.628	5.353	5.101	4.870

FORMULAE

Annuity

Present value of an annuity of £1 per annum, receivable or payable for n years, commencing in one year, discounted at r% per annum:

$$PV = \frac{1}{r} \left[1 - \frac{1}{(1+r)^n} \right]$$

Perpetuity

Present value of £1 per annum, payable or receivable in perpetuity, commencing in one year, discounted at r% per annum:

$$PV = \frac{1}{r}$$

Growing Perpetuity

Present value of £1 per annum, receivable or payable, commencing in one year, growing in perpetuity at a constant rate of g% per annum, discounted at r% per annum:

$$PV = \frac{1}{r-g}$$

Meaning of CIMA's examination requirements

CIMA use precise words in the requirements of their questions. In the schedule below we reproduce the precise meanings of these words from the CIMA syllabus. You must learn these definitions and make sure that in the exam you do precisely what CIMA requires you to do.

Learning objective	Verbs used	Definition
1 Knowledge What you are expected to know	List	Make a list of
	State	Express, fully or clearly, the details of/facts of
	Define	Give the exact meaning of
2 Comprehension What you are expected to understand	Describe	Communicate the key features of
	Distinguish	Highlight the differences between
	Explain	Make clear or intelligible/state the meaning of
	Identify	Recognise, establish or select after consideration
	Illustrate	Use an example to describe or explain something
3 Application Can you apply your knowledge?	Apply	To put to practical use
	Calculate/compute	To ascertain or reckon mathematically
	Demonstrate	To prove with certainty or to exhibit by practical means
	Prepare	To make or get ready for use
	Reconcile	To make or prove consistent/compatible
	Solve	Find an answer to
	Tabulate	Arrange in a table
4 Analysis Can you analyse the detail of what you have learned?	Analyse	Examine in detail the structure of
	Categorise	Place into a defined class or division
	Compare and contrast	Show the similarities and/or differences between
	Construct	To build up or compile
	Discuss	To examine in detail by argument
	Interpret	To translate into intelligible or familiar terms
	Produce	To create or bring into existence
5 Evaluation Can you use your learning to evaluate, make decisions or recommendations?	Advise	To counsel, inform or notify
	Evaluate	To appraise or assess the value of
	Recommend	To advise on a course of action

Examinable Documents

Listed below are the examinable documents for this Paper, referenced to the place in the text where they are primarily covered.

Statements of Standard Accounting Practice (SSAPs)

No	Title	Issue date	Page
4	Accounting for government grants (revised)	July 1990	249
5	Accounting for value added tax	April 1974	263
9	Stocks and long-term contracts (revised)	Sept 1988	322
19	Accounting for investment properties (revised)	July 1994	243
20	Foreign currency translation	April 1983	115
21	Accounting for leases and hire purchase contracts (revised)	Feb 1997	301
25	Segmental reporting	June 1990	363

(Tutorial note. Although SSAP 13 and SSAP 17 are not listed in the examinable documents identified by CIMA, they are assumed knowledge for this paper and so are included in this text, SSAP 13 on page 253 and SSAP 17 on page 321.)

Financial Reporting Standards (FRSs)

No	Title	Issue date	Page
FRS 1	Cash flow statements (revised)	Oct 1996	162
FRS 2	Accounting for subsidiary undertakings	July 1992	14
FRS 3	Reporting financial performance	Oct 1992	203
FRS 4	Capital instruments	Dec 1993	287
FRS 5	Reporting the substance of transactions	April 1994	282
FRS 6	Acquisitions and mergers	Sept 1994	73
FRS 7	Fair values in acquisition accounting	Sept 1994	65
FRS 8	Related party disclosures	Oct 1995	321
FRS 9	Associates and joint ventures	Nov 1997	36
FRS 10	Goodwill and intangible assets	Dec 1997	251
FRS 11	Impairment of fixed assets and goodwill	July 1998	258
FRS 12	Provisions, contingent liabilities and contingent assets	Sept 1998	218
FRS 13	Derivatives and other financial instruments: disclosures	Sept 1998	291
FRS 14	Earnings per share	Oct 1998	355
FRS 15	Tangible fixed assets	Feb 1999	243
FRS 16	Current tax	Dec 1999	265
FRS 17	Retirement benefits	Nov 2000	275
FRS 18	Accounting policies	Dec 2000	200
FRS 19	Deferred tax	Dec 2000	272
FRSSE	Financial reporting standard for smaller entities	Dec 2001	221

UITF Abstracts

Title			Issue date	Page
UITF	Abstract 4	Presentation of long-term debtors in current assets	July 1992	202
UITF	Abstract 5	Transfers from current assets to fixed assets	July 1992	249
UITF	Abstract 9	Accounting for operations in hyper-inflationary economies	June 1993	140
UITF	Abstract 19	Tax on gains and losses on foreign currency borrowings that hedge an investment in a foreign enterprise	Feb 1998	140
UITF	Abstract 21	Accounting issues arising from the proposed introduction of the euro	Mar 1998	140
UITF	Abstract 27	Revisions to estimates of the useful economic life of goodwill and intangible assets	Dec 2000	253
UITF	Abstract 29	Website development costs	Feb 2001	249

Other documents

Title			Issue date	Page
Statement of principles			Dec 1999	195
Operating and financial review			Jan 2003	327

Financial Reporting Exposure Drafts (FREDs)

FRED 22	Revision of FRS 3 'Reporting financial performance'		Dec 2000	217
FRED 23	Financial instruments: hedge accounting		May 2002	297
FRED 24	The effects of changes in foreign exchange rates; Financial reporting in hyperinflationary economies		May 2002	141
FRED 25	Related party disclosures		May 2002	321
FRED 26	Earnings per share		May 2002	361
FRED 27	Events after the balance sheet date		May 2002	321
FRED 28	Inventories; Construction and service contracts		May 2002	322
FRED 29	Property, plant and equipment; Borrowing costs		May 2002	248
FRED 30	Financial instruments: Disclosure and presentation; Recognition and measurement		June 2002	298
FRED 31	Share-based payment		Nov 2002	223
	Amendment to FRS 5: revenue recognition		Feb 2003	286

Discussion papers

		Issue date	Page
Business combinations		Dec 1998	79
Review of the FRSSE		Feb 2001	222
Leases: implementation of a new approach		Dec 1999	312
Year-end financial reports: improving communication		Feb 2000	216
Reporting financial performance: proposals for change		June 1999	216
Statement of Principles for financial reporting: Proposed interpretation for public benefit entities		May 2003	200

Objective test questions

The objective test questions will comprise a question with four possible answers. For example,

1   What is the world's tallest mountain?

      A   Ben Nevis

      B   K2

      C   Mount Everest

      D   Mount Snowdon

You have to select the correct answer (which in the above example is of course C).

In the examination, however, the incorrect answers, called distractors, may be quite plausible and are sometimes designed if not exactly to mislead you, they may nevertheless be the result of fairly common mistakes.

The following is a suggested technique for answering these questions, but as you practise for the examination you have to work out a method which suits you.

Step 1

Read all the questions, but not necessarily the answers. Select the ones which you think are the most straightforward and do them first.

Step 2

For more awkward questions, some people prefer to work the question without reference to the answers which increases your confidence if your answer then matches one of the options. However some people prefer to view the question with the four answers as this may assist them in formulating their answer.

This is a matter of personal preference and you should perhaps practise each to see which you find most effective.

Step 3

If your answer does not match one of the options you must:

(a)   Re-read the question carefully to make sure you have not missed some important point.

(b)   Re-work your solution eliminating any mistakes.

(c)   Beware the plausible distractors but do not become paranoid. The examiner is not trying to trip you up and the answer should be a straightforward calculation from the question.

Step 4

Time allocation. As with all questions you must not overrun your time. The questions are technically worth only two marks each which is about three to four minutes per question. It is very easy to get bogged down. If you cannot get one of the right answers then move on to the next question.

Step 5

When you have finished all the questions go back to the ones you have not answered.

Keep an eye on the clock – don't overrun the time allocation.

If you really cannot do it, **have a guess**. You are not penalised for wrong answers. **Never leave any questions unanswered.**

xviii

CHAPTER 1

The consolidated balance sheet: basic principles

EXAM FOCUS

Group accounts is considered by the examiner to be a core topic on the Paper 7a syllabus. It makes up 45% of the syllabus and the examiner has said that half of the multiple choice questions in Section A and the whole of the compulsory question in Section B will concern consolidations.

It is therefore vital to understand the rationale behind group accounts and to be able to prepare a consolidated balance sheet (CBS) and a consolidated profit and loss account (CPL).

LEARNING OUTCOMES

This chapter covers the following Learning Outcomes of the CIMA syllabus:

> Prepare a consolidated balance sheet for a group of companies
> Explain the conditions required for an undertaking to be a subsidiary of a group
> Explain and apply the rules for the exclusion of subsidiaries from consolidation

In order to cover these Learning Outcomes the following topics are included.

> The nature of group accounts
> Buying shares in another company
> Minority interests
> Control and ownership
> Accounting for reserves
> Accounting for intra-group balances
> Conditions for an undertaking to be a subsidiary
> Exemption from preparing consolidated accounts
> Exclusion of subsidiaries from consolidation

1 The nature of group accounts

1.1 Accounting issues

 If one company owns more than 50% of the ordinary shares of another company this will usually give the first company 'control' of the second company. (Note there are other criteria for control. These are covered later in this chapter).

This is because the first company (P Ltd, say) has enough voting power to appoint all the directors of the second company (S Ltd, say). P Ltd is, in effect, able to manage S Ltd as if it were merely a department of P Ltd, rather than a separate entity. In strict legal terms P Ltd and S Ltd remain distinct, but in economic substance they can be regarded as a single unit (a 'group').

The key issue underlying group accounts is the need to reflect the economic substance of the relationship.

We call the first company the 'parent' or 'holding' company and the second the 'subsidiary'. In examples and illustrations we will often use 'P Ltd' (or 'H Ltd') to denote a parent or holding company, and 'S Ltd' to denote a subsidiary company.

To reflect the true economic substance of a group of companies we need to produce group accounts in addition to the individual accounts prepared for each company within the group. One of the main methods of doing this is to prepare 'consolidated' accounts and this is the subject of the present chapter.

Consolidated accounts present the group as though it were a 'single economic entity'.

1.2 The single entity concept

Consolidated accounts consolidate the results and net assets of group members so as to display the group's affairs as those of a single economic entity. As already mentioned, this conflicts with the strict legal position that each company is a distinct entity.

Figure 1 The group as a single entity

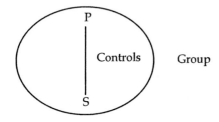

1.3 The mechanics of consolidation

A standard group accounting question will present you with the accounts of the parent company and the accounts of the subsidiary and will require you to prepare consolidated accounts.

To tackle questions of this kind we will use a formal pattern of five workings. These are listed below. In a complex example all five of these workings may be needed, but we will begin with simpler cases.

We are going to use this formal pattern of workings to illustrate the approach to these questions, starting with basic examples and gradually building in complications.

(W1) Establish the group structure

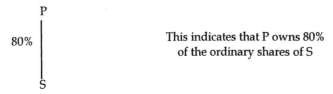

This indicates that P owns 80% of the ordinary shares of S

(W2) Set out the net assets of S

	At date of acquisition £	At the balance sheet (B/S) date £
Share capital	X	X
Profit and loss account	X	X
	X	X

(W3) **Calculate the goodwill on acquisition**

	£
Cost of shares acquired	X
Less share of net assets at acquisition (see W2)	(X)
	X

(W4) **Calculate the minority interest**

	£
Share of net assets at balance sheet date (see W2)	X

(W5) **Calculate the profit and loss reserve**

	£
P Ltd profit and loss reserve (100%)	X
S Ltd – group share of post-acquisition profits	X
Less goodwill amortised to date	(X)
	X

2 Buying shares in another company

2.1 Example

When one company buys shares in another company the cash paid is recorded as an investment in the acquiring company's balance sheet.

Example

Draft balance sheets of Polar and Squirrel on 31 December 20X1 are as follows.

	Polar Ltd £000	Squirrel Ltd £000
Tangible fixed assets	90	80
Investment in Squirrel at cost	110	
Current assets	50	30
	250	110
Creditors: amounts falling due within one year	(30)	(10)
Total assets less current liabilities	220	100
Capital and reserves		
Share capital	100	100
Profit and loss account	120	-
	220	100

Polar Ltd had just bought 100% of the shares of Squirrel on the balance sheet date.

Required

Prepare a consolidated balance sheet as at 31 December 20X1.

Exam technique

- ♦ Get organised
- ♦ Always present the answer first, supported by workings
- ♦ Set up two sheets of A4 paper

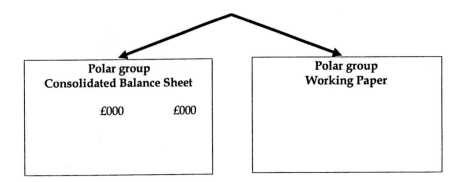

♦ Start with the workings. Then use your workings to construct the balance sheet.

2.2 Approach to the example

The starting point is to establish the group structure. We are told that Polar owns 100% of Squirrel and therefore (W1) will look like this.

(W1) Group structure

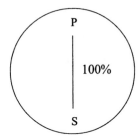

(Tutorial note. P controls S and therefore we need to prepare group accounts.)

Our second step is to focus on the net assets of the subsidiary. We calculate net assets by remembering that:

Net assets = Share capital + reserves

Squirrel Ltd has no reserves and so net assets = share capital. The balance sheet date is the same as the date of acquisition.

(W2) will look like this.

Net assets of Squirrel Ltd

	At date of acquisition	*At balance sheet date*
	£000	£000
£1 shares	100	100

The reason for preparing (W2) is so that we can go on to calculate the goodwill arising on consolidation. This is a key mark-earning calculation.

The difference between the amount P paid to acquire S ('the purchase consideration') and the share of the tangible net assets acquired is the amount P paid for goodwill. This is normally, but not always, a positive figure. In other words, P usually pays an amount greater than the value of the tangible net assets, the excess being the amount paid for the intangible asset 'goodwill'.

We use (W3) to calculate the goodwill.

(W3) *Goodwill*	£000
Purchase consideration (from P's balance sheet)	110
For 100% of net assets (£100,000) acquired (W2)	(100)
Goodwill	10

The positive goodwill is a further asset which P has paid for. It will appear as an intangible fixed asset in the consolidated balance sheet.

We are now in a position to produce a consolidated balance sheet.

Watch out for the following key points.

♦ The investment in S at cost will *never* appear in the consolidated balance sheet.

♦ The share capital of S will *never* appear in the consolidated balance sheet.

♦ The investment in S has been cancelled against the share capital on consolidation and it is only the difference between the two (ie goodwill) which appears in the consolidated balance sheet as an intangible fixed asset.

We include 100% of the assets and liabilities of both the parent and subsidiary because by definition we control these net assets. They belong to the group and must be disclosed in full in the consolidated balance sheet.

You can now produce an answer which is cross-referenced to the workings.

2.3   Solution to the example

POLAR GROUP CONSOLIDATED BALANCE SHEET AS AT 31 DECEMBER 20X1

	£000	£000
Goodwill (W3)		10
Tangible fixed assets (90 + 80) 100% P + S		170
		180
Current assets (50 + 30) 100% P + S	80	
Creditors: amounts due within one year (30 + 10) 100% P+S	(40)	
Net current assets		40
Total assets less current liabilities		220
Capital and reserves		
Share capital (100% P only)		100
Profit and loss reserve (100% P)		120
		220

2.4   Working paper

(W1)   *Group structure*

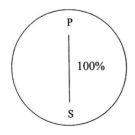

(W2)	Net assets of S	At date of acquisition £000	At balance sheet date £000
£1 shares		100	100

(W3) Goodwill	£000
Purchase consideration	110
For 100% net assets acquired	(100)
Goodwill	10

Practice question 1 *(The answer is in the final chapter of this book)*

Puffin (I)

Draft balance sheets of Puffin and Seagull on 31 December 20X1 are as follows.

	Puffin Ltd £000	Seagull Ltd £000
Tangible fixed assets	146	35
Investment in Seagull at cost	90	
Current assets	24	15
	260	50
Creditors: amounts falling due within one year	(30)	(10)
	230	40
Capital and reserves		
Share capital	100	40
Profit and loss account	130	–
	230	40

Puffin Ltd had just bought 100% of the shares of Seagull on the balance sheet date.

Required

Prepare a consolidated balance sheet as at 31 December 20X1.

3   Minority interests

3.1   Control

We said earlier that we can 'control' a company without necessarily owning it 100%. In fact any holding of more than 50% of the equity shares is usually sufficient to give control. If we own more than 50%, but less than 100%, of the equity shares of another company we need an additional working: (W4) minority interest. This calculation is necessary to reflect the third-party ownership in the net assets of the subsidiary.

3.2   Example

Suppose that Polar's investment in Squirrel represents only 80% of Squirrel's equity, not 100%. All other details remain the same.

Required

Prepare a consolidated balance sheet as at 31 December 20X1.

3.3   Approach to the example

We use exactly the same technique as before, following our standard pattern of workings.

(W1) *Group structure*

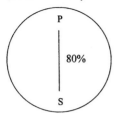

(W2) *Net assets of Squirrel*	*At date of acquisition* £000	*At balance sheet date* £000
£1 shares	100	100

(W3) *Goodwill*	£000
Purchase consideration	110
For 80% of net assets (£100,000) acquired	(80)
Goodwill	30

Note that the application of the 80% in (W3) gives us a different goodwill figure.

We now move on and calculate the third-party ownership in the net assets of Squirrel. Again, (W2) is a sub-working which will feed into (W4), minority interest. This time however it is the net assets at the balance sheet date which concerns us.

(W4) *Minority interest*	£000
20% of net assets at balance sheet date (£100,000) (W2)	20

(*Tutorial note.* If we own 80% of the shares of Squirrel, third parties own the rest (20%). In other words 20% of Squirrel's net assets at the balance sheet date are 'owned' by third parties and this will need to be reflected in the consolidated balance sheet.)

We are now in a position to prepare a consolidated balance sheet. Note the position of the minority interest figure.

3.4 Solution to the example

POLAR GROUP CONSOLIDATED BALANCE SHEET AS AT 31 DECEMBER 20X1

	£000	£000
Fixed assets		
Intangible assets (W3)		30
Tangible assets (90 + 80)		170
		200
Current assets (50 + 30)	80	
Creditors: amounts falling due within one year (30 + 10)	(40)	
Net current assets		40
Total assets less current liabilities		240
Capital and reserves		
£1 shares (100% P only)		100
Profit and loss reserves (100% P)		120
Shareholders' capital		220
Minority interest (W4)		20
		240

Practice question 2 *(The answer is in the final chapter of this book)*

Puffin (II)

Facts as before, but now assume that Puffin's investment in Seagull represents only an 80% interest.

Required

Prepare a consolidated balance sheet as at 31 December 20X1.

4   Control and ownership

4.1   Introduction

Usually, any holding greater than 50% of the ordinary shares will give P *control* of S. However, P does not *own* all of S unless the shareholding is 100%.

The part of S's net assets and results included in the consolidation which is not owned by P is owned by the minority interests (MI).

4.2   Reflecting control and ownership in group accounts

When preparing the consolidated accounts, we need to reflect P's *control* of S and the *ownership* interests of P and MI in S. Group accounts reflect both control and ownership, as shown in Figure 2.

Figure 2   Control and ownership in the consolidated balance sheet

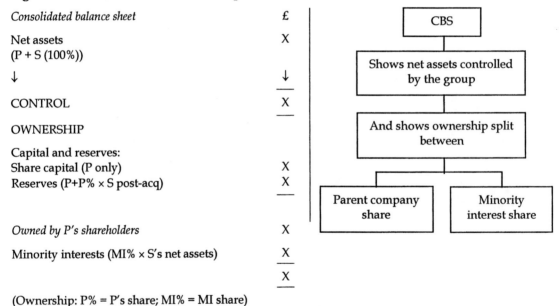

(Ownership: P% = P's share; MI% = MI share)

5   Accounting for reserves

5.1   Pre-acquisition reserves

The reserves which exist in a subsidiary company at the date when it is acquired are called its 'pre-acquisition' reserves. These are capitalised at the date of acquisition by including them in the goodwill calculation.

To see what this means, remember that we calculate the value of net assets acquired not by totalling the value of individual assets, but instead (as a short cut) by referring to the other side of the balance sheet (capital and reserves). Thus the value of net assets acquired is the value of share capital acquired plus the value of (pre-acquisition) profits acquired. By comparing this total with the amount of the purchase consideration we arrive at the value of goodwill.

5.2   Example

Draft balance sheets of Piper and Swans on 31 December 20X1 are as follows.

	Piper Ltd £000	Swans Ltd £000
Fixed assets	90	100
Investment in Swans at cost	110	
Current assets	50	30
	250	130
Creditors: amounts falling due within one year	(30)	(10)
Total assets less current liabilities	220	120
Capital and reserves		
Share capital	100	100
Profit and loss account	120	20
	220	120

Piper Ltd had just bought 80% of the shares of Swans on the balance sheet date.

Required

Prepare a consolidated balance sheet as at 31 December 20X1.

5.3   Method

We use our standard workings as before, but when we calculate net assets at the date of acquisition we include share capital and *reserves at the date of acquisition*.

(W2) will look like this.

Net assets of Swans Ltd	*At date of acquisition* £000	*At balance sheet date* £000
£1 shares	100	100
Profit and loss account	20	20
	120	120

If we follow our standard workings our answer will be as follows.

5.4   Solution to the example

PIPER GROUP CONSOLIDATED BALANCE SHEET AS AT 31 DECEMBER 20X1

	£000	£000
Fixed assets		
Intangible assets (W3)		14
Tangible assets (90 + 100)		190
		204
Current assets (50 + 30)	80	
Current liabilities (30 + 10)	(40)	
Net current assets		40
Total assets less current liabilities		244
Capital and reserves		
£1 shares (100% P only)		100
Profit and loss reserves (W5)		120
Shareholders' capital		220
Minority interest (W4)		24
		244

5.5   Working paper

(W1)   Group structure

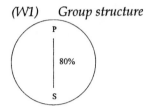

(W2)   Net assets of Swans

	At date of acquisition £000	At balance sheet date £000
£1 shares	100	100
Reserves	20	20
	120	120

(W3)   Goodwill

	£000
Purchase consideration	110
For 80% of net assets (£120,000) acquired	(96)
Goodwill	14

(W4)   Minority interests

20% of net assets at balance sheet date (£120,000)	24

5.6   Post-acquisition reserves

Profits earned by the subsidiary after the date of acquisition are called 'post-acquisition reserves'. We include the group's share of the subsidiaries' post-acquisition reserves in the consolidated balance sheet, which gives us our final standard working (W5): the group profit and loss account reserve.

(W5)   Group Profit and Loss reserve

	£000
100% Parent	120

20
pre-acquisition

20
subsidiary

Post acquisition
nil × 80%

	£000
	–
	120

If the subsidiary has other reserves (eg, a revaluation reserve, a share premium, a general reserve) we use the same basic calculation for each reserve separately.

Practice question 3 *(The answer is in the final chapter of this book)*

Pluto

Draft balance sheets of Pluto and Snoopy on 31 December 20X8 are as follows.

	Pluto Ltd £000	Snoopy Ltd £000
Fixed assets	120	150
Investment in Snoopy at cost	140	–
Current assets	40	50
	300	200
Creditors: amounts falling due within one year	(40)	(30)
	260	170
Capital and reserves		
Share capital	100	100
Profit and loss account	160	70
	260	170

Pluto had purchased 75% of the shares of Snoopy on 1 January 20X8 when Snoopy's profit and loss account had stood at £50,000.

Required

Prepare a consolidated balance sheet as at 31 December 20X8. Leave the goodwill arising on consolidation at cost in the consolidated balance sheet.

6   Accounting for intra-group balances

6.1   The single entity concept

The objective of consolidated accounts is to present the group as a single entity. Hence the effects of transactions between group members need to be eliminated as the group has not transacted with any third party.

Figure 3   **The single entity concept**

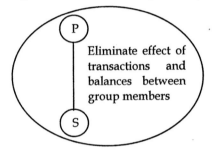

Reflecting the group as a single entity means that items which are assets in one group company and liabilities in another need to be cancelled out; otherwise group assets and liabilities will be overstated.

Intra-group balances result from, for example:

♦   loans and debentures between group companies
♦   intra-group trading
♦   dividends from S to P.

To eliminate such balances, cancel the credit balance in one company against the debit balance in the other, before summing the net assets line-by-line.

6.2   Example

Draft balance sheets of Plant and Shrub on 31 March 20X7 are as follows.

	Plant Ltd £000	Shrub Ltd £000
Tangible fixed assets	100	140
Investment in S at cost	180	
Current assets		
Stock	30	35
Debtors	20	10
Bank	10	5
	340	190
Creditors: amounts falling due within one year	(25)	(40)
Total assets less current liabilities	315	150
Creditors: amounts falling due after one year		
10% debentures	(65)	–
	250	150

Capital and reserves		
Share capital: £1 shares	250	100
Share premium	-	30
Profit and loss reserve	-	20
	250	150

Notes

1   Plant bought 80,000 shares in Shrub in 20X1 when S's reserves included a share premium of £30,000 and a profit and loss reserve of £5,000.

2   Plant owes Shrub £8,000 and this is reflected in both their accounts.

Required

Prepare a consolidated balance sheet as at 31 March 20X7. Leave the purchased goodwill at cost in the consolidated balance sheet.

(Tutorial note. We will need to cancel inter-company balances on consolidation. This means that we must exclude £8,000 from both group debtors and group creditors.)

You are now in a position to prepare a consolidated balance sheet. Remember you need to do a (W5) for each reserve in the subsidiary.

6.3   Solution to the example

PLANT GROUP CONSOLIDATED BALANCE SHEET AS AT 31 MARCH 20X7

	£000	£000
Fixed assets		
Intangible assets (W3)		72
Tangible assets (100 + 140)		240
		312
Current assets		
Stock (30 + 35)	65	
Debtors (20 + 10 – 8)	22	
Bank (10 + 5)	15	
	102	
Current liabilities		
Creditors (25 + 40 – 8)	57	
Net current assets		45
Creditors: amounts due after more than one year		
10% debentures		(65)
Total assets less current liabilities		292
Capital and reserves		
Share capital		250
Profit and loss reserve (W5)		12
		262
Minority interests (W4)		30
		292

6.4   Workings

(W1)   *Group structure*

(W2) Net assets of Shrub	At date of acquisition	At balance sheet date
	£000	£000
£1 shares	100	100
Share premium	30	30
Profit and loss account	5	20
Net assets	135	150

(W3) Goodwill	£000
Purchase consideration	180
For 80% of net assets (£135,000) acquired	(108)
Goodwill	72

(W4) Minority interests	£000
20% of net assets at balance sheet date	30
(20% × £150,000)	

(W5) Group profit and loss account	£000
100% P	NIL

Pre-acquisition £5,000

S £20,000

£15,000 × 80%
Post-acquisition   **12**

Group profit and loss reserve	12

Group share premium account	£000
100% P	NIL

Pre-acquisition £30,000

S £30,000

NIL × 80%
Post-acquisition   **NIL**

Group share premium	NIL

Practice questions 4 and 5 *(The answers are in the final chapter of this book)*

4   Top Dog

The balance sheets of Top Ltd and Dog Ltd at 31 December 20X8 were as follows.

	Top Ltd	Dog Ltd
	£	£
Tangible fixed assets	65,000	31,700
Investment in Dog Ltd	48,000	–
Current assets	120,200	61,700
	233,200	93,400
Current liabilities	58,200	28,400
Total assets less current liabilities	175,000	65,000
Capital and reserves		
Ordinary share capital – £1 ordinary shares	100,000	40,000
Profit and loss account	75,000	25,000
	175,000	65,000

Top Ltd acquired the entire share capital of Dog Ltd several years ago when the accumulated profits of Dog Ltd amounted to £6,000.

Required

Prepare the consolidated balance sheet of Top Ltd and its subsidiary as at 31 December 20X8 showing goodwill as a permanent intangible asset.

5   Top Dog (MI)

In the previous question, assume that the investment in Dog Ltd related to only 24,000 £1 ordinary shares and that the accumulated profits at acquisition amounted to £16,000.

Required

Prepare the consolidated balance sheet at 31 December 20X8 showing goodwill as a permanent intangible asset.

6.5   Learning outcome

You have now covered the first of the learning outcomes for this chapter:

Prepare a consolidated balance sheet for a group of companies.

7   Conditions for an undertaking to be a subsidiary

7.1   Requirements of the Companies Act 1985

FRS 2 and the Companies Act 1985 define the requirements for a company to be the parent company of another company:

(a)   It holds a majority of the voting power, or

(b)   It is a member of the company and has the power to appoint or remove a majority of the directors, or

(c)   The memorandum of association of the company or a control contract gives the parent the right to exercise a dominant influence over the company, or

(d)   It holds a participating interest (normally at least 20%) of the shares and exercises a dominant influence over the company.

In computational questions the criterion is usually (a) based on holding more than 50% of the shares. A question could however give you details of one of the other conditions listed above and expect you to consolidate a company on that basis.

7.2   Learning outcome

You have now covered the following learning outcome of the CIMA syllabus:

Explain the conditions required for an undertaking to be a subsidiary of a group.

8   Exemption from preparing consolidated accounts

8.1   Exempt groups

♦   **Small or medium sized groups**

A group meeting any two of the following three criteria need not prepare consolidated accounts:

Turnover	Not exceeding £11.2m net* or £13.44m gross*
Gross assets	Not exceeding £5.6m net* or £6.72m gross*
Average number of employees	Not exceeding 250

*Total turnover or gross assets may be calculated "net" (after consolidation adjustments) or "gross" (before consolidation adjustments).

The limits must be exceeded in the current year and the previous year before the exemption is lost.

This exemption does not apply if any group member is:

- a public company

- a banking company

- an insurance company

- an authorised person under the Financial Services and Markets Act 2000 (ie authorised to carry on an investment business)

♦ **Wholly owned subsidiary**

A parent company which is a wholly owned subsidiary of another company within the European Union need not prepare consolidated accounts. The company must disclose the name of the ultimate parent company in its financial statements:

P must prepare consolidated accounts for P, S and SS.

S does **not** need to prepare consolidated accounts for S and SS because there is no minority interest concerned with the results of the sub-group.

This exemption is not available to listed companies.

♦ **Majority-owned subsidiary**

A majority-owned subsidiary may claim the same exemption as a wholly owned subsidiary subject to the right of its minority shareholders to require separate consolidated accounts for the sub-group:

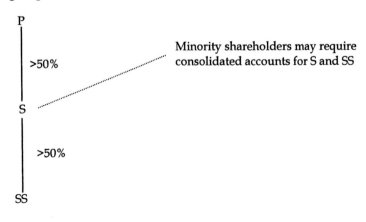

Minority shareholders demanding consolidated accounts must hold:

- 5% of the total shares in the company, or
- more than half of the total minority shares.

♦ **All subsidiaries qualify for exclusion**

No consolidated accounts are required if all the subsidiaries are excluded – see next section.

9 Exclusion of subsidiaries from consolidation

9.1 Conditions for exclusion

FRS 2 and the Companies Act 1985 allow the exclusion of some subsidiaries from consolidation. The chart below summarises the conditions:

Grounds	FRS 2	CA 85	Comment/accounting treatment
Non-materiality	No mention	Allows exclusion	One or more subsidiaries may be excluded if collectively they are not material
Severe long-term restrictions on control are in place	Subsidiary **must** be excluded on this ground	Subsidiary **may** be excluded on this ground	Use the equity method of accounting* (see Chapter 3)
Disproportionate expense or delay	Not acceptable	Allows exclusion	Not acceptable
Interest held for imminent sale; subsidiary **not** previously consolidated.	Subsidiary **must** be excluded on this ground	Subsidiary **may** be excluded on this ground	Show in consolidated balance sheet as current asset at lower of cost and net realisable value
Activities of a subsidiary are so different that consolidation would be misleading	Exclusion only allowed in exceptional cases	Subsidiary must be excluded on this ground	Use the equity method of accounting* (see Chapter 3)

*Note: you will learn about the equity method of accounting in Chapter 3. Briefly, the equity method of accounting means that the investing company's share of the net assets and profit or loss of the investee company are included in one line in the consolidated balance sheet (assets) and profit and loss account (profit or loss).

9.2 Learning outcome

You have now covered the final learning outcome for this chapter:

Explain and apply the rules for the exclusion of subsidiaries from consolidation.

10 Summary

You should now be familiar with the basic principles and techniques involved in preparing a consolidated balance sheet and with the criteria for the inclusion of subsidiaries in the consolidation. Notice in particular the underlying purpose of the consolidation process: the aim is to reflect the true economic substance of the group by displaying its assets and liabilities as those of a single entity.

Multiple choice questions *(The answers are in the final chapter of this book)*

1   Vaynor plc acquired 100,000 ordinary shares in Weeton Ltd and 40,000 ordinary shares in Yarlet Ltd some years ago. No goodwill arose on the acquisitions.

Extracts from the balance sheets of the three companies as on 30 September 20X7 were:

	Vaynor plc £000	Weeton Ltd £000	Yarlet Ltd £000
Ordinary shares of £1 each	500	100	50
Reserves	90	40	70

At acquisition the reserves of Weeton Ltd showed a deficit of £10,000 and of Yarlet Ltd a credit balance of £30,000.

The consolidated reserves of Vaynor plc on 30 September 20X7 were:

A   £162,000

B   £170,000

C   £172,000

D   £180,000

2   Holder plc acquired 150,000 £1 ordinary shares in Sub plc on 1 July 20X6 at a cost of £300,000. Sub plc's reserves at 1 July 20X6 were £36,000 and its issued ordinary share capital was £200,000.

The amount of goodwill arising on consolidation is:

A   £64,000

B   £84,000

C   £123,000

D   £138,000

3   Castor plc acquires 75% of the share capital of Pollux Ltd on 1 December 20X1. The consideration given is £1 million in cash and 300,000 £1 ordinary shares of Castor plc. The market value of each of Castor plc's shares on 1 December is 300 pence. On 1 December the fair value of Pollux Ltd's net tangible assets is £1 million.

What is the amount of goodwill on acquisition to be dealt with in Castor plc's consolidated accounts?

A   £300,000

B   £550,000

C   £900,000

D   £1,150,000

4   Harwich Ltd holds 70,000 £1 preference shares in Sall Ltd. These are non-voting but rank *pari passu* with the ordinary shares in a winding-up.

Felixstowe Ltd holds 20,000 £1 voting ordinary shares in Sall Ltd.

The share capital of Sall Ltd is made up of the following:

	£
100,000 preference shares of £1 each	100,000
30,000 ordinary shares of £1 each	30,000
	130,000

Sall Ltd is a subsidiary undertaking of:

A   both Harwich Ltd and Felixstowe Ltd

B   Harwich Ltd

C   Felixstowe Ltd

D   Neither Harwich Ltd nor Felixstowe Ltd

CHAPTER 2

The consolidated balance sheet: further issues

EXAM FOCUS

The previous chapter has introduced the basic principles of a consolidated balance sheet. However, exam questions typically involve more than the simple situations so far described. It is usual to find that one or more complications are introduced by the examiner and this chapter discusses those that crop up frequently.

LEARNING OUTCOMES

This chapter covers the following Learning Outcomes from the CIMA syllabus

    Prepare a consolidated balance sheet for a group of companies

    Prepare financial statements when a subsidiary is acquired part way through an accounting period; to include the effective date of acquisition and dividends out of pre-acquisition profits

In order to cover these Learning Outcomes the following topics are included.

    The treatment of goodwill
    Unrealised profit in stock
    Preference shares in a subsidiary
    Dividends from a subsidiary
    Acquisition of a subsidiary in mid-year
    Dividends paid out of pre-acquisition profits.

1   The treatment of goodwill

1.1   FRS 10: Goodwill and Intangible Assets

Definition of purchased goodwill in FRS 10:

    Purchased goodwill is the difference between the cost of an acquired entity and the aggregate of the fair values of that entity's identifiable assets and liabilities.

Non-purchased (or inherent) goodwill is never to be recognised or included in the accounts at all, due to the necessary subjectivity in measuring it.

Purchased goodwill (including goodwill arising on consolidation) is shown as an intangible fixed asset on the balance sheet. It is amortised over its estimated useful economic life.

Negative goodwill is shown as a negative asset in the fixed assets section of the balance sheet, just below any positive goodwill. (Negative goodwill arises if a subsidiary is purchased for an amount *less than* the total value of its separable net assets).

FRS 10 contains a presumption that the useful life of goodwill is a maximum of 20 years. If the estimated useful economic life of goodwill is *20 years or less*, the goodwill is required to be amortised over its estimated useful economic life. The amortisation should be charged in the profit and loss account.

At the end of the first full year after the acquisition a limited impairment review should be performed to confirm that the goodwill is still of value.

If the estimated useful economic life of goodwill is *more than 20 years* the goodwill is required to be written off over its estimated useful economic life, with the amortisation charged in the profit and loss account. If the estimated useful economic life is indefinite, the goodwill should not be amortised.

In both the cases described in the previous paragraph, at the end of each financial year a full impairment review must be performed. Contrast this with the limited impairment review that is required when the estimated life is 20 years or less.

1.2 Example

Consider the example of Faye Ltd below.

BALANCE SHEETS AT 31 DECEMBER 20X9

	Faye Ltd		Garbo Ltd	
	£	£	£	£
Fixed assets				
Tangible assets		33,000		20,000
Investments: shares in Garbo Ltd at cost		12,000		
Current assets	5,000		15,000	
Creditors: amounts falling due within one year	(9,000)		(10,000)	
Net current (liabilities)/assets		(4,000)		5,000
Total assets less current liabilities		41,000		25,000
Creditors: amounts falling due after more than one year				
8% Debenture loans		20,000		9,000
		21,000		16,000
Capital and reserves				
Called up share capital (£1 ordinary shares)		10,000		4,000
Share premium account		5,000		–
Profit and loss account		6,000		12,000
		21,000		16,000

On 1 January 20X3 Faye Ltd acquired 3,000 shares of Garbo Ltd. At that date the balance on Garbo Ltd's profit and loss account was £8,000.

Required

Prepare the consolidated balance sheet of Faye Ltd at 31 December 20X9, assuming the group policy is to amortise goodwill arising on consolidation over a period of ten years.

1.3 Approach to the solution

Note two points of exam technique.

♦ Watch the date of acquisition carefully.
♦ Make sure you use the correct number of years for the amortisation charge on goodwill.

We use our standard workings for (W1), (W2) and (W3).

1.4   Workings

(W1)   Group structure

(W2)   Net assets of Garbo Ltd

	At date of acquisition £	At balance sheet date £
Share capital	4,000	4,000
Profit and loss account	8,000	12,000
	12,000	16,000

(W3)   Goodwill

	£
Purchase consideration	12,000
Net assets acquired (75% × £12,000)	(9,000)
Goodwill	3,000
Amortised to date (7/10)	(2,100)
Intangible fixed asset remaining	900

We now recognise that at 31 December 20X9, seven years' worth of the purchased goodwill (ie 70%) would have been written off to the profit and loss account, leaving three years' worth (ie 30%) as an asset in the balance sheet.

(W4)   Minority interest

	£
Minority interest (25% × 16,000 (W2))	4,000

But now (W3) will feed into (W5) showing the write-off of the goodwill to the profit and loss account.

(W5)   Profit and loss account

	£
Faye Ltd	6,000
Less accumulated amortisation of goodwill (70% × 3,000)	(2,100)
	3,900
Garbo Ltd (75% × (12,000 – 8,000) (W2))	3,000
	6,900

The remaining part of the goodwill will appear in the consolidated balance sheet.

1.5 Solution

The consolidated balance sheet will now look as follows.

FAYE LTD
CONSOLIDATED BALANCE SHEET AT 31 DECEMBER 20X9

	£	£
Fixed assets		
Intangible asset: goodwill (30% × £3,000)		900
Tangible assets (33,000 + 20,000)		53,000
Current assets (5,000 + 15,000)	20,000	
Creditors: amounts falling due within one year	(19,000)	
Net current assets		1,000
Total assets less current liabilities		54,900
Creditors: amounts falling due after more than one year		
8% Debenture loans (20,000 + 9,000)		(29,000)
		25,900
Capital and reserves		
Called up share capital		10,000
Share premium account		5,000
Profit and loss account (W5)		6,900
		21,900
Minority interest (W4)		4,000
		25,900

Practice question 1 *(The answer is in the final chapter of this book)*

Dublin

The following are the summarised balance sheets of Dublin and Shannon at 31 December 20X9.

	Dublin Ltd £	Shannon Ltd £
Fixed assets		
Tangible assets	100,000	60,000
Investments:		
24,000 shares in Shannon Ltd	50,000	
Current assets	215,000	50,000
	365,000	110,000
Creditors: amounts falling due within one year	(150,000)	(20,000)
	215,000	90,000
Capital and reserves		
Called up share capital (£1 ordinary)	190,000	40,000
Profit and loss account	25,000	50,000
	215,000	90,000

Dublin Ltd purchased its shares in Shannon Ltd on 1 January 20X9, when there was a credit balance on that company's profit and loss account of £40,000.

The accounting policy of Dublin Ltd is to amortise goodwill over 5 years.

Required

Prepare the consolidated balance sheet as at 31 December 20X9.

2   Unrealised profit in stock

2.1   The accounts of individual companies

Each company within a group prepares its own accounts. The asset values shown in these accounts are established on normal historical cost principles. In particular, any stock held by an individual company will normally be valued at the amount it cost to acquire.

From the group's point of view this can cause a slight accounting problem if there is trading between members of the group. Often such trade is conducted on an arm's length basis: the selling company treats the buying company just like any other customer and charges an amount which includes a profit element.

In the buying company's accounts stock will be valued at acquisition cost, including the profit element earned by the selling company. The problem is that from the group's point of view this profit has not yet been realised because no sale has been made outside the group.

Remember that the objective of consolidated accounts is to reflect the financial results and position of the group *as a single entity*. To achieve this, we need to make an adjustment on consolidation.

2.2   The consolidation adjustment for unrealised profit

The first step is to calculate how much profit is included in closing stock.

♦   Determine the value of closing stock included in an individual company's accounts which has been purchased from another company in the group.

♦   By manipulating mark-up or profit percentages calculate how much of that value represents profit earned by the selling company.

For example, if you are given the selling company's rate of mark-up, apply the following formula:

$$\text{Value of stock} \times \frac{\text{Mark–up percentage}}{100 + \text{mark–up percentage}}$$

 The next step depends on who is selling to whom. The main possibilities are as follows.

♦   Holding company selling to subsidiary — the profit element is included in the holding company's accounts and relates entirely to the group.

♦   Subsidiary selling to holding company — the profit element is included in the subsidiary company's accounts and relates partly to the group, partly to minority interests (if any).

In the first case the adjustment is as follows.

♦   Debit   Group profit and loss account
♦   Credit   Group stock

In the second case the adjustment is as follows.

♦   Debit   Group profit and loss account (group share)
♦   Debit   Minority interest (MI share)
♦   Credit   Group stock (total)

Practice question 2 *(The answer is in the final chapter of this book)*

P and S

P Ltd owns 80% of S Ltd. During the current accounting period, S Ltd sold goods to P Ltd for £18,000 which gave S Ltd a profit of £6,000. At the balance sheet date, half of these goods are included in P Ltd's stocks.

At the balance sheet date, P Ltd's accounts showed retained profits of £100,000, and S Ltd's accounts showed net assets of £75,000, including retained profits of £65,000. S Ltd had retained profits of £20,000 at acquisition.

Required

Show how the adjustment to eliminate unrealised profits will appear in the consolidation workings for P Ltd.

3 Preference shares in a subsidiary

3.1 Accounting issues

By definition, a parent company (P) owns equity shares in a subsidiary company. However, if the subsidiary company also has preference shares in issue, these too — or some of them — may be owned by the parent company.

When calculating group reserves this factor has no effect at all. The reserves of the subsidiary belong to its equity shareholders only.

However, when calculating goodwill and minority interest it is important to take account of preference shares.

♦ To the extent that S's preference shares are owned by outsiders they should be transferred to the minority interest account.

♦ Any remaining preference shares — owned by P — should be cancelled against P's 'investment in preference shares of S'. Any difference on cancellation represents goodwill — the difference between the amount paid by P and the nominal value of preference shares acquired.

3.2 Example

Consider the example of Motor Ltd below.

Several years ago, Motor Ltd acquired the following shares in Bike Ltd.

	£
75,000 ordinary shares of £1 – cost	93,100
15,000 6% preference shares of £1 – cost	16,050
	109,150

At the date of acquisition, the accumulated profits of Bike Ltd amounted to £11,000. The summarised balance sheets of the two companies at 31 December 20X8 were as follows.

	Motor Ltd £	Bike Ltd £
Fixed assets		
Tangible fixed assets	431,100	219,350
Investments	109,150	–
Current assets		
Stock	143,070	71,120
Debtors	89,200	36,230
Cash at bank	19,300	17,150
	791,820	343,850
Sundry creditors	93,400	51,150
	698,420	292,700
Capital and reserves		
Ordinary shares of £1	350,000	100,000
6% preference shares of £1	–	60,000
Profit and loss account	348,420	132,700
	698,420	292,700

During the year, Motor Ltd sold goods whose invoice value was £24,000 to Bike Ltd. These goods were invoiced at cost plus 25%, and one-quarter were still in Bike's stock at the year end.

Goodwill has been fully amortised.

Required

Prepare the consolidated balance sheet of Motor Ltd as at 31 December 20X8.

3.3   Approach to the solution

Note the following points of exam technique.

- ♦ You must recognise that a holding in preference shares exists as well as a holding in ordinary shares.

- ♦ You achieve this by doing an 'active' read of the question, ie. asking yourself 'do we own preference shares as well as ordinary shares?'

- ♦ You may find it useful to use a highlighter pen to highlight key facts on the face of the question.

When you do your (W1) group structure you should realise that the holding in preference shares does not affect the standard group structure working.

(W1)   Group structure

However you need to note any minority interest in preference shares.

Ordinary shares		
Motor	75%	Bike
Minority interest	25%	Bike
	100%	
Preference shares		
Motor	25%	Bike
Minority interest	75%	Bike
	100%	

Now you have recognised the complication of a holding in preference shares, you must keep them separate from ordinary shares in your net assets working.

(W2)   Net assets

	At date of acquisition £	At balance sheet date £
Share capital	100,000	100,000
Profit and loss account	11,000	132,700
	111,000	232,700
Preference shares	60,000	60,000

When you now work goodwill you should cancel the entire purchase consideration (ie the amount paid for both ordinary shares and preference shares) against:

♦   75% net assets acquired — attributable to the ordinary shareholders.
♦   25% net assets acquired — attributable to the preference shareholders.

(W3)   Goodwill

	£
Purchase consideration	109,150
for	
75% net assets acquired (£111,000) (ordinary shares)	(83,250)
25% net assets acquired (£60,000) (preference shares)	(15,000)
Goodwill	10,900

The minority interest is also calculated in two parts.

(W4)   Minority interests

	£
25% (£232,700)	58,175
75% (£60,000)	45,000
	103,175

At this point it is a good idea to consider unrealised profit in stock in case it affects minority interest. In this example the entire profit is made by the group, as the parent is selling to the subsidiary so there is no impact on minority interest.

(W5)   Unrealised profit in stock

$$£6,000 \times \frac{25}{125} = £1,200$$

		£
Debit	Group profit and loss account	1,200
Credit	Group stock	1,200

You can now prepare the profit and loss account working, remembering that goodwill is fully amortised and to reduce the total reserves by the unrealised profit in stock.

(W6)   Group profit and loss account

	£
100% Parent	348,420

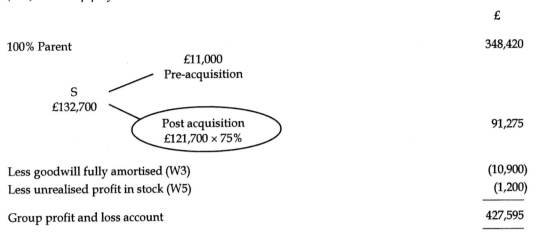

	£
Post acquisition £121,700 × 75%	91,275
Less goodwill fully amortised (W3)	(10,900)
Less unrealised profit in stock (W5)	(1,200)
Group profit and loss account	427,595

3.4   Solution

The answer can now be prepared as follows.

MOTOR LTD CONSOLIDATED BALANCE SHEET AS AT 31 DECEMBER 20X8

	£	£
Fixed assets (431,100 + 219,350)		650,450
Current assets		
Stock (143,070 + 71,120) – 1,200	212,990	
Debtors (89,200 + 36,230)	125,430	
Cash at bank (19,300 + 17,150)	36,450	
	374,870	
Creditors: amounts falling due within one year		
(93,400 + 51,150)	(144,550)	
Net current assets		230,320
		880,770
Capital and reserves		
Called up share capital		350,000
Profit and loss account (W6)		427,595
		777,595
Minority interest (W4)		103,175
		880,770

Practice question 3 *(The answer is in the final chapter of this book)*

Christian

Christian Ltd acquired 80% of the equity share capital of Dior Ltd for £35,000 and 30% of the preference share capital for £5,000 on 31 December 20X3, when the profit and loss reserve of Dior Ltd was £25,000. The net assets of Dior Ltd at 31 December 20X6 were as follows.

	£
Called up share capital	
Preference shares of £1 each	20,000
Ordinary shares of £1 each	10,000
Profit and loss account	40,000
	70,000

Required

Calculate goodwill on acquisition and minority interests at 31 December 20X6.

4 Dividends from a subsidiary

4.1 Accounting issues

Care is needed when dealing with proposed dividends not yet paid by the subsidiary. A two-step approach is recommended.

Step 1. Ensure that the draft accounts of both the subsidiary and the parent company are up-to-date and reflect the proposed dividend. You may be presented with draft balance sheets in which one or both of the companies have omitted to make the necessary entries. In this case you need to adjust the draft balance sheets.

♦ If the subsidiary has not yet accrued for the proposed dividend the adjustment is as follows.

Debit   Revenue reserves
Credit   Dividends payable

with the full amount of the dividends payable, whether to parent company or to minority shareholders.

Often this entry has already been done.

♦ If the parent company has not yet accrued for its share of the proposed dividend the adjustment is as follows.

Debit   Debtors (dividends receivable)
Credit   Revenue reserves

with the parent company's share of the dividends receivable.

Often it is this entry that needs to be done.

Step 2. On consolidation the dividend payable in S Ltd's accounts will cancel out with the dividend receivable in P Ltd's accounts.

♦ If S is wholly owned, there will be a complete cancellation.

♦ If S is only partly owned, there is only part cancellation. The uncancelled portion will be the amount of dividend payable to minority interests and this will appear in the consolidated balance sheet as a current liability.

Note the following points of exam technique:

♦ As soon as you recognise that proposed dividends have not been accounted for, you must do the bookkeeping.

♦ The key is to amend the question paper before you do any workings.

4.2 Example

P plc owns 80% of S.

	P plc £000		S plc £000
Fixed assets	100		50
Debtors	30	**+4**	10
Proposed dividend creditor	(10)		(5)
	120		55
Share capital			
	100		50
Profit and loss account	20	**+4**	5
	120		55

P accounts for dividends only when actually received.

4.3   Solution

Calculate P's share of S's dividend — £5,000 × 80% = £4,000. Update your question paper by writing the adjustment next to debtors and profit and loss account.

Practice question 4 *(The answer is in the final chapter of this book)*

Hewey

Hewey plc acquired 80% of the ordinary share capital of S plc for £150,000 and 50% of the issued 10% cumulative preference shares for £10,000, both purchases being effected on 1 May 20X7. There have been no changes in the issued share capital of S plc since that date. The following balances are taken from the books of the two companies at 30 April 20X8.

	Hewey plc £000	S plc £000
Freehold property at cost	86	55
Plant and machinery at cost	272	168
Investment in S plc	160	–
Stocks	111	65
Debtors	30	15
Cash	19	2
	678	305
Ordinary share capital (£1 shares)	300	100
10% cumulative preference shares (50p shares)	–	20
Share premium account	20	10
General reserve	68	15
Profit and loss account	50	35
Trade creditors	35	22
Taxation	50	30
Proposed dividends	15	10
Provision for depreciation		
Freehold property	40	15
Plant and machinery	100	48
	678	305

The following additional information is available.

♦   Stocks of Hewey plc include goods purchased from S plc for £20,000. S plc charged out these stocks at cost plus 25%.

♦   Proposed dividend of S plc includes a full year's preference dividend. No interim dividends were paid during the year by either company.

♦   Creditors of Hewey plc include £6,000 payable to S plc in respect of stock purchases. Debtors of S plc include £10,000 due from Hewey plc. The holding company sent a cheque for £4,000 to its subsidiary on 29 April 20X8 which was not received by S plc until May 20X8.

♦   At 1 May 20X7 the balances on the reserves of S plc were as follows.

	£000
Share premium	10
General reserve	20
Profit and loss account	30

♦   Goodwill is to be amortised over ten years.

♦   Dividends are not accounted for until the cash is received.

Required

Prepare a consolidated balance sheet for Hewey plc and its subsidiary S plc at 30 April 20X8.

(Notes to the accounts are not required. Workings must be shown.)

5 Acquisition of a subsidiary in mid-year

5.1 Date of acquisition

The date on which a company becomes a subsidiary is the date on which control passes to the parent.

5.2 The accounting problem

P may not acquire S at the start or end of a year. If S is acquired mid-year, we will need to calculate the net assets at the date of acquisition.

We usually assume that S's profit after tax accrues evenly over time.

5.3 Example

P acquired 80% of S on 31 May 20X2 for £20,000.

S's net assets at 31 December 20X1 were as follows.

	£
Share capital	1,000
Profit and loss account	15,000
	16,000

During the year to 31 December 20X2, S made a profit after tax of £600.

Required

(a) Calculate S's net assets at acquisition.
(b) Calculate goodwill on consolidation.
(c) Show what profits from S will be included in the consolidated profit and loss reserve.

5.4 Solution

(a) **Net assets at acquisition**

	£	£
Share capital		1,000
Profit and loss account		
At 31 December 20X1	15,000	
1 January 20X2 – 31 May 20X2 (5/12 × 600)	250	
		15,250
		16,250

(b) **Goodwill**

	£
Cost of investment	20,000
Less share of net assets acquired (£16,250 × 80%)	(13,000)
	7,000

(c) **Profit and loss reserve includes**

	£
Share of post-acquisition reserves of S: 80% × (15,600 – 15,250)	£280

Practice question 5 *(The answer is in the final chapter of this book)*

Hugh

On 1 July 20X7 Hugh plc acquired 120,000 £1 ordinary shares of Sheila plc.

During the year to 31 December 20X7 Sheila plc made a profit after tax of £22,000. The following information is available.

♦ The stock of Sheila plc includes goods purchased from Hugh plc for £16,000. Hugh plc invoiced those goods at cost plus 25%.

♦ Goodwill is to be amortised over five years.

The following balance sheets have been prepared as at 31 December 20X7.

	Hugh plc £	Sheila plc £
Freehold land	130,000	87,000
Plant	22,000	57,600
Cost of shares in Sheila plc	203,000	–
Stock at cost	130,000	59,400
Debtors	75,000	84,000
Bank balance	52,000	8,000
	612,000	296,000
£1 ordinary share capital	400,000	160,000
Profit and loss account	160,000	112,000
Creditors	52,000	24,000
	612,000	296,000

Required

Prepare the consolidated balance sheet of Hugh plc as at 31 December 20X7.

6   Dividends paid out of pre-acquisition profits

6.1   Two possible accounting treatments

When a subsidiary company is acquired, the next dividend paid by the subsidiary may be paid partially out of pre-acquisition profits.

There are two possible treatments of pre-acquisition dividends in the books of the parent company.

♦ Treat in the normal way as income.

> Dr Dividend receivable debtor/cash
>   Cr P&L account

This is appropriate if the question states no permanent diminution in the carrying value of the investment has occurred. Otherwise the alternative approach should be taken.

♦ Treat the pre-acquisition dividend as a return on the cost of investment.

> Dr Dividend receivable debtor/cash
>   Cr Cost of investment account

6.2 Learning outcomes

This chapter has continued to cover the following learning outcome of the CIMA syllabus:

Prepare a consolidated balance sheet for a group of companies

and has also dealt with the following learning outcome:

Prepare financial statements when a subsidiary is acquired part way through an accounting period; to include the effective date of acquisition and dividends out of pre-acquisition profits.

7 Summary

In this chapter we have examined some of the complications frequently included by the examiner in consolidated balance sheet questions.

Goodwill – purchased goodwill should be amortised over its estimated economic life.

Unrealised profit – when sales are made between group companies any unrealised profit in year-end stock must be eliminated from the consolidated balance sheet.

Preference shares in a subsidiary – these do not affect the calculation of consolidated reserves, but do affect the goodwill on consolidation (and possibly the minority interest).

Dividends proposed by the subsidiary – before proceeding to consolidate, ensure that the balance sheets of both parent and subsidiary reflect the proposed dividend.

Multiple choice questions (The answers are in the final chapter of this book)

1   Sansom plc has two subsidiaries, Mabbutt Ltd and Waddle Ltd. It purchased 10,000 £1 shares in Mabbutt Ltd on 1 January 20X1 for £35,000 when the reserves of Mabbutt Ltd stood at £21,000. It purchased 15,000 £1 shares in Waddle Ltd for £20,000 on 31 December 20X1, when the reserves of Waddle Ltd stood at £16,000.

The issued share capital of the two subsidiaries is as follows:

Mabbutt Ltd	£15,000
Waddle Ltd	£20,000

It is the group's policy to amortise/recover goodwill over ten years on a time apportioned basis.

What is the net book value of goodwill in the consolidated balance sheet at 31 December 20X4?

	Goodwill	Negative goodwill
A	£11,000	£7,000
B	£11,000	£4,900
C	£6,600	£7,000
D	£6,600	£4,900

2   The following is balance sheet information of Ho plc and Su Ltd as on 30 September 20X2.

	Ho plc £000	Su Ltd £000
Ordinary £1 shares	2,600	1,000
Profit and loss account	750	700
Trade creditors	350	900
Proposed dividend	-	100
	3,700	2,700
Sundry assets	3,700	2,700
	3,700	2,700

Ho plc acquired 60% of the share capital of Su Ltd several years ago when Su Ltd's reserves were £300,000. No goodwill arose on this acquisition. Ho plc does not account for dividends until received.

The consolidated profit and loss account balance on 30 September 20X2 is:

A   £990,000

B   £1,050,000

C   £1,170,000

D   £1,230,000

3   Dollin plc is the sole subsidiary of Newlyn plc. The net current assets as at 31 December 20X1 of Newlyn plc and Dollin plc were £25 million and £20 million respectively. During the year ended 31 December 20X1 Newlyn plc sold goods which cost £3 million to Dollin plc for £5 million on credit. Dollin plc had neither sold nor paid for these goods as at 31 December 20X1.

What is the total for consolidated net current assets?

A   £40 million

B   £42 million

C   £43 million

D   £45 million

4   Lynton Ltd acquired 75% of the 200,000 £1 ordinary shares and 50% of the 100,000 £1 preference shares of Pinner Ltd when its reserves were £24,000. No goodwill arose on this acquisition. The reserves of Lynton Ltd and Pinner Ltd are now £500,000 and £60,000 respectively.

What are the figures for minority interest and consolidated reserves in the consolidated balance sheet?

	Minority interest	Consolidated reserves
A	£109,000	£527,000
B	£109,000	£545,000
C	£115,000	£527,000
D	£115,000	£545,000

CHAPTER 3

The consolidated balance sheet: associates and joint ventures

EXAM FOCUS

So far we have looked at groups consisting of a parent company and a subsidiary company. However, the examiner frequently complicates matters by including a company which does not qualify as a subsidiary, but over which the parent company exercises significant influence. To deal with exam questions of this type you need to be thoroughly familiar with the equity method of accounting, and that is the subject of the present chapter.

LEARNING OUTCOMES

This chapter covers the following Learning Outcomes of the CIMA Syllabus.

> Explain the conditions required for an undertaking to be an associate of a group
>
> Explain the concept of an associate and a joint venture
>
> Prepare consolidated financial statements to include an associate or joint venture within the group

In order to cover these Learning Outcomes the following topics are included.

> Defining an associated undertaking
> The equity method of accounting
> Joint ventures

1 Defining an associated undertaking

1.1 Associates and subsidiaries

A group of companies consists of a parent company and its subsidiaries. Subsidiaries are those companies over which the parent exercises *control* by virtue of holding more than 50% of the equity shares.

Often a group will be able to exercise *significant influence* over another company by virtue of a substantial shareholding which, however, falls short of 50%. Such a company is called an *associated undertaking* of the group. When we use the term 'group companies' we are referring to the parent company and its subsidiaries; an associated undertaking is *not* a group company.

 An associated undertaking is therefore defined as an entity over which the group exercises long-term significant influence, but not control. If the group holds 20% or more of the company's equity we assume that significant influence exists unless there is a clear indication to the contrary.

The relationship between a group and its associate(s) is shown in Figure 1.

Figure 1 **A group with an associated undertaking**

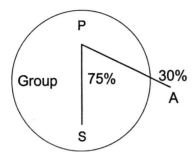

Note that the shares in A may be owned either by P or by S.

1.2 Learning outcome

You have now covered the following learning outcome of the syllabus:

> Explain the conditions required for an undertaking to be an associate of a group

1.3 FRS 9

The rules on accounting for associated undertakings are contained mainly in an accounting standard, FRS 9 *Associates and Joint Ventures*.

FRS 9 requires the use of the equity method to account for associates. The investing group must disclose its share of associates' operating results, amortisation of goodwill, non-operating exceptional items and interest, all separately on the face of the profit and loss account.

 In the investing company's *individual accounts* the balance sheet shows the investment in associated undertaking(s) — called *participating interests* — as a fixed asset investment, stated (usually) at cost. The individual company's profit and loss account shows dividend income received from associates under the heading 'income from participating interests'.

In the *consolidated accounts* we use the equity accounting method and refer to A as an associated undertaking. This is described below.

2 *The equity method of accounting*

2.1 Definition

 The equity method of accounting is a method of accounting for an investment that brings into the consolidated profit and loss account the investor's share of the investment undertaking's **results** (instead of merely bringing in the dividends receivable) and that records the investment in the consolidated balance sheet at the investor's share of the investment undertaking's **net assets**, including goodwill not yet written off (instead of merely bringing in the cost of the investment).

The equity method of accounting is used for:

♦ Associated undertakings, as explained in this chapter and the next

♦ Subsidiaries excluded from consolidation because of:

- Restrictions on control
- Different activities (see Chapter 1)

An expanded form of the equity method (called the gross equity method) is used to account for joint ventures in the consolidated accounts (see later in this chapter).

2.2 The consolidated balance sheet

In fixed asset investments, we replace the investment shown in the individual company balance sheet with the group share of A's net assets at the balance sheet date, in one line. The caption is 'Interests in associated undertakings'.

In group reserves, we include P's share of A's post-acquisition reserves (just as we do for a subsidiary).

Next, we cancel the investment in A in the individual company's books against the share of A's net assets acquired (at fair value). The difference is a premium or discount on acquisition (in effect, goodwill).

To calculate these amounts, do a net assets working for A (just as we did for a subsidiary).

Goodwill must be calculated and treated in the same way as for subsidiaries but presented within the 'investments in associates' caption and separately disclosed.

2.3 Example

Below are the balance sheets of three companies as at 31 December 20X9.

	Dipsy Ltd £000	LaaLaa Ltd £000	Po Ltd £000
Fixed assets			
Tangible assets	1,120	980	840
Investments			
672,000 shares in LaaLaa	644	-	-
168,000 shares in Po	224	-	-
Current assets	605	1,008	336
Creditors: amounts falling due within one year	(353)	(588)	(196)
	2,240	1,400	980
Capital and reserves			
£1 ordinary shares	1,120	840	560
Profit and loss account	1,120	560	420
	2,240	1,400	980

You are also given the following information.

♦ Dipsy Ltd acquired its shares in LaaLaa Ltd on 1 January 20X9 when LaaLaa Ltd had a debit balance on its profit and loss account of £56,000.

♦ Dipsy Ltd acquired its shares in Po Ltd on 1 January 20X9 when Po Ltd had a credit balance on its profit and loss account of £140,000.

♦ Creditors include the final proposed dividends of the three companies, which are as follows.

	£
Dipsy Ltd	112,000
LaaLaa Ltd	42,000
Po Ltd	28,000

♦ Dipsy Ltd has not accounted for any dividends receivable.

♦ Goodwill/premium is being amortised over five years.

Required

Prepare the consolidated balance sheet for the year ended 31 December 20X9 for Dipsy Ltd and its subsidiary, incorporating its associated company in accordance with FRS 9.

2.4   Approach to the solution

We tackle a group which has an associated company in exactly the same way as we do basic groups.

We start with the group structure in the normal way. However we reflect the associate as being external to the group.

(W1)   Group structure

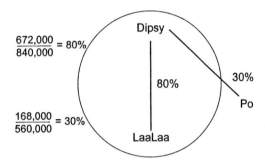

We must remember to adjust for the dividends which have not been accounted for. Remember: the easiest method is to amend the face of the question, as shown below.

	Dipsy Ltd £000		LaaLaa Ltd £000	Po Ltd £000
Fixed assets				
Tangible assets	1,120		980	840
Investments				
672,000 shares in LaaLaa	644		-	-
168,000 shares in Po	224	+33.6	-	-
Current assets	605	+8.4	1,008	336
Creditors: amounts falling due within one year	(353)		(588)	(196)
	2,240		1,400	980
Capital and reserves				
£1 ordinary shares	1,120	+33.6	840	560
Profit and loss account	1,120	+8.4	560	420
	2,240		1,400	980

We can then prepare the net assets working in the normal way for both the subsidiary and the associate.

Watch out: the balance on LaaLaa's profit and loss account at the date of acquisition was a *debit*.

(W2)   Net assets − LaaLaa

	At date of acquisition £000	At balance sheet date £000
£1 shares	840	840
Profit and loss account	(56)	560
	784	1,400

Net assets — Po

	At date of acquisition	At balance sheet date
	£000	£000
£1 shares	560	560
Profit and loss account	140	420
	700	980

We can then calculate goodwill on acquisition in the standard way.

(W3)   Goodwill/Premium

	£000
Laa Laa	
Purchase consideration	644
For 80% of net assets (£784,000)	(627.2)
	16.8
Amortised to date (16.8 × ⅕)	(3.36)
Intangible fixed asset remaining	13.44

	£000
Po	
Purchase consideration	224
For 30% of net assets (£700,000)	(210)
Premium	14
Amortised to date (14 × ⅕)	(2.8)
Add to – investment in associated company	11.2

We calculate minority interest in the subsidiary only.

(W4)   Minority interest

20% of £1,400,000   £280,000

The group profit and loss account reserve works in the usual way. We include our share of the post-acquisition reserves of the associate just as we do for a subsidiary.

(W5)   Group profit and loss account

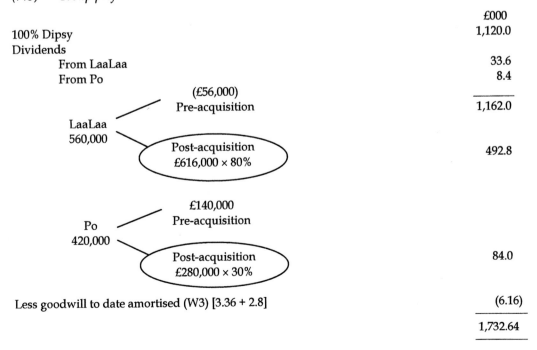

	£000
100% Dipsy	1,120.0
Dividends	
From LaaLaa	33.6
From Po	8.4
	1,162.0
Post-acquisition £616,000 × 80%	492.8
Post-acquisition £280,000 × 30%	84.0
Less goodwill to date amortised (W3) [3.36 + 2.8]	(6.16)
	1,732.64

We then have one final working to calculate the investment in the associated company. Use (W2) as the sub-working for net assets at the balance sheet date.

(W6)   Investment in associated company

	£
Share of net assets £980,000 × 30%	294,000
Add unamortised premium	11,200
	305,200

When we consolidate we have to remember that the dividend debtor from the associate *does not cancel on consolidation* – it is not part of the group.

The solution should now look like this.

CONSOLIDATED BALANCE SHEET AT 31 DECEMBER 20X9

	£000	£000
Fixed assets		
Intangible assets (W3)		13.44
Tangible assets (1,120 + 980)		2,100
Investment in associated company (W6)		305.2
		2,418.64
Current assets (605 + 33.6 + 8.4 + 1,008 – 33.6)	1,621.4	
Creditors: amounts falling due within one year (353 + 588 – 33.6)	(907.4)	714
		3,132.64
Capital and reserves		
£1 ordinary shares		1,120
Profit and loss account (W5)		1,732.64
		2,852.64
Minority interest (W4)		280
		3,132.64

Practice question 1 *(The answer is in the final chapter of this book)*

Haley

The draft balance sheets as at 31 December 20X9 of three companies are set out below.

	Haley plc £000	Socrates Ltd £000	Aristotle Ltd £000
Fixed assets			
Tangible assets	300	100	160
Investments at cost			
18,000 shares in Socrates Ltd	75	–	–
18,000 shares in Aristotle Ltd	30	–	–
Net current assets	345	160	80
	750	260	240
Loans	(100)	(50)	(80)
	650	210	160
Capital and reserves			
Ordinary shares of £1 each	250	30	60
Profit and loss account	400	180	100
	650	210	160

The reserves of Socrates Ltd and Aristotle Ltd when the investments were acquired were £70,000 and £30,000 respectively.

Goodwill/premium on acquisition has been fully amortised.

Required

Prepare the consolidated balance sheet as at 31 December 20X9. Notes are not required.

---

3   *Joint ventures*

3.1   *Definition*

A joint venture exists when two or more companies jointly control another company, but with no individual participant holding a controlling interest. For example, company X is a joint venture in the example below.

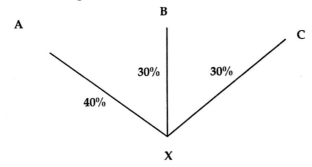

 A joint venture is a contractual arrangement whereby no one party can exercise control but together they can do so. Decisions are taken only after the consent of all parties to the arrangement, each party holding the power of veto to ensure decisions are made on the basis of unanimity.

Joint ventures are accounted for using gross equity accounting.

3.2   *Features of gross equity accounting*

Gross equity accounting is the same as equity accounting summarised above except that:

♦ the investment in the joint venture is included in the consolidated balance sheet as a fixed asset investment disclosed as:

Share of gross assets	X
Share of gross liabilities	(X)
	X

♦ the group share of the joint venture turnover should be disclosed on the face of the consolidated profit and loss account as a memorandum item (see next chapter).

3.3   *Joint arrangements*

This has the appearance of a joint venture but does not conduct its own business activities and exists to provide a service to the participants. The arrangement is thus not an entity in its own right and has been established to enable the participants to pursue their own business activities.

FRS 9 distinguishes such arrangements from joint ventures, which have their own trading activities, and requires them to be accounted for by each party accounting for their own share of the assets, liabilities and costs. This is essentially line by line **proportional consolidation**.

Proportional consolidation means that the group's share of each balance sheet item (and profit and loss account item) of the joint arrangement is included in the corresponding item in the consolidated balance sheet (and consolidated profit and loss account).

3.4 Learning outcomes

You have now covered the final two learning outcomes of this chapter.

Explain the concept of an associate and a joint venture.

Prepare consolidated financial statements to include an associate or joint venture within the group.

4 Summary

This short chapter first described the equity method of accounting for associated companies in preparing a consolidated balance sheet. You need to remember that associated undertakings are *not* members of the group. As a consequence, the consolidated balance sheet does *not* incorporate the group's share of A's assets and liabilities line by line. Instead, the consolidated balance sheet reflects the group's interest in A by means of a single line 'Investment in associated undertaking(s)'.

FRS 9 also covers the accounting for joint ventures. Investments in joint ventures are included in the consolidated accounts using the gross equity method, a development of the equity method used for accounting for associates. The same principles are applied but with greater disclosures.

Multiple choice questions *(The answers are in the final chapter of this book)*

1   Durie plc has many subsidiary companies. On 1 January 20X6 Durie plc bought 30% of the share capital of Edberg Ltd for £6,660. The balance on the profit and loss account of Edberg Ltd at that date was £13,000 and the fair value of its net assets was £20,000. The excess of fair value over book value related to a plot of land which was still owned at 31 December 20X9. The fair value was not reflected in the books of Edberg Ltd.

The summarised draft balance sheet of Edberg Ltd on 31 December 20X9 was as follows:

	£
Sundry net assets	22,000
Share capital - £1 ordinary shares	5,000
Profit and loss account	17,000
	22,000

It is the policy of Durie plc to amortise goodwill over its useful life of ten years.

At what value will the investment in Edberg Ltd be shown using the equity method on 31 December 20X9?

A   £6,996

B   £7,596

C   £7,656

D   £8,256

2   Three companies, Beed plc, Transformer plc and Berlin plc each have share capital of £10,000, profit and loss reserves of £20,000 and net assets at fair value of £30,000.

Beed plc subscribed at par value for 60% of Transformer plc on its incorporation 7 years ago and has just acquired 40% of Berlin plc for £32,000. Beed plc's policy is to amortise all goodwill over 10 years on a time apportioned basis.

What figures will be identical in the consolidated balance sheet?

A   Minority interest and investment in associate, but not consolidated revenue reserves

B   Minority interest and consolidated revenue reserves, but not investment in associate

C   Consolidated revenue reserves and investment in associate, but not minority interest

D   Minority interest, consolidated revenue reserves and investment in associate

3   On 1 January 20X0 Adam Ltd purchased 30% of Eve Ltd for £55,000. At this date the balance on the profit and loss account of Eve Ltd stood at £60,000 and the fair value of net assets, which has not been reflected in the books, was £170,000. The excess of fair value over book value related to a plot of land which was still owned at 31 December 20X4.

During the year ended 31 December 20X4 Adam Ltd sold goods to Eve Ltd for £6,000 which are still in stock at the year end. Adam Ltd makes a gross profit margin of 10%.

The balance sheet of Eve Ltd on 31 December 20X4 showed the following.

	£
Net assets	310,000
Share capital	100,000
Profit and loss account	210,000
	310,000

It is the policy of Adam Ltd to treat goodwill as being of infinite life.

At what amount should Adam Ltd's investment in Eve Ltd be stated in its consolidated balance sheet on 31 December 20X4?

A   £92,820

B   £95,820

C   £96,000

D   £99,820

4   On 31 December 20X1 the Jan plc group bought 40% of Nikki Ltd. The investment in Nikki Ltd is classed as an associated undertaking per FRS 9. Jan plc paid £150,000 for the shares in Nikki Ltd when Nikki Ltd's profit and loss account stood at £125,000.

The balance sheet of Nikki Ltd at 31 December 20X2 shows the following.

	£
Sundry net assets	450,000
Ordinary share capital	300,000
Profit and loss account	150,000
	450,000

The group policy is to capitalise all goodwill and transfer it to the profit and loss account over ten years.

At what amount will the investment in Nikki Ltd be stated in the consolidated balance sheet at 31 December 20X2?

A   £160,000

B   £162,000

C   £180,000

D   £198,000

CHAPTER 4

The consolidated profit and loss account

EXAM FOCUS

Questions on consolidated accounts are a staple part of the Paper 7a examination. A question on preparing a consolidated profit and loss account is just as likely to feature as a question requiring a consolidated balance sheet.

LEARNING OUTCOMES

This chapter covers the following Learning Outcomes of the CIMA Syllabus.

> Prepare a consolidated profit and loss account for a group of companies

> Prepare consolidated financial statements to include an associate or joint venture within the group

In order to cover these Learning Outcomes the following topics are included.

> Accounting for subsidiary companies
> Accounting for associated companies
> Advanced topics
> Joint ventures
> Disclosure requirements of FRS 9

---

1   Accounting for subsidiary companies

1.1   Control and ownership

 A profit and loss account shows the profit generated by resources disclosed in the related balance sheet.

♦   P's individual profit and loss account includes dividend income receivable from S.

♦   The consolidated profit and loss account (CPL) shows all incomes generated by the group's resources (ie by the net assets shown in the consolidated balance sheet).

To reflect this we must prepare the CPL on a basis consistent with the consolidated balance sheet. In particular, the CPL must show incomes generated from the net assets under P's control.

To do this, we include in the CPL all of S's income and expenses (100%), line by line, down to and including profit after tax. This is the case even if our equity share in S is less than 100%.

To reflect our ownership in S we must then adjust for any minority interest in S's profits. We do this by deducting the appropriate share of S's profits after tax as a separate line in the CPL. The balance of profit remaining at this stage is the profit attributable to P's shareholders.

Since the CPL includes all of the income generated by S we must take care to exclude dividends payable by S to P from P's individual profit and loss account before consolidating. Otherwise, we are double counting.

Indeed, this is just one example of intra-group transactions that must be eliminated from the consolidated accounts. We have already dealt with such transactions in the consolidated balance sheet (eg unrealised profit in closing stock). We now look at the impact of intra-group transactions on the CPL.

1.2   *Intra-group transactions*

Intra-group transactions (intra = within) are those which take place within the group and do not involve outside entities. An equivalent term is *inter-company transactions* (inter = between): transactions between members of the group, not involving outsiders.

 The objective of consolidated accounts is to display the group as a single entity. Intra-group transactions have a nil effect on the group as a whole and must be excluded from the consolidated accounts. We have just seen one example of this: payment of a dividend by S to P. Similarly, if S pays loan interest to P this too must be excluded.

The effect of this on the CPL is that:

♦ any dividends paid or proposed in CPL are the dividends paid by P to P's shareholders

♦ any dividend income shown in the CPL must arise from trade investments, *not* investments in S or A.

The minority interest in S is calculated on the profit after tax and before dividends. The figure therefore includes the minority's share of S's dividends and S's retained profits.

Inter-company trading must also be eliminated from the CPL. Such trading will be included in the turnover of one group company and the purchases of another. To cancel these transactions on consolidation:

♦ add across P and S turnover and cost of sales to get the consolidated figure
♦ deduct the value of the inter-company sale from consolidated turnover and cost of sales.

If any items sold by one group company to another are included in closing stocks, their value must be adjusted to the lower of cost and net realisable value to the group. This is consistent with our treatment of stock in the consolidated balance sheet.

We take the following steps.

♦ Increase the cost of sales by a provision for unrealised profit (PURP) on closing stocks (100%, to reflect *control*).

♦ Reduce cost of sales by unrealised profit in opening stocks (100%).

♦ If the unrealised profit arises on sales made by S, deduct the minority interest share from the minority interest in S's profit after tax (to reflect *ownership*).

1.3   A proforma CPL

Here is a proforma CPL for a holding company with an 80% subsidiary and a 30% associate.

CONSOLIDATED PROFIT AND LOSS ACCOUNT FOR THE YEAR ENDED........

	£000	£000
Turnover (100% of P and S, less inter-company sales)		X
Cost of sales		(X)
Gross profit (100% of P and S, less unrealised profit in stock)		X
Distribution costs (100% of P and S)		(X)
Administrative expenses (100% of P and S)		(X)
Operating profit (cast down)		X
Share of profits of associated company (30% of A's profit before tax)		X
Investment income (external only)		X
Profit before tax (cast down)		X
Taxation (100% P & S, plus 30% of A's tax)		(X)
Profit after tax (cast down)		X
Less minority interests (20% of S's profit after tax)		(X)
Profit attributable to members of investing company (cast down)		X
Dividends (100% of P only)		(X)
Retained profit (cast down)		X
Retained profit brought forward		
100% P	X	
+ 80% of S's post-acquisition profit	X	
+ 30% of A's post-acquisition profit	X	
Less goodwill amortised to date	(X)	X
Retained profit carried forward (cast down)		X

1.4   Example

Given below are the profit and loss statements for P plc and its subsidiary L Ltd for the year ended 31 December 20X5.

	P plc	*L Ltd*
	£000	£000
Turnover	3,200	2,560
Cost of sales	(2,200)	(1,480)
Gross profit	1,000	1,080
Distribution costs	(160)	(120)
Administrative expenses	(400)	(80)
	440	880
Investment income	160	–
Profit before tax	600	880
Taxation	(400)	(480)
Profit after tax	200	400
Dividend	(96)	(200)
Retained profit for year	104	200
Retained profit brought forward	1,200	1,120
Retained profit carried forward	1,304	1,320

- ◆ P plc paid £1.5m on 31 December 20X1 for 80% of L Ltd's share capital of £800,000. The balance on L Ltd's profit and loss account was £600,000 at that time. Goodwill has been fully amortised.

- ◆ P plc made sales to L Ltd which were worth a total of £600,000 during the year. Not all of the goods had been resold by the year end. The profit element included in L Ltd's closing stock was £30,000.

- ◆ The figure for investment income in P plc's profit statement comprises the parent company's share of the subsidiary's total dividend for the year.

Required

Prepare a consolidated profit and loss account for the year ended 31 December 20X5 for the P group.

1.5 Approach to the solution

Note the following points of exam technique

- ◆ You need to learn your format, including the position of minority interest.

- ◆ Remember you do not need a full set of balance sheet workings for a consolidated profit and loss account.

- ◆ You will, however, still need to calculate group structure and goodwill.

(W1)   Group structure

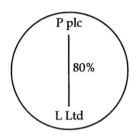

(W2)   Net assets – P plc

This is only needed at the date of acquisition (unless you are doing both a balance sheet and a CPL).

	Date of acquisition £000
Share capital	800
Profit and loss account	600
	1,400

(W3)   Goodwill

	£000
Purchase consideration	1,500
For 80% net assets acquired (£1,400,000)	(1,120)
Goodwill	380

You can now work down the profit and loss account using the proforma.

1.6   *Solution*

CONSOLIDATED PROFIT AND LOSS ACCOUNT OF P PLC
FOR THE YEAR ENDED 31 DECEMBER 20X5

	£000
Turnover (3,200 + 2,560 – 600)	5,160
Cost of sales (balancing figure)	(3,110)
Gross profit (1,000 + 1,080 – 30)	2,050
Investment income (external only)	–
Distribution costs (160 + 120)	(280)
Administrative expenses (400 + 80)	(480)
Profit on ordinary activities before tax (cast down)	1,290
Taxation (400 + 480)	(880)
Profit on ordinary activities after tax (cast down)	410
Less minority interests (400 × 20%)	(80)
Group profit after tax (cast down)	330
Dividends (100% P only)	(96)
Retained profit (cast down)	234

You now just need to calculate the balance of profits brought forward. This follows the same basic workings as for the profits carried forward, as shown on the balance sheet.

(W4)   Profit and loss account brought forward

	£000
P plc 100%	1,200

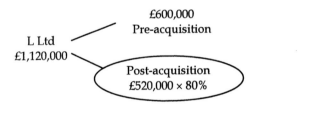

	£000
	416
	1,616
Less goodwill (W3) fully amortised	(380)
Retained profit brought forward	1,236

This now allows you to complete your solution.

	£000
Retained profit for the year	234
Retained profit brought forward	1,236
Retained profit carried forward	1,470

Practice question 1 *(The answer is in the final chapter of this book)*

Humphrey

The following are the profit and loss accounts for the year ended 30 September 20X5 of Humphrey plc and its subsidiary Stanley plc.

	Humphrey plc £000	Stanley plc £000
Turnover	1,100	400
Cost of sales	(600)	(240)
Gross profit	500	160
Distribution costs	(60)	(50)
Administration costs	(65)	(55)
Operating profit	375	55
Investment income	20	5
Interest	(25)	(6)
Profit before tax	370	54
Taxation	(160)	(24)
Profit after tax	210	30
Dividends paid and proposed	(100)	(20)
Retained profit for year	110	10
Retained profit brought forward	90	30
Retained profit carried forward	200	40

The following information is relevant.

- ◆ Humphrey plc acquired 80% of Stanley plc many years ago, when the reserves of that company were £5,000.

- ◆ Total intra-group sales in the year amounted to £100,000, Humphrey plc selling to Stanley plc.

- ◆ At the year end the balance sheet of Stanley plc included stock purchased from Humphrey plc. Humphrey plc had taken a profit of £2,000 on this stock.

- ◆ The investment income of Humphrey plc includes £16,000 from Stanley plc.

Required

Prepare a consolidated profit and loss account for the year ended 30 September 20X5.

1.7   Learning outcome

You have now covered the following learning outcome for this chapter:

> Prepare a consolidated profit and loss account for a group of companies.

2   Accounting for associated companies

2.1   Equity accounting in the CPL

The treatment of associated companies in the CPL is consistent with their treatment in the balance sheet. The main steps are as follows.

- ◆ The investing company's individual profit and loss account includes dividend income from the investment in A. In the CPL, replace this with the group's share of A's profit before tax, and disclose it as 'income from interests in associated undertakings'.

♦ Include the group's share of A's tax charge in the group tax charge, and disclose the amount separately in a note to the accounts.

♦ If A was acquired in mid-year, time-apportion its profit or loss.

FRS 9 requires the investing group's share of A's operating results, amortisation of goodwill, non-operating exceptional items, and interest to be shown separately on the face of the CPL.

2.2 Dealing with intra-group transactions

Do not cancel inter-company balances and trading with A, as A is not part of the group.

For dividends from A, ensure that dividends payable and receivable are fully accounted for in the books of the individual companies. The consolidated balance sheet will show a debtor for dividends due to the group from A.

Eliminate unrealised profit on sales from P to A or A to P by adjusting the net assets of A so as to eliminate profit prior to equity accounting.

2.3 Example

Below are the profit and loss accounts of the Barbie group and its associated company, as at 31 December 20X8.

	Barbie plc £000	Ken Ltd £000	Shelly Ltd £000
Turnover	385	100	60
Cost of sales	(185)	(60)	(20)
Gross profit	200	40	40
Expenses	(50)	(15)	(10)
Profit before tax	150	25	30
Tax	(50)	(12)	(10)
Profit after tax	100	13	20
Dividends	(40)	–	(10)
Retained profit for the year	60	13	10
Retained profit brought forward	190	60	140
Retained profit carried forward	250	73	150

You are also given the following information.

♦ Barbie plc acquired 60,000 shares in Shelly Ltd for £80,000 when that company had a credit balance on its profit and loss account of £50,000 a number of years ago. Shelly Ltd has 200,000 £1 ordinary shares.

♦ Barbie plc acquired 45,000 shares in Ken Ltd for £70,000 when profit and loss reserves were £20,000. Ken Ltd has 50,000 £1 ordinary shares.

♦ The dividends of Barbie and Shelly are final proposed dividends and Barbie plc has not accounted for any dividends receivable.

♦ Any goodwill has been fully amortised.

Required

Prepare the consolidated profit and loss account for Barbie plc including the results of its associated company.

2.4 Solution

CONSOLIDATED PROFIT AND LOSS ACCOUNT
FOR THE YEAR ENDED 31 DECEMBER 20X8

	£000
Turnover (385 + 100)	485
Cost of sales (balancing figure)	(245)
Gross profit (200 + 40)	240
Investment income (external only)	–
Administrative expenses (50 + 15)	(65)
Share of profits of associated company (30% of Shelly's profit before tax)	9
Profit before tax	184
Taxation: group (50 + 12)	(62)
Shelly (30% × 10)	(3)
Profit after tax	119
Minority interest (10% of Ken's profit after tax)	(1.3)
Profit attributable to members of Barbie	117.7
Dividends (Barbie only, 100%)	(40)
Retained profit for the year	77.7
Retained profit brought forward (W4)	241
Retained profit carried forward	318.7

2.5 Workings

(1) Group structure

Ken   Shelly

$$\frac{45,000}{50,000} = 90\% \qquad \frac{60,000}{200,000} = 30\%$$

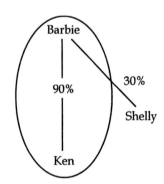

(2) Net assets

Shelly	*At the date of acquisition*
	£000
Share capital	200
Reserves	50
	250

Ken	£000
Share capital	50
Reserves	20
	70

(3)   *Goodwill/premium*

		Shelly £000	Ken £000
Purchase consideration		80	70
For 30% (250)		(75)	
90% (70)			(63)
Premium/goodwill		5	7

(4)   *Retained profit b/f*

	£000
100% Barbie	190

Ken
60

20 Pre-acquisition

Post-acquisition
40 ───── 90%

36

Shelly
140

50 Pre-acquisition

Post-acquisition
90 ───── 30%

27

	253
Less goodwill fully amortised (W3: 5 + 7)	(12)
	241

Practice question 2 *(The answer is in the final chapter of this book)*

King

King Ltd acquired shares in two other companies many years ago as follows.

Company	Shares acquired %	Goodwill on acquisition £	Balance on reserves at acquisition £
Prawn Ltd	80	90,000	260,000
Madras Ltd	25	62,000	340,000

The results of the three companies for the year ended 30 September 20X9 are as follows.

	King Ltd £000	Prawn Ltd £000	Madras Ltd £000
Turnover	800	430	600
Cost of sales and expenses	(550)	(255)	(440)
Profit before tax	250	175	160
Taxation	(80)	(45)	(60)
Profit after tax	170	130	100
Proposed dividends	(70)	(50)	(40)
Retained profit	100	80	60
Retained profit brought forward	600	320	540
Retained profit carried forward	700	400	600

During the year King Ltd made sales of £80,000 to Prawn Ltd at a gross profit of 25%. At the year end Prawn Ltd still held £36,000 of these goods in stock.

Required

Prepare the consolidated profit and loss account for the King Ltd group for the year ended 30 September 20X9. All goodwill has been fully amortised.

3 Advanced topics

3.1 Preference shares in subsidiary

Where there are preference shares in the subsidiary company the calculation of minority interest in the CPL becomes slightly more difficult.

You should adopt the following format for your computation.

	£
Minority share of preference dividends	X
(MI% in prefs × preference dividend)	
Minority interest in profit attributable to ordinary shareholders	X
(MI% in ords × (S's profit after tax – preference dividend))	
Minority interest in CPL	X

3.2 Example

On 1 January 20X9 Z plc acquired 60% of the ordinary shares of X Ltd and 25% of its preference shares. The issued capital of X Ltd on this date was £1,000,000 ordinary shares of £1 each, fully paid, and £400,000 of 6% preference shares of £1 each, fully paid.

The following draft profit and loss accounts have been produced by Z plc and X Ltd for the year ended 31 December 20X9, before Z plc recognised any dividends receivable from X Ltd.

	Z plc £000	X Ltd £000
Turnover	1,260	520
Cost of sales	(420)	(210)
Gross profit	840	310
Distribution costs	(180)	(60)
Administration expenses	(120)	(90)
Profit before taxation	540	160
Taxation	(130)	(26)
Profit after taxation	410	134
Dividends proposed		
Preference	–	(24)
Ordinary	(150)	(60)
Retained profit for the year	260	50
Retained profits brought forward	1,350	78
Retained profits carried forward	1,610	128

During the year ended 31 December 20X9 Z plc had sold £84,000 worth of goods to X Ltd. These goods had cost Z plc £56,000. On 31 December 20X9 X Ltd still had £36,000 worth of these goods in stock (valued at selling price).

Required

Prepare the consolidated profit and loss account for Z plc for the year ended 31 December 20X9.

Note. Any goodwill arising on acquisition should be ignored.

3.3   *Approach to the solution*

The only added difficulty is in calculating the minority interest figure in the CPL. We therefore tackle (W3) first.

(W3)   Minority interest

First deal with the balance available to ordinary shareholders.

	£000
Subsidiary's profit after tax	134
Less preference dividend	(24)
	——
Balance available to ordinary shareholders	110
	——
Minority interests = 40%	44
Minority interest in preference dividend (75% of pref dividend)	18
	——
	62
	——

(W1)   Group structure

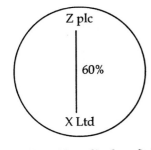

Note that Z plc also holds 25% of X Ltd's preference shares

$$\left(\frac{100,000}{400,000} = 25\% \right)$$

(W2)   Unrealised profit in stock

	£000
Selling price	84
Cost	56
	——
Total profit	28
	——

The profit mark-up is therefore one third of the selling price $\left[\frac{28}{84} = \frac{1}{3} \right]$. Since closing stock at selling price is £36,000 the unrealised profit is $\frac{1}{3} \times £36,000 = £12,000$.

(W4)   Retained profits brought forward

	£000
100% Z	1,350
X – All pre-acquisition (look at dates)	–
	——
	1,350
	——

3.4 Solution

Z PLC
CONSOLIDATED PROFIT AND LOSS ACCOUNT
FOR THE YEAR ENDED 31 DECEMBER 20X9

	£000
Turnover (1,260 + 520 – 84)	1,696
Cost of sales (balancing figure)	(558)
Gross profit (840 + 310 – 12) (W2)	1,138
Distribution costs (180 + 60)	(240)
Administrative expenses (120 + 90)	(210)
Profit before tax	688
Taxation (130 + 26)	(156)
Profit after tax	532
Minority interest (W3)	(62)
Profit attributable to group	470
Dividends	(150)
Retained profit	320
Retained profits brought forward (W4)	1,350
Retained profits carried forward	1,670

Practice question 3 *(The answer is in the final chapter of this book)*

High

High plc acquired its 80% interest in the ordinary capital and 25% interest in the preference capital of Tension plc some years ago for £10,000. At that time Tension plc's profit and loss reserve stood at £4,000 (credit) and there were no other reserves. The following are the draft profit and loss accounts of High plc and Tension plc for the year ended 31 March 20X3. Goodwill has been fully amortised.

	High plc £	Tension plc £
Turnover	274,500	181,250
Cost of sales	(126,480)	(86,520)
Gross profit	148,020	94,730
Distribution costs	(67,315)	(42,885)
Administration costs	(25,555)	(17,295)
	55,150	34,550
Dividends from Tension plc		
Ordinary	4,800	–
Preference	150	–
Bank interest receivable	250	100
Profit before tax	60,350	34,650
Corporation tax	(29,000)	(15,100)
Profit after tax	31,350	19,550
Transfers to reserves	6,000	5,000
Preference dividend paid	–	300
Ordinary dividend paid	3,000	2,000
Preference dividend proposed	–	300
Ordinary dividend proposed	5,000	4,000
Retained profit for the year	17,350	7,950
Retained profit brought forward	28,000	17,250
Retained profit carried forward	45,350	25,200

The following information is also available.

♦ Stock of High plc at 31 March 20X3 includes goods purchased from Tension plc at a profit to that company of £700. Total intra-group sales for the year amounted to £37,500.

♦ Tension plc's issued share capital comprises 10,000 50p ordinary shares and 4,000 £1 15% preference shares.

Required

Prepare the consolidated profit and loss account for the year ended 31 March 20X3.

3.5 *Acquisition of a subsidiary in mid-year*

If we acquire a subsidiary in mid-year the CPL includes S's results only from the date of acquisition, ie the date on which control is obtained.

We adopt the following drill.

♦ Consolidate S from date of acquisition.

♦ Identify the net assets of S at the date of acquisition in order to calculate goodwill.

♦ Assume that revenue and expenses accrue evenly over the year unless the contrary is indicated.

♦ Time-apportion the results of S in the year of acquisition.

♦ Time-apportion the totals for turnover and cost of sales, then deduct inter-company items.

3.6 *Example*

The following profit and loss accounts were prepared for the year ended 31 March 20X9.

	Ethos plc £	Pathos Ltd £
Sales	303,600	217,700
Cost of sales	(143,800)	(102,200)
Gross profit	159,800	115,500
Operating costs	(71,200)	(51,300)
Operating profit	88,600	64,200
Dividends receivable		
Quoted investments	2,800	1,200
Pathos Ltd	15,000	–
Profit before tax	106,400	65,400
Taxation	(46,200)	(32,600)
Profit after tax	60,200	32,800
Transfer to general reserve	(15,000)	(5,000)
Proposed ordinary dividend	(30,000)	(20,000)
Retained profit for the year	15,200	7,800
Retained profits brought forward	79,300	38,650
Retained profits carried forward	94,500	46,450

On 30 November 20X8 Ethos plc acquired 75% of the issued ordinary capital of Pathos Ltd.

The profits of both companies are deemed to accrue evenly over the year.

Required

(a) Prepare the consolidated profit and loss account for the year ended 31 March 20X9. (Ignore the disclosure requirements of FRS 3.)

(b) Explain why only four months of Pathos Ltd's profit and loss account is included in the consolidated profit and loss account.

3.7   Solution

CONSOLIDATED PROFIT AND LOSS ACCOUNT FOR THE YEAR ENDED 31 MARCH 20X9

	£
Turnover (W2)	376,167
Cost of sales (W2)	(177,867)
Gross profit	198,300
Operating costs (W2)	(88,300)
Operating profit	110,000
Investment income (W2)	3,200
Profit on ordinary activities before tax	113,200
Corporation tax (W2)	(57,067)
Profit on ordinary activities after tax	56,133
Minority interest (W3)	(2,733)
Profit attributable to members of Ethos plc	53,400
Dividend	(30,000)
Transfers to reserves (W4)	(16,250)
Retained profit for the year	7,150
Retained profit at 1 April 20X8	79,300
Retained profit at 31 March 20X9	86,450

3.8   Time apportionment

The results of a subsidiary are included in the consolidated accounts from the date control is achieved.

Ethos plc acquired 75% of the issued ordinary capital of Pathos Ltd on 30 November 20X8. This is the date on which control passed and hence the date from which the results of Pathos Ltd should be reflected in the consolidated profit and loss account.

All reserves earned by Pathos Ltd in the four months since that date are post-acquisition reserves.

The remaining previous eight months' profit from 1 April 20X8 to 30 November 20X8 are all pre-acquisition reserves and will be included in the calculation of goodwill on consolidation.

3.9   Workings

(W1)   *Group structure*

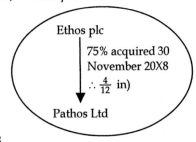

(W2) Consolidation schedule	Ethos plc	Pathos Ltd $\frac{4}{12}$	Consolidated
	£	£	£
Turnover	303,600	72,567	376,167
Cost of sales	(143,800)	(34,067)	(177,867)
Operating costs	(71,200)	(17,100)	(88,300)
Investment income	2,800	400	3,200
Tax	(46,200)	(10,867)	(57,067)
Profit after tax		10,933	

(Tutorial note. Alternative calculation for profit after tax of Pathos Ltd

Profit after tax per question £32,800 × 4/12	(10,933)

(W3) Minority interest	
25% × 10,933	2,733

(W4) Transfer to reserves	
Ethos plc	15,000
Pathos Ltd 75% × 5,000 × 4/12	1,250
	16,250

Practice question 4 *(The answer is in the final chapter of this book)*

Simon

The draft profit and loss accounts of the three companies for the year ended 31 December 20X4 were as follows.

	Simon plc £	Butterworth Ltd £	Tolley Ltd £
Turnover	5,100,000	2,050,000	960,000
Cost of sales	(4,210,000)	(1,750,000)	(720,000)
Gross profit	890,000	300,000	240,000
Distribution costs and administrative expenses	(400,000)	(275,000)	(180,000)
Operating profit	490,000	25,000	60,000
Dividends received and receivable	8,000	–	–
Interest payable	(10,000)	–	–
Profit on ordinary activities before taxation	488,000	25,000	60,000
Tax on profit on ordinary activities	(210,000)	(5,000)	(30,000)
Profit on ordinary activities after taxation	278,000	20,000	30,000
Dividends	(50,000)	(10,000)	–
Retained profit for year	228,000	10,000	30,000
Profit and loss account brought forward	1,528,475	469,000	375,000
Profit and loss account carried forward	1,756,475	479,000	405,000

You are also given the following information.

♦   During the year Simon plc sold to Butterworth Ltd goods invoiced at £45,000 upon which a 20% gross profit was made. This was the only intra-group trading and none was unsold at the year-end.

♦   Simon plc had owned 80% of the equity share capital of Butterworth Ltd for many years. At acquisition, Butterworth Ltd's profit and loss account stood at £210,000 and the goodwill arising was £35,000.

♦ On 31 March 20X4, Simon plc acquired 60% of the £100,000 equity share capital of Tolley Ltd for £402,000.

♦ It is the group's policy to carry goodwill as a permanent intangible asset.

Required

Prepare the consolidated profit and loss account of Simon plc for the year ended 31 December 20X4.

Note. Ignore the disclosure requirements of FRS 3 *Reporting Financial Performance*.

4 Joint ventures

4.1 Introduction

When the parent company has an interest in a joint venture the consolidated profit and loss account should include:

♦ The group's share of the profit or loss of the joint venture
♦ **As a memorandum,** the group's share of the turnover of the joint venture

4.2 Example

An extract from a consolidated profit and loss account is given below, illustrating the disclosure of joint ventures and associates.

CONSOLIDATED PROFIT AND LOSS ACCOUNT FOR THE YEAR ENDED 31 DECEMBER 20X4

		£m	£m
Turnover: group and share of joint ventures			320
Less share of joint ventures' turnover			(120)
Group turnover			200
Cost of sales			(120)
Gross profit			80
Expenses			(40)
Group operating profit			40
Share of operating profit of:	Joint ventures	30	
	Associates	24	
		54	
			54
			94
Interest receivable (group)			6
Interest payable:	Group	26	
	Joint ventures	10	
	Associates	12	
			(48)
Profit before tax			52
Tax:	Group	5	
	Joint ventures	5	
	Associates	2	
			(12)
Profit after tax			40

5   Further disclosure requirements of FRS 9

5.1   Disclosures

For all associates and joint ventures, a note to the consolidated financial statements must disclose:

♦   Proportion of shares held
♦   Accounting date if different from group
♦   Nature of business

Additional disclosures are required if the group interests in associates or joint ventures exceed 15% or 25% of total group assets, turnover or profit.

The 15% rule applies when the totals for **all** associates or **all** joint ventures exceed 15%. The 25% rule applies to **individual** associates or joint ventures which exceed 25%.

Additional disclosures by note

Disclosable item	For total of all associates or joint ventures exceeding 15%	For individual associate or joint venture exceeding 25%
Turnover	✓ (associates only)	✓
Profit before tax		✓
Taxation		✓
Profit after tax		✓
Fixed assets	✓	✓
Current assets	✓	✓
Liabilities due within one year	✓	✓
Liabilities due after more than one year	✓	✓

5.2   Learning outcome

You have now covered the final learning outcome for this chapter.

> Prepare consolidated financial statements to include an associate or joint venture within the group.

6   Summary

In preparing a CPL we include the results of S in full, down to and including profit after taxation. We then strip out any minority share in S's profit after tax. All inter-company transactions between P and S are eliminated.

With associates, the CPL includes a share of A's profit or loss before tax, disclosed as 'Income from interests in associated undertakings'. The group's share of A's tax charge is added to the group's own tax charge. Inter-company items are *not* eliminated because A is not part of the group.

Joint ventures are included in the CPL in a similar way to associates, though with additional disclosures.

Multiple choice questions *(The answers are in the final chapter of this book)*

1   Barley Ltd has owned 100% of the issued share capital of Oats Ltd for many years. Barley Ltd sells goods to Oats Ltd at cost plus 20%. The following information is available for the year.

        Turnover

Barley Ltd	£460,000
Oats Ltd	£120,000

During the year Barley Ltd sold goods to Oats Ltd for £60,000, of which £18,000 were still held in stock by Oats Ltd at the year end.

At what amount should total turnover appear in the consolidated profit and loss account?

A   £520,000

B   £530,000

C   £538,000

D   £562,000

2   Ufton plc is the sole subsidiary of Walcot plc. The cost of sales figures for 20X1 for Walcot plc and Ufton plc were £11 million and £10 million respectively. During 20X1 Walcot plc sold goods which had cost £2 million to Ufton plc for £3 million. Ufton plc has not yet sold any of these goods.

What is the consolidated cost of sales figure for 20X1?

A   £16 million

B   £18 million

C   £19 million

D   £20 million

3   Shaw Ltd owns 75% of the ordinary share capital and 40% of the preference share capital of Wilde Ltd.

The following details are extracted from the books of Wilde Ltd.

Profit after tax	£70,000
Proposed ordinary dividend	£20,000
8% £1 preference shares	£125,000

Shaw Ltd has profit after tax (excluding any inter-company items) of £80,000 in its own accounts.

What is the total retained profit for the group for the year?

A   £121,500

B   £125,000

C   £129,000

D   £136,500

CHAPTER 5

Fair values in acquisition accounting

EXAM FOCUS

Our assumption so far has been that the book values of a subsidiary's assets at the date when it is acquired are a fair indication of their true value. This is an important point when calculating the goodwill on acquisition: remember that the price we pay for the subsidiary, less the value of the tangible assets we acquire, is the value of the intangible asset 'goodwill'.

In the exam — as in real life — things are often more complicated than this. Often an exam question will give us details about the fair values of the subsidiary's assets at the date of acquisition. It is these fair values — *not* the book values — that you must use when calculating goodwill on acquisition.

LEARNING OUTCOMES

This chapter covers the following Learning Outcome of the CIMA Syllabus.

> Explain and apply the concept of fair value at the point of acquisition

In order to cover this Learning Outcome the following topics are included.

> The requirements of FRS 7
> Dealing with fair value adjustments

---

1 The requirements of FRS 7

1.1 The accounting problem

So far in dealing with the acquisition of a subsidiary we have assumed that the net assets shown in the subsidiary's balance sheet are stated at fair value. This is not always the case, owing to the limitations of historical cost accounting.

At the date of acquisition the assets and liabilities of the subsidiary must be stated at fair value if a correct goodwill figure is to be produced.

Group accounting questions at Paper 7 may therefore include a requirement to put through basic fair value adjustments. The governing standard in this area is FRS 7 *Fair Values in Acquisition Accounting*.

1.2 Objective and definitions of FRS 7

FRS 7 deals with how to calculate the fair values used to compute goodwill. (As we have already seen, once goodwill has been calculated, its accounting treatment is governed by FRS 10.)

The objective of FRS 7 is to ensure that assets and liabilities of an acquired business are recorded at fair value on the date of acquisition and that all changes to acquired assets and liabilities after the acquisition are reported in the post-acquisition results of the acquiring group.

FRS 7 includes the following key definitions.

♦ *Fair value:* the amount at which an asset or liability could be exchanged in an arm's length transaction other than in a forced or liquidation sale.

♦ *Identifiable assets and liabilities:* assets and liabilities of an acquired entity that are capable of being disposed of or settled separately without disposing of a business of the entity.

♦ *Recoverable amount:* the greater of an asset's net realisable value and its value in use.

♦ *Value in use:* the present value of future cash flows from continued use of the asset, including its ultimate disposal.

1.3 Accounting treatment

Identifiable assets and liabilities recognised in the accounts are those of the acquired entity that existed at the date of acquisition.

Assets and liabilities are measured at fair values reflecting conditions at the date of acquisition.

The following do not affect fair values at the date of acquisition and are therefore dealt with as post-acquisition items.

♦ Changes resulting from the acquirer's intentions or future actions

♦ Changes resulting from post-acquisition events

♦ Provisions for future operating losses or reorganisation costs incurred as a result of the acquisition.

2 Dealing with fair value adjustments

2.1 Calculating fair values

The rules for calculating fair values of different classes of assets are summarised in Table 1.

Table 1 Rules for calculating fair values

Category of asset	Valuation
Tangible fixed assets	Lower of: ♦ market value or depreciated replacement cost, and ♦ recoverable amount
Intangible fixed assets	Estimated market value
Stocks and work in progress	Lower of replacement cost and net realisable value
Quoted investments	Market value
Monetary assets and liabilities	The amount expected to be received or paid, taking into account the timing
Contingencies	Fair value, where this can be determined. Reasonable estimates may be used.
Pension funds	Liability: fair value of deficiency Asset: surplus, to the extent that it is reasonably expected to be realised.
Deferred tax assets and liabilities	Value by considering the enlarged group as a whole

Contingent assets and liabilities are not normally recognised except on acquisition. Acquisition makes it necessary to identify and recognise all assets and liabilities provided they can be reliably valued. If this is not done, reporting of post-acquisition performance will be distorted.

The fair value exercise should be completed, if possible, by the date on which the first post-acquisition financial statements of the acquirer are approved by directors. If this is not possible, revise as necessary for the next financial statements and adjust goodwill.

2.2   Calculating the cost of acquisition

The cost of acquisition includes the following elements.

♦ Cash paid
♦ Fair value of any other consideration
♦ Fees and similar incremental costs incurred directly in making the acquisition.

Issue costs of shares or other securities must be deducted from the proceeds of the issues (FRS 4), so are not part of the cost of acquisition.

Deferred consideration should be discounted, using a rate at which the acquirer could obtain similar borrowing.

Any contingent consideration should be included at a reasonable estimate of the fair value of amounts expected to be payable in future. Adjust the cost of acquisition and goodwill when estimates are revised.

Where contingent consideration involves the issue of shares there is no liability (obligation to transfer economic benefits). Recognise this as part of shareholders' funds under a separate caption representing shares to be issued.

2.3   Example

Joynt plc acquired 85% of Goulding Ltd.

♦ At acquisition the balance sheet of Goulding Ltd showed net assets with a book value of £1,305,000. Included in this total are freehold land with a book value of £300,000 (market value £720,000), patents with a book value of £175,000 (market value £200,000) and goodwill (arising on the acquisition of an unincorporated business some years ago) with a book value of £350,000. The fair value of all other assets and liabilities is approximately equal to book value.

♦ The directors of Joynt plc intend to close down one of the divisions of Goulding Ltd and wish to provide for operating losses up to the date of closure which are forecast as £29,000.

♦ An investment in plant and machinery will be required to bring the remaining production line of Goulding Ltd up to date. This will amount to £220,000 in the next 12 months.

♦ In addition, the costs of reorganising Goulding Ltd to reflect the corporate image of Joynt plc are estimated at £70,000.

♦ The consideration comprised cash of £90,000 and 900,000 shares with a nominal value of 25p and fair value of 130p each.

♦ The costs of the share issue were £37,000, and professional fees to bankers and solicitors in respect of the acquisition amounted to £75,000. In addition, the finance director of Joynt plc has estimated that the time and expenses incurred by the directors of Joynt plc in negotiating and completing the deal amounted to £16,000.

Required

Calculate goodwill arising on consolidation.

2.4   Exam technique

The best way to deal with fair value adjustments is at (W2) — net assets acquired.

Remember that both the purchase consideration and the net assets acquired need to be reflected at fair value.

You will need to read through the question line by line and consider each piece of information given in the light of the rules laid down by FRS 7.

2.5 Approach to the example

(W1)   Group structure

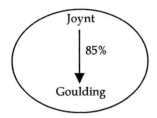

(W2)   Net assets

We start net assets in the normal way. We then put through any fair value adjustments.

	Net assets at the date of acquisition
	£
Net assets at book value (given in question)	1,305,000
Fair value adjustments	
Freehold land (720-300)	420,000
Patents (200-175)	25,000
Goodwill	(350,000)
Net assets at fair value	1,400,000

The fair value adjustments derive from FRS 7 requirements.

♦   Freehold land is valued at market value.

♦   Intangibles (patents) are valued at estimated market value.

♦   Goodwill is not an identifiable asset and must therefore be written off.

♦   The closure of the division, the investment in plant, and the reorganisation costs are quite clearly post-acquisition and will therefore be specifically excluded.

Once we have adjusted net assets to fair value we can then move on to calculate goodwill.

(W3)   Goodwill

Purchase consideration	£
Cash	90,000
Shares (900,000 × £1.30)	1,170,000
Professional fees	75,000
	1,335,000
For 85% of net assets acquired at fair value (£1,400,000)	(1,190,000)
Goodwill	145,000

Explanation

♦   Cash is always fair value!
♦   Shares are valued at market value.
♦   Direct fees only are allowed.
♦   The costs of issuing shares are excluded.

Practice question 1 *(The answer is in the final chapter of this book)*

Hut

On 1 January 20X8 Hut plc acquired 128,000 ordinary shares of Shed plc. The following balance sheets have been prepared as at 31 December 20X8.

	Hut plc £	Shed plc £
Freehold land at cost	80,000	72,000
Plant at cost	120,000	80,000
Cost of shares in Shed plc	203,000	–
Stock at cost	112,000	74,400
Debtors	104,000	84,000
Bank balance	41,000	8,000
	660,000	318,400
£1 ordinary share capital	400,000	160,000
Profit and loss account	160,000	112,000
Plant depreciation at 31 December 20X8	48,000	22,400
Creditors	52,000	24,000
	660,000	318,400

The following information is available.

♦   At 1 January 20X8 Shed plc had a debit balance of £11,000 on profit and loss account.

♦   In fixing the bid price for the shares of Shed plc, Hut plc valued the freehold at £90,000. Ignore depreciation on the freehold. All Shed plc's plant was acquired since 1 January 20X8.

♦   The stock of Shed plc includes goods purchased from Hut plc for £16,000. Hut plc invoiced those goods at cost plus 25%.

♦   Goodwill on consolidation is to be amortised over ten years.

Required

Prepare the consolidated balance sheet of Hut plc as at 31 December 20X8.

2.6   *Learning outcome*

You have now covered the learning outcome for this chapter:

Explain and apply the concept of fair value at the point of acquisition

3   *Summary*

You should now be able to put through simple fair value adjustments in group accounting.

You must remember when you calculate purchased goodwill to include the net assets of the subsidiary at fair value at the date of acquisition.

Multiple choice questions (The answers are in the final chapter of this book)

1   Which of the following items would be included in assessing the fair value of net assets acquired for the purposes of consolidations in accordance with FRS 7 *Fair values in acquisition accounting*?

    A   Provision for future losses

    B   Contingent gain due to subsidiary

    C   Provision for costs of integrating new business

    D   Provision for costs of reorganisation once a new business is incorporated

2   The books of Tiny Ltd contain a provision for reorganisation. The reorganisation is under way and the provision is to cover costs to be incurred in the next six months to complete the reorganisation.

Huge plc is considering acquiring Tiny Ltd. If it does so, the reorganisation of Tiny Ltd will continue.

In assessing the fair value of net assets, the directors of Huge plc wish to make a provision for future trading losses and include the existing provision for reorganisation costs.

In accordance with FRS 7 *Fair values in acquisition accounting*, which provisions, if any, may be included?

	Provision for trading losses	*Provision for reorganisation costs*
A	Include	Include
B	Exclude	Include
C	Include	Exclude
D	Exclude	Exclude

3   Which of the following is/are acceptable when assessing fair values on acquisition in accordance with FRS 7 *Fair values in acquisition accounting*?

(1)   Valuation of fixed assets at market value where this is higher than book value.

(2)   Discounting debtors to present values where the debt is not due to be recovered for two years.

(3)   Inclusion of contingencies where the probability of the outcome would lead to the acquired company only disclosing the contingency, not including amounts in the accounts.

A   (1) only

B   (2) only

C   (1) and (2) only

D   (1), (2) and (3)

4   Leeds Ltd acquired the whole of the issued share capital of Cardiff Ltd for £12 million in cash. In arriving at the purchase price Leeds Ltd had taken into account in respect of Cardiff Ltd future reorganisation costs of £1 million and anticipated future losses of £2 million. The fair value of the net assets of Cardiff Ltd before taking into account these matters was £7 million.

In accordance with FRS 7 *Fair values in acquisition accounting*, what is the amount of goodwill on the acquisition?

A   £8 million

B   £7 million

C   £6 million

D   £5 million

CHAPTER 6

Accounting for mergers

EXAM FOCUS

Most exam questions on consolidated accounts are based on the acquisition method of accounting, and it is this method that we have been discussing so far. However, there are circumstances in which another method — merger accounting — is more appropriate.

Although merger accounting is less frequently examined than acquisition accounting it is important to be thoroughly familiar with it. This is because when it *does* make an appearance there are too many marks at stake for you to overlook it.

LEARNING OUTCOMES

This chapter covers the following Learning Outcomes of the CIMA Syllabus.

> Explain the merger method of consolidation
> Compare and contrast merger, acquisition and equity methods of accounting
> Prepare consolidated financial statements under the merger method

In order to cover these Learning Outcomes the following topics are included.

> Distinguishing a merger from an acquisition
> Legal requirements and FRS 6

---

1 Distinguishing a merger from an acquisition

1.1 Accounting issues

When one company acquires the share capital of another, we normally have an acquisition. The common features of an acquisition are as follows.

- The first company pays out resources (ie cash) and the cash holdings of the group are therefore reduced following the deal.

- There is a change of ownership. The previous shareholders have taken their cash and left the group.

The acquisition method of accounting is designed to reflect the substance of the deal, normally that one company has acquired the other.

However, there are some business combinations which do not have the substance of an acquisition. This is illustrated below.

1.2   *Illustration*

Suppose that A plc wishes to purchase shares in B plc. The situation *before* this transaction is as follows.

A plc now acquires the entire share capital of B plc from B plc's shareholders and pays for them by issuing shares in A plc in exchange. The situation now looks like this.

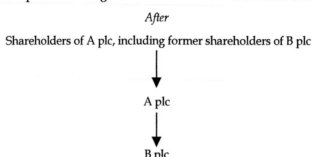

 In this scenario the key features of an acquisition are missing.

◆   B plc's former shareholders retain an interest in the group after the merger (ie share for share exchange has taken place).

◆   A plc has not paid out resources (ie cash) in exchange for B plc.

The substance of the transaction is that A plc and B plc have combined to pool their interests under common ownership. The combination would be the same in substance if B plc had become the parent company.

1.3   *Key features of merger accounting*

To overcome problems with acquisition accounting in a merger, the concept of an acquisition needs to be replaced with a concept of 'pooling of interests' where there is, in substance, no purchase.

There is therefore a need for an alternative method to reflect the substance of the circumstances.

 The main features which distinguish merger accounting from acquisition accounting are as follows.

◆   The net assets of the combining parties need not be adjusted to fair value, though they must use uniform accounting policies.

◆   Profits/losses and cash flows are consolidated from the start of the accounting period in which the combination occurs, even if the merger was in mid-year. Comparatives are restated to achieve uniformity.

◆   The difference between the nominal value of equity shares issued (plus the fair value of any other consideration) and the nominal value of shares acquired in exchange is shown as a movement on other reserves in the group accounts.

◆   Existing balances on the share premium account of the new subsidiary are included in group reserves (not capitalised as part of the goodwill calculation).

◆   Merger expenses should be charged to the profit and loss account as reorganisation or restructuring expenses.

Despite these differences there are areas in which acquisition accounting coincides with merger accounting.

♦ Uniform accounting policies must be used.

♦ Group companies should have uniform year-ends and accounting periods.

♦ Inter-company transactions and balances are cancelled on consolidation.

♦ Unrealised profits must be eliminated and ownership of eliminated profit recorded by subsidiary must be apportioned between group and minority interests (FRS 2).

Dividends paid by the subsidiary prior to combination are shown as dividends in the consolidated profit and loss account because the merged entity is treated as having been always in existence. The dividend would have been paid to shareholders of the subsidiary, who are now shareholders of the parent and are treated as always having been so.

1.4 Comparison with equity accounting

Both the acquisition method and the merger method are methods of consolidating subsidiaries into consolidated accounts. All the assets of the parent are added to all the assets of the subsidiary to show the total assets under the control of the parent.

In the equity method, a one-line item in the consolidated balance sheet shows the parent's share of the net assets of an associate. The associate is not controlled by the parent, so it is not appropriate to present the associate's net assets individually in the consolidated balance sheet. That is why the equity method is appropriate for associates, where the parent has significant influence but not control.

1.5 Learning outcomes

You have now covered the first two learning outcomes for this chapter:

> Explain the merger method of consolidation
> Compare and contrast merger, acquisition and equity methods of accounting

2 Legal requirements and FRS 6

2.1 Regulations on merger accounting

To prevent companies using the merger method when in substance the combination is an acquisition there are rules to govern the use of this method. They come from two sources.

♦ The Companies Act 1985, Schedule 4A.
♦ FRS 6 *Acquisitions and Mergers*. It is vital that you learn these rules.

The following requirements are contained in CA 1985 Schedule 4A (and restated in FRS 6, Appendix 1). Unless these requirements are satisfied the combination ranks as an acquisition, not a merger.

♦ After the combination at least 90% of the nominal value of shares carrying unrestricted rights to participate in distributions (and in assets on liquidation) is held by or on behalf of the parent or its subsidiaries.

♦ The shareholding was attained through an arrangement providing for the issue of equity shares by a parent or its subsidiaries.

♦ The fair value of any consideration other than the issue of equity shares is not greater than 10% of the nominal value of equity shares issued.

♦ Adoption of the merger method of accounting accords with generally accepted accounting principles (ie it must comply with FRS 6).

The following criteria for merger accounting are set out in FRS 6.

♦ Criterion 1: No party to the combination is portrayed as acquirer or acquiree.

♦ Criterion 2: All parties to the combination participate in establishing the management structure, and decisions are made by consensus.

♦ Criterion 3: Relative sizes are not so disparate that one entity dominates by virtue of size.

♦ Criterion 4: Consideration

(a) Consideration for equity shares obtained comprises primarily equity shares in the combined entity.

(b) Any non-equity consideration is an immaterial proportion of the fair value of consideration.

(c) Take into account consideration for equity shares acquired in the two years prior to combination. (This will have been recorded at fair value.)

♦ Criterion 5: No equity shareholders retain any material interest in the future performance of only part of the combined entity.

 If these criteria are satisfied merger accounting *must* be used (unless it would be forbidden by CA 1985).

2.2 The merger relief provisions of the Companies Act

If a company issues shares at a premium (whether for cash or other consideration, eg shares in another company), it must credit the premium to share premium account (s130 CA 1985). The uses of a share premium account are very restricted.

Where a company issues ordinary shares in a share-for-share exchange to take its holding in another company to 90%, it need not apply s130 to this issue. Instead, s131 permits the company to credit the premium to a capital reserve (often called a *merger reserve*).

2.3 Example

A plc offers to exchange shares with Z plc on a one-for-one basis and the offer is accepted by all except 4% of the shareholders of Z. At the date of the offer the market price of a share in A is £3.

Before the offer neither company owned any shares in the other.

The summarised balance sheets, before the proposed exchange of shares, are given below.

	A plc £000	Z plc £000
Fixed assets		
Land and buildings	1,600	1,150
Plant, fixtures, furniture	2,200	1,350
Vehicles	1,150	650
	4,950	3,150
Current assets		
Stocks and work in progress	800	300
Debtors	650	250
Other assets	200	450
	1,650	1,000
Creditors	750	1,050
Net current assets/(liabilities)	900	(50)
	5,850	3,100

Capital and reserves		
Share capital (£1 ordinary shares)	3,600	1,250
Surplus on revaluation	600	
Profit and loss account	1,650	1,850
	5,850	3,100

The fair value of the assets of Z were as follows.

- Land and buildings £1,650,000
- Plant, fixtures and furniture £1,300,000
- Vehicles £620,000
- Stocks and work in progress £290,000
- Debtors £240,000

Required

(a)   Prepare a consolidated balance sheet using the acquisition method for each of the following situations.

    (i)   Assuming the details given above.

    (ii)   Assuming A plc paid 10 pence per share for Z plc in addition to a one-for-one exchange of shares.

(b)   Prepare a consolidated balance sheet using the merger method for each of the two situations in (a) above.

You will need to learn the rules for the use of the merger method of accounting in case the question does not tell you which method to use.

If the purchase consideration is a 'share swap', not cash, you will need to have two extra workings.

- To calculate the fair value of the purchase consideration
- To calculate the new number of shares in the parent company

2.4   *Approach to the example: acquisition method*

We use our standard approach for (W1) and (W2).

(W1)   Group structure

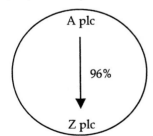

(W2)   Net assets – Z

	Date of acquisition £000	Balance sheet date £000
Share capital	1,250	1,250
Profit and loss account	1,850	1,850
Net assets – book value	3,100	3,100
Fair value adjustments		
Land and buildings	500	500
Plant	(50)	(50)
Vehicles	(30)	(30)
Stocks	(10)	(10)
Debtors	(10)	(10)
Net assets – fair value	3,500	3,500

However when we calculate goodwill we see that the purchase consideration was not cash but shares (with a little bit of cash in the second scenario).

(W3)   Goodwill

	(i) £000	(ii) £000
Purchase consideration		
For 96% of Z's net assets acquired at fair value	(3,360)	(3,360)

This means we will need a supporting working to calculate the fair value of the purchase consideration: use the market value of £3.

(W4)   Purchase consideration

(i)   1,250,000 × 96% =   1,200,000 shares obtained
        1,200,000 × 1/1 =   1,200,000 new shares in A plc issued
        1,200,000 × £3   =   £3,600,000

(ii)   £3,600,000 + (1,200,000 × 10p) = £3,720,000

We can now slot this into (W3).

(W3)   Goodwill

	(i) £000	(ii) £000
Purchase consideration (W4)	3,600	3,720
For 96% of Z's net assets	(3,360)	(3,360)
	240	360

(W5)   is a standard minority interest working.

(W5)   Minority interest

4% of net assets (£3,500,000)	£140,000

(W6)   Group reserves is the standard working.

(W6)   Group reserves

	(i) £000	(ii) £000
100% of A's reserves		
Revaluation reserve	600	600
Profit and loss account	1,650	1,650

Z's reserves are all pre-acquisition.

We will then need two extra workings to calculate the new share capital of A plc and the share premium on the new issue.

(W7)   *Share capital*

	(i) £000	(ii) £000
Existing share capital of A	3,600	3,600
New issue	1,200	1,200
	4,800	4,800

(W8)   *Share premium*

	(i) £000	(ii) £000
Face value	1,200	1,200
Issue price	3,600	3,600
	2,400	2,400

(As this combination meets the section 131 merger relief requirements we could credit the share premium to the merger reserve.)

We are now in a position to consolidate in the usual way.

		(i) £000	(ii) £000
(a)	**Consolidated balance sheets**		
	Fixed assets		
	Goodwill (W3)	240	360
	Land and buildings	3,250	3,250
	Plant and fixtures and fittings	3,500	3,500
	Vehicles	1,770	1,770
		8,760	8,880
	Current assets		
	Stock and work in progress	1,090	1,090
	Debtors	890	890
	Other assets	650	530*
		2,630	2,510
	Creditors	(1,800)	(1,800)
	Net current assets	830	710
	Total assets less current liabilities	9,590	9,590
	Capital and reserves		
	Share capital (W7)	4,800	4,800
	Share premium (W8)	2,400	2,400
	Revaluation reserve (W6)	600	600
	Profit and loss account (W6)	1,650	1,650
		9,450	9,450
	Minority interest (W5)	140	140
		9,590	9,590

* Remember the cash adjustment in the second scenario.

We are then in a position to do the same example using the merger method.

Remember these points of exam technique.

◆ Ignore fair values for the merger method.

◆ The top half of the balance sheet will simply be the net assets of both companies added together.

	(i) £000	(ii) £000
Net assets	8,950	8,830

◆ We include 100% of A's share capital in both methods.

◆ Merger relief provisions allow us to ignore share premium.

When we calculate group reserves there is no split between pre- and post-acquisition reserves. We simply include 100% of A plc and our share of all the reserves of Z plc, ie 96% of Z plc. This means there is only one new working — the merger adjustment.

We calculate this as follows.

	(i) £000	(ii) £000
Nominal value of subsidiary's shares obtained in a share swap	1,200	1,200
Less nominal value of new shares issued	(1,200)	(1,200)
Fair value of any other consideration	-	(120)
Merger adjustment	Nil	(120)

This can then be taken to reserves.

	(i) £000	(ii) £000
Profit and loss account		
100% A plc	1,650	1,650
96% Z plc	1,776	1,776
	3,426	3,426
Merger adjustment		(120)
	3,426	3,306

We are now in a position to prepare a consolidated balance sheet using the merger method.

		(i) £000	(ii) £000
(b)	**Consolidated balance sheets**		
	Net assets	8,950	8,830
	Share capital	4,800	4,800
	Revaluation reserve	600	600
	Profit and loss account	3,426	3,306
	Minority interest (4% × 3,100)	124	124
		8,950	8,830

Practice questions 1 and 2 *(The answers are in the final chapter of this book)*

1   A plc

(a)   Refer back to the example of A plc above. You are required to prepare a consolidated balance sheet using the acquisition method for each of the following situations.

  (i)   Assuming that the offer was three shares in A plc for two shares in Z plc.
  (ii)   Assuming that the offer was two shares in A plc for three shares in Z plc.

(b)   Prepare a consolidated balance sheet using the merger method for each of the two situations in (a) above.

2   Coll

Set out below are the summarised balance sheets of two companies, Coll plc and Tiree plc.

	Coll plc £000	Tiree plc £000
Net assets	5,000	4,000
Share capital — £1 ordinary shares	1,000	1,000
Profit and loss account	4,000	3,000
	5,000	4,000

Coll plc is to combine with Tiree plc by acquiring 100% of Tiree plc's shares. The consideration consists of 1,000,000 £1 ordinary shares valued at £6 each. The fair value of Tiree plc's assets is £4,600,000.

Required

(a)   Assuming that the combination is to be accounted for as an acquisition:

  (i)   prepare the balance sheet of Coll plc reflecting the issue of shares
  (ii)   prepare the consolidated balance sheet of the Coll group after the combination.

(b)   Assuming that the combination is to be accounted for as a merger:

  (i)   prepare the balance sheet of Coll plc reflecting the issue of shares
  (ii)   prepare the consolidated balance sheet of the Coll group after the combination.

(c)   Show how the answer to (b) (ii) above would differ if:

  (i)   the consideration consisted of 800,000 £1 ordinary shares and
  (ii)   the consideration consisted of 1,200,000 £1 ordinary shares.

3   Discussion paper: 'Business combinations'

3.1   Introduction

In December 1998 the ASB issued a discussion paper 'Business combinations' seeking views on the future of accounting in this area. The paper is based on an international appraisal of current methods of accounting for business combinations prepared by members of the US Financial Accounting Standards Board. The current split of combinations between acquisitions and mergers has always been thought to be unsatisfactory by some commentators, who point out that unscrupulous accountants will try and use merger accounting (with its higher reported profits since fixed assets do not have to be revalued on acquisition which would lead to higher depreciation) in a situation which is really an acquisition.

Should a single method of accounting be required for all combinations, eg acquisition accounting or merger accounting or some new method?

It is a similar debate to lease accounting, where the current split of leases into finance leases and operating leases tempts some accountants into trying to classify their leases as operating leases rather than finance leases to avoid having to show the obligation to the lessor in the lessee's balance sheet.

3.2 Recommendations

The discussion paper considers three methods of accounting for business combinations:

(a)   The merger method (also known as the pooling-of-interests method).

(b)   The acquisition method (also known as the purchase method).

(c)   The fresh-start method.

Under the fresh-start method, the reporting entity is treated as a new entity with all of its assets and liabilities being re-measured to fair value at the date of the combination, and its history starts on that date. This method is not in current use in any major standard-setting country in the world.

 The discussion paper concludes that in principle it would be preferable to have a single method of accounting for business combinations, and proposes that the single method should be the acquisition method.

3.3 Reaction to the discussion paper

In the UK most responses to the discussion paper have been unfavourable. Most respondents want to retain the use of the merger method for genuine mergers, ie to keep the status quo as per FRS 6. So this is another area where the UK might become out-of-step with international accounting developments. As with pension scheme accounting and deferred tax accounting, the ASB may have to bow to international pressure in the end.

The USA has recently banned the use of the merger method and the IASB is proposing to ban the merger method by issuing a new international accounting standard in the future. The days of the merger method are numbered, and the UK will have little choice other than to fall in line and ban the use of the merger method in the UK. All business combinations will then have to be accounted for using the acquisition method.

3.4 Learning outcome

You have now covered the final learning outcome for this chapter:

> Prepare consolidated financial statements under the merger method

4 Summary

The key points to take from this chapter are as follows.

♦ The circumstances in which use of merger accounting is obligatory — these are defined in FRS 6.

♦ The main principles of the merger accounting method — these are set out in Section 1 above.

Multiple choice questions *(The answers are in the final chapter of this book)*

1   A company acquires in separate transactions the entire share capital of another company over a period of time as follows.

Firstly	20% for consideration of 1,000 £1 shares (market value £2 each)
Secondly	40% for consideration of 1,500 £1 shares (market value £3 each)
Thirdly	40% for consideration of 2,000 £1 shares (market value £4 each)

After the entire share capital has been acquired, what will be the minimum permissible balance on the share premium account of the acquiring company?

A   £10,000

B   £4,000

C   £1,000

D   Nil

2   Blue plc has an issued share capital of £1 million in ordinary shares of £1 each. Green plc purchased 90% of Blue plc by issuing its own £1 ordinary shares as follows.

Date	No of shares in Blue plc	No of shares in Green plc
30 June 20X1	600,000	500,000
30 June 20X2	300,000	350,000

The fair values of Green plc's shares on 30 June 20X1 and 30 June 20X2 were £1.30 and £1.50 respectively.

What amount must be credited to the share premium account of Green plc in respect of these transactions?

A   Nil

B   £150,000

C   £175,000

D   £325,000

3   Jenson Ltd offers to exchange shares on a one for one basis with Ferrari Ltd and this offer is accepted by 95% of the shareholders of Ferrari Ltd. At the date of the offer the balances on the profit and loss accounts of Jenson Ltd and Ferrari Ltd are £750,000 and £320,000 respectively.

Immediately after the share exchange has taken place, what would be the consolidated profit and loss account reserve figure under acquisition accounting and under merger accounting?

	Acquisition accounting	*Merger accounting*
A	£750,000	£1,054,000
B	£750,000	£1,070,000
C	£1,054,000	£750,000
D	£1,070,000	£750,000

CHAPTER 7

Group accounts: complex structures

EXAM FOCUS

If you are competent at dealing with consolidations for a simple group, it is relatively straightforward to make the step up to deal with a complex group. Make sure you are really familiar with the simple groups covered in previous chapters before embarking on this one.

LEARNING OUTCOMES

This chapter covers the following Learning Outcome of the CIMA Syllabus.

> Prepare a consolidated profit and loss account and a consolidated balance sheet for a group of companies (more advanced aspects)

In order to cover this Learning Outcome the following topics are included

> Vertical groups
> Adjustments on consolidation
> D-shaped groups
> The consolidated profit and loss account

---

1   Vertical groups

1.1   Control and ownership

There are four main methods of accounting for an investing company's interest in another undertaking.

♦   Merger accounting
♦   Acquisition accounting
♦   Proportional consolidation
♦   Equity accounting

The main features of each method are summarised in Table 1 below.

Table 1 **Accounting for investments in group accounts**

	Merger accounting	*Acquisition accounting*	*Proportional consolidation*	*Equity accounting*
Investment in subsidiary/joint venture/associate	Replace with 100% of net assets at year-end (caption by caption).	Replace with 100% of separable net assets at year-end (caption by caption).	Replace with parent's share of net assets at year-end (caption by caption).	Restate to reflect parent's share of net assets at the year-end (single caption).
Minority interest	Show, as a source of finance, the interests of minorities in those net assets at the year-end.	Show, as a source of finance, the interests of minorities in those net assets at the year-end.	N/A	N/A
Goodwill/ difference/ premium on acquisition	Compute and account for difference arising on consolidation (*book values*).	Compute and account for goodwill arising on consolidation (*fair values*).	Compute and account for premium arising on acquisition (*fair values*).	Compute and account for premium arising on acquisition (*fair values*).
Reserves Include:	Parent's share of any change in any of the subsidiary's reserves since incorporation of the subsidiary.	Parent's share of any change in any of the subsidiary's reserves since acquisition of the subsidiary.	Parent's share of any change in any of the investee's reserves since acquisition of the investee.	Parent's share of any change in any of the associate's reserves since acquisition of the associate.

Used to account for subsidiaries   Not in common use in the UK   Used for associates

1.2 Investments by a subsidiary company

A parent may have a subsidiary which has investments of its own. These may be trade investments, associates, or subsidiaries. As the parent controls its subsidiaries, it will also control their holdings in other companies. To show the group as a single economic entity, we need to consolidate subsidiaries which are indirectly held as well as those held by the parent directly.

We do this by applying the principles of group accounts already familiar from earlier chapters. A starting point is to identify *control* relationships to determine the status of investments. Actual shareholdings determine control.

Figure 1 A vertical group

In this illustration:

♦   A controls B and B controls C.
♦   As A controls B, it also controls B's holdings in other companies.
♦   Hence, B and C are subsidiaries of A as they are controlled by A.

Company C is often called a sub-subsidiary.

In a vertical group of this kind, use the group structure to determine the status of investments.

♦   The key is to identify control relationships.

♦   The parent controls its subsidiaries' holdings in other companies but does not control an associate's holdings.

The date of acquisition by A is the date on which A gains control. If B already held C, treat B and C as being acquired on the same day.

The group structure is vital – always identify this first and determine the status of investments. Also look carefully at dates to identify when the parent obtained control.

1.3   Ownership

Using the earlier group structure:

♦   A owns 60% of B and B owns 70% of C.
♦   In effect, A owns 42% of C (60% × 70%).
♦   Minority interests own 58% of C.

The minority interest can be analysed as follows.

	%
Owned by outside shareholders in C	30
Owned by outside shareholders in B (40% × 70%)	28
Effective minority interest	58

Use effective interest to ascertain *ownership* of net assets and profits. But note that the treatment of the investment is determined by the *control* relationship, not the effective interest. Despite the fact that A owns only 42% of C, C is treated as a subsidiary (not an associate) because B controls C.

1.4   Example

The following details relate to the A Ltd group.

	A Ltd £	B Ltd £	C Ltd £
Investment in B Ltd	720	-	-
Investment in C Ltd	-	300	-
Sundry net assets	1,200	1,200	960
	1,920	1,500	960
Share capital	500	480	240
Profit and loss account	1,420	1,020	720
	1,920	1,500	960

A Ltd purchased 60% of B Ltd when B Ltd's profit and loss account stood at £400. Later B Ltd purchased 70% of C Ltd when C Ltd's profit and loss stood at £120.

Required

Prepare the consolidated balance sheet, ignoring the need to amortise goodwill.

1.5 Approach to the example

Observe the following points of exam technique.

- ◆ Apply the same principles as for simple groups but with extra considerations.

- ◆ Prepare group accounts for the parent company's shareholders.

- ◆ Hence, look at the accounts from the parent's point of view.

- ◆ Remember always to present your answer first, supported by a working paper.

- ◆ Always prepare five standard workings: group structure; net assets at balance sheet date and at date of acquisition; goodwill; minority interest; profit and loss reserve.

We start by identifying the *control* relationship.

A   A controls B

| 60%

B   B controls C

| 70%

C

The ultimate parent of both B and C is therefore A. A can control C through its holding in B.

Now we calculate A's *ownership* in C. A owns 60% of B, B owns 70% of C, A effectively owns 60% × 70% = 42% of C.

Working 1 will therefore look like this.

(W1)   Group structure

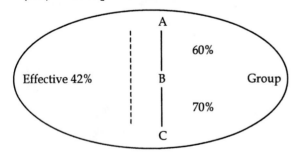

We then need a net asset working for both the subsidiary and the sub-subsidiary.

(W2)   Net assets

	At date of acquisition £	At balance sheet date £
B Ltd		
Share capital	480	480
Profit and loss	400	1,020
	880	1,500

	At date of acquisition £	At balance sheet date £
C Ltd		
Share capital	240	240
Profit and loss	120	720
	360	960

To calculate goodwill in B Ltd we use a standard calculation.

(W3)   Goodwill — B Ltd

	£
Purchase consideration	720
For 60% of net assets acquired (880)	(528)
Goodwill	192

The first complication arises when we calculate the goodwill in the sub-subsidiary, C Ltd. The key is to remember to do it *from the point of view of the ultimate parent.*

Goodwill — C Ltd

	£
Purchase consideration (60% × 300)	180
For 42% of net assets acquired (360)	(151)
Goodwill	29

We are saying that B paid £300 for its share of C Ltd and therefore effectively A paid 60% of £300 for its effective ownership of 42%.

The next complication comes when we try to calculate the minority interest in B Ltd.

We start in the normal way by calculating 40% × £1,500 = £600. However we have a double counting problem because the net assets at the balance sheet date of £1,500 *include* the purchase consideration. We need to exclude this from the working.

The minority interest in B Ltd is therefore as follows.

	£
40% × £1,500	600
Less minority share of B's investment in C Ltd (40% × £300)	120
	480

To calculate the minority interest in C Ltd we use the basic working: 58% × £960 = £557.

(W4)   Minority interests

	£
B Ltd	480
C Ltd	557
	1,037

We also use the standard working for (W5).

(W5)   Profit and loss account

	£
A Ltd	1,420
Share of post-acquisition reserves:	
B Ltd (60% × (1,020 - 400))	372
C Ltd (42% × (720 - 120))	252
	2,044

We can now prepare the answer.

A LTD CONSOLIDATED BALANCE SHEET	£
Intangible fixed assets: goodwill (192 + 29) (W3)	221
Sundry net assets (1,200 + 1,200 + 960)	3,360
	3,581
Called up share capital	500
Profit and loss account (W5)	2,044
	2,544
Minority interests (W4)	1,037
	3,581

1.6 Associate held by subsidiary

Consider the group structure in Figure 2.

Figure 2 Subsidiary invests in associated company

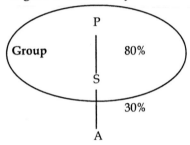

The group (ie P and S considered as a single entity) has a 30% interest in A. Therefore assume that the group has significant influence over A: A is an associate of the group.

P effectively *owns* 24% (80% × 30%) of A.

The minority interest in S own part of the group's interest in A (20% × 30% = 6% effective).

1.7 Example

The balance sheets of three companies at 31 December 20X8 are as follows.

	P Ltd £	S Ltd £	A Ltd £
Fixed asset investments			
80,000 shares in S Ltd	130,000		
3,000 shares in A Ltd		5,000	
Sundry net assets	120,000	225,000	25,000
	250,000	230,000	25,000
Share capital (£1 ordinary shares)	100,000	100,000	10,000
Profit and loss account	150,000	130,000	15,000
	250,000	230,000	25,000

P Ltd acquired its investment in S Ltd when S Ltd's reserves were £50,000. S Ltd later acquired its investment in A Ltd when A Ltd's reserves were £5,000.

Required

Prepare the consolidated balance sheet of P Ltd at 31 December 20X8. All goodwill has been fully amortised.

1.8   Approach to the example

We need to equity account for A in the group accounts and apportion ownership between P and the minority interest in S.

To deal with the associate in the consolidated balance sheet proceed as follows.

♦   Consolidate P and S, leaving investment in associate at cost in subsidiary's net assets.

♦   Equity account for associate in the group accounts and apportion ownership interest between P and minority interests in S.

♦   Include the group share of A's net assets in 'Interests in associated undertakings' in the consolidated balance sheet.

Calculate the premium on acquisition as follows.

	£
Cost of investment : P's share (80% of S's investment in A)	X
Less share of net assets acquired (24% of A's net assets at acquisition)	(X)
	X

Calculate group reserves as follows.

♦   Include P's share (24% effective) of A's post-acquisition reserves in the group profit and loss reserve.

♦   Amortise premium on acquisition over its useful life.

In the minority interest calculation:

♦   include their share (6%) of A's net assets at the balance sheet date

♦   deduct their share (20%) of S's investment in A, to avoid double-counting the investment and net assets of A.

1.9   Solution

The final balance sheet and workings can now be prepared.

P LTD CONSOLIDATED BALANCE SHEET AT 31 DECEMBER 20X8

	£
Interests in associated undertakings (30% × 25,000 (W2))	7,500
Sundry net assets (120,000 + 225,000)	345,000
	352,500
Called up share capital — £1 ordinary shares	100,000
Profit and loss account (W5)	206,000
	306,000
Minority interests (W4)	46,500
	352,500

Workings

(1)   **Group structure**

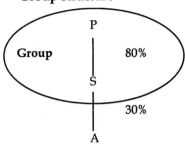

	%
Group interest in A Ltd	30
	—
Ownership of group interest	
P Ltd effective interest (80% × 30%)	24
Minority interests	6
	—
	30
	—

(2)   **Net assets**

	At date of acquisition £	At balance sheet date £
S Ltd		
Share capital	100,000	100,000
Profit and loss account	50,000	130,000
	150,000	230,000

	At date of acquisition £	At balance sheet date £
A Ltd		
Share capital	10,000	10,000
Profit and loss account	5,000	15,000
	15,000	25,000

(3)   **Goodwill**

	£
S Ltd	
Cost of investment	130,000
Share of net assets acquired (80% × 150,000)	(120,000)
	10,000

	£
A Ltd	
Cost of investment (80% × 5,000)	4,000
Share of net assets acquired (24% × 15,000(W2))	(3,600)
	400

(4)   **Minority interests**

	£
S Ltd (20% × 230,000 (W2))	46,000
Share of net assets of A Ltd (6% × 25,000 (W2))	1,500
Less share of cost of investment in A Ltd (20% × 5,000 (W3))	(1,000)
	46,500

(5)   **Profit and loss account**

	£
P Ltd	150,000
Share of S Ltd (80% × (130,000 - 50,000) (W2))	64,000
Share of A Ltd (24% × (15,000 - 5,000) (W2))	2,400
Goodwill on S Ltd (W3) fully amortised	(10,000)
Premium on A Ltd (W3) fully amortised	(400)
	206,000

Practice question 1 *(The answer is in the final chapter of this book)*

H group

BALANCE SHEETS AT 31 DECEMBER 20X8

	H plc £	S Ltd £	T Ltd £
Shares in S Ltd (75%)	65,000	-	-
Shares in T Ltd (60%)	-	50,000	-
Sundry net assets	145,000	70,000	75,000
	210,000	120,000	75,000
Ordinary share capital	120,000	70,000	40,000
Reserves	90,000	50,000	35,000
	210,000	120,000	75,000

Both investments were acquired on 31 December 20X1 when S Ltd reserves were £10,000 and T Ltd reserves were £12,000. Goodwill on consolidation is now fully amortised.

Required

Prepare the consolidated balance sheet at 31 December 20X8.

---

2   Adjustments on consolidation

2.1   Dividends

Adjustments to record dividends affect individual companies' books of account.

♦   Actual shareholdings determine who receives dividends.

♦   In the earlier example, since A does not own shares in C, it does not receive any dividends from C.

Therefore, effective interests are irrelevant and should be ignored when dealing with dividends.

To deal with dividends, follow the same steps as with a simple group.

♦   Record the dividend in the paying company's books.

♦   Record the dividend receivable in the receiving company's books.

♦   Cancel the inter-company balance to leave the dividend creditor in the consolidated balance sheet as the parent's dividend plus dividends due to minority interests.

2.2   Example

Using the earlier example of A Ltd, B Ltd and C Ltd, show the impact on the consolidated workings of the following dividends.

		£
Proposed dividends		
	B Ltd	200
	C Ltd	100

2.3   Approach to the example

The key thing to remember is that these adjustments *must* be put through before you work out net assets; otherwise it all goes horribly wrong.

Put through the adjustments on the face of the questions: see below.

	A Ltd £	B Ltd £	C Ltd £
Investment in B Ltd	720	-	-
Investment in C Ltd	-	300	-
Debtors (60% × 200/70% × 100)	**120**	**70**	
Sundry net assets	1,200	1,200	960
Creditors (proposed dividend)	——	**(200)**	**(100)**
	1,920	1,500	960
Share capital	500	480	240
Profit and loss account	1,420 **+120**	1,020 **-200** **+70**	720 **-100**
	1,920	1,500	960

When we calculate net assets we now get different figures at the balance sheet date. Net assets at the date of acquisition are unaffected.

(2)   **Net assets at balance sheet date**

	B Ltd £	£	C Ltd £	£
Share capital		480		240
Profit and loss	1,020		720	
Proposed dividend	(200)		(100)	
Dividends receivable	70		-	
		890		620
		1,370		860

This will give us a different minority interest working.

(4)   **Minority interests**

	£
In B Ltd (40% × £1,370)	548
In C Ltd (58% × £860)	499
Cost of investment in C Ltd (as before)	(120)
	927

The profit and loss account working will also change (in detail, though not in total).

(5) **Profit and loss account**

	£
A Ltd	1,420
Dividend receivable from B Ltd	120
Share of post-acquisition profits	
B Ltd (60% × (890 - 400))	294
C Ltd (42% × (620 - 120))	210
	2,044

The dividend receivable debtors will then cancel against the proposed dividend creditor.

The final balance sheet looks as follows.

A LTD CONSOLIDATED BALANCE SHEET	£
Intangible fixed assets : goodwill	221
Sundry net assets (1,200 + 120 + 1,200 + 70 - 200 + 960 - 100)	3,250
	3,471
Called up share capital	500
Profit and loss account	2,044
	2,544
Minority interests	927
	3,471

Practice question 2 *(The answer is in the final chapter of this book)*

Gucci

The following balance sheets relate to Gucci Ltd and its group companies at 31 December 20X9.

	Gucci Ltd		Dior Ltd		Yves Ltd	
	£	£	£	£	£	£
Fixed assets						
Tangible assets		5,000		7,000		6,000
Shares in Dior Ltd		6,500				
Shares in Yves Ltd				3,500		
Debentures of Dior Ltd		500				
		12,000		10,500		6,000
Current assets						
Stocks	2,000		3,000		3,000	
Debtors	3,000		3,500		3,750	
Cash at bank and in hand	500		–		–	
	5,500		6,500		6,750	
Creditors: amounts falling due within one year						
Bank loans and overdrafts	–		1,000		900	
Trade creditors	2,500		1,700		2,100	
Proposed dividends	–		3,000		2,000	
	2,500		5,700		5,000	
Net current assets		3,000		800		1,750
Total assets less current liabilities		15,000		11,300		7,750
Creditors: amounts falling due after more than one year						
10% debenture loans		(2,000)		(1,000)		–
		13,000		10,300		7,750

Capital and reserves

Called up share capital (£1 shares)	1,000	5,000	1,000
Share premium account	–	2,500	–
Profit and loss account	12,000	2,800	6,750
	13,000	10,300	7,750

The following information is relevant.

♦ Dior Ltd bought 80% of Yves Ltd on 1 January 20X5 when the latter's profit and loss account stood at £3,000.

♦ Gucci Ltd bought 75% of Dior Ltd on 1 January 20X5 when the latter's profit and loss account stood at £1,000.

♦ Gucci Ltd and Dior Ltd do not account for dividends until they are received.

♦ The directors of Gucci Ltd wish to propose a dividend of £2,000.

♦ Goodwill has been fully amortised.

Required

Produce the consolidated balance sheet of Gucci Ltd at 31 December 20X9.

2.4 Unrealised profit

Use *effective interests* when determining ownership for unrealised profit adjustments.

Example

Using the group structure as previously, C Ltd sells goods to A Ltd for £300, which originally cost C Ltd £200. If the goods are still in stock at the year-end, the adjustment in the consolidated balance sheet is:

		£	£
Debit	Profit and loss account (42% × £100)	42	
Debit	Minority interests (58% × £100)	58	
Credit	Stocks (consolidated balance sheet)		100

3 D-shaped groups

3.1 Introduction

Sometimes the parent company also holds a direct interest in the sub-subsidiary. We call this a 'D'-shaped or mixed group.

Figure 3 A D-shaped group

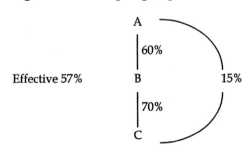

3.2   Example

The following are the summarised balance sheets of T Ltd, P Ltd and A Ltd as at 31 December 20X4.

	T Ltd £	P Ltd £	A Ltd £
Fixed assets	140,000	61,000	170,000
Investments	200,000	65,000	-
Net current assets	10,000	14,000	10,000
	350,000	140,000	180,000
Ordinary shares of £1 each	200,000	80,000	100,000
Revenue reserves	150,000	60,000	80,000
	350,000	140,000	180,000

On 1 January 20X3 P Ltd acquired 35,000 ordinary shares in A Ltd at a cost of £65,000 when the revenue reserves of A Ltd amounted to £40,000.

On 1 January 20X4 T Ltd acquired 64,000 shares in P Ltd at a cost of £120,000 and 40,000 shares in A Ltd at a cost of £80,000. The revenue reserves of P Ltd and A Ltd amounted to £50,000 and £60,000 respectively on 1 January 20X4.

Required

Prepare the consolidated balance sheet of the T Ltd group as at 31 December 20X4. Ignore the need to amortise goodwill.

3.3   Approach to the example

Apply the same principles as for a vertical group.

Note that the dates on which the investments are made are important. A good technique is to build up the group structure in chronological order and look at the status of investments at each stage to decide how to deal with them.

Remember that the parent has an indirect holding through its subsidiary as well as a direct holding through the shares it owns itself.

3.4   Solution

(1)   **Group structure**

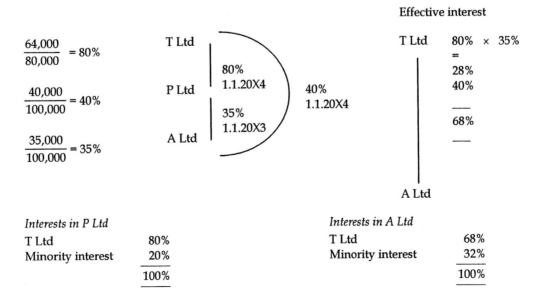

Interests in P Ltd		Interests in A Ltd	
T Ltd	80%	T Ltd	68%
Minority interest	20%	Minority interest	32%
	100%		100%

Working 1 is the key – look for the control relationship and then the effective ownership.

The net assets working remains standard.

(2)   **Net assets of P Ltd**

	At date of acquisition £	At balance sheet date £
£1 shares	80,000	80,000
Reserves	50,000	60,000
	130,000	140,000

Net assets of A Ltd

	At date of acquisition £	At balance sheet date £
£1 shares	100,000	100,000
Reserves	60,000	80,000
	160,000	180,000

For goodwill in the subsidiary we use the standard working.

(3)   **Goodwill – P Ltd**

	£
Purchase consideration	120,000
For 80% of net assets (£130,000)	(104,000)
Goodwill	16,000

The first complication arises when we calculate the goodwill in the sub-subsidiary. There is a two-part purchase consideration — a direct amount and an indirect amount.

Goodwill – A Ltd

	£
Direct consideration	80,000
Indirect consideration (80% × 65,000)	52,000
Total consideration	132,000
For 68% of net assets (£160,000)	(108,800)
Goodwill	23,200

Minority interest and group profit and loss account remain the same as for a vertical group.

(4)   **Minority interest**

	£
P Ltd	
20% × £140,000	28,000
Less share of P Ltd's investment in A Ltd (20% × £65,000)	(13,000)
Minority interest	15,000
A Ltd	
32% × £180,000	57,600
	72,600

(5)   **Group profit and loss account**

	£
T Ltd	150,000
P Ltd (share of post-acquisition profits)	
(60,000 - 50,000) × 80%	8,000
A Ltd (share of post-acquisition profits)	
(80,000 - 60,000) × 68%	13,600
	171,600

The final balance sheet can now be prepared.

T LTD CONSOLIDATED BALANCE SHEET AS AT 31 DECEMBER 20X4

	£
Intangible fixed assets: goodwill	39,200
Fixed assets	371,000
Net current assets	34,000
	444,200
£1 shares	200,000
Group reserves (W5)	171,600
	371,600
Minority interests (W4)	72,600
	444,200

Practice question 3 *(The answer is in the final chapter of this book)*

Pace

The summarised balances extracted from the accounting records of Pace Ltd, Slow Ltd and Stop Ltd at 30 November 20X7 are as follows.

	Pace Ltd	Slow Ltd	Stop Ltd
	£	£	£
Land and buildings	447,500	230,950	52,000
Plant and machinery	600,500		61,750
Fixtures and fittings	54,500	41,000	8,800
Investments at cost			
420,000 shares in Slow Ltd	367,500		
70,000 shares in Stop Ltd	49,000		
35,000 shares in Stop Ltd		24,500	
Stock	526,610	163,290	85,700
Debtors	241,920	129,680	29,750
Cash	88,200	4,725	8,105
Creditors	(95,480)	(86,645)	(88,605)
	2,280,250	507,500	157,500
£1 shares	1,750,000		175,000
75p shares		420,000	
Other reserves	350,000	70,000	
Profit and loss account	180,250	17,500	(17,500)
	2,280,250	507,500	157,500

Further information

1. Pace Ltd purchased its interest in Slow Ltd and Stop Ltd on 1 December 20X4 at which date there was an adverse balance on Stop Ltd's profit and loss account of £35,000 and a credit balance of the same amount on the profit and loss account of Slow Ltd.

2. Stop Ltd had an adverse balance of £52,500 on profit and loss account when Slow Ltd purchased 35,000 shares in 20X3.

3. Neither Slow Ltd or Stop Ltd had any other reserves when their shares were purchased by Pace Ltd and Slow Ltd.

You are required to prepare the consolidated balance sheet of Pace Ltd and its subsidiaries at 30 November 20X7. Assume that all goodwill has been fully amortised.

4 The consolidated profit and loss account

4.1 Introduction

Complex group structures lead to only one additional complication as far as the profit and loss account is concerned. This is the calculation of minority interests. We illustrate the approach below.

Example

The A Ltd group is structured as follows.

Profits for the year are as follows (ignoring tax).

	A Ltd	B Ltd	C Ltd
	£	£	£
Operating profit	500	400	300
Dividend from B	60	–	–
Dividend from C	-	70	-
Profit for year	560	470	300
Dividends (paid)	(200)	(100)	(100)
Retained profit	360	370	200

Required

Calculate the minority interests in the consolidated profit and loss account.

4.2 Approach to the example

As already stated, the only extra complication concerns the minority interest. This should be calculated using *effective* interests.

To avoid counting C's profits *both* in C's effective minority interest *and* in B's minority interest, first deduct B's share of dividends from C from B's profit after tax. Use this *adjusted* figure for B's profit after tax to compute the minority interest in B's profit.

4.3 Solution

Minority interests in the consolidated profit and loss account will be as follows.

	£
Minority interests in B (40% × (470 - 70))	160
Minority interests in C (58% × 300)	174
	334

4.4 Example

A Ltd owns 75% of B Ltd and B Ltd owns 90% of C Ltd. Summary profit and loss accounts for the year are as follows.

	A Ltd £	B Ltd £	C Ltd £
Operating profit	100,000	80,000	20,000
Dividend from B Ltd	6,000		
Dividend from C Ltd		1,800	
Profit before taxation	106,000	81,800	20,000
Taxation	(40,000)	(30,000)	(7,000)
Profit after taxation	66,000	51,800	13,000
Dividends paid	(35,000)	(8,000)	(2,000)
Retained profit for the year	31,000	43,800	11,000

Required

Prepare the consolidated profit and loss account for the year.

4.5 Solution

A LTD CONSOLIDATED PROFIT AND LOSS ACCOUNT

	£
Profit on ordinary activities before taxation (100 + 80 + 20)	200,000
Tax on profit on ordinary activities (40 + 30 + 7)	(77,000)
Profit on ordinary activities after taxation	123,000
Minority interests (W2)	(16,725)
Profit for the financial year attributable to the shareholders of A Ltd	106,275
Dividends (paid)	(35,000)
Retained profit for the financial year	71,275

Workings

(1)   **Group structure**

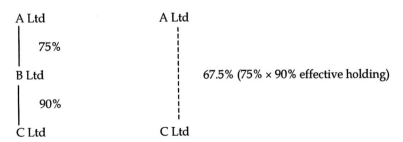

A Ltd

|
75%

B Ltd

|
90%

C Ltd

A Ltd

67.5% (75% × 90% effective holding)

C Ltd

(2)   Minority interests

	£		£
In B Ltd			
Profit after taxation	51,800		
Less dividend from C Ltd	(1,800)		
	50,000	× 25% =	12,500
In C Ltd (32.5% × £13,000)			4,225
			16,725

Practice question 4 *(The answer is in the final chapter of this book)*

Lamb

Lamb Ltd purchased 60% of Tikka Ltd in 20X2, when the balance on the profit and loss account of Tikka Ltd was £24,000, giving rise to goodwill of £28,000. In 20X4 Tikka Ltd acquired 80% of Biryani Ltd when the balance on the profit and loss account of Biryani Ltd was £36,000. The goodwill on acquisition of Biryani Ltd (calculated on the effective interest of Lamb Ltd) was £42,000. All goodwill has been fully amortised.

The draft results of the three companies for the year ended 30 June 20X7 are as follows.

	Lamb Ltd	Tikka Ltd	Biryani Ltd
	£	£	£
Turnover	197,000	100,000	128,000
Cost of sales and expenses	(96,600)	(52,000)	(78,000)
Operating profit	100,400	48,000	50,000
Dividends receivable	9,600	8,000	-
Profit before tax	110,000	56,000	50,000
Taxation	(40,000)	(17,000)	(14,000)
Profit after tax	70,000	39,000	36,000
Dividends	(30,000)	(16,000)	(10,000)
Retained profit	40,000	23,000	26,000
Retained profit b/f	120,000	70,000	52,000
Retained profit c/f	160,000	93,000	78,000

All group companies have correctly accounted for dividends payable and receivable. Tikka Ltd has yet to account for the gain on disposal of freehold property shortly before the year-end. The profit amounts to £14,000. There are no tax implications.

Required

Prepare the consolidated profit and loss account of the Lamb Ltd group for the year ended 30 June 20X7.

4.6   Learning outcome

You have now covered the learning outcome for this chapter:

> Prepare a consolidated profit and loss account and a consolidated balance sheet for a group of companies (more advanced aspects).

5 Summary

We have looked at two main group structures: vertical groups and D-shaped (also called "mixed") groups. In each case we used *control* relationships to determine the status of investments (ie whether or not they rank as subsidiaries or associates). We used *effective* relationships to determine ownership and minority interests.

The consolidation adjustments that arise frequently relate to inter-company dividends and unrealised profits.

In the consolidated profit and loss account the only figure that must be treated with extra care is the minority interest.

Multiple choice questions *(The answers are in the final chapter of this book)*

1   Gregus Ltd acquired 60,000 shares in Petra Ltd on 1 January 20X1 for £240,000 when Petra Ltd's profit and loss account stood at £280,000. Petra Ltd's share capital is made up of 100,000 £1 ordinary shares.

    Petra Ltd acquired 120,000 shares in Empus Ltd on 1 January 20X2 for £100,000 when Empus Ltd's profit and loss account stood at £50,000. Empus Ltd's share capital is made up of 200,000 50 pence ordinary shares.

    Goodwill is written off over 3 years.

    What is the net book value of goodwill in the consolidated balance sheet as at 31 December 20X2?

    A   £8,000

    B   £18,000

    C   £10,667

    D   £34,667

2   Given below are the balance sheets of A Ltd, B Ltd and C Ltd as at 31 March 20X2.

	A Ltd £	B Ltd £	C Ltd £
Investment in B Ltd	1,200	-	-
Investment in C Ltd	-	840	-
Net assets	3,000	1,400	1,250
	4,200	2,240	1,250
Share capital	2,000	1,000	800
Profit and loss account	2,200	1,240	450
	4,200	2,240	1,250

A Ltd acquired 75% of B Ltd when B Ltd's profit and loss account stood at £400. B Ltd then acquired 80% of C Ltd when C Ltd's profit and loss account stood at £200. These purchases were a number of years ago and any goodwill has been fully amortised.

What is the figure for the consolidated profit and loss account reserve in the consolidated balance sheet as at 31 March 20X2?

A   £2,800

B   £2,850

C   £2,980

D   £3,030

3   Given below are the net assets of three companies as at 30 June 20X2.

D Ltd	£780,000
E Ltd	£340,000
F Ltd	£300,000

D Ltd owns 80% of the shares of E Ltd. E Ltd owns 60% of the shares of F Ltd.

What is the minority interest in the consolidated balance sheet as at 30 June 20X2?

A   £92,000

B   £188,000

C   £212,000

D   £224,000

4   G Ltd owns 60% of the share capital of H Ltd and 25% of the share capital of J Ltd. H Ltd owns 60% of J Ltd.

What is the total minority interest percentage in J Ltd?

A   15%

B   24%

C   39%

D   49%

CHAPTER 8

Group accounts: piecemeal acquisitions

EXAM FOCUS

In some questions the shares in a subsidiary company have been acquired in several stages, rather than in one go.

In order to calculate goodwill and reserves at acquisition, the net assets at the date of acquisition must be established. With a piecemeal acquisition there will be more than one date to deal with. This is a frequent complication in exam questions and the present chapter shows how to deal with it.

LEARNING OUTCOMES

This chapter covers the following Learning Outcome of the CIMA Syllabus.

Prepare consolidated financial statements where the shareholdings, or control, are acquired in stages

In order to cover this Learning Outcome the following topics are included.

Piecemeal acquisition: the possibilities
Increasing the stake in a subsidiary
An associate becoming a subsidiary

---

1 Piecemeal acquisitions: the possibilities

1.1 Introduction

There are several piecemeal acquisition possibilities, depending on the size of the stake purchased at each stage. These are summarised in Table 1 with example percentages.

Table 1 Piecemeal acquisitions

First acquisition		Second acquisition	
Percentage acquired	Status of investment	Percentage acquired	Status of investment
15%	Trade investment	45%	Subsidiary (total: 60%)
15%	Trade investment	20%	Associate (total: 35%)
60%	Subsidiary	20%	Subsidiary (total: 80%) (increased stake)
30%	Associate	50%	Subsidiary (total: 80%)

1.2 Trade investment becoming a subsidiary

We illustrate this possibility by means of an example.

1.3 Example

Solar Ltd acquired its holding in Hoover Ltd as follows.

	%	
31 December 20X4	15	when Hoover Ltd's reserves were £40,000
30 June 20X5	50	when Hoover Ltd's reserves were £80,000
31 December 20X5	-	when Hoover Ltd's reserves were £120,000

Required

Calculate the pre-acquisition and post-acquisition reserves of Hoover Ltd at 31 December 20X5.

1.4 Solution

The rule is that the date of acquisition is the date on which control is gained. We ignore the previous status as a trade investment.

The pre-acquisition reserves are therefore £80,000 and post-acquisition reserves are (£120,000-£80,000) £40,000.

1.5 Trade investment becoming an associate

The rule here is similar: the date of acquisition is the date on which significant influence is attained. We ignore the previous status as a trade investment.

As an example, suppose that Solar's second acquisition of shares in Hoover amounted to 20% (not 50%). In this case we say that significant influence was attained on 30 June 20X5 and we calculate pre-acquisition reserves at that date.

Table 1 also illustrates two other possibilities: increasing our stake in a subsidiary (eg from 60% to 80%) and converting an associate into a subsidiary (eg by increasing our stake from 30% to 80%). Each of these cases is discussed below.

2 Increasing the stake in a subsidiary

2.1 The technique illustrated

We illustrate the technique by means of an example.

Example

The balance sheets of Portion Ltd and its subsidiary Slice Ltd at 31 December 20X1 are as follows.

	Portion Ltd	Slice Ltd
	£000	*£000*
Investment in Slice Ltd	400	-
Sundry net assets	600	550
	1,000	550
Share capital: £1 ordinary shares	200	100
Profit and loss account	800	450
	1,000	550

Portion Ltd acquired its holding in Slice Ltd as follows.

Date	Proportion acquired	Cost of investment	Slice Ltd profit and loss reserve
	%	£000	£000
30 September 20X0	60	250	300
31 July 20X1	20	150	400

Goodwill on consolidation is to be amortised over ten years with a full year's charge made in the year of acquisition.

Required

Prepare the consolidated balance sheet of Portion Ltd at 31 December 20X1.

2.2   Approach to the example

Where we have an increased stake in a subsidiary we will need a three column net assets working.

(W2)   Net assets

	At date of acquisition		*At balance sheet date*
	30.9.X0	*31.7.X1*	*31.12.X1*

We then proceed with our usual workings.

(W1)   Group structure

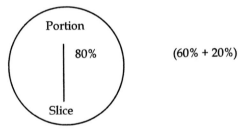

    (60% + 20%)

As soon as you see it is a piecemeal increase in stake in subsidiary, switch to a three column working for net assets.

(W2)   Net assets – Slice

	At date of acquisition		*At balance sheet date*
	30.9.X0	*31.7.X1*	*31.12.X1*
	£000	*£000*	*£000*
Share capital	100	100	100
Profit and loss account	300	400	450
Net assets	400	500	550

We will now be able to calculate goodwill using net assets at each stage separately.

(W3)   Goodwill

	£000	£000
Purchase consideration	250	150
For 60% net assets acquired (400) 30.9.X0	(240)	–
For 20% net assets acquired (500) 31.7.X1	–	(100)
Goodwill	10	50
Amortisation (2/10; 1/10)	2	5
Balance carried forward	8	45

Minority interest is calculated by means of our standard working.

(W4)   Minority interest

	£000
20% (550)	110

The group reserves of Slice, as with goodwill, will also need to be calculated in two chunks.

(W5)   Profit and loss account

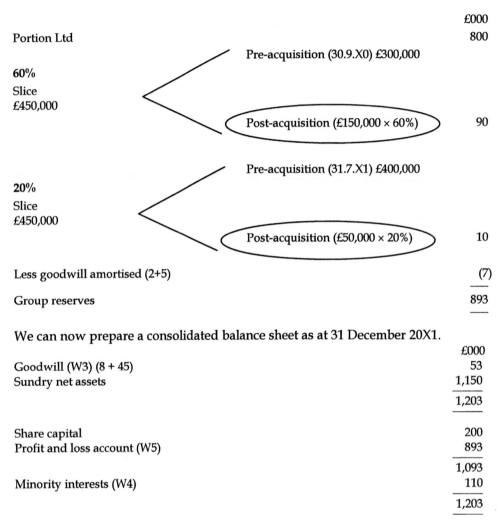

	£000
Portion Ltd	800
60% Slice £450,000 — Post-acquisition (£150,000 × 60%)	90
20% Slice £450,000 — Post-acquisition (£50,000 × 20%)	10
Less goodwill amortised (2+5)	(7)
Group reserves	893

Pre-acquisition (30.9.X0) £300,000

Pre-acquisition (31.7.X1) £400,000

We can now prepare a consolidated balance sheet as at 31 December 20X1.

	£000
Goodwill (W3) (8 + 45)	53
Sundry net assets	1,150
	1,203
Share capital	200
Profit and loss account (W5)	893
	1,093
Minority interests (W4)	110
	1,203

Practice question 1 *(The answer is in the final chapter of this book)*

Dolland

Dolland Ltd has two subsidiary companies, Contact Ltd, in which it has a 75% holding, and Hard Ltd, in which it holds 60% of the equity share capital.

The holdings were acquired as follows.

	Company	Number of shares	Cost £	Profit and loss balance £
1 January 20X0	Contact Ltd	120,000	195,000	110,000
30 June 20X0	Hard Ltd	60,000	84,000	31,000
1 January 20X2	Contact Ltd	30,000	65,000	212,000

The draft balance sheets of the companies at 31 December 20X7 were as follows.

	Dolland Ltd £	Contact Ltd £	Hard Ltd £
Fixed assets			
Tangible	368,000	400,000	100,200
Investments	344,000	-	-
	712,000	400,000	100,200
Net current assets	106,540	165,000	50,400
	818,540	565,000	150,600
Capital and reserves			
Called up share capital — £1 ordinary shares	500,000	200,000	100,000
Profit and loss account	318,540	365,000	50,600
	818,540	565,000	150,600

The following adjustments are required.

(1)   Dolland Ltd and Contact Ltd wish to propose a 5% dividend.

(2)   Hard Ltd wishes to propose a 15% dividend.

Group policy is to amortise goodwill over five years.

Required

Prepare the consolidated balance sheet of Dolland Ltd as at 31 December 20X7.

3   *An associate becoming a subsidiary*

3.1   *The basic method*

There are two methods of calculating net assets at the date of acquisition.

♦   The basic rule (Companies Act 1985)

♦   An alternative method described in FRS 2 (paragraph 89)

We first of all illustrate the basic (CA 85) method by means of an example.

3.2   *Example*

Long Ltd, whose year end is 31 December, had balance sheets as follows.

	20X2 £	20X1 £
Investment in Ashton Ltd	168,000	60,000
Other net assets	528,000	560,000
	696,000	620,000
Share capital	50,000	50,000
Profit and loss account	646,000	570,000
	696,000	620,000

The shares in Ashton Ltd had been acquired as follows.

Acquisition date	Shares acquired		Cost £	Net assets at acquisition £	Net assets at year-end £
1 February 20X1	5,000	(25%)	60,000	115,000	140,000
1 July 20X2	7,000	(35%)	108,000	160,000	165,000

The above balance sheets already consolidate a wholly owned subsidiary but the investment in Ashton Ltd is shown at cost.

Required

(a)   Prepare the consolidated balance sheet of Long Ltd at 31 December 20X1.

(b)   Prepare the consolidated balance sheet of Long Ltd at 31 December 20X2, applying the Companies Act 1985 method of computing goodwill relating to Ashton Ltd.

Note   Goodwill is to be carried as a permanent intangible fixed asset.

3.3   *Approach to the example*

Part (a) is simply revision of accounting for associates, which is assumed prior knowledge from earlier in this text.

To tackle this, we use equity accounting – a modified form of the consolidation procedure. Instead of accounting for the company's net assets 100% we only account for the group share. We will therefore have no minority interests.

(W1)   Group structure

Ashton

Assuming that Long has significant influence over Ashton we will need to equity account.

(W2)   Net assets — Ashton

	At date of acquisition	At balance sheet date
Net assets (given in question)	£115,000	£140,000

We calculate goodwill/premium in the normal way.

(W3)   Goodwill

	£
Purchase consideration	60,000
For 25% of net assets acquired (115,000)	(28,750)
Goodwill	31,250

 Remember: there is no minority interest in equity accounting.

We bring in our share of the associate's post-acquisition reserves in the normal way.

(W4) Group reserves

	£
100% Long	570,000

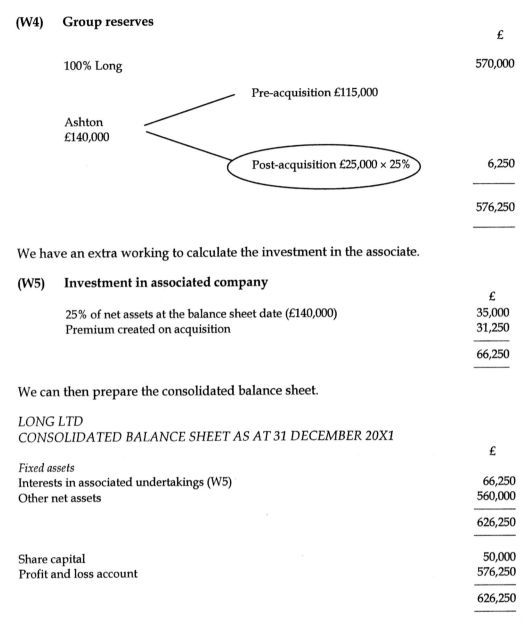

Pre-acquisition £115,000

Ashton
£140,000

Post-acquisition £25,000 × 25%   6,250

	£
	576,250

We have an extra working to calculate the investment in the associate.

(W5) Investment in associated company

	£
25% of net assets at the balance sheet date (£140,000)	35,000
Premium created on acquisition	31,250
	66,250

We can then prepare the consolidated balance sheet.

LONG LTD
CONSOLIDATED BALANCE SHEET AS AT 31 DECEMBER 20X1

	£
Fixed assets	
Interests in associated undertakings (W5)	66,250
Other net assets	560,000
	626,250
Share capital	50,000
Profit and loss account	576,250
	626,250

We then move on a year at part (b). By this time, Long group have purchased another 35% taking their total holding to 60%. We have a piecemeal acquisition in which an associate becomes a subsidiary.

The basic (CA85) rule is that the date of acquisition is the date on which control is gained. We *ignore* the previous status as an associate.

This leads to the following workings.

(W1) Group structure

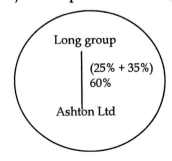

Long group

(25% + 35%)
60%

Ashton Ltd

(W2) **Net assets**

	Date of acquisition	Balance date
Net assets (given in question)	£160,000	£165,000

(W3) **Goodwill**

	£
Purchase consideration (£60,000 + £108,000)	168,000
For 60% of net assets acquired (£160,000)	(96,000)
	£72,000

(W4) **Minority interest**

40% (£165,000)	£66,000

(W5) **Group profit and loss account**

	£
100% Long	646,000

£160,000
Pre-acquisition

Ashton
£165,000

Post-acquisition
£5,000 × 60% — 3,000

Group profit and loss	649,000

We can now prepare the consolidated balance sheet.

CONSOLIDATED BALANCE SHEET AS AT 31 DECEMBER 20X2

	£
Goodwill (W3)	72,000
Other net assets (528 + 165)	693,000
	765,000
Share capital	50,000
Profit and loss account (W5)	649,000
	699,000
Minority interests (W4)	66,000
	765,000

3.4 The alternative method (FRS 2)

FRS 2 argues that in some circumstances the basic CA85 method will fail to give a true and fair view. It argues that a truer figure for goodwill is obtained using the 'three column net assets' approach.

We will apply this approach to the example of the Long group.

Our (W1) is unchanged but (W2) will now look like this.

Net assets

	Date of acquisition		Balance sheet date
	1.2.X1 (25%)	1.7.X2 (35%)	
Net assets (given in question)	£115,000	£160,000	£165,000

Goodwill is calculated in the piecemeal way.

	£
Purchase consideration	168,000
For 25% of net assets acquired on 1.2.X1 (£115,000)	(28,750)
For 35% of net assets acquired on 1.7.X2 (£160,000)	(56,000)
Goodwill	83,250

This gives us a more accurate figure for goodwill.

The minority interest calculation (W4) remains unchanged but the group profit and loss account will also be calculated in a piecemeal way.

(W5)   Group profit and loss account

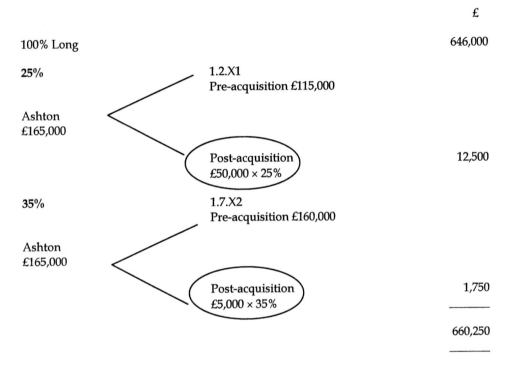

	£
100% Long	646,000
25%	
1.2.X1 Pre-acquisition £115,000	
Ashton £165,000	
Post-acquisition £50,000 × 25%	12,500
35%	
1.7.X2 Pre-acquisition £160,000	
Ashton £165,000	
Post-acquisition £5,000 × 35%	1,750
	660,250

The balance sheet will then be as follows.

CONSOLIDATED BALANCE SHEET AS AT 31 DECEMBER 20X2

	£
Goodwill	83,250
Other net assets	693,000
	776,250
Share capital	50,000
Profit and loss account	660,250
	710,250
Minority interest	66,000
	776,250

Practice question 2 *(The answer is in the final chapter of this book)*

Harrods

The summarised balance sheets as at 30 June 20X5 of Harrods Ltd, Selfridges Ltd and Allders Ltd are given below.

	Harrods Ltd £	Selfridges Ltd £	Allders Ltd £
Tangible fixed assets	25,500	22,200	18,450
Investment in Selfridges Ltd	15,450		
Investment in Allders Ltd	5,700		
Stock	11,150	4,300	1,350
Debtors	5,200	1,100	250
Cash	1,000	500	–
	64,000	28,100	20,050
Share capital — 50p ordinary shares	20,000	10,000	5,000
Profit and loss account brought forward	38,200	6,400	1,800
Retained profit for the year	200	1,800	600
	58,400	18,200	7,400
Debenture loans	–	4,000	6,000
Creditors	2,100	2,200	1,250
Bank overdraft		2,500	5,100
Proposed dividend	3,500	1,200	300
	64,000	28,100	20,050

The following additional information is given.

(1) Harrods Ltd paid £10,000 to acquire 60% of the ordinary share capital of Selfridges Ltd on 30 June 20X1 when the profit and loss account of Selfridges Ltd stood at £2,500. Harrods Ltd acquired an additional 30% of the ordinary share capital on 1 November 20X4.

(2) Harrods Ltd acquired 4,000 ordinary shares in Allders Ltd on 1 October 20X3 when the balance on Allders Ltd's profit and loss account stood at £1,500.

The directors of Harrods Ltd are of the opinion that the freehold land included in Allders Ltd's balance sheet at the date of acquisition was undervalued by £1,000. Allders Ltd has not reflected this valuation in its own books. The company still owns the land at the balance sheet date.

(3) Harrods Ltd has not yet accounted for dividends receivable from either Selfridges Ltd or Allders Ltd.

(4) The stock figure in the balance sheet of Selfridges Ltd at 30 June 20X5 includes an item purchased from Harrods for £1,200 which had not been paid for at that date. Harrods Ltd had accounted for it as a sale in the normal way at its standard mark up of 300% on cost.

(5) Goodwill arising on consolidation is to be amortised over ten years with a full year's charge in the year of acquisition.

Required

Prepare the consolidated balance sheet of Harrods Ltd at 30 June 20X5, together with your consolidation schedules.

3.5   *Learning outcome*

You have now covered the learning outcome for this chapter:

> Prepare consolidated financial statements where the shareholdings, or control, are acquired in stages.

4   Summary

There are four main problem areas to consider when an investing company increases its stake in another undertaking.

- A trade investment becomes a subsidiary
- A trade investment becomes an associate
- We increase our stake in an existing subsidiary
- An associate becomes a subsidiary

In general, we treat the new status as having come into being on the date of the second acquisition, but things are not always that simple. Notice in particular:

- the three-column net assets calculation required in the case where we increase our stake in a subsidiary

- the similar calculation recommended by FRS 2 in the case where an associate becomes a subsidiary, when the normal method would fail to give a true and fair view.

Multiple choice questions *(The answers are in the final chapter of this book)*

1   Loud Ltd purchased shares in Quiet Ltd as follows.

1 July 20X6. 10% of the ordinary shares when the reserves of Quiet Ltd were £80,000. There was no intention to acquire control at this stage.

31 December 20X6. A further 50% of the ordinary shares when the reserves of Quiet Ltd were £100,000.

30 June 20X7. A further 20% of the ordinary shares when the reserves of Quiet Ltd were £120,000.

The group share of the pre-acquisition reserves of Quiet Ltd as at 30 June 20X7 under the acquisition method of consolidation is:

A   £60,000

B   £82,000

C   £84,000

D   £96,000

2   Large Ltd has held 50% of the equity voting rights of Little Ltd, its associated undertaking, for a number of years. During the year ended 31 December 20X9, Large Ltd purchased the remaining equity voting rights of Little Ltd for £15,000. On the effective date of acquisition of the remaining shares, Little Ltd had net liabilities of £25,696.

What is the goodwill arising on the acquisition in 20X9?

A   £40,696

B   £27,848

C   £10,696

D   £2,152

3   Hartlepool Ltd acquired the following shareholdings in Southend Ltd:

31 December 20W7	10% for £50,000 when Southend's reserves totalled £300,000
31 December 20X0	60% for £350,000 when Southend's reserves totalled £400,000

Southend Ltd has a total share capital of 100,000 £1 ordinary shares.

What is the goodwill arising on consolidation?

A   £50,000

B   £100,000

C   £110,000

D   £120,000

CHAPTER 9

Foreign currency: direct transactions

EXAM FOCUS

This is a difficult topic but one likely to be the subject of regular examination questions.

LEARNING OUTCOMES

This chapter covers the following Learning Outcomes of the CIMA Syllabus.

> Explain and apply foreign currency translation principles
> Explain the correct treatment for foreign loans financing foreign equity investments

In order to cover these Learning Outcomes the following topics are included.

> Dependent and non-dependent operations
> Direct business transactions
> Hedging

---

1 Dependent and non-dependent operations

1.1 An analysis of foreign currency operations

There are various ways in which a business may engage in foreign currency operations. In most cases these transactions give rise to problems of translating amounts expressed in foreign currencies into equivalent sterling amounts. The accounting procedures in this area are laid down by SSAP 20 *Foreign Currency Translation*.

In the simplest case, a business may wish to sell goods direct to overseas customers or buy goods direct from overseas suppliers (exporting and importing respectively).

Another possibility is to set up a dependent operation of some kind in an overseas country. For example, a UK business might establish a production plant in Germany. This might have tax advantages, or perhaps geographical advantages if much of the company's turnover is exported to continental Europe. The overseas operation functions as just an extension of the UK business, similar to a branch.

At the other extreme, the UK business might set up a non-dependent operation in Germany — for example, an autonomous subsidiary. Although investment funds may be provided by the UK parent, the German subsidiary might well function as an independent company in its own right.

The reason for distinguishing between these possibilities is that two different methods have been devised to account for the translation of overseas currencies. A major criterion for determining which method is appropriate is the nature of the trading carried out by the UK company. The possibilities are summarised in Figure 1.

Figure 1 The temporal method and the closing rate method

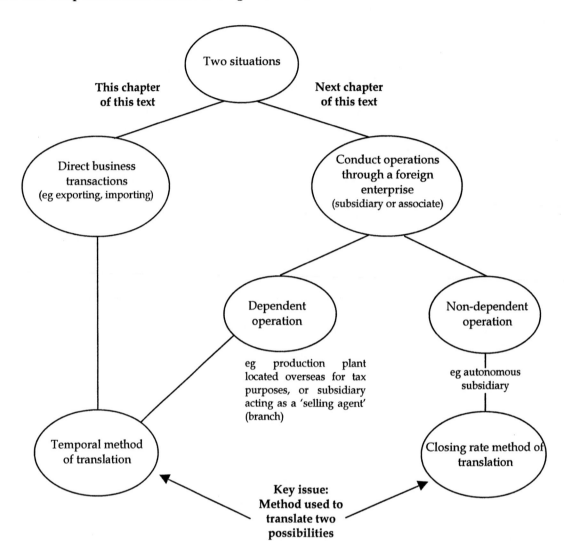

2   *Direct business transactions*

2.1   *The temporal method of translation*

All the following transactions rank as 'direct business transactions' to which the temporal method applies.

♦ A UK business sells goods direct to a US customer. If the customer pays in sterling, there is no problem with currency translation. However, if the debt is denominated in dollars, the UK company will eventually receive payment in dollars.

♦ A UK business buys goods direct from a Swiss supplier. Again, if the debt is denominated in sterling, no problem arises. But if the debt is expressed in francs there is a translation problem.

♦ A UK business raises a loan of one million Japanese yen. The liability must be expressed in sterling in the UK accounts and again there is a translation problem.

In all of these cases the UK company must prepare a profit and loss account and a balance sheet expressed in sterling. This means that transactions expressed in other currencies must be translated into a sterling equivalent. The problem is that the rate of exchange between, say, sterling and US dollars is not a fixed quantity; on the contrary, it fluctuates from day to day. So what exchange rate should the UK company use?

The temporal method is one solution to this problem. As its name suggests, the method is based on the timing of transactions.

♦ In the profit and loss account we use the actual rate prevailing on the day when the transaction took place. We may simplify this by treating all transactions with the average exchange rate for the accounting period, but only if the exchange rate was fairly stable during the period.

♦ In the balance sheet, we translate *monetary* assets and liabilities (these are money held and amounts to be received or paid in money, eg bank balances, cash holdings, loans, debtors, creditors etc) using the closing rate, ie the rate prevailing on the balance sheet date.

♦ We translate *non-monetary* items (all other assets and liabilities) in the balance sheet – eg investments, fixed assets, stocks - at their historical rate, ie the rate prevailing when the balances first arose. We make no attempt to re-translate these balances at subsequent balance sheet dates.

It is easy to see that *exchange differences* may arise as a result of this procedure. For example, suppose we buy goods for US$ 100,000 on 15 December when the exchange rate is US$ 1.5 = £1. We record this in the profit and loss account as a purchase valued at £66,667. At 31 December – our balance sheet date – the exchange rate is US$ 1.4 = £1. We show our balance sheet liability as £71,429. There is a difference of £4,762.

Using the temporal method, all exchange differences are routed through the profit and loss account.

♦ Those that relate to trading items are disclosed as 'other operating income or expense'.

♦ Those that relate to financing items are disclosed as 'interest payable and similar charges' or 'other interest receivable and similar income'.

2.2   The rationale for the temporal method

We translate transactions in the profit and loss account using the actual rate at the date the transactions took place to be consistent with basic accounting principles, ie historical cost accounting.

For the same reason we leave non-monetary items in the balance sheet at historical cost (stock, fixed assets).

However, it would be inappropriate to leave monetary items at historical cost as this may fail to give us a true and fair view. At the balance sheet date the translation of a foreign currency loan may give us a bigger liability than we had when we took out the loan, because of fluctuations in the exchange rate. It is important, therefore, that we report the true amount of the liability at the balance sheet date, not a historical figure.

2.3   Example

The following transactions were undertaken by Jeyes plc in the accounting year ended 31 December 20X1.

Date	Narrative	Amount $
1 January 20X1	Purchase of a fixed asset	100,000
31 March 20X1	Payment for the fixed asset	100,000
	Purchases on credit	50,000
30 June 20X1	Sales on credit	95,000
30 September 20X1	Payment for purchases	50,000
30 November 20X1	Long-term loan taken out	200,000

Exchange rates	$	:	£
1 January 20X1	2.0	:	1
31 March 20X1	2.3	:	1
30 June 20X1	2.1	:	1
30 September 20X1	2.0	:	1
30 November 20X1	1.8	:	1
31 December 20X1	1.9	:	1

Required

Prepare journal entries to record the above transactions.

2.4 Approach to the example

Remember that this is just basic accounting. Don't let the $ sign confuse the issue — the double entries don't change!

Remember the basic rules for the temporal method.

◆ Translate at the *actual* date when the transaction took place.
◆ All exchange differences are taken to the profit and loss account.

Then set up your journal and work logically through the transactions.

2.5 Solution

Date	Journal	Debit	Credit
1 January 20X1	Fixed assets	£50,000	
	Creditors		£50,000
	Being purchase of fixed asset ($100,000/2)		

On 1 January Jeyes plc buys an asset for $100,000. The recording is done in the normal way with the translation done at the exchange rate of $2.0 : £1.

The asset is not paid for until 31 March, by which time the exchange rate has shifted to $2.3 : £1. We will therefore have to pay only £43,478, not the £50,000 creditor we set up. We have therefore made an exchange gain of £6,522. This will be taken to the profit and loss account.

Date	Journal	Debit	Credit
31 March 20X1	Creditors	£50,000	
	Cash		£43,478
	Profit and loss account – exchange gain		£6,522
	Being payment for fixed asset ($100,000/2.3)		

We use the same approach for the remaining transactions.

Date	Journal	Debit	Credit
31 March 20X1	Purchases	£21,739	
	Creditors		£21,739
	Purchases on credit $\dfrac{\$50,000}{2.3}$		
30 June 20X1	Debtors	£45,238	
	Sales		£45,238
	Sales on credit $\dfrac{\$95,000}{2.1}$		
30 September 20X1	Creditors	£21,739	
	Profit and loss account – exchange loss	£3,261	
	Cash		£25,000
	Payment for purchases $\dfrac{\$50,000}{2}$		
30 November 20X1	Cash	£111,111	
	Loan account		£111,111
	Loan taken out $\dfrac{\$200,000}{1.8}$		

At the year end we need to consider any foreign currency balance sheet items.

We need to re-translate the debtors and the loan (monetary items) to the closing rate at the balance sheet date. The debtors are currently held at £45,238. At the balance sheet date the debtors are now worth $\frac{\$95,000}{1.9} = \text{£}50,000$.

We therefore need to journalise the difference £50,000 – £45,238 = £4,762. We increase debtors and take the exchange difference to the profit and loss account.

Date	Journal	Debit	Credit
31 December 20X1	Debtors	£4,762	
	Profit and loss account – exchange gain		£4,762
	Being re-translation of foreign currency debtors at year end		

We also need to re-translate the loan to the closing rate at the balance sheet date. The loan is currently held at £111,111. At the balance sheet date the liability is now $\frac{\$200,000}{1.9} = \text{£}105,263$.

Again we need to journalise the difference £105,263 - £111,111 = £5,848. We need to reduce the loan account and therefore we have made an exchange gain which we take to the profit and loss account.

Date	Journal	Debit	Credit
31 December 20X1	Loan	£5,848	
	Profit and loss account – exchange gain		£5,848
	Being re-translation of foreign currency loan at year end		

Practice questions 1 - 3 *(The answers are in the final chapter of this book)*

1   Aston

Aston plc has a year end of 31 December 20X1. On 25 October 20X1 Aston plc buys goods from a Swedish supplier for SwK 286,000.

On 16 November 20X1 Aston plc pays the Swedish supplier in full.

The goods remain in stock at the year end.

Exchange rates

25 October 20X1	£1 = SwK 11.16
16 November 20X1	£1 = SwK 10.87
31 December 20X1	£1 = SwK 11.02

Required

Show the accounting entries for these transactions.

2   Moye

Moye Ltd has a year end of 31 December 20X1.

On 25 October 20X1 Moye Ltd buys goods from a Swedish supplier for SwK 286,000.

The goods remain in stock and the creditor remains unpaid at the year end.

Exchange rates

25 October 20X1	£1 = SwK 11.16
31 December 20X1	£1 = SwK 11.02

Required

Show the accounting entries for these transactions.

3   Warrilow

Warrilow plc has a year end of 31 December 20X1.

On 29 November 20X1 Warrilow plc receives a loan from a Swiss bank of SFr 2,217,000.

The proceeds are used to partly finance the purchase of a new office block.

The loan remains unsettled at the year end.

Exchange rates

29 November 20X1   £1 = SFr 2.217
31 December 20X1   £1 = SFr 2.424

Required

Show the accounting entries for these transactions.

2.6   Learning outcome

You have now covered the following learning outcome of the CIMA syllabus:

Explain and apply foreign currency translation principles

3   Hedging

3.1   The problem

A common practice among companies acquiring a foreign currency equity investment is to safeguard against losses by financing the investment using a foreign currency loan.

The company is recognising that any loss on the investment will be matched by a gain on the loan and vice versa.

The problem arises because the investment is a non-monetary item, whereas the loan is a monetary item. Under the temporal method the two items are treated differently in the balance sheet, as shown in Figure 2.

Figure 2 The normal temporal method

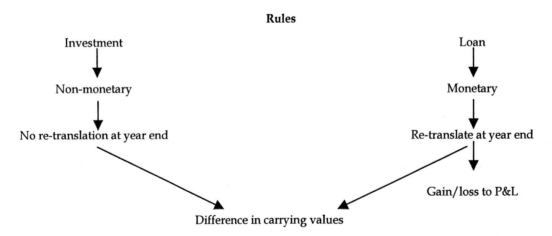

This treatment fails to reflect the true substance as the loan and investment are directly related. Any gain/loss on one is, in principle, cancelled out by an equivalent loss/gain on the other, and no 'true' exchange difference arises.

3.2 The solution

 SSAP 20 allows an exception to the basic rules in such circumstances. The conditions are as follows.

♦ The loan can be seen as financing the investment.

♦ The investment will generate enough cash (eg dividends, disposal proceeds) to cover the loan.

♦ The accounting treatment must be applied consistently.

If these conditions are met the hedging provisions may be applied (SSAP 20, paragraph 51).

♦ Both the investment and the loan are treated as monetary items and re-translated at the year end.

♦ Any gain or loss on the investment goes to reserves (not to profit and loss account).

♦ Any gain or loss on the loan also goes to reserves to be offset against the above movement on the investment. Any 'excess' movement on the loan goes to the profit and loss account.

3.3 Example

On 1 January 20X5 P borrows 200,000 Francland Francs and uses this to help fund the acquisition of 80% of S, at a cost of $80,000.

Exchange rates are as follows.

	FF	:	£	$	:	£
1 January 20X5	8	:	1	2.0	:	1
31 December 20X5	7	:	1	1.8	:	1
31 December 20X6	6	:	1	1.7	:	1

Prepare the journal entries as at 1 January 20X5, 31 December 20X5 and 31 December 20X6 assuming P applies the hedging provisions of SSAP 20.

3.4 Solution

We record the initial transactions in the normal way.

Date	Journal	Debit	Credit
1 January 20X5	Cash	£25,000	
	Loan account		£25,000
	Being loan taken out FF $\dfrac{200,000}{8}$		
1 January 20X5	Investment	£40,000	
	Cash		£40,000
	Purchase of 80% in an American		
	subsidiary $\dfrac{\$80,000}{2}$		

As the company applies the hedging provisions we treat both the investment and the loan as monetary items.

At 31 December 20X5, we re-translate the investment at the year end and take the exchange difference to reserves. The investment is currently held at £40,000. Its carrying value at 31 December 20X5 is $\dfrac{80,000}{1.8} = £44,444$.

We will journalise the difference of £4,444.

Date	Journal	Debit	Credit
31 December 20X5	Investment	£4,444	
	Reserves		£4,444
	Being exchange gain on the investment		

We then re-translate the loan and can take any loss to reserves in so far as it matches against the gain on the investment. The loan is currently held at £25,000. Its carrying value at 31 December 20X5 is $\dfrac{200,000}{7} = £28,571$.

We will journalise the difference of £3,571.

Date	Journal	Debit	Credit
31 December 20X5	Reserves	£3,571	
	Loan		£3,571
	Exchange loss on loan		

We then move on a year and do the same again. Re-translating the investment:

$\dfrac{80,000}{1.7} = £47,059$.

Date	Journal	Debit	Credit
31 December 20X6	Investment (£47,059 - £44,444)	£2,615	
	Reserves		£2,615
	Being exchange gain on loan		

Re-translating the loan: $\dfrac{200,000}{6} = £33,333$.

The loan is currently held at £28,571, so we have an exchange loss of £4,762.

We are only allowed to take the loss to reserves in so far as it matches with the gain on the investment. The excess has to go to the profit and loss account.

Date	Journal	Debit	Credit
31 December 20X6	Profit and loss account	£2,147	
	Reserves	£2,615	
	Loan account		£4,762
	Being exchange loss on loan		

Watch out for the following points.

♦ Hedging can take place even if the loan and the investment are in different currencies.

♦ When calculating exchange differences on long-term items remember to look from one balance sheet to the next, not from the original date of the transaction.

Practice question 4 (The answer is in the final chapter of this book)

Karpal

Karpal Ltd has a foreign equity investment which is financed by foreign borrowings. It has consistently adopted the provisions of paragraph 51 of SSAP 20. The cash generated by the investment is expected to exceed the amount of the borrowings.

	Situation 1	Situation 2	Situation 3
Exchange gain on investment	£4,293	£4,293	£4,293
Exchange gain (loss) on borrowings	£(5,039)	£(3,500)	£2,586

Required

Show the accounting entries for these transactions.

3.5 Learning outcome

You have now covered the final learning outcome for this chapter:

Explain the correct treatment for foreign loans financing foreign equity investments

4 Summary

The temporal method is used when direct business transactions give rise to foreign currency balances. The rules are as follows.

♦ In the profit and loss account use the actual rate (or approximate this by using an average rate, provided that fluctuations in the period are insignificant).

♦ In the balance sheet, use the closing rate for monetary items and the historical rate for non-monetary items.

♦ All exchange differences are accounted for in the profit and loss account.

The rules of the temporal method may be relaxed when a transaction falls within paragraph 51 of SSAP 20. In this case, an overseas investment and the related overseas financing are both translated at the closing rate. Any exchange difference on the investment is taken to reserves. Any exchange difference on the loan is taken to reserves to the extent that it matches the exchange difference on the investment; any excess difference is taken to the profit and loss account.

Multiple choice questions *(The answers are in the final chapter of this book)*

1   Buffy Ltd purchased a machine from a US company for $200,000 cash on 1 October 20X2 and on the same date sold goods on credit to another US company for $50,000. The latter US company was still a debtor at the year end of 31 December 20X2. The exchange rates were:

1 October 20X2	$1.60 : £1
31 December 20X2	$1.70 : £1

What exchange difference will be recognised in the profit and loss account for the year ending 31 December 20X2?

A   £1,838 gain

B   £1,838 loss

C   £9,191 gain

D   £9,191 loss

2   Demon Ltd purchased goods from a US supplier for $64,000 and sold goods to a French customer for 40,000 euros. Both transactions took place on 1 February 20X2. On 15 March the French customer paid the amount due but at the year end of 31 March 20X2 Demon Ltd had not yet paid the US supplier.

The exchange rates were as follows:

	$: £	Euros : £
1 February	1.5	1.6
15 March	1.6	1.7
31 March	1.7	1.5

What net exchange difference will appear in the profit and loss account for the year ending 31 March 20X2?

A   £1,471 loss

B   £3,549 gain

C   £3,549 loss

D   £5,020 gain

3   Daffy Ltd took out a hedging loan of $200,000 on 1 January 20X2 in order to finance an equity investment in a German company at a cost of 300,000 euros. Exchange rates were as follows:

	$: £	Euros : £
1 January 20X2	1.5	1.5
31 December 20X2	1.3	1.4

What exchange difference would appear in the profit and loss account for the year ending 31 December 20X2?

A   None

B   £6,227 loss

C   £14,286 gain

D   £20,513 loss

CHAPTER 10

Foreign currency: indirect transactions

EXAM FOCUS

A common question for Paper 7a is likely to be to prepare consolidated accounts where the parent company has a subsidiary or an associate denominated in a foreign currency.

The key issue is which exchange rate to use in translating the overseas entity's balance sheet before we can carry out the consolidation. As we saw in the previous chapter, we use the temporal method in cases where the overseas entity is essentially an extension of the UK company. In the alternative case, where the overseas entity is essentially independent, the closing rate method is used.

LEARNING OUTCOMES

This chapter covers the following Learning Outcome of the CIMA Syllabus.

> Explain the difference between the closing rate/net investment method and the temporal method

In order to cover this Learning Outcome the following topics are included.

> The closing rate method: balance sheet
> The temporal method: balance sheet
> The profit and loss account
> Hyper-inflationary economies

1 The closing rate method: balance sheet

1.1 Temporal method vs closing rate method

In the previous chapter, Figure 1 showed the three main scenarios in which a UK company engages in overseas operations. For the sake of convenience, we repeat this below as Figure 1.

Figure 1 The temporal method and the closing rate method

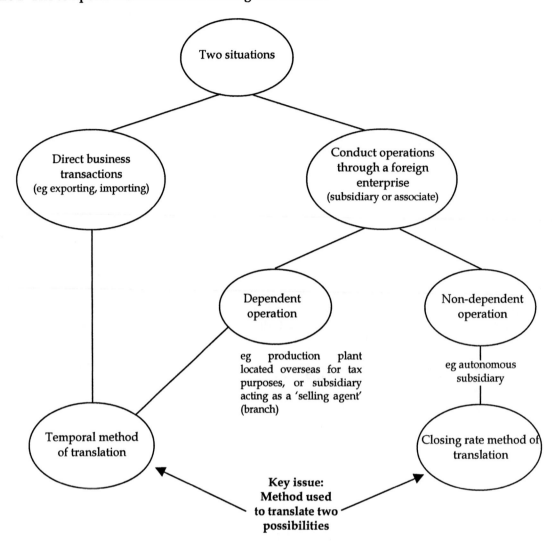

In the previous chapter we examined direct business transactions – the left hand arm of the diagram. In this chapter we take the right hand fork and investigate situations where the UK's overseas operations are conducted *indirectly*, ie through the medium of an entity established overseas.

In these cases, the overseas entity (a branch, a subsidiary or an associated company) will be preparing its own accounts expressed in the local currency. Before we can consolidate, we must translate these accounts into sterling. As usual, the question arises: 'Which method should we use?'

 As the diagram suggests, the key factor is the relationship between the UK company and the overseas entity.

♦ If the overseas entity is essentially an extension, or agency, of the UK company, then the economic substance is the same as if the UK company is engaged in direct business transactions. In this case the temporal method is appropriate.

♦ If the overseas entity is essentially independent of the UK company, then the economic substance is that we are not engaged in direct business transactions with our overseas customers and suppliers. Instead, we have made an investment in an entity that deals with those external organisations. Our interest is not directly in the individual transactions of the overseas entity; rather, we have invested in the overall net assets of that entity. In this case the closing rate method (also called the net investment method) is appropriate.

To determine whether the overseas enterprise is more dependent on the economic environment of the investing company's currency than on that of its own reporting currency, consider the following factors.

- The impact of cash flows
- Functional dependence
- The trading currency
- The financing currency

1.2   Mechanics of the closing rate method

The main rules are as follows.

- Translate profit and loss items at average rate or closing rate.

- Translate balance sheet items (monetary and non-monetary) at closing rate.

- Show exchange differences as a reserve movement (and also in the statement of total recognised gains and losses).

Detailed rules for the balance sheet are as follows.

- Split out pre-and post-acquisition reserves of the subsidiary in foreign currency.

- Translate share capital and pre-acquisition reserves at the historical rate. This will give the net assets at the date of acquisition in sterling.

- Translate the remaining items at closing rate, letting post-acquisition reserves of subsidiary in sterling be the balancing figure.

In the profit and loss account, translate at average rate or closing rate depending on the accounting policy. Either is permitted by SSAP 20.

In the statement of total recognised gains and losses, show exchange differences arising in the year.

1.3   Example

Gobbo Ltd bought 80% of Sly Inc on 31 December 20X2 for $6,000 when the exchange rate was $4 = £1. The reserves of Sly Inc at that date were $2,000.

Gobbo Ltd does not trade.

On 31 December 20X3 the balance sheets were as follows.

	Gobbo Ltd £	Sly Inc $
Investment in Sly	1,500	–
Sundry other net assets	500	9,300
	2,000	9,300
Share capital	2,000	4,000
Profit and loss account	–	5,300
	2,000	9,300

The rate of exchange on 31 December 20X3 was $2.5 = £1.

Required

Prepare a consolidated balance sheet.

Carry goodwill as a permanent intangible asset.

1.4 *Approach to the example*

Remember that a lot of the marks are available for the standard consolidation workings.

You will need two extra workings.

♦ Translation of Sly's accounts
♦ Exchange differences

We start in the standard way.

(W1) Group structure

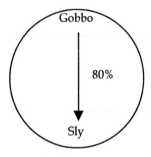

We will however need an extra working at this point to translate the balance sheet of Sly. We need to ensure that we separate out pre- and post-acquisition reserves in this translation.

(W1A) Translation of the balance sheet

	Sly Inc $	Rate	Sly Inc £
Sundry net assets	9,300		
	9,300		
Share capital	4,000		
Profit and loss account			
– pre-acquisition	2,000		
– post-acquisition (balancing figure)	3,300		
	9,300		

Translate the entire top half of the balance sheet (net assets) using the exchange rate at the balance sheet date, ie the closing rate of $2.5 = £1.

	Sly Inc $	Rate	Sly Inc £
Sundry net assets	9,300	2.5	3,720
	9,300		3,720 *
Share capital	4,000		
Profit and loss account			
– pre-acquisition	2,000		
– post-acquisition	3,300		
	9,300		3,720

* This means we have calculated net assets at the balance sheet date £3,720. This will be used to calculate the minority interests.

We translate the share capital and the pre-acquisition profit and loss reserve using the exchange rate at the date of acquisition, ie the historical rate of $4 = £1.

	Sly Inc $	Rate	Sly Inc. £
Sundry net assets	9,300	2.5	3,720
	9,300		3,720
Share capital	4,000	4	1,000 *
Profit and loss account			
– pre-acquisition	2,000	4	500 *
– post-acquisition	3,300		
	9,300		3,720

*   This means we have calculated net assets at the date of acquisition £1,500. This will be used to calculate goodwill.

We then include the post-acquisition reserves as the balancing figure.

	Sly Inc. $	Rate	Sly Inc. £
Sundry net assets	9,300	2.5	3,720
	9,300		3,720
Share capital	4,000	4	1,000
Profit and loss account			
– pre-acquisition	2,000	4	500
– post-acquisition	3,300	bal fig	2,220 *
	9,300		3,720

*   This means we have calculated the post-acquisition reserves of Sly Inc which we will need to calculate group reserves.

We now continue with our consolidation.

(W2)   Net assets

	At date of acquisition £	At balance sheet date £
Share capital	1,000	1,000
Profit and loss account	500	2,720
Net assets	1,500	3,720

(W3)   Goodwill

	£
Purchase consideration	1,500
For 80% of net assets (1,500)	(1,200)
Goodwill	300

(W4)   Minority interests

	£
20% of net assets at balance sheet date (3,720)	744

(W5)   Group profit and loss account

		£
100% Gobbo		–
80% of post-acquisition reserves of Sly (2,220)		1,776
Group profit and loss account		1,776

1.5   Solution

We can then prepare a consolidated balance sheet.

	£
Intangible fixed assets: goodwill (W3)	300
Sundry other net assets (500+3,720)	4,220
	4,520
Share capital	2,000
Group profit and loss account (W5)	1,776
Shareholders' funds	3,776
Minority interests (W4)	744
	4,520

Practice question 1 *(The answer is in the final chapter of this book)*

Gobbo CRM

Moving on from the original example, on 31 December 20X4 the balance sheets of Gobbo and Sly were as follows.

	Gobbo Ltd	Sly Inc
	£	$
Investment in Sly	1,500	–
Sundry other net assets	500	12,900
	2,000	12,900
Share capital	2,000	4,000
Profit and loss account	–	8,900
	2,000	12,900

The rate of exchange on 31 December 20X4 was $3.0 = £1.

Required

Prepare a consolidated balance sheet at 31 December 20X4, using the closing rate method. Carry goodwill as a permanent intangible asset.

2   The temporal method: balance sheet

2.1   The temporal method

So far we have assumed that the relationship between Gobbo and Sly justifies use of the closing rate method. However, if we decide that Sly is effectively dependent on Gobbo we should use the temporal method instead. This is illustrated below.

Example

Gobbo Ltd bought 80% of Sly Inc on 31 December 20X2 for $6,000 when the exchange rate was $4 = £1. The reserves of Sly Inc at that date were $2,000. Gobbo Ltd does not trade.

On 31 December 20X3 the balance sheets were as follows.

	Gobbo Ltd £	Sly Inc $
Fixed assets		
Tangible	–	13,500
Investment in Sly	1,500	–
Current assets		
Stock	–	1,200
Other	500	3,300
	2,000	18,000
Long-term loans	–	8,700
	2,000	9,300
Capital and reserves		
Share capital	2,000	4,000
Profit and loss account	–	5,300
	2,000	9,300

The rate of exchange when the stock was purchased was $2.4 = £1. There were no additions or disposals of fixed assets during the year.

The rate of exchange on 31 December 20X3 was $2.5 = £1.

Required

Prepare a consolidated balance sheet at 31 December 20X3.

Carry goodwill as a permanent intangible asset.

2.2 Approach to the example

We adopt our standard approach

(W1)   Group structure

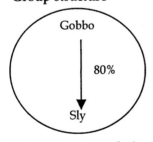

(W1A) Set out your translation

	Sly Inc $	Rate	Sly Inc £
Fixed assets	13,500		
Current assets			
Stock	1,200		
Other	3,300		
	18,000		
Long-term loans	(8,700)		
	9,300		

Capital and reserves

Share capital	4,000
Profit and loss account	
– pre-acquisition	2,000
– post-acquisition	3,300
	9,300

Remember to split out pre- and post-acquisition reserves.

The rules of the temporal method include the following.

♦ Split out individual non-monetary assets.

♦ Translate monetary items at closing rates and non-monetary items at historical rates.

	Sly Inc $	Rate	Sly Inc £
Fixed assets			
Tangible (historical)	13,500	4	3,375
Current assets			
Stock (historical)	1,200	2.4	500
Other (closing)	3,300	2.5	1,320
	18,000		
Long-term loans (closing)	(8,700)	2.5	(3,480)
	9,300		1,715
Share capital	4,000		
Profit and loss account			
– pre-acquisition	2,000		
– post-acquisition	3,300		
	9,300		1,715

Translate share capital and pre-acquisition reserves at historical rate. This will give the net assets at date of acquisition in sterling. Let post-acquisition reserves in sterling be the balancing figure.

	Sly Inc $	Rate	Sly Inc £
Fixed assets			
Tangible	13,500	4	3,375
Current assets			
Stock	1,200	2.4	500
Other	3,300	2.5	1,320
	18,000		5,195
Long-term loans	(8,700)	2.5	(3,480)
	9,300		1,715
Share capital	4,000	4	1,000
Profit and loss			
– pre-acquisition	2,000	4	500
– post-acquisition	3,300	bal fig	215
	9,300		1,715

We can now continue our consolidation.

(W2)   Net assets

	At date of acquisition £	At balance sheet date £
Share capital	1,000	1,000
Profit and loss	500	715
	1,500	1,715

(W3)   Goodwill

	£
Purchase consideration (6,000 ÷ 4)	1,500
For 80% of net assets acquired (1,500)	(1,200)
Goodwill	300

(W4)   Minority interest

	£
20% of £1,715	343

(W5)   Group profit and loss account

	£
100% of Gobbo	–
80% post-acquisition reserve of Sly (£215 × 80%)	172
	172

This leads to the following balance sheet.

Consolidated balance sheet as at 31 December 20X3

	£
Intangible fixed assets: goodwill (W3)	300
Tangible fixed assets	3,375
Current assets	
Stock	500
Other	1,820
Long-term loans	(3,480)
	2,515
Capital and reserves	
Share capital	2,000
Profit and loss account (W5)	172
	2,172
Minority interest (W4)	343
	2,515

Practice question 2 *(The answer is in the final chapter of this book)*

Gobbo TM

Moving on from the original example, on 31 December 20X4 the balance sheets were as follows.

	Gobbo Ltd £	Sly Inc $
Fixed assets		
Tangible	–	12,000
Investment in Sly	1,500	–
Current assets		
Stock	–	1,914
Other	500	4,986
	2,000	18,900
Long-term loans	–	6,000
	2,000	12,900
Share capital	2,000	4,000
Profit and loss account		
– pre-acquisition	–	2,000
– post-acquisition	–	6,900
	2,000	12,900

The rate of exchange on 31 December 20X4 was $3 = £1. The stocks of Sly Inc were purchased when the rate of exchange was $2.9 = £1. There were no additions or disposals of fixed assets during the year.

Required

Prepare a consolidated balance sheet at 31 December 20X4 using the temporal method. Carry goodwill as a permanent intangible asset.

---

3 The profit and loss account

3.1 The closing rate method

We illustrate the profit and loss account by continuing with the example of Gobbo and Sly.

3.2 Example

The profit and loss account of Sly for the year ended 31 December 20X4 was as follows.

	Sly Inc $
Profit before tax	7,200
Tax	3,600
Profit after tax	3,600

The average rate of exchange for the year (which should be used to translate the profit and loss account) was $2.85 = £1.

Required

Prepare a consolidated profit and loss account for the year ended 31 December 20X4.

3.3 Approach to the example

Translate profit and loss items at the average rate or closing rate. In this case we are told to use the average rate.

(W1)   Translation

	Sly Inc $	Rate	Sly Inc £
Profit before tax	7,200	2.85	2,526
Tax	(3,600)	2.85	(1,263)
Profit after tax	3,600		1,263
Dividends	–		–
Retained profit	3,600	2.85	1,263

3.4 Solution

You can now prepare a consolidated profit and loss account in the normal way.

Consolidated profit and loss account

	£
Profit before tax	2,526
Tax	(1,263)
Profit after tax	1,263
Minority interest [£1,263 × 20%]	(253)
Group profit retained	1,010

The statement of reserves must include the exchange difference if we are to reconcile. Remember to work from $ to £.

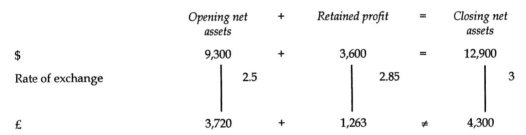

	Opening net assets	+	Retained profit	=	Closing net assets
$	9,300	+	3,600	=	12,900
Rate of exchange		2.5		2.85		3
£	3,720	+	1,263	≠	4,300

The balancing figure is the exchange difference of £683, of which 80% will be taken to reserves.

3.5 Statement of reserves

	£
Profit and loss on 1 January 20X4 (opening balance)	1,776
Retained profit (profit and loss account)	1,010
Exchange difference (683 × 80%)	(546)
Profit and loss on 31 December 20X4	2,240

Practice question 3 *(The answer is in the final chapter of this book)*

Grofine I

Grofine Ltd bought 75% of S Inc on 31 December 20X1 when the net assets of S Inc were $12,000,000 and the exchange rate was $3 = £1.

At 31 December 20X3 the balance sheets were as follows.

	Grofine Ltd £000	S Inc $000
Fixed assets	–	2,400
Investment in S Inc	5,000	–
Net current assets	652	20,800
	5,652	23,200
Share capital	5,000	4,000
Pre-acquisition reserves	–	8,000
Post-acquisition reserves	652	11,200
	5,652	23,200

The rate of exchange at 31 December 20X3 was $2.5 = £1.

The profit and loss account of S Inc for the year ended 31 December 20X3 was as follows.

	S Inc $000
Turnover	22,000
Cost of sales	(11,490)
Gross profit	10,510
Distribution and admin expenses	(3,910)
Profit	6,600
Dividend paid during year	(2,000)
Retained profit	4,600

The average rate of exchange for the year was $2.3 = £1. This should be used to translate the profit and loss account.

The dividend was paid when the rate of exchange was $2.3 = £1.

Grofine Ltd did not trade during the year.

The rate of exchange at 31 December 20X2 was $2 = £1.

Required

Using the closing rate method prepare the consolidated balance sheet of Grofine Ltd as at 31 December 20X3, together with the consolidated profit and loss account and statement of reserves for the year ended 31 December 20X3. Carry goodwill as a permanent intangible asset.

3.6 The temporal method

Again we use the example of Gobbo.

3.7   Example

The profit and loss account for the year ended 31 December 20X4 was as follows.

	Sly Inc $
Turnover	28,215
Cost of sales and other expenses	(19,515)
Depreciation	(1,500)
	7,200
Exchange differences	–
Profit before tax	7,200
Tax	(3,600)
Profit after tax	3,600

The average rate of exchange was $2.85 = £1.

Required

Prepare a consolidated profit and loss account for the year ended 31 December 20X4.

3.8   Approach to the example

The rules for the temporal method are as follows.

♦   Split out opening stock, closing stock and depreciation.

♦   Translate sales, purchases, expenses and taxation at average rate (approximation to actual). Translate opening and closing stock and depreciation at historical rate.

♦   Calculate exchange differences by reconstructing the opening balance sheet of the subsidiary in foreign currency to get opening net monetary assets. Take to face of profit and loss account.

We begin by translating Sly's profit and loss account.

	Sly Inc $	Rate	Sly Inc £
Turnover	28,215	2.85	9,900
Cost of sales and other expenses	(19,515)	(W1)	(6,938)
Depreciation	(1,500)	4.0	(375)
			2,587
Exchange difference		*	283
Profit before tax	7,200		
Tax	(3,600)	2.85	(1,263)
Profit after tax	3,600		1,607

*   The exchange difference (a gain) is proved below.

(W1)   Cost of sales and other expenses

	Sly Inc $	Rate	Sly Inc £
Opening stock	1,200	2.4	500
Purchases	20,229	2.85	7,098
Closing stock	(1,914)	2.9	(660)
	19,515		6,938

This leads to the following consolidated profit and loss account.

	£
Turnover	9,900
Cost of sales	(6,938)
Depreciation	(375)
	2,587
Exchange difference	283
Profit before tax	2,870
Tax	(1,263)
Profit after tax	1,607
Minority interest (20% × £1,607)	(321)
Profit attributable to group	1,286

The exchange differences are calculated as follows.

	Opening net monetary assets $	+	Retained net monetary assets $	=	Closing net monetary assets $
	3,300 - 8,700		28,215 - 19,515		4,986 - 6,000
			-3,600 - 714 (stock)		
	= (5,400)		= 4,386		= (1,014)
Rate	2.5		2.85		3.0
	(£2,160)	+	£1,539	≠	(£338)

What this means is that we might have expected closing net monetary assets of (£621), ie (£2,160) + £1,539. In fact, our closing net monetary assets are (£338), which means that we have an exchange gain of £283. This is taken to the face of the profit and loss account.

Practice question 4 *(The answer is in the final chapter of this book)*

Grofine II

Grofine Ltd bought 75% of S Inc on 31 December 20X1 when the net assets of S Inc were $12,000,000 and the exchange rate was $3 = £1.

At 31 December 20X3 the balance sheets were as follows.

	Grofine Ltd £000	S Inc $000
Fixed assets	–	2,400
Investment in S Inc	5,000	–
Stocks	–	1,710
Other net current assets	652	19,090
	5,652	23,200
Share capital	5,000	4,000
Pre-acquisition reserves	–	8,000
Post-acquisition reserves	652	11,200
	5,652	23,200

The rate of exchange at 31 December 20X3 was $2.5 = £1 and the stocks were purchased when the rate was $2.4 = £1.

The profit and loss account of S Inc for the year ended 31 December 20X3 was as follows.

	S Inc $000
Turnover	22,000
Opening stock	2,200
Purchases	11,000
	13,200
Closing stock	(1,710)
Cost of sales	11,490
Gross profit	10,510
Distribution and admin expenses	(3,610)
Depreciation	(300)
Exchange differences	–
Profit	6,600
Dividend paid during year	(2,000)
Retained profit	4,600

The average rate of exchange for the year was $2.3 = £1.

The dividend was paid when the rate of exchange was $2.3 = £1. Grofine Ltd did not trade during the year.   The rate of exchange at 31 December 20X2 was $2 = £1.

Stock at 31 December 20X2 was $2,200,000; this was purchased when the exchange rate was $2.2 = £1. No fixed assets were purchased during the year.

Required

Using the temporal method prepare the consolidated balance sheet of Grofine Ltd as at 31 December 20X3 together with the consolidated profit and loss account for the year ended 31 December 20X3. Carry goodwill as a permanent asset.

3.9   Learning outcome

You have now covered the learning outcome for this chapter:

> Explain the difference between the closing rate/net investment method and the temporal method.

4   Hyper-inflationary economies

4.1   Introduction

Where a foreign enterprise operates in a country with a very high level of inflation (hyper-inflation), applying the usual translation methods to historical cost accounts may not be satisfactory.

For example, consider a subsidiary acquired in Zedland for Z10,000, representing the fair value of the land owned by the subsidiary at the date of acquisition, 1 January 20X1, when £1 = Z10.

By the balance sheet date, 31 December 20X5, there has been hyper-inflation in Zedland, so that now there is £1 = Z100. Without any special rules, the overseas net assets would be translated at the closing rate to a sterling equivalent of

$$\frac{Z10,000}{100} = £100$$

This illustrates the problem: the overseas net assets will translate to a smaller and smaller sterling value if their historical cost in local currency is translated at the closing exchange rate.

4.2 UITF Abstract 9

UITF Abstract 9 'Accounting for operations in hyper-inflationary economies' was issued to combat this problem of 'disappearing assets'.

Abstract 9 requires that, where the cumulative inflation rate over three years approaches or exceeds 100%, then the local currency financial statements should be adjusted to reflect current price levels before the translation process is carried out.

Abstract 9 suggests two possible ways that such an adjustment can be made:

(a)   revalue the net assets to their fair value in local currency terms, before doing the translation, or

(b)   use a relatively stable currency (eg, the US $) as the functional currency of the overseas operations, rather than the local currency.

4.3 Example

A fuller example based on the earlier figures is shown below.

On 1 January 20X1 AB plc established an overseas subsidiary in Zedland, a country with high inflation. The subsidiary bought land for Z10,000 on its incorporation.

On 1 January 20X1, £1 = Z10 = $1.50.

By the balance sheet date, 31 December 20X5, £1 = Z100 = $1.40.

The Zedland general price index was 100 on 1 January 20X1 and 900 on 31 December 20X5.

Show the sterling amount at which the land would be included in the 20X5 consolidated balance sheet:

(a)   without adjustment for Abstract 9
(b)   revaluing to reflect fair prices in local terms
(c)   using US dollars as the functional currency.

4.4 Solution

(a)   Z10,000 ÷ 100 = £100

(b)   At 31 December 20X5, the land has a current price value of:

$$Z10,000 \times \frac{900}{100} = Z90,000$$

In sterling, this is translated to Z90,000 ÷ 100 = £900

(c)   The cost of the land was originally Z10,000 = $1,500. By 31 December 20X5, this is $1,500 ÷ 1.40 = £1,071.

4.5 Conclusion

Part (a) illustrates the 'disappearing asset' phenomenon. Either of the sterling values from parts (b) and (c) (£900 or £1,071) show a fairer view of the value of the land at the balance sheet date.

5   Hedging in group accounts

5.1   Introduction

One final problem area to consider is where a parent company has financed the purchase of an overseas subsidiary by raising a foreign currency loan in its own (the parent's) accounts. SSAP 20 permits hedging in the consolidated accounts, similar to the hedging in individual accounts that you met in the previous chapter.

5.2   The position without hedging

If the group hedging provisions are not adopted, then consider the exchange differences that will arise in the group accounts when an overseas subsidiary is financed by the parent raising a foreign loan.

The loan as a monetary item will be re-translated at each balance sheet date, with the exchange difference recognised in the parent's profit and loss account.

The exchange difference arising on re-translating the opening net assets will usually be recognised in reserves, in accordance with the likely situation of the closing rate method being applied.

But in substance the loan is financing the overseas net assets, so it is illogical to treat the two exchange differences differently.

5.3   The SSAP 20 group hedging provisions

Where the closing rate method is being applied, and the parent company finances the purchase of an overseas investment by raising a foreign currency loan in its own accounts, then the gain or loss on re-translating the loan can be offset in reserves against the gain or loss on re-translating the opening net assets (ie the exchange difference arising on consolidation).

Necessary conditions are:

(a)   the investment must be one such that the closing rate method is applicable.

(b)   the total borrowings do not exceed the cashflows to be generated from the investment.

(c)   the exchange difference on the borrowings can only be offset to a maximum of the exchange difference on the opening net assets.

(d)   the accounting treatment must be consistently applied.

6   Other relevant UITF Abstracts

6.1   Abstract 19: Tax on gains and losses on foreign currency borrowings that hedge an investment in a foreign enterprise

We have seen that exchange differences on foreign hedging borrowings can be taken to reserves and reported in the STRGL.

The UITF decision is that tax charges or credits that are directly and solely attributable to such exchange differences should also be taken to reserves and reported in the STRGL.

6.2   Abstract 21: Accounting issues arising from the proposed introduction of the euro

Costs associated with the introduction of the euro should be written off to the profit and loss account, unless they relate to necessary modifications to assets and the entity already has a policy to capitalise assets of this type, or the expenditure clearly enhances rather than maintains the asset.

6.3 Appendix to Abstract 21

The UITF issued further guidance on the introduction of the euro in an Appendix to Abstract 21 issued in 1998. With effect from 1 January 1999 the currencies of participating countries are fixed against one another, having floated up until that date.

The UITF confirm that the principles of SSAP 20 remain applicable following the introduction of the euro. For example, a company with a year end of 30 November 1998 should not anticipate the fixed exchange rate to be applied from the end of 1998, but should use the actual closing rate at the balance sheet date as normal.

7 Future developments

7.1 The publication of FRED 24

In May 2002 the ASB issued FRED 24 which contains two new proposed FRSs to replace SSAP 20 and UITF Abstract 9. The planned approach is as follows:

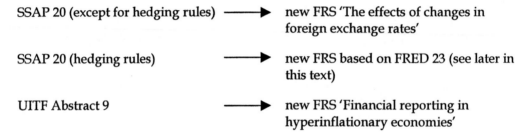

SSAP 20 (except for hedging rules) ⟶ new FRS 'The effects of changes in foreign exchange rates'

SSAP 20 (hedging rules) ⟶ new FRS based on FRED 23 (see later in this text)

UITF Abstract 9 ⟶ new FRS 'Financial reporting in hyperinflationary economies'

The purpose behind FRED 24 is to align UK accounting with the relevant IASs on foreign currency translation, as far as the ASB believe is appropriate. The main changes from current UK accounting would be as follows:

- ♦ SSAP 20 does not specifically address the question of the currency in which financial statements are presented; it is assumed that they will be presented in the parent company's local currency. FRED 24 clarifies the distinction between a functional currency and a presentation currency. Each entity must determine its functional currency (that of its primary economic environment) and must first measure its results in that currency. However FRED 24 then permits the entity to report those results in any currency (the presentation currency) it chooses.

- ♦ when using the closing rate method, SSAP 20 allows the profit and loss account to be translated using either the closing rate or an average rate. FRED 24 in principle requires the actual rate to be used, although in practice an average rate should be an acceptable approximation. The closing rate is no longer acceptable.

- ♦ UITF Abstract 9 allows two possible approaches to adjusting local currency financial statements: revalue in local currency terms before translation, or use a stable currency as the functional currency. FRED 24 proposes that only the first approach should be acceptable. The use of a hard proxy currency is not permitted by international standards so is no longer acceptable.

7.2 Commentary on FRED 24

Neither of the two new standards in FRED 24 dealing with foreign currency translation are particularly controversial. The changes reduce the choices in standards so will improve the consistency and comparability of financial statements.

8   Summary

In this chapter we have considered overseas operations conducted through the medium of an entity established in the overseas country.

♦   If the overseas entity is dependent on the UK investor, use the temporal method.

♦   Otherwise, use the closing rate method.

The overseas entity will have prepared its own accounts. Before we can consolidate we must translate these accounts using the appropriate method. You are advised to follow the 'drills' laid out in this chapter as a logical means of arriving at accurate consolidated accounts.

Multiple choice questions (*The answers are in the final chapter of this book*)

1   Henly Ltd has a French subsidiary which receives goods from the UK company, sells the goods in France and remits the profits back to Henly Ltd. The subsidiary is totally financed by the UK company.

When the subsidiary is consolidated with Henly Ltd's financial statements, what method should be used to translate the financial statements of the subsidiary?

A   Closing rate method

B   Net investment method

C   Temporal method

D   Indirect method

Using the following information answer questions 2 and 3.

Hardy Ltd purchased 60% of the share capital of Saint Ltd on 1 January 20X1 for $105,000 when the exchange rate was $1.5 to £1. The reserves of Saint Ltd at that date were $35,000.

The balance sheet of Saint Ltd at 31 December 20X2 is given below:

	$
	$
Fixed assets	160,000
Net monetary assets	20,000
	180,000
Share capital	100,000
Profit and loss account	80,000
	180,000

The exchange rate at 31 December 20X2 was $1.25 to £1. The profit and loss account of Hardy Ltd totalled £440,000 on 31 December 20X2. Goodwill has a useful economic life of four years.

2   What are the consolidated profit and loss account reserves as at 31 December 20X2 using the closing rate method?

    A   £464,400

    B   £472,400

    C   £486,000

    D   £494,000

3   What are the consolidated profit and loss account reserves as at 31 December 20X2 using the temporal method?

    A   £451,600

    B   £459,600

    C   £464,667

    D   £472,667

CHAPTER 11

Group accounts: disposals

EXAM FOCUS

The standard group accounts question concerns the production of consolidated accounts where a parent controls a subsidiary. One complication is where the parent sells shares in its investee during the accounting period.

Questions are to be expected from time to time on this topic.

LEARNING OUTCOMES

This chapter covers the following Learning Outcomes of the CIMA Syllabus.

> Prepare financial statements when a subsidiary is disposed of part way through an accounting period
>
> Prepare accounts for a demerger

In order to cover these Learning Outcomes the following topics are included.

> The different types of disposal
> Accounting for disposals in group accounts
> Tackling examination questions on disposals
> Demergers

---

1   The different types of disposal

1.1   The investing company's accounts

When a group disposes of all or part of its interest in a subsidiary undertaking this must be reflected both in the investing company's individual accounts and in the group accounts. Most of this chapter is concerned with group accounts, but we begin by looking briefly at the investing company's own accounts.

The parent company will carry its investment in subsidiary in its own balance sheet as a fixed asset investment, usually at cost.

When all or part of the investment is sold, this is recorded as a fixed asset disposal in the parent's own accounts, and will usually give rise to a profit or loss on disposal (proceeds - cost of investment sold). An accrual may also be necessary for tax on any profit on disposal.

To record the disposal we make the following entries.

	£	£
Debit Cash/debtors (proceeds)	X	
Credit Investment in S (cost of investment sold)		X
Debit Loss on disposal or	X	
Credit Profit on disposal		X
Debit Profit and loss tax charge (tax on gain on disposal)	X	
Credit Tax creditor		X

1.2   *Treatment in the consolidated accounts*

In the group accounts, we must deal with the following factors.

♦ Inclusion of results and cash flows of the entity disposed of
♦ Calculation and presentation of profit or loss on disposal
♦ Inclusion of any remaining interest in the company after a part disposal

In dealing with these matters in the group accounts, the single entity concept must be applied and the effect on the group as a whole considered.

We must also consider deemed disposals (where the group's interest is reduced other than by selling shares), and demergers (where an existing group divides into two separate groups).

The main sources of regulation in this area are as follows.

♦ FRS 1 Cash Flow Statements (for cash flow aspects)
♦ FRS 2 Accounting for Subsidiary Undertakings
♦ FRS 3 Reporting Financial Performance
♦ FRS 10 Goodwill and Intangible Assets

Cash flow statement aspects will be dealt with in a later chapter.

The accounting treatment depends largely on whether we have a full disposal (of the entire holding) or a part disposal (retaining some interest in the undertaking).

Part disposal possibilities include the following situations.

♦ Retention of control (ie the undertaking remains a subsidiary)
♦ Retention of significant influence (ie the undertaking becomes an associate)
♦ Retention of little or no influence (ie the undertaking becomes a trade investment)

The main accounting procedures are summarised in Table 1.

Table 1 Accounting treatment in group accounts

Status of investment		Treatment in consolidated profit and loss account	Treatment in consolidated balance sheet
Before disposal	*After disposal*		
Subsidiary → Subsidiary (eg 90%) (eg 60%)		Consolidate for the whole year Calculate minority interest in two pieces eg $\frac{x}{12}$ profit × 10% + $\frac{12-x}{12}$ profit × 40%	Consolidate as normal with closing minority interest based on year end holding
Subsidiary → Associate (eg 90%) (eg 40%)		Pro-rata S's results and consolidate up to the date of disposal After disposal, equity account	Equity account as at the year end based on year end holding
Subsidiary → Trade investment (eg 90%) (eg 10%)		Pro-rata S's results and consolidate up to the date of disposal After disposal, only include dividend income	Freeze in consolidated balance sheet at equity value at date of disposal. Reduce for any impairment in value

In all cases we must consider the impact of FRS 3 on the consolidated profit and loss account.

2   Accounting for disposals in group accounts

2.1   The consolidated profit and loss account

The consolidated profit and loss account shows the group's results over a period of time. Hence, it must include:

♦   the subsidiary's results up to the date on which it ceases to be a subsidiary undertaking
♦   the profit or loss arising on disposal.

This is summarised in Figure 1.

Figure 1   The consolidated profit and loss account

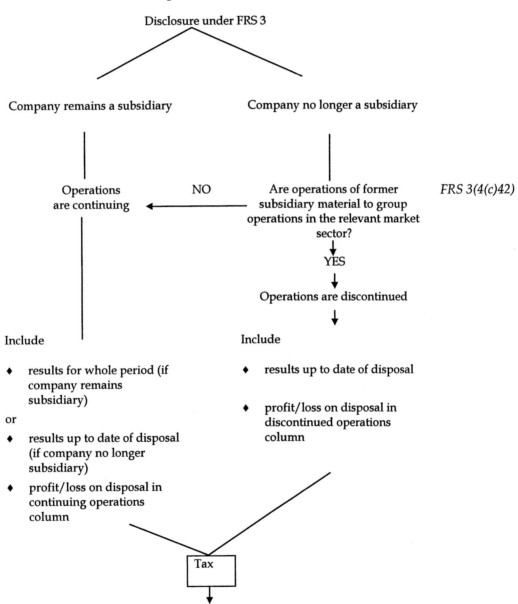

2.2   *Calculation of the profit or loss on disposal*

On disposal, the group transacts with a third party and disposes of all or part of its ownership of the subsidiary's net assets.

FRS 2 requires the profit or loss on disposal to be calculated as the difference between:

♦   the group share of the subsidiary's net assets before disposal, and

♦   the group share of the subsidiary's net assets after disposal together with any proceeds received.

Net assets compared should include any related goodwill not previously written off through the consolidated profit and loss account for any year.

Profit or loss on disposal is therefore calculated as follows.

		£
Proceeds		X
Less	Share of S's net assets at date of disposal attaching to stake disposed of	(X)
	Goodwill not previously written off through consolidated profit and loss account for any year attaching to stake disposed of	(X)
Profit or (loss) on disposal		X/(X)

The net assets of S at disposal are calculated as follows.

	£
Net assets at beginning of period	X
Add Profit before dividends $\times \dfrac{x}{12}$	X
Less Dividends paid prior to disposal	(X)
	X

2.3   *Disclosures*

Profit or loss on disposal will normally be an exceptional item on the face of the consolidated profit and loss account below operating profit. Related tax should be disclosed in a note.

Profit or loss should be classified as continuing or discontinued in line with the classification of results (see above).

For each material disposal of a previously acquired business, disclose the following information.

♦   The name of the undertaking that has ceased to be a subsidiary, showing any ownership interest retained

♦   The amount of profit or loss shown in the consolidated profit and loss account attributable to that undertaking

♦   An explanation of the circumstances where the undertaking has ceased to be a subsidiary other than by the disposal of (part of) the interest held by the group

♦   The profit or loss on the disposal

♦   The amount of goodwill attributable to the business disposed of

3 Tackling examination questions on disposals

We illustrate the above by working through a comprehensive question.

3.1 Example

The draft accounts of two companies at 31 March 20X1 were as follows.

BALANCE SHEETS

	Cagney Group £	Lacey Ltd £
Investment in Lacey Ltd at cost	3,440	-
Sundry net assets	36,450	6,500
	39,890	6,500
Sale proceeds of disposal (suspense account)	(8,890)	-
	31,000	6,500
Share capital (£1 ordinary shares)	20,000	3,000
Profit and loss account	11,000	3,500
	31,000	6,500

PROFIT AND LOSS ACCOUNTS FOR YEAR

	Cagney Group £	Lacey Ltd £
Profit before tax	12,950	3,800
Tax	(5,400)	(2,150)
Profit after tax	7,550	1,650
Profit and loss account brought forward	3,450	1,850
Profit and loss account carried forward	11,000	3,500

Cagney Ltd had acquired 90% of Lacey Ltd when the reserves of Lacey Ltd were £700. Goodwill of £110 has been fully amortised. The Cagney Ltd group includes other 100% owned subsidiaries.

On 31 December 20X0, Cagney Ltd sold shares in Lacey Ltd.

Required

Prepare extracts from the Cagney Group balance sheet and Cagney Group profit and loss account on the basis that Cagney Ltd sold the following shares in Lacey Ltd.

(a)   Its entire holding
(b)   A 15% holding
(c)   A 50% holding (significant influence retained)
(d)   An 80% holding (significant influence not retained).

Note   Ignore tax on the disposal.

3.2 Disposal of an entire holding

We first deal with part (a) — a full disposal.

◆   The consolidated balance sheet is a 'snapshot' at an instant of time. Look at the group structure at the balance sheet date, excluding the subsidiary disposed of.

♦ In the consolidated profit and loss account, bring in the subsidiary's results while it was a member of the group (up to the date of disposal). Time apportion turnover etc (including minority interest) and calculate profit or loss on disposal.

Set out your answer as usual, heading up one sheet of paper for the balance sheet, one for the profit and loss account, and one for workings.

We will work the consolidated profit and loss account first. Start with the group structure as normal, but note the date of disposal and the period for which it was a subsidiary.

(W1)   Group structure

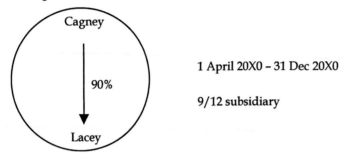

1 April 20X0 – 31 Dec 20X0

9/12 subsidiary

You will need to calculate net assets at the date of disposal in order to calculate the profit or loss on disposal.

(W2)   Net assets at disposal 31 December 20X0

	£
Share capital	3,000
Profit and loss brought forward	1,850
Profit for the year (pro rata — £1,650 × 9/12)	1,238
	6,088
Group share 90%	5,479

(W3)   Profit on disposal

Disposal — subsidiary

	£		£
Net assets disposed of (W2)	5,479	Proceeds	8,890
Profit on disposal	3,411		
	8,890		8,890

You can then calculate the minority interest for the profit and loss account.

(W4)   Minority interest

	£
Lacey's profit after tax (£1,650 × 9/12)	1,238
Minority share (10%)	124

We have a standard working for profit and loss brought forward.

(W5)   Profit brought forward

	£
100% Cagney	3,450

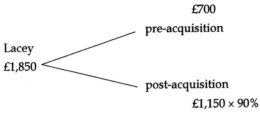

	£
post-acquisition £1,150 × 90%	1,035
Less goodwill fully amortised	(110)
	4,375

You can then prepare the consolidated profit and loss account in the normal way.

PROFIT AND LOSS ACCOUNT EXTRACT FOR THE YEAR ENDED 31 MARCH 20X1

	£
Operating profit [£12,950 + (£3,800 × 9/12)]	15,800
Profit on disposal (W3)	3,411
Profit before tax	19,211
Taxation [£5,400 + (£2,150 × 9/12)]	(7,012)
Profit after tax	12,199
Minority interest (W4)	(124)
Profit for year	12,075
Profit brought forward (W5)	4,375
Profit carried forward	16,450

We can then prove the profit carried forward in the profit and loss account.

(W6)   Reconciliation of profit carried forward

	£
100% Cagney	11,000
Profit on disposal [£8,890 - £3,440]	5,450
	16,450

You can now prepare a consolidated balance sheet in the normal way.

CAGNEY GROUP BALANCE SHEET EXTRACT AS AT 31 MARCH 20X1

	£
Sundry net assets (Cagney only)	36,450
Share capital	20,000
Profit and loss account (W6)	16,450
	36,450

3.3 *Partial disposal: retaining control*

We now move on to part (b), in which Lacey remains a subsidiary even after the disposal.

The approach is the same as for a full disposal, but we must recognise that Lacey is a subsidiary for the full year.

♦ Once again, the consolidated balance sheet is a 'snapshot' at an instant of time. Look at the group structure at the balance sheet date, including Lacey as a subsidiary.

♦ In the consolidated profit and loss account, bring in 100% of Lacey's results while a subsidiary (ie the whole year). Take out the minority interest in two parts (before and after disposal). Calculate the profit or loss on disposal.

(W1)   **Group structure**

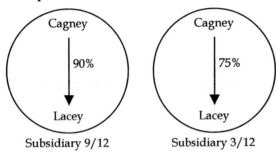

| | Subsidiary 9/12 | Subsidiary 3/12 |

(W2)   **Net assets at disposal**

	£
As in part (a)	6,088
Proportion disposed of (15%)	913

(W3)   **Profit on disposal**

Disposal — subsidiary

	£		£
Net assets disposed of (W2)	913	Proceeds	8,890
Profit on disposal	7,977		
	8,890		8,890

(W4)   **Minority interest**

	£
Lacey's profit after tax	
(£1,650 × 9/12 × 10%)	124
(£1,650 × 3/12 × 25%)	103
	227

You can now prepare the consolidated profit and loss account as before.

PROFIT AND LOSS ACCOUNT EXTRACT FOR THE YEAR ENDED 31 MARCH 20X1

	£
Operating profit (12,950 + 3,800)	16,750
Profit on disposal (W3)	7,977
Profit before tax	24,727
Tax (5,400 + 2,150)	(7,550)
Profit after tax	17,177
Minority interest (W4)	(227)
Profit for the year	16,950
Profits brought forward (as before)	4,375
Profits carried forward	21,325

You can now reconcile the profit and loss carried forward figure. Remember that Lacey is still a 75% subsidiary.

(W5)   Reconciliation of profit and loss carried forward

	£
100% Cagney	11,000
Profit on disposal (£8,890 – (3,440 × 15/90))	8,317
Less Goodwill (£110 - £110 × 15/90)	(92)

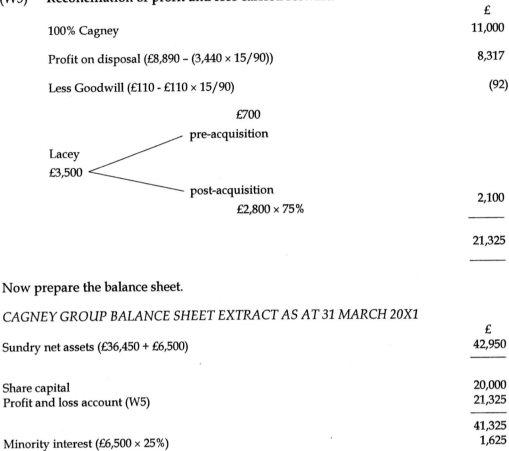

	£
post-acquisition £2,800 × 75%	2,100
	21,325

Now prepare the balance sheet.

CAGNEY GROUP BALANCE SHEET EXTRACT AS AT 31 MARCH 20X1

	£
Sundry net assets (£36,450 + £6,500)	42,950
Share capital	20,000
Profit and loss account (W5)	21,325
	41,325
Minority interest (£6,500 × 25%)	1,625
	42,950

3.4   *Partial disposal: retaining significant influence*

We now move on to part (c), in which the size of the disposal means that Lacey is no longer a subsidiary, but does qualify as an associate.

As usual, the balance sheet is a 'snapshot'. At the balance sheet date Lacey is an associate, not a subsidiary, so we do not consolidate its net assets; we equity account instead. There is no minority interest.

In the consolidated profit and loss account we distinguish two separate time periods.

Up to disposal	*After disposal*
♦ Bring in all results up to disposal (time apportion)	♦ Bring in group share of profit before tax
♦ Take out minority interest	♦ Group share of tax
♦ Calculate profit/loss on disposal	♦ Time apportioned

The approach is similar to previously, but we recognise a subsidiary for part of the year and an associate for the remainder.

(W1) **Group structure**

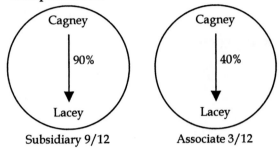

| Subsidiary 9/12 | Associate 3/12 |

(W2) **Net assets at disposal**

	£
As before	6,088
Proportion disposed of (50%)	3,044

(W3) **Profit on disposal**

Disposal — subsidiary

	£		£
Net assets disposed of (W2)	3,044	Proceeds	8,890
Profit on disposal	5,846		
	8,890		8,890

(W4) **Minority interest**

Lacey's profit after tax (£1,650 × 9/12 × 10%)	124

PROFIT AND LOSS EXTRACT FOR THE YEAR ENDED 31 MARCH 20X1

	£
Operating profit (£12,950 + 9/12 × £3,800)	15,800
Income from interest in associate (£3,800 × 3/12 × 40%)	380
	16,180
Profit on disposal (W3)	5,846
Profit before tax	22,026
Tax — group [(£5,400 + (9/12 × £2,150)]	(7,012)
— associate (£2,150 × 3/12 × 40%)	(215)
Profit after tax	14,799
Minority interest (W4)	(124)
Profit for the year	14,675
Profits brought forward (as before)	4,375
Profits carried forward	19,050

Then reconcile, remembering that Lacey is an associate at the balance sheet date.

(W5) **Reconciliation of profit and loss carried forward**

	£
100% Cagney	11,000
Profit on disposal (£8,890 – (£3,440 × 50/90))	6,979
	17,979
Less goodwill written off (£110 – (£110 × 50/90))	(49)

Lacey £3,500

£700 pre-acquisition

post-acquisition £2,800 × 40%

£2,800 × 40%	1,120
	19,050

The balance sheet is as follows.

CAGNEY GROUP BALANCE SHEET EXTRACT AS AT 31 MARCH 20X1

	£
Investment in associate (£6,500 × 40%)	2,600
Sundry net assets (Cagney only)	36,450
	39,050
Share capital	20,000
Profit and loss account (W5)	19,050
	39,050

3.5   *Partial disposal: retaining a trade investment*

We now move on to part (d), in which the size of the disposal means that Lacey is no longer even an associate, but merely a trade investment.

In the balance sheet, we do not consolidate or equity account for Lacey. We just treat it as a trade investment, with its equity value frozen as at the date of the disposal.

In the consolidated profit and loss account we again distinguish two separate time periods.

♦ In the first period we have a subsidiary and consolidate its results (using time apportionment). We take out a minority interest and we calculate a profit or loss on disposal.

♦ In the second period we have a trade investment. We take no account of Lacey's profit for this period in the consolidated profit and loss account.

We adopt our usual approach.

(W1)   **Group structure**

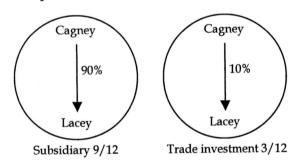

Subsidiary 9/12   Trade investment 3/12

(W2)   **Net assets at disposal**

	£
As before	6,088
Proportion disposed of (80%)	4,870

(W3)   **Profit on disposal**

Disposal — subsidiary

	£		£
Net assets disposed of (W2)	4,870	Proceeds	8,890
Profit on disposal	4,020		
	8,890		8,890

PROFIT AND LOSS EXTRACT FOR THE YEAR ENDED 31 MARCH 20X1

	£
Operating profit [£12,950 + (£3,800 × 9/12)]	15,800
Profit on disposal (W3)	4,020
	19,820
Tax [£5,400 + (£2,150 × 9/12)]	(7,012)
Profit after tax	12,808
Minority interest (£1,650 × 9/12 × 10%)	(124)
Profit for the year	12,684
Profits brought forward (as before)	4,375
	17,059

(W4) **Proof of profit and loss carried forward**

	£	£
100% Cagney		11,000
Profit on disposal [£8,890 - (£3,440 × 80/90)]		5,832
		16,832
Less goodwill (£110 – (£110 × 80/90))		(12)
Lacey reserves brought forward	1,850	
Profits in year £1,650 × 9/12	1,238	
Reserves at date of disposal	3,088	

£3,088 —
- £700 pre-acquisition
- post-acquisition £2,388 × 10%   239

| | | 17,059 |

CAGNEY GROUP BALANCE SHEET AS AT 31 MARCH 20X1

	£
Fixed asset investments (£6,088 × 10%)	609
Sundry net assets	36,450
	37,059
Share capital	20,000
Profit and loss account (W4)	17,059
	37,059

Practice question 1 *(The answer is in the final chapter of this book)*

Burrelli

The summarised draft balance sheets of Burrelli Ltd and Dawes Ltd on 31 December 20X5 are as follows.

	Burrelli Ltd £000	Dawes Ltd £000
Tangible fixed assets	1,740	840
Investments — 960,000 shares in Dawes Ltd at cost	1,200	-
Net current assets	1,010	600
	3,950	1,440

Capital and reserves

Called up share capital — £1 ordinary shares	2,400	960
Profit and loss account	1,150	480
Proceeds of sale of shares	400	-
	3,950	1,440

Burrelli Ltd owned 960,000 shares in Dawes Ltd which cost £1.2m. When the investment was acquired the reserves of Dawes Ltd amounted to £190,000. On 30 June 20X5 Burrelli Ltd sold 25% of its holding for £400,000. Apart from crediting the sale proceeds in the balance sheet, Burrelli Ltd has made no other entries to reflect the disposal.

The balances on reserves at 1 January 20X5 were as follows.

Burrelli Ltd	£750,000
Dawes Ltd	£400,000

Dawes Ltd has proposed a dividend of 10p per share for the year ended 31 December 20X5 and has provided for this. Burrelli Ltd only accounts for dividends when received.

Goodwill has been fully amortised. Ignore tax.

Required

Prepare the consolidated balance sheet of Burrelli Ltd on 31 December 20X5.

3.6 Deemed disposals

Instead of a group reducing its interest in a subsidiary by selling some or all of its shares (a direct disposal), the group may reduce its interest by means of a deemed disposal, ie where the group's interest is reduced other than by selling shares.

Deemed disposals may arise (for example) where:

♦ a subsidiary makes a rights issue and the group does not take up its full allocation of shares

♦ another party exercises options which give it an increased stake in the subsidiary (and hence reduce the group's interest)

♦ a subsidiary issues shares to a third party.

A deemed disposal is treated in the same way as a direct disposal. Calculate profit or loss on disposal as proceeds (if any) less share of net assets disposed of (compare group's share of net assets before and after) together with any related goodwill not yet amortised.

3.7 Example

P plc has owned 100% of S Ltd since incorporation of S Ltd. The capital and reserves of S Ltd at 31 December 20X4 are as follows.

	£000
Share capital — £1 ordinary shares	3,000
Profit and loss account	7,000
	10,000

S Ltd then issues 1,000,000 shares to a third party for £3,000,000. S Ltd's share capital and reserves will now be as follows.

	£000
Share capital — £1 ordinary shares	4,000
Share premium account	2,000
Profit and loss account	7,000
	13,000

Required

Calculate the profit or loss on disposal in the consolidated profit and loss account of P plc.

3.8 Solution

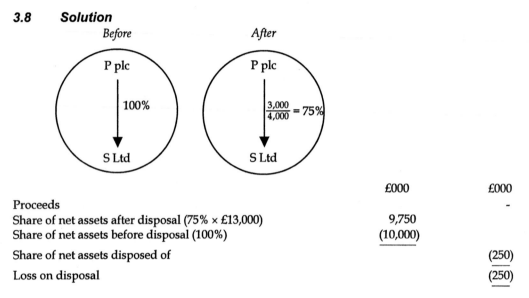

	£000	£000
Proceeds		-
Share of net assets after disposal (75% × £13,000)	9,750	
Share of net assets before disposal (100%)	(10,000)	
Share of net assets disposed of		(250)
Loss on disposal		(250)

S Ltd's net assets change at disposal because shares are being issued.

3.9 Learning outcome

You have now covered the first learning outcome for this chapter:

> Prepare financial statements when a subsidiary is disposed of part way through an accounting period.

4 Demergers

4.1 Accounting issues

A demerger occurs where an existing group divides into two or more separate groups. This is illustrated in Figure 2.

Figure 2   A demerger

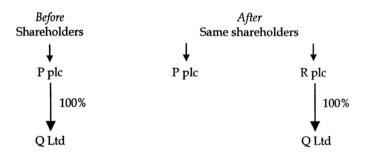

P plc has owned Q Ltd since incorporation. P plc incorporates a new company, R plc, which issues shares to P plc's shareholders in exchange for P plc's shares in Q Ltd. P plc then retains no significant interest in R plc.

(P plc also has other subsidiary undertakings.)

The key accounting issues are as follows.

♦   How should the transaction be reflected in the individual company and group accounts of P plc?

♦   How should R plc record the shares issued to the shareholders of P plc and its investment in Q Ltd in its own accounts?

♦   How should R plc consolidate Q Ltd in its group accounts?

Note that as an alternative to setting up a new company, P plc could distribute the shares in Q Ltd to its own shareholders directly.

4.2   Treatment by P plc

The substance of the transaction is that P plc has made a distribution (ie a dividend) to its shareholders.

In P plc's individual accounts, this represents a distribution of the investment in Q Ltd. The value of the distribution is equal to the carrying value of the investment in Q Ltd in P plc's balance sheet.

The value of the distribution from the perspective of the P plc group is equal to the net assets of Q Ltd at the date of demerger.

These amounts could be shown in the profit and loss account as dividends or (more commonly) as movements on the profit and loss reserve.

Another possibility is to show the transaction as a disposal for nil consideration of the investment in Q Ltd. However, this would show a loss to P plc and the group whereas the substance is that there has been a distribution to the owners of P plc. Hence, this approach is not normally adopted.

4.3   Treatment by R plc

R plc has issued shares in exchange for 100% of Q Ltd. R plc can therefore record the issue of shares at nominal value using the s131 CA85 merger relief provisions and need not record its investment in Q Ltd at fair value.

Provided that the CA85 and FRS 6 criteria are met, R plc should consolidate Q Ltd using merger accounting as this reflects the substance of the combination.

4.4   Learning outcome

You have now covered the final learning outcome for this chapter:

Prepare accounts for a demerger

5 Summary

The key steps in dealing with a disposal are as follows.

♦ Check that the disposal has been properly dealt with in the parent's own accounts.

♦ Prepare a consolidated balance sheet at the required date subsequent to disposal, based on the group structure at that time.

♦ Prepare a consolidated profit and loss account for the period including the disposal, consolidating the subsidiary up to the date of disposal (or for the whole year if control is retained).

♦ Calculate profit or loss on disposal from the group perspective, including any related goodwill not previously amortised. Show the profit or loss on disposal as an exceptional item on the face of the consolidated profit and loss account below operating profit.

♦ Classify results and profit/loss on disposal as discontinued only if FRS 3 criteria are met.

Multiple choice questions (The answers are in the final chapter of this book)

1   Yogi plc has held an 80% investment in Bear Ltd for many years. On 31 December 20X6 it disposed of all of its investment. Details for the acquisition and disposal are as follows.

	£000
Cost of investment	7,380
Fair value of Bear Ltd's net assets at acquisition (reflected in Bear Ltd's books)	9,000
Sale proceeds on 31 December 20X6	9,940

Goodwill arising on acquisition has been fully amortised.

The summarised balance sheet of Bear Ltd on 31 December 20X6 showed the following.

	£000
Net assets	10,350
Called up share capital	3,000
Profit and loss account	7,350
	10,350

What is the profit/(loss) on disposal of the shares in Bear Ltd that will be included in the consolidated profit and loss account of Yogi plc for the year ended 31 December 20X6?

(Ignore taxation and make all calculations to the nearest thousand pounds.)

A   £(410,000)

B   £(1,220,000)

C   £1,480,000

D   £1,660,000

2   Bill Group held a 40% interest in Ben Ltd for 5 years. Original cost was £120,000 and goodwill arising on acquisition was £50,000. Sales proceeds were £250,000, and this has been posted to a suspense account in Bill Ltd's individual accounts. Ben Ltd had net assets of £100,000 on disposal.

Goodwill is amortised over ten years.

What is the profit on disposal which will be included within the consolidated profit and loss account of Bill Group?

A   £130,000

B   £150,000

C   £185,000

D   £210,000

3   Tom plc acquired 75% of Bill plc on 1 January 20X4. The goodwill arising on this acquisition was £125,000 which was capitalised and amortised over 20 years in the group accounts.

On 1 January 20X9 Tom plc disposed of its entire holding in Bill plc for £820,000. On this date the net assets of Bill plc amounted to £790,000.

What is the profit/(loss) on disposal which should be included in the consolidated profit and loss account of Tom plc?

A   £(63,750)

B   £102,500

C   £196,250

D   £133,750

4   The Gill Group disposed of the following mid way through the financial year.

Tracey Ltd	100% subsidiary for	£150,000
Debbie Ltd	40% associate for	£70,000

Goodwill arising on acquisition has been fully amortised. The reserves of the companies are as follows.

	At acquisition	*At disposal*
Tracey Ltd	£70,000	£100,000
Debbie Ltd	£25,000	£40,000

The consolidated reserves of the remaining Gill Group, including the profit made on the disposal of the investments in the year, were £230,000 at 31 December 20X6.

What will be the figure for reserves included in the consolidated balance sheet for the Gill Group as at 31 December 20X6?

A   £230,000

B   £260,000

C   £266,000

D   £275,000

CHAPTER 12

Group accounts:
cash flow statements

EXAM FOCUS

Cash flow statements are examinable at both Paper 6 and Paper 7a. The difference is that at Paper 7a you may well be expected to prepare such a statement for a group, rather than for an individual company. We assume in this chapter that you are already familiar with the individual company situation and we concentrate on the specific complications that arise in group situations. You may find it useful to look back at your Paper 6 books to revise basic procedures.

LEARNING OUTCOMES

This chapter covers the following Learning Outcome of the CIMA Syllabus.

> Prepare a group cash flow statement with appropriate notes

In order to cover this Learning Outcome the following topics are included.

> The need for cash flow statements
> The FRS 1 format
> Group cash flow statements
> Interpretation of a cash flow statement
> Cash flow statements with an overseas investment

1 The need for cash flow statements

1.1 Limitations of accruals-based statements

 The balance sheet and profit and loss account are prepared on an accruals basis. They provide information about profitability and financial position, but do not show how the company has generated and used cash.

The profit and loss account may show profits on an accruals basis even if the company is suffering severe cash flow problems. This presents a misleading picture, because a business will not continue in existence if it cannot generate cash to meet its liabilities as they fall due.

A cash flow statement provides users of accounts with information on how a business has generated and used cash so that users can obtain a fuller picture of liquidity and financial adaptability (ie ability to alter amounts and timing of cash flows to respond to unexpected needs or opportunities).

A cash flow statement also supports the profit and loss account by providing information on the quality of profits (ie whether operating profits are matched by cash generation).

1.2 FRS 1 Cash flow statements

FRS 1 (Revised 1996) was published by the ASB to replace the original FRS 1 issued in 1991. A cash flow statement now shows the movements in pure cash that have taken place during the period.

You should learn certain definitions laid down in FRS 1.

Cash is defined as cash in hand and deposits repayable on demand, less overdrafts repayable on demand. Cash includes cash in hand and deposits denominated in foreign currencies.

Liquid resources are defined as current asset investments held as readily disposable stores of value. A readily disposable investment is one that:

♦ is disposable by the entity without curtailing or disrupting its business, and

♦ is readily convertible into known amounts of cash at or close to its carrying amount, or is traded in an active market.

Net debt is defined as borrowings (debt plus related derivatives and obligations under finance leases) less cash and liquid resources. 'Net debt' is replaced by 'net funds' if cash and liquid resources exceed borrowings.

The objective of FRS 1 is to ensure that entities:

♦ report their cash generation and cash absorption for a period by highlighting the significant components of cash flow in a way that facilitates comparison with other businesses

♦ provide information that assists in the assessment of their liquidity, solvency and financial adaptability.

2 The FRS 1 format

2.1 The main headings

You should learn the main headings in an FRS 1 cash flow statement, and the order in which they appear.

♦ Operating activities
♦ Dividends from joint ventures and associates
♦ Returns on investments and servicing of finance
♦ Taxation
♦ Capital expenditure and financial investment
♦ Acquisitions and disposals
♦ Equity dividends paid
♦ Management of liquid resources
♦ Financing

2.2 Reconciliations to be provided

Two reconciliations are required. These may either be presented adjoining the cash flow statement (but it must be clear that they are not part of the statement), or alternatively they can be shown in notes.

In the exam you could show these reconciliations as notes 1 and 2. Note 1 is the reconciliation of operating profit to net cash flow from operating activities. Note 2 is the reconciliation of net cash flow to movement in net debt.

In note 1, disclose the depreciation charge as well as the movements in stocks, debtors and creditors.

In note 2, show how the increase or decrease in cash for the period can be reconciled to the movement in net debt for the period. FRS 1 requires an analysis of changes in net debt to be provided, say as note 3. These changes must be categorised showing separately those arising from:

♦   the entity's cash flows

♦   the acquisition or disposal of subsidiaries

♦   other non-cash changes, such as recognition of changes in market value and exchange rate movements.

2.3   Presentation of operating cash flows

Operating cash flows can be presented by:

♦   the direct method (showing the relevant constituent cash flows); or

♦   the indirect method (calculating operating cash flows by adjustment to the operating profit reported in the profit and loss account).

You should use the indirect method unless told otherwise.

If using the direct method, the cash flow from operating activities will be calculated in working as follows.

	£
Operating activities	
Cash received from customers	X
Cash payments to suppliers	(X)
Cash paid to and on behalf of employees	(X)
Other cash payments	(X)
Net cash inflow from operating activities	X

2.4   Classification of cash flows by standard headings

Classify each cash flow according to the substance of the transaction giving rise to it. An exception is that interest paid is always classified under 'returns on investments and servicing of finance' even if capitalised in other primary statements. The main headings are shown in Table 1.

Table 1 The standard headings in an FRS 1 cash flow statement

Standard heading	*Include*
Operating activities	Cash flows re operating items including those relating to provisions (whether or not the provision is included in operating profit)
Dividends from joint ventures and associates	Dividends from equity accounted entities
Returns on investments and servicing of finance	Receipts resulting from ownership of investments, including interest received and dividends received (but not those from equity accounted entities)
	Payments to providers of debt finance, non-equity shareholders and minority interests including:

♦   interest paid (even if capitalised)
♦   FRS 4 finance costs
♦   interest element of finance lease rental payments
♦   non-equity dividends paid
♦   dividends paid to minority interests

Standard heading	Include
Taxation	Corporation tax paid
Capital expenditure and financial investment	Cash flows re:

♦ acquisition or disposal of fixed assets (other than those to be classified under 'Acquisitions and disposals')

♦ current asset investment not included in liquid resources

Cash inflows include receipts from:

♦ disposal of fixed assets
♦ repayment of loans
♦ sales of debt instruments

Cash outflows include:

♦ payments to acquire fixed assets
♦ loans made
♦ payments to acquire debt instruments

Acquisitions and disposals	Cash flows re acquisition or disposal of any:

♦ trade or business
♦ subsidiary
♦ associate

For acquisition or disposal of a subsidiary show separately any balances of cash and overdrafts transferred as part of the purchase or sale

Equity dividends paid	Dividends paid on reporting entity's (or, in a group, the parent's) equity shares
Management of liquid resources	Cash flows re liquid resources

Explain what is included in liquid resources and any changes in policy

Cash inflows include:

♦ withdrawals from short-term deposits

♦ inflows from disposal or redemption of other investments held as liquid resources

Cash outflows include:

♦ payments into short-term deposits
♦ outflows to acquire other investments held as liquid resources

Financing	Cash flows re receipts or repayments of principal from or to external providers of finance

Cash inflows include receipts from issue of shares, debentures, loans, notes, bonds and other borrowings

Cash outflows include

♦ repayments of amounts borrowed
♦ capital element of finance lease rental payments
♦ payments of expenses or commissions on issue of equity shares

Disclose separately any financing cash flows with equity accounted entities

2.5 Benefits of FRS 1 (revised)

FRS 1 as revised focuses attention on pure cash. A business has to generate cash in order to remain viable.

It is generally accepted that a cash flow statement under FRS 1 (revised) is more useful than both a statement of source and application of funds and the form of cash flow statement in FRS 1 as originally issued.

It is intended to give indications of liquidity and viability. This is important, because it is possible for companies to fail from lack of cash while apparently generating profits.

It gives an indication of financial adaptability (ie ability to generate cash by selling assets or raising additional capital).

Cash flows are a matter of fact and difficult to manipulate. The accruals-based financial statements are more subjective.

The note reconciling operating profit to net cash flow from operating activities highlights techniques which enhance profit performance with no cash flow advantage (eg sales to slow payers). The cash flow statement shows how much cash has actually been generated from operating activities and therefore the ability to turn profit into cash. Cash flow information has predictive value (likely to have many common components from year to year).

2.6   Criticisms of FRS 1

Additional disclosure of gross cash flows is optional. Most businesses do not report them, therefore depriving users of accounts (and themselves) of vital information.

Current cash flows may not be a reliable indicator of future cash flows.

There is a danger of information overload – the cash flow statement (unlike its predecessor, the statement of source and application of funds) is supported by detailed notes.

3   Group cash flow statements

3.1   Introduction

The group cash flow statement is prepared from the consolidated financial statements and therefore reflects the cash flows of the group (ie the parent and its subsidiaries). Intra-group cash flows are eliminated; only cash flows external to the group remain.

The method of preparation is the same as for the individual company cash flow statement but additional cash flows may arise as follows.

♦   Acquisition or disposal of a subsidiary
♦   Dividends paid to minority interests or received from associates

3.2   Example

Reproduced below are extracts from the annual accounts of Baton Ltd.

Consolidated balance sheet as at 30 September

	Notes	20X5		20X4	
		£000	£000	£000	£000
Fixed assets					
Intangible assets: goodwill	(3)		28		35
Tangible assets	(4)		859		770
Investments: shares in associated undertakings	(5)		216		218
			1,103		1,023
Current assets					
Stocks		1,354		1,285	
Debtors		484		440	
Investments (treasury bills)		20		15	
Cash at bank and in hand		300		284	
		2,158		2,024	
Creditors: amounts falling due within one year					
Trade creditors		685		570	
Proposed dividend		77		79	
Taxation		107		103	
		869		752	

	Notes	20X5		20X4	
		£000	£000	£000	£000
Net current assets			1,289		1,272
Total assets less current liabilities			2,392		2,295
Creditors: amounts falling due after more than one year					
Debenture loans			(494)		(528)
Provisions for liabilities and charges					
Deferred taxation			(12)		(15)
Provisions for unfunded pensions			(148)		(138)
			1,738		1,614
Capital and reserves					
Called up share capital	(6)		105		90
Share premium account	(7)		35		–
Profit and loss account	(8)		1,484		1,414
			1,624		1,504
Minority interest			114		110
			1,738		1,614

Consolidated profit and loss account for the year ended 30 September 20X5

	Notes	£000	£000
Turnover			3,120
Cost of sales and staff costs	(1)		(2,674)
Distribution costs and administrative expenses	(2)		(42)
Operating profit			404
Income from associated undertakings			61
Interest payable			(32)
Profit on ordinary activities before taxation			433
Tax on profit on ordinary activities			
Group		162	
Associated undertakings		27	
			(189)
Profit on ordinary activities after taxation			244
Minority interest			(25)
Profit attributable to shareholders of Baton Ltd			219
Dividends			(149)
Retained profit for the financial year			70

Notes

(1)   Staff costs

	£000
Wages and salaries	200
Social security	22
	222

(2)   Distribution costs and administrative expenses

This includes depreciation and amortisation charges, profits on disposals of fixed assets and movements in pension provisions.

(3)   **Intangible assets: goodwill**

Goodwill arising on acquisitions is amortised over its expected useful life of nine years. Goodwill relating to acquisitions of subsidiaries is as follows.

	£000
Cost	
At 1 October 20X4 and 30 September 20X5	62
Accumulated amortisation	
At 1 October 20X4	27
Charge for year	7
At 30 September 20X5	34
Net book value	
At 30 September 20X5	28
At 1 October 20X4	35

(4)   **Tangible fixed assets**

	Land and buildings	Plant and machinery	Total
Cost	£000	£000	£000
At 1 October 20X4	502	708	1,210
Expenditure	64	168	232
Disposals	(58)	(43)	(101)
At 30 September 20X5	508	833	1,341
Depreciation			
At 1 October 20X4	121	319	440
Charge for year	14	65	79
Adjustments on disposals	(14)	(23)	(37)
At 30 September 20X5	121	361	482
Net book value			
At 30 September 20X5	387	472	859
At 1 October 20X4	381	389	770

Proceeds on disposals of land and buildings were £75,000 and of plant and machinery were £45,000.

(5)   **Investments**

	20X5		20X4	
Interests in associated undertakings	£000	£000	£000	£000
Share of net assets		213		213
Premium on acquisition				
At acquisition	12		12	
Less Amortisation to date	(9)		(7)	
		3		5
		216		218

(6) **Called up share capital**

	£000
Ordinary shares of £1 each	
Authorised	150
Issued and fully paid	
At 1 October 20X4	90
Rights issue	15
At 30 September 20X5	105

(7) **Share premium account**

	£000
Premium on rights issue during year	35
Balance 30 September 20X5	35

(8) **Profit and loss account**

	£000
Balance 1 October 20X4	1,414
Retained profit for the year	70
Balance 30 September 20X5	1,484
Of which retained by: Group	1,330
Associated undertakings (20X4: £149,000)	154
	1,484

Required

Prepare a consolidated cash flow statement for the year ended 30 September 20X5 insofar as the given information permits.

3.3   *Approach to the question*

A common complaint from students attempting cash flow statement questions is that they simply do not have enough time to make a good attempt at the question.

It is essential, even before you do a detailed read, to prepare your answer booklet. Presentation is important: you will need to prepare the following.

♦ A sheet headed 'Baton Ltd Consolidated cash flow statement for the year ended 30 September 20X5' with the main FRS 1 headings on it.

♦ A sheet headed 'Notes to the cash flow statement'

♦ A sheet for workings

Then you need an 'active read'. By the time you have finished your detailed read you should have ascertained:

♦ any acquisition or disposal in the period
♦ any exchange differences
♦ any other non-cash items
♦ any associated companies

In this example there is no acquisition or disposal or any exchange differences. We will therefore start with Note 1.

We start with operating profit and then pick up any non-cash transactions:

♦ depreciation
♦ amortisation
♦ book profits and losses
♦ provisions
♦ movements on stock, debtors and creditors.

3.4 Baton Ltd Notes to the cash flow statement

(1) *Reconciliation of operating profit to net cash inflow from operating activities*

	£000
Operating profit	404
Amortisation of goodwill (7+2)	9
Depreciation charges	79
Less profit on disposal (25+31)	(56)
Increase in stocks (1,354 - 1,285)	(69)
Increase in debtors (484 - 440)	(44)
Increase in creditors (685 - 570)	115
Increase in provisions for unfunded pensions	10
	448

The dividend from the associate is calculated as follows.

(W1)   **Interests in associated undertakings**

	£000		£000
Brought forward	218	Profit and loss account – share of tax	27
Profit and loss account share of profit before tax	61	Goodwill amortised in the year	2
		Dividends received from associate (balance)	34
		Carried forward	216
	279		279

We continue to work down the cash flow format. The next section of the cash flow statement is 'returns on investments and servicing of finance'. You will need to calculate dividends paid to minority interests at this point.

(W2)   **Minority interests**

	£000		£000
Dividend paid to the minority (balance)	21	Brought forward	110
Carried forward	114	Profit and loss account	25
	135		135

If we now include interest paid we can complete this section.

The next section is 'taxation'. Use the usual 'T' account working.

(W3)   **Taxation**

	£000		£000
Cash paid (balance)	161	Brought forward	
Carried forward		Corporation tax	103
Deferred tax	12	Deferred tax	15
Corporation tax	107	Profit and loss account – group tax	162
	280		280

The next section is 'capital expenditure'. Pick up the payments to acquire tangible fixed assets and the receipts from disposal from Note 4. In the present question, there is no acquisition or disposal.

We next use the standard working to calculate equity dividend paid.

(W4)   **Dividend creditor**

	£000		£000
Cash paid (balance)	151	Balance brought forward	79
		Profit and loss account	149
Balance carried forward	77		
	——		——
	228		228
	——		——

'Management of liquid resources' comes next. If the company has pushed any cash into short-term investments (eg treasury bills) it will be reflected in this section.

The final section 'financing' will then include cash flows from shares and long-term liabilities.

3.5 Solution

Your answer will now look like this.

BATON LTD
CONSOLIDATED CASH FLOW STATEMENT FOR THE YEAR ENDED 30 SEPTEMBER 20X5

	£000	£000
Net cash inflow from operating activities (Note 1)		448
Dividends from associate		34
Returns on investments and servicing of finance		
Dividends paid to minority interests (W2)	(21)	
Interest paid	(32)	
	——	
		(53)
Taxation (W3)		(161)
Capital expenditure		
Payments to acquire tangible fixed assets	(232)	
Receipts from sales of tangible fixed assets	120	
	——	
		(112)
Equity dividends paid (W4)		(151)
Management of liquid resources		
Purchase of treasury bills (20 - 15)		(5)
Financing		
Issue of ordinary share capital (15 + 35)	50	
Redemption of debenture loans (528 - 494)	(34)	
	——	
		16
		——
Increase in cash		16
		——

We then need to provide the reconciliation of net cash flow to the movement in net debt. It is easiest however to work Note 3 first as this will provide the working for Note 2.

(3) Analysis of changes in net debt

	At 1 October 20X4	Cash flows	At 30 September 20X5
	£000	£000	£000
Cash at bank and in hand	284	16	300
Debt due after one year	(528)	34	(494)
Current asset investments	15	5	20
	——	——	——
Total	(229)	55	(174)
	——	——	——

(2)   **Reconciliation of net cash flow to movement in net debt (Note 3)**

	£000	£000
Increase in cash in the period	16	
Cash to repurchase debenture	34	
Cash used to increase liquid resources	5	
Change in net debt		55
Net debt at 1 October 20X4 (528 – 15 – 284)		(229)
Net debt at 30 September 20X5 (494 – 20 – 300)		(174)

You should now have a cash flow statement with notes supported by and cross-referenced to a working paper.

Practice question 1 *(The answer is in the final chapter of this book)*

Field

Given below are the summarised balance sheets for the Field plc group at 31 December 20X5 and 20X6 and the summarised profit and loss account for 20X6.

BALANCE SHEET	20X6	20X5
	£000	£000
Fixed assets	4,700	3,700
Investments in associated undertakings	2,100	2,000
Stocks	1,700	1,400
Debtors	2,600	2,400
Bank balances and cash	50	100
	11,150	9,600
Trade creditors	2,000	1,500
Bank overdraft	150	350
Taxation	250	200
Proposed dividend	70	60
Deferred taxation	140	180
Share capital	4,900	4,300
Loans	1,400	1,250
Reserves	2,010	1,580
Minority interest	230	180
	11,150	9,600

PROFIT AND LOSS ACCOUNT	£000	£000
Operating profit for the year		640
Share of associated undertaking's profits		200
		840
Interest paid		(110)
		730
Taxation – Group	120	
– Associate	50	
		(170)
		560
Minority interest		(60)
		500
Dividend		(70)
Retained profit for the year		430

Depreciation for the year on fixed assets was £70,000 and there were no disposals in the year.

Required

Prepare the cash flow statement for the Field plc group for the year ended 31 December 20X6.

3.6   Acquisitions and disposals

 In an FRS 1 cash flow statement you must show separately the cash flow relating to acquisition or disposal of

♦   a trade or business
♦   a subsidiary
♦   an associate

Also disclose separately any balances of cash or overdrafts transferred as part of the acquisition or disposal of a subsidiary.

These disclosures should be made under the heading 'acquisitions and disposals'.

In the notes to the cash flow statement, disclose:

♦   a summary of the effect of the acquisition or disposal, indicating how much of the consideration comprised cash

♦   material effects on amounts under each standard heading (this could be done by dividing cash flows between continuing and discontinued operations and acquisitions or by a simple statement)

♦   any net debt (excluding cash and overdrafts) acquired or disposed of with a subsidiary in the analysis of changes in net debt.

4   Interpretation of a cash flow statement

4.1   Techniques to apply

Consider unusual or discretionary cash flows, specifically:

♦   discontinued activities
♦   unsuccessful takeover bid
♦   cash inflows from an acquisition.

Watch for non-cash changes:

♦   Shares issued to purchase a subsidiary
♦   Major investment in fixed assets via a lease
♦   Non-cash share issue.

Compare operating profit to operating cash flows. This is a measure of the quality of profits: if operating cash flows are significantly lower, the company may run into liquidity problems.

Compare interest in the profit and loss account to interest cash flows. Capitalised interest does not appear in the profit and loss account but is still shown in the cash flow statement. Interest cover should always include capitalised interest.

Compare earnings with the cash equivalent, ie operating flows plus returns on investments less servicing of finance and taxation. Cash EPS can be calculated in this way.

Practice question 2 *(The answer is in the final chapter of this book)*

Tender

The summarised consolidated profit and loss account for Tender Ltd and its subsidiaries for the year ended 30 June 20X5 is as follows.

	£000
Turnover	14,620
Cost of sales and other operating expenses	(12,960)
Operating profit	1,660
Profit on disposal of investment (Note 2)	306
Interest paid and similar charges	(320)
Profit on ordinary activities before taxation	1,646
Tax on profit on ordinary activities	(470)
Profit on ordinary activities after taxation (Note 1)	1,176
Minority interest	(24)
	1,152
Dividends paid - ordinary	(192)
	960
Profit and loss account at 1 July 20X4	5,600
Profit and loss account at 30 June 20X5	6,560

The summarised consolidated balance sheets for Tender Ltd and its subsidiaries at 30 June 20X5 and 30 June 20X4 are as follows.

	30 June 20X5		30 June 20X4	
	£000	£000	£000	£000
Tangible fixed assets (Note 3)		5,712		6,580
Current assets				
Stocks	2,802		2,935	
Debtors	2,203		1,924	
Investments (corporate bonds)	1,290		1,010	
Cash at bank and in hand	1,488		756	
	7,783		6,625	
Creditors: amounts falling due within one year (Note 4)	(1,910)		(1,980)	
		5,873		4,645
		11,585		11,225
Creditors: amounts falling due after more than one year		(3,000)		(3,000)
Provisions for liabilities and charges				
Deferred taxation		(517)		(763)
		8,068		7,462
Called up share capital		1,000		1,000
Profit and loss account		6,560		5,600
Minority interest		508		862
		8,068		7,462

The notes to the accounts include the following.

(1)   Profit on ordinary activities

	£000
Profit after taxation is stated after charging	
Depreciation	1,094

(2)   Profit on sale of investment

At 30 June 20X4 the group held 75% of the issued share capital of Gentle Ltd. On 1 July 20X4 the group sold all of its holding for £1,440,000 cash. The original holding was purchased when the profit and loss account of Gentle Ltd was £100,000. All goodwill arising on the acquisition of Gentle Ltd has been amortised through the profit and loss account.

The balance sheet of Gentle Ltd at 30 June 20X4 was as follows.

	£000	£000
Tangible fixed assets		1,104
Current assets		
Stocks	504	
Debtors	346	
Cash	134	
	984	
Creditors: amounts falling due within one year		
Trade creditors	(576)	
		408
		1,512
Called up share capital		720
Profit and loss account		792
		1,512

(3)   Tangible fixed assets

	£000
Cost	
At 1 July 20X4	11,772
Additions during year	1,954
Disposals	(2,136)
At 30 June 20X5	11,590
Depreciation	
At 1 July 20X4	5,192
Charge for the year	1,094
Relating to disposals	(408)
At 30 June 20X5	5,878
Net book value	
At 30 June 20X5	5,712
At 1 July 20X4	6,580

The proceeds on the sale of the fixed assets were equal to their net book value at the time of disposal.

(4)   Creditors: amounts falling due within one year

	20X5	20X4
	£000	£000
Creditors include taxation of	750	630

Required

Prepare a consolidated cash flow statement and supporting notes for the year ended 30 June 20X5, insofar as the information allows.

5 Cash flow statements with an overseas investment

5.1 Introduction

Retranslation exchange differences are not cash flows. They should therefore be excluded from the consolidated cash flow statement.

 When using the temporal method, the treatment of exchange differences may be summarised as follows.

Exchange differences arising on	Included in the profit and loss account	To deal with in cash flow statement
Debtors/creditors and settlement	Operating profit	Ignore (exchange differences are in operating profit and balance sheet movement, operating cash flow is correct)
Cash (operating)	Operating profit	Remove in reconciliation
Loan retranslation	Interest	Exclude from ♦ returns on investments and servicing of finance ♦ balance sheet movement on loans (via analysis of changes in net debt note)

When using the closing rate method, FRS 1 requires the inclusion of cash flows of the foreign entity at the rate used to translate the foreign entity's profit and loss account.

If the profit and loss account is translated at the closing rate, we need an analysis of exchange differences on opening net assets. Adjust the opening consolidated balance sheet to closing rate and prepare the cash flow statement as usual.

5.2 Example

Set out below is a summary of the accounts of Picketing plc for the year ended 31 December 20X4.

CONSOLIDATED PROFIT AND LOSS ACCOUNT
FOR THE YEAR ENDED 31 DECEMBER 20X4

	£000	£000
Turnover		33,374
Cost of sales and other expenses		(28,233)
Operating profit		5,141
Income from associated undertakings		70
Interest payable and similar charges		(325)
Profit on ordinary activities before taxation		4,886
Tax on profit on ordinary activities		
Group	2,038	
Share of associated undertaking	40	
		(2,078)
Profit attributable to the group		2,808
Minority interests		(3)
Profit attributable to the group		2,805
Dividends — proposed		(383)
Retained profit for the financial year		2,422

Statement of retained profits	£000
Profit and loss account brought forward	5,896
Retained profit for the year	2,422
Exchange differences	302
Profit and loss account carried forward	8,620

CONSOLIDATED BALANCE SHEETS AS AT 31 DECEMBER

	Note	20X4 £000	20X4 £000	20X3 £000	20X3 £000
Fixed assets					
Intangible assets			435		
Tangible assets	(1)		11,157		8,995
Investment in associated undertaking			300		270
			11,892		9,265
Current assets					
Stocks		9,749		7,624	
Debtors		6,897		5,161	
Cash at bank and in hand		927		394	
		17,573		13,179	
Creditors: amounts falling due within one year	(2)	(9,628)		(6,109)	
Net current assets			7,945		7,070
Total assets less current liabilities			19,837		16,335
Creditors: amounts falling due after more than one year					
Debenture loans			(2,102)		(1,682)
Provisions for liabilities and charges	(3)		(1,290)		(935)
			16,445		13,718
Capital and reserves					
Called up share capital (£1 ords)			1,997		1,997
Share premium account			5,808		5,808
Profit and loss account			8,620		5,896
			16,425		13,701
Minority interest			20		17
			16,445		13,718

Notes to the accounts

(1)   Tangible assets: net book value summary

	£000
At 31 December 20X3	8,995
Exchange rate adjustment	138
Additions	3,107
Disposals	(288)
Depreciation charge for the year	(795)
At 31 December 20X4	11,157

The profit on the disposal of fixed assets was £318,000.

(2)   Creditors: amounts falling due within one year

	20X4 £000	20X3 £000
Bank overdrafts	1,228	91
Trade creditors	4,295	3,007
Corporation tax	3,722	2,566
Proposed dividend	383	445
	9,628	6,109

(3)   Provisions for liabilities and charges

	Pensions £000	Deferred taxation £000	Total £000
At 31 December 20X3	246	689	935
Exchange rate adjustment	29	–	29
Increase in provision	460	–	460
Decrease in provision	–	(134)	(134)
At 31 December 20X4	735	555	1,290

(4)   Quince Ltd

During the year the company acquired the entire issued share capital of Quince Ltd for a cash consideration of £1,268,000. The fair values of the assets of Quince Ltd were as follows.

	£000
Fixed assets	208
Stocks	612
Trade debtors	732
Trade creditors	(407)
Debenture loans	(312)
	833

Additional information

Exchange gains in the statement of retained profits comprise differences on the retranslation of the following.

	£000
Fixed assets	138
Pensions	(29)
Stocks	116
Debtors	286
Creditors	(209)
	302

Required

Prepare a consolidated cash flow statement for the year ended 31 December 20X4.

5.3   *Approach to the example*

If there is an acquisition or disposal in the period you must immediately sort it out. Prepare Note 4 (purchase of subsidiary undertaking). Remember that each item in the note will feature in your answer.

(4)   Purchase of subsidiary undertaking

	£000
Net assets acquired	
Fixed assets (additions to fixed assets)	208
Stocks (Note 1)	612
Trade debtors (Note 1)	732
Trade creditors (Note 1)	(407)
Debenture loans (Financing note)	(312)
	833
Goodwill	435
(Non-cash adjustment if carried as intangible asset, Note 1 if amortised)	
	1,268
Satisfied by cash	1,268

Remember that exchange differences are not cash flows and must be excluded when comparing balance sheets for cash flow calculations.

Proforma working for Note 1	Stock £000	Debtors £000	Creditors £000
Closing balance	9,749	6,897	4,295
Opening balance	(7,624)	(5,161)	(3,007)
Acquired with subsidiary	(612)	(732)	(407)
Exchange gains	(116)	(286)	(209)
Increase/(decrease) in the period	1,397	718	672

Search for any other non-cash items: for example, the increase for pension provisions, the depreciation charge and profits/losses on disposal of fixed assets. (Although it is not relevant to this example, remember to watch out for amortisation of goodwill). You are now in a position to prepare Note 1 as usual.

Notes to the cash flow statement

(1)   Reconciliation of operating profit to net cash inflow from operating activities

	£000
Operating profit	5,141
Depreciation charges	795
Profit on sale of fixed assets	(318)
Increase in pension provision	460
Increase in stocks (2,125 - 612 - 116)	(1,397)
Increase in debtors (1,736 - 732 - 286)	(718)
Increase in creditors (1,288 - 407 - 209)	672
Net cash inflow from operating activities	4,635

Where you have an associated undertaking, you will need to work out how much dividend was received from it in the period. The easiest approach is to use a T account. Open an associated undertaking T account.

Investment in associate

	£000		£000
Balance brought forward	270	Share of tax	40
Share of profit before tax	70	Dividends received (balance)	Nil
		Balance carried forward	300
	340		340

 You can also prepare Notes 2 and 3. You must remember that, although it is not relevant to this question, if the exchange gain had included a gain on cash, this must have been excluded from the movement. It is best exam technique to work Note 3 first.

(3)   Analysis of changes in net debt

	At 1 January 20X4 £000	Cash flows £000	Acquisition (excl cash and overdrafts) £000	At 31 December 20X4 £000
Cash at bank and in hand	394	533		927
Bank overdrafts	(91)	(1,137)		(1,228)
		(604)		
Debt due after one year	(1,682)	(108)	(312)	(2,102)
Total	(1,379)	(712)	(312)	(2,403)

(2)   Reconciliation of net cash flow to movement in net debt (Note 3)

	£000	£000
Decrease in cash in period	(604)	
Cash inflow from increase in debt financing	(108)	
		(712)
Debt acquired with subsidiary		(312)
Movement in net debt in the period		(1,024)
Net debt at 1 January 20X4		(1,379)
Net debt at 31 December 20X4		(2,403)

At this point you can also consider dividend paid to minority interests, using the same approach as for associates.

Dividend paid to minority interests

	£000		£000
Dividend paid (balance)	Nil	Balance brought forward	17
Balance carried forward	20	Profit and loss account	3
	20		20

You are now in a position to complete the next section of the cash flow statement — 'returns on investments and servicing of finance'.

Use the usual T account working for taxation.

Tax account

	£000		£000
Tax paid (balance)	1,016	Brought forward	
Carried forward		Corporation tax	2,566
Corporation tax	3,722	Deferred tax	689
Deferred tax	555	Charge for the year	2,038
	5,293		5,293

On payments to acquire tangible fixed assets, remember to exclude the fixed assets acquired with the subsidiary (Note 4).

Acquisitions – payments to acquire subsidiary undertakings can be picked up directly from Note 4.

Then calculate the dividend paid by the holding company and you are ready to complete the next section of the cash flow statement – 'equity dividends paid'.

Dividend paid by the holding company

	£000		£000
Dividend paid (balance)	445	Balance brought forward	445
Balance carried forward	383	Profit and loss account	383
	828		828

Finally you can complete the last section – 'financing'. Remember to exclude the debentures acquired with the subsidiary.

Your answer should then look as follows, supported by appropriate notes and a neat working paper.

PICKETING PLC
CONSOLIDATED CASH FLOW STATEMENT FOR THE YEAR ENDED 31 DECEMBER 20X4

	£000	£000
Net cash inflow from operating activities (Note 1)		4,635
Returns on investments and servicing of finance: interest paid		(325)
Taxation		(1,016)
Capital expenditure		
Payments to acquire tangible fixed assets	(2,899)	
Receipts from sale of tangible fixed assets (318 + 288)	606	
		(2,293)
Acquisitions and disposals: purchase of subsidiary undertaking (Note 4)		(1,268)
Equity dividends paid		(445)
Financing: new debenture loans issued (2,102 - 1,682 - 312)		108
Decrease in cash		(604)

5.4 Learning outcome

You have now covered the learning outcome for this chapter:

> Prepare a group cash flow statement with appropriate notes.

6 Summary

You should now be able to calculate the amounts to be included in cash flow statements, recommend the headings under which they should be included and draft appropriate notes in respect of:

- taxation
- minority interests
- associated undertakings
- acquisition and disposal of subsidiary.

You should also be able to discuss the merits and shortcomings of FRS 1.

Multiple choice questions *(The answers are in the final chapter of this book)*

1   The consolidated balance sheet of Bugs Ltd shows a minority interest of £640,000 at 31 March 20X1 and £700,000 at 31 March 20X2. The consolidated profit and loss account shows a minority interest of £100,000.

What amount should appear in the group cash flow statement for minority interest?

A   Receipt of £40,000

B   Payment of £40,000

C   Payment of £60,000

D   Receipt of £100,000

Using the following information answer questions 2 and 3.

Given below is an extract from the consolidated balance sheet of Fraser Ltd group.

	31 Dec 20X2 £000	31 Dec 20X1 £000
Investment in associate	400	360
Creditors: amounts falling due within one year		
Corporation tax	120	110

You are also given a summarised consolidated profit and loss account for the year ending 31 December 20X2.

	£000	£000
Operating profit		240
Income from associated undertakings		80
		320
Tax on profit on ordinary activities		
Group	60	
Associated undertakings	20	
		80
Profit after tax		240

2   What figure would appear in the group cash flow statement for the associated undertaking?

   A   Receipt of £20,000

   B   Payment of £20,000

   C   Receipt of £60,000

   D   Payment of £80,000

3   What figure would appear in the group cash flow statement for tax paid?

   A   £50,000

   B   £60,000

   C   £70,000

   D   £90,000

CHAPTER 13

Capital reconstruction schemes

EXAM FOCUS

The Paper 7a syllabus does not require you to **devise** a capital reconstruction scheme but you may have to prepare accounts to implement a given scheme.

LEARNING OUTCOMES

This chapter covers the following Learning Outcome of the CIMA Syllabus.

> Prepare accounts for a capital reconstruction scheme

In order to cover this Learning Outcome the following topics are included.

> Reasons for reorganisation or capital reconstruction
> Share reduction under s135 CA 1985
> Reconstruction under s425 CA 1985
> External reconstructions

---

1 Reasons for reorganisation or capital reconstruction

1.1 Financial difficulties

If a company is in financial trouble it may have no recourse but to accept liquidation as the final outcome.

However it may be in a position to survive, and indeed flourish, by taking up some future contract or opening in the market.

The only hindrance to this may be that its future operations need a cash injection.

This cash injection cannot be raised because the present structure and status of the company will not be attractive to outside investors.

The typical profile is as follows.

- ◆ Large accumulated losses
- ◆ Large arrears of debenture interest
- ◆ Large arrears of dividends on cumulative preference shares
- ◆ No payment of ordinary dividends
- ◆ A market share price below nominal value
- ◆ Lack of market confidence in its future

To get a cash injection the company will need to reorganise or reconstruct.

1.2   The interests of stakeholders in the company

The capital structure protects stakeholders in the company (shareholders and creditors).

Any changes to this structure are therefore restricted by company law to protect these stakeholders. Some of the ways in which this is achieved are explained below.

A company with accumulated losses is prevented from paying ordinary dividends, possibly for several years, because of the Companies Acts rules on distribution. This will not make the company an attractive proposition for prospective equity investors.

Large arrears of debenture interest and preference share dividends are also a negative factor.

♦   They tie up any future resources which could be used for expansion.

♦   They tie up any future profits which could be used for distribution.

♦   They make it difficult to obtain new debenture or preference financing as past arrears will make new issues unattractive to the market.

Non-payment of ordinary dividends on existing ordinary shares will make any new issue unattractive.

If the market value of a company's shares is below their nominal value the company will be unable to issue new shares because the investor wants to pay *market price*.

(The company cannot issue at this price as it is below *nominal value*. Issuing shares at a discount is not allowed under the Companies Acts.)

1.3   Possible reconstructions

The changing or reconstruction of the company's capital could alleviate these problems. The company can take any or all of the following steps.

♦   Write off the accumulated losses
♦   Write off the debenture and preference share arrears
♦   Write down the nominal value of the shares.

To do this the company must ask all or some of its existing stakeholders to surrender existing rights and amounts owing in exchange for new rights under a new or reformed company.

Why would stakeholders be willing to do this? The main reason is that it may be preferable to the alternatives, which are:

♦   To remain as they are, with the prospect of no return from their investment and no growth in their investment, or

♦   To accept whatever return they could be given in a liquidation.

It is helpful to look in turn at the situation faced by each group of stakeholders.

Ordinary shareholders These are the last to be allocated funds in liquidation, and therefore have a high chance of no return at all.

Preference shareholders usually rank before ordinary shareholders in liquidation, but there is still a possibility of loss of capital and arrears.

Debentureholders have a better chance under liquidation than others (because their loan is secured) but the full amount of their debt may not be received.

Trade creditors have a low chance of repayment under liquidation.

Faced with these alternatives, it is clear why stakeholders may prefer to acquiesce in a scheme of reconstruction.

They give up existing rights and amounts owing (which are unlikely to be met) for the opportunity to share in the growth in profits which may arise from the extra cash which can be generated as a consequence of their actions.

1.4 Classifying the possible schemes

There are several ways in which a scheme of reorganisation or reconstruction may be effected. Figure 1 illustrates the main possibilities.

Figure 1 Classifying the possible schemes

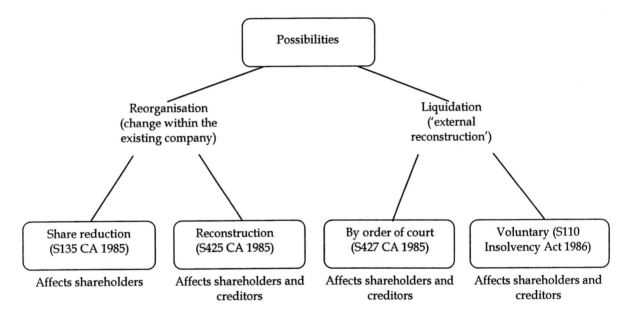

We look at each of these possibilities in turn in the remainder of this chapter.

2 Share reduction under s135 CA1985

2.1 How the scheme works

Using s135 a company may:

(a)   write off unpaid share capital
(b)   write off any share capital which is lost or not represented by available assets
(c)   write off any paid up share capital which is in excess of requirements.

Under (a), the company is effectively reducing the nominal value of its share capital. For example, ordinary shares of £1 each 80p paid may be reclassified as ordinary shares of 80p each fully paid.

Under (b) – the most common situation – the company has a debit balance on the profit and loss reserve. This prevents any dividend payments. The company can write off those losses against equity and other capital reserves, thus allowing distribution to take place once profits have been built up.

Under (c) the company is using surplus cash to repay its shareholders.

2.2   Illustration

A Ltd has the following balance sheet as at 31 December 20X2.

	£000
Assets	200
Creditors	(50)
	150
Ordinary share capital:	
1,000,000 ordinary shares of 20p	200
Share premium account	100
Profit and loss account	(150)
	150

A Ltd has a debit balance on the profit and loss account of £150,000.

 It may write this off under s135 using the share premium account and some of its share capital. Write off the maximum amount possible against share premium account (here £100,000) and the balance (here £50,000) against share capital.

This leads to the following balance sheet.

	£000
Assets	200
Creditors	(50)
	150
Share capital: 750,000 shares of 20p each	150

In effect for every four shares held the company has cancelled one.

2.3   The advantage to shareholders

Although one share has been cancelled any new profit can be distributed whereas before it would just reduce the losses brought forward. In effect all this does is to formalise what has already happened.

Equity interest is eroded by accumulated losses. Court approval is needed so creditors can object if they wish.

3   Reconstruction under s425 CA1985

3.1   Introduction

Section 425 reconstruction extends the s135 idea to include creditors, debentureholders and other stakeholders.

In addition to a reduction on share capital the arrangement may:

♦ write off debenture interest arrears
♦ replace existing debentures with a lower interest debenture
♦ write off preference dividend arrears
♦ write off amounts owing to trade creditors.

It is important to recognise the trade off which is being made by the stakeholders. They sacrifice existing rights (eg dividends, repayments and interest) in return for new rights (new openings, new contracts, share in increased profits).

3.2   Example

The balance sheet of Milner Ltd is shown below.

	£	£
Fixed assets		
Goodwill		50,000
Other		220,000
		270,000
Current assets	50,000	
Current liabilities		
Bank overdraft	(20,000)	
Trade creditors	(100,000)	
Net current liabilities		(70,000)
		200,000
Capital and reserves		
Ordinary shares of £1 each, fully paid		100,000
Preference shares of £1 each, fully paid		125,000
Share premium		75,000
Profit and loss account		(100,000)
		200,000

Milner Ltd wishes to put the following reconstruction scheme into effect.

1   A new ordinary share of 25p nominal value will be created.

2   The ordinary shares will be written off and the shareholders will be offered one new ordinary share for every old share held.

3   The preference shares will be written off and the shareholders will be offered four new ordinary shares for every preference share held.

4   Existing ordinary shareholders will be invited to subscribe for three fully paid new ordinary shares at par for every old ordinary share held.

5   Goodwill and reserves are to be written off.

Required

Show the balance sheet of the company immediately after the scheme has been put into effect, assuming that the shareholders take up all the new shares to which they are entitled.

3.3   Solution

Open a reconstruction account

All adjustments which occur because of the scheme must be accounted for in the reconstruction account.

Any balance on this account remaining after implementing the scheme will be transferred to a capital reserve.

Reconstruction account

	£		£
New ordinary shares (100,000 × £0.25) (2)	25,000	Ordinary shares (2)	100,000
New ordinary shares (125,000 × 4 × £0.25) (3)	125,000	Preference shares (3)	125,000
Goodwill (5)	50,000	Share premium (5)	75,000
Profit and loss account (5)	100,000		
	300,000		300,000

(1)   New ordinary share of 25p nominal value is to be created.

(2)   The ordinary shares are written off and shareholders offered a new ordinary share for every old share held.

(3)   Preference shares are to be written off and shareholders offered four new ordinary shares for every preference share held.

(4)   Existing ordinary shareholders will be invited to subscribe for three fully paid new ordinary shares at par for every old ordinary share held.

£100,000 × 3 × 25p = £75,000

Dr Cash   £75,000
Cr Share capital   £75,000

(5)   Goodwill and reserves to be written off.

This leads to the following balance sheet.

	£	£
Fixed assets		
Tangible assets		220,000
Current assets		
(£50,000 + £75,000 – £20,000)	105,000	
Current liabilities	(100,000)	
Net current assets		5,000
		225,000
Share capital		
900,000 25p shares (£25,000 + £125,000 + £75,000)		225,000

Practice question 1 *(The answer is in the final chapter of this book)*

Bethany

Bethany Ltd is a company that carries on business as film processors. For the past few years it has been making losses owing to the intense price competition.

The company's balance sheet as at 30 June 20X1 was as follows.

	£000
Fixed assets	7,200
Net current assets	7,550
	14,750
11% redeemable debentures 20X8	(7,000)
	7,750
Share capital	
Ordinary shares of £1 each fully paid	20,000
8% cumulative preference shares of £1 each, fully paid	5,000
Reserves	
Profit and loss balance	(17,250)
	7,750

The company has changed its marketing strategy and is now aiming at the specialist portrait print market. It is expected that the company will earn annual profits after tax of £3,000,000 for the next five years (the figure is before an interest charge). Corporation tax is assumed to be at a rate of 31%.

The directors are proposing to reconstruct the company and have produced the following proposal for discussion.

(a) The existing ordinary shares to be cancelled

(b) The 11% debentures to be redeemed and the debentureholders issued in exchange with

　　(i)　£6,000,000 14% redeemable debentures 20Y8, and
　　(ii)　4,000,000 ordinary shares of 25p each, fully paid up

(c) The 8% cumulative preference shareholders to be issued with 4,000,000 ordinary shares of 25p each, fully paid up, in payment of the four years' arrears of preference dividend

(d) The existing ordinary shareholders to be issued with 7,000,000 ordinary shares of 25p each, fully paid up

In the event of a liquidation, it is estimated that the net realisable value of the assets would be £6,200,000 for the fixed assets and £7,000,000 for the net current assets.

Required

(a) Prepare a balance sheet as at 1 July 20X1 after the reconstruction has been effected and describe the legal process required.　　　　**(6 marks)**

(b) Prepare computations to show the effect of the proposed reconstruction scheme on each of the debentureholders, preference shareholders and ordinary shareholders.

(8 marks)

(c) Write a brief report to advise a shareholder who owns 10% of the issued ordinary share capital on whether to agree to the reconstruction as proposed. The shareholder has informed you that he feels the proposals are unfair.　　　　**(8 marks)**

(Total : 22 marks)

4　*External reconstructions*

4.1　*Liquidation by order of the court (s427 CA1985)*

This involves the assets and liabilities of the old company being transferred to a new company.

Old stakeholders are offered shares in the new company. Full liquidation rights are maintained.

4.2　*Voluntary liquidation under s110 Insolvency Act 1986*

The procedure is similar to the above but court sanction is not needed. A special resolution is needed to approve it.

This is not as common as s427 as the company must be solvent. Basic principles are the same.

4.3　*Example*

A plc agrees to acquire the net assets, excluding the bank balance, of B plc. The purchase consideration comprises the following.

	£
50,000 £1 ordinary shares issued at a premium of 10p	55,000
£30,000 8% debentures issued at 90	27,000
Cash	18,000
	100,000

When computing the consideration the directors of A plc valued B's land and buildings at £40,000, the stock at £15,000 and the debtors at book value subject to 3% doubtful debt provision.

After the sale B plc is liquidated. The preference shares are redeemed at a premium of 5%, and the shares and debentures in A plc together with the remaining cash are distributed to the ordinary shareholders of B plc.

The balance sheet of B plc prior to the acquisition appears as follows.

B plc balance sheet

	Cost £	Dep'n £	£
Fixed assets			
Freehold land and buildings	24,000		24,000
Plant and machinery	32,000	10,000	22,000
	56,000	10,000	46,000
Current assets			
Stock		19,000	
Debtors		20,000	
Bank		5,000	
		44,000	
Current liabilities			
Trade creditors		14,000	
			30,000
			76,000
Capital and reserves			
£1 ordinary shares			30,000
£1 6% preference shares			20,000
Share premium account			10,000
Revenue reserves			16,000
			76,000

Required

(a) Show the closing entries in the books of B plc.
(b) Show the opening entries in the books of A plc.

4.4 *Solution*

(a) *Books of B*

Realisation account

	£		£
Land and buildings	24,000	Creditors	14,000
Plant and machinery	22,000	Purchase consideration	100,000
Stock	19,000		
Debtors	20,000		
Profit on realisation	29,000		
	114,000		114,000

Bank and cash

	£		£
Balance b/f	5,000	Preference shares	21,000
Cash	18,000	Cash to shareholders	2,000
	23,000		23,000

Sundry capital

	£		£
Cash – redemption	21,000	Share capital	30,000
Ordinary shares	55,000	Preference shares	20,000
Debtors	27,000	Share premium	10,000
Cash	2,000	Revenue reserves	16,000
		Profit on realisation	29,000
	105,000		105,000

Debtor account – A plc

	£		£
Realisation account	100,000	Ordinary shares	55,000
		Debtors	27,000
		Cash	18,000
	100,000		100,000

(b)   *Books of A plc*

Purchase of business account

	£		£
Doubtful debt provision (£20,000 × 3%)	600	Land and buildings	40,000
		Plant and machinery	22,000
Trade creditors	14,000	Stock	15,000
Ordinary shares	50,000	Debtors	20,000
Share premium (less discount)	2,000	Goodwill (balance)	17,600
Debentures	30,000		
Cash	18,000		
	114,600		114,600

4.5   Learning outcome

You have now covered the learning outcome for this chapter:

Prepare accounts for a capital reconstruction scheme.

5   Summary

Companies in financial difficulties may effect a reorganisation or capital reconstruction. Stakeholders agree to give up their existing entitlements in exchange for new rights.

The main mechanisms are as follows.

♦   Share reduction under s135 CA1985
♦   Reconstruction under s425 CA1985
♦   Liquidation by order of the court (s427 CA1985)
♦   Voluntary liquidation (s110 Insolvency Act 1986)

Multiple choice questions *(The answers are in the final chapter of this book)*

1   Which of the following is not an allowable capital reconstruction under S135 Companies Act?

  A   Write off of unpaid share capital

  B   Write off of preference dividend arrears

  C   Write off of any share capital not represented by available assets

  D   Write off of any paid up share capital in excess of requirements

2   Bisto Ltd has the following balance sheet as at 31 March 20X2.

	£000
Assets	350
Liabilities	(150)
	200
Ordinary share capital	
1,200,000 25 pence ordinary shares	300
Share premium	50
Profit and loss account	(150)
	200

The directors of Bisto Ltd are to reconstruct the capital by writing off the losses and cancelling the share premium account and the necessary share capital.

How many 25 pence ordinary shares will remain after the capital reconstruction?

  A   150,000

  B   200,000

  C   600,000

  D   800,000

3   Given below is the balance sheet of Frank Ltd at 30 June 20X2.

	£
Fixed assets	284,000
Stock	16,000
Debtors	12,000
Cash	4,000
Current liabilities	(22,000)
	294,000
Ordinary share capital	200,000
Share premium	50,000
Profit and loss account	44,000
	294,000

Lily Ltd has agreed to acquire the net assets (except cash) of Frank Ltd by issuing 400,000 50 pence ordinary shares at a premium of 20% and £80,000 5% debentures issued at 80.

Lily Ltd values the fixed assets at £300,000 and the stock, debtors and creditors at £6,000 in total. After the sale Frank Ltd is liquidated and the shares and debentures in Lily Ltd and the cash balance are distributed to the ordinary shareholders of Frank Ltd.

What is the profit or loss on realisation of Frank Ltd?

A   £2,000 loss

B   £10,000 loss

C   £10,000 profit

D   £14,000 profit

CHAPTER 14

Conceptual framework

EXAM FOCUS

Any answer you write to a discussion question in the exam will be improved if you can bring in accounting principles and concepts. The main sources are the ASB's 'Statement of Principles' and FRS 18 (which has replaced SSAP 2).

LEARNING OUTCOMES

This chapter covers the following Learning Outcome of the CIMA Syllabus.

Discuss emerging developments in financial reporting

In order to cover this Learning Outcome the following topics are included.

The Statement of Principles
FRS 18: Accounting policies

1 The Statement of Principles

1.1 Introduction

The ASB has published a Statement of Principles, which is intended to lay out the conceptual underpinning of the accounting standards that are issued. The idea is that, if we can all agree on a uniform set of basic accounting principles, then there should be less disagreement on the contents of accounting standards developed from those principles.

The Statement of Principles is split up into eight chapters, each of which deals with a particular topic.

♦ Chapter 1: The objective of financial statements
♦ Chapter 2: The reporting entity
♦ Chapter 3: The qualitative characteristics of financial information
♦ Chapter 4: The elements of financial statements
♦ Chapter 5: Recognition in financial statements
♦ Chapter 6: Measurement in financial statements
♦ Chapter 7: Presentation of financial information
♦ Chapter 8: Accounting for interests in other entities

1.2 Chapter 1: The objective of financial statements

The objective is stated as to provide information useful to a wide range of users. Information is required on:

♦ financial position   – balance sheet
♦ performance   – profit and loss account and statement of total recognised gains and losses
♦ financial adaptability – cash flow statement and certain notes to the accounts

Each category of user has a different set of interests:

Users	Need information to assess ability of enterprise to
Investors (primary users)	pay dividends, manage resources
Employees	provide employment/remuneration
Customers	continue in operational existence
Suppliers	repay debts, continue in operational existence
Lenders	pay interest, repay loans
Government	pay tax, manage and account for resources
Public	provide goods and services, provide employment
	Need information on
All	financial position, performance and financial adaptability

1.3 Chapter 2: The reporting entity

This chapter considers the issue of which entities should be required to prepare and publish their financial statements, so that the users of accounts (as previously identified) can be satisfied. It is clearly important that those entities that ought to publish their financial statements do in fact do so.

The chapter concludes that an entity should prepare and publish financial statements if there is a legitimate demand for the information, and it is a cohesive economic unit.

The boundary of the reporting entity is determined by the scope of its control. Therefore, for example, a parent company should publish group accounts containing all the net assets under the parent's control. This is consistent with the normal principles of group accounting as described earlier in this text.

1.4 Chapter 3: The qualitative characteristics of financial information

Threshold quality

Information is only useful if it is *material* (ie if its omission or mis-statement could influence economic decisions taken by users on the basis of the information).

Subject to the threshold quality of materiality, the chapter identifies four characteristics that make financial information useful to users:

♦ relevance

♦ reliability

♦ comparability

♦ understandability

Relevance	Reliability
relevant = can influence decisions	reliable = a complete and faithful representation
Information is relevant if	Information is reliable if it is:
- it possesses predictive and/or confirmatory value; and - it is provided in time to influence the decisions	- faithful representation (reflecting the substance of the transactions) - neutral (free from bias) - free from material error - complete, and - prudent
Comparability	**Understandability**
comparable → for an enterprise over time and between enterprises	understandable → to a user with - a reasonable knowledge of business, economic activities and accounting; and - a willingness to study the information with diligence
Aspects of comparability: - consistency - disclosure (eg accounting policies, corresponding amounts) - compliance with accounting standards	Aspects of understandability: - users' abilities - aggregation and classification

1.5   Chapter 4: The elements of financial statements

This chapter identifies seven elements of financial statements:

Assets

=   Rights or other access to future economic benefits controlled by an entity as a result of past transactions or events.

Liabilities

=   An entity's obligations to transfer economic benefits as a result of past transactions or events.

Ownership interest

=   The residual amount found by deducting all liabilities of the entity from all of the entity's assets.

Gains

=   Increases in ownership interest other than those relating to contributions from owners.

Losses

=   Decreases in ownership interest other than those relating to distributions to owners.

Contributions from owners

=   Increases in ownership interest resulting from investments made by owners in their capacity as owners.

Distributions to owners

=   Decreases in ownership interest resulting from transfers made to owners in their capacity as owners.

1.6 Chapter 5: Recognition in financial statements

An item should be recognised in financial statements if:

- the item meets the definition of an element of financial statements (asset, liability, gain, loss etc.), and

- there is sufficient evidence that the *change in assets or liabilities* inherent in the item has occurred (including where appropriate, evidence that a future inflow or outflow of benefit will occur); and

- the item can be *measured* at a monetary amount with sufficient *reliability*.

Reliable measurement

Methods of reliable measurement include transaction price (historic cost), market-based measures (eg replacement costs, net realisable value) and the expected value of a group of items.

Recognition in profit and loss account

For gains to be recognised in the profit and loss account rather than in the statement of total recognised gains and losses, certain additional criteria must be satisfied:

- the gain must be earned;
- the gain must be realised.

The idea is that a gain which is earned but not yet realised will be dealt with in the statement of total recognised gains and losses. When such a gain is subsequently realised, it will still not feature in the profit and loss account as it has already been reported in the statement of total recognised gains and losses.

1.7 Chapter 6: Measurement in financial statements

When preparing financial statements, a measurement basis has to be chosen for each category of assets and liabilities. Possible bases are:

- historical cost
- replacement cost
- present value of future cash flows (= economic value = value in use)
- net realisable value

This chapter does not specify a single measurement basis which must be adopted, but states that the basis chosen should be the one that best meets the objective of financial statements and the demands of the qualitative characteristics of financial information.

Historical cost is usually more reliable than measures of current value, though arguably current values are more relevant.

1.8 Chapter 7: Presentation of financial information

Financial statements comprise the primary financial statements plus supporting notes.

Individual primary statements

These comprise:

- the profit and loss account;
- the statement of total recognised gains and losses;
- the balance sheet; and
- the cash flow statement.

statements of financial performance

Statements of financial performance

Statements of financial performance contribute to financial reporting by:

♦ giving an account of the results of the stewardship of management to enable users to assess the past performance of management and to form a basis for developing future expectations about financial performance; and

♦ providing feedback to users so that they can check the accuracy of their previous assessments of the financial performance for past periods and, if necessary, modify their assessments for future periods.

Balance sheet

The balance sheet and notes provide information on and the interrelationships between its:

♦ **resource structure** - major classes and amounts of assets; and
♦ **financial structure** - major classes and amounts of liabilities and ownership interest.

It is helpful to users if assets, liabilities and ownership interest are reported in classes.

Presentation of information in the balance sheets can help a user to assess future cash flows. For example, assets held for sale should be reported separately from those held on a continuing basis.

A balance sheet does not purport to show the value of a business enterprise. However, together with other financial statements and other information, balance sheets should provide information that is useful to those who wish to make their own assessment of a company's value.

Cash flow statement

A cash flow statement reflects cash receipts classified by major sources and cash payments classified by major uses. It provides useful information on a company's activities in:

♦ generating cash through operations;
♦ using cash to repay debt;
♦ using cash to distribute dividends; and
♦ re-investing to maintain or expand operations.

This helps in the assessment of a company's risk, liquidity, viability, adaptability and the way in which profits are converted to cash. Assessment of prospects for future cash flows is hindered by the effect of timing differences between, for example, cash receipts and sales. Therefore, cash flow statements should be useful in conjunction with the other primary statements when assessing future cash flow prospects.

Features of financial statements that help them to communicate clearly

♦ **Aggregation** - the simplification, condensation and structuring of voluminous transactions and other events into amounts and totals in the financial statements.

♦ **Classification** - the grouping of items by their nature or function.

♦ **Structure** - the presentation of the components resulting from the process of aggregation and classification in individual statements of financial performance, financial position and cash flows along with related notes.

♦ **Articulation** - the interrelation of the financial statements because they reflect different aspects of the same transactions or events.

♦ **Accounting policies** – should be disclosed clearly

♦ **Notes to financial statements** - amplifying or explaining items in the primary statements. The notes and primary statements provide an integrated whole, but misrepresentation in the primary statements corrected by disclosure in the notes will not give a true and fair view.

♦ **Supplementary information** - such as alternative asset values from those in the financial statements and statistical information, positioned outside the primary statements and notes.

1.9 Chapter 8: Accounting for interests in other entities

This chapter reiterates the standard method of accounting for investments owned by the parent company, when preparing the parent's individual accounts and the parent's group accounts.

In the individual accounts, investments are shown as assets, with dividends receivable credited to the profit and loss account.

In the group accounts, the method of accounting depends on the level of the parent's influence over the investment:

♦ If the parent controls the investment, the investment should be consolidated

♦ If the parent exercises significant influence over the investment, the equity method is appropriate

♦ If the parent exercises little or no influence over the investment, it should be treated like any other investment asset.

1.10 Application of the Statement to public benefit entities

The Statement of Principles is primarily intended to apply to profit-oriented entities, but it is desirable that a common set of accounting principles should be applied to the financial reporting of all entities including public benefit entities (defined as entities whose primary objective is to provide goods or services for the general public or social benefit and where any risk capital has been provided to support that primary objective rather than to earn a financial return for equity shareholders).

The ASB is therefore engaged on a project to produce guidance on the Statement of Principles that is drafted where necessary to be of specific relevance to public benefit entities (such as charities). In May 2003 the ASB issued a discussion paper on this topic.

Many parts of the original Statement require no additional material to clarify their application to public benefit entities. However, there are areas where further guidance would be useful. For example, many of the assets held by public benefit entities do not result in inflows of cash, but are used instead to provide goods or services for the entity's beneficiaries. The original Statement might therefore be interpreted as suggesting that such assets should be reported at a value of zero, since no future inflow of cash is expected. The discussion paper argues that this is incorrect. The economic benefits that arise from the assets are the services that are provided to the beneficiaries.

Thus, while the wording of the definitions of assets and liabilities are not proposed to be amended, the discussion paper offers guidance on their interpretation in the financial statements of public benefit entities.

The ASB will review the comments received on this discussion paper and then plans to issue in due course an official Interpretation of the Statement of Principles to provide guidance on the application and interpretation of the principles by public benefit entities.

2 FRS 18: Accounting policies

2.1 Introduction

After the Statement of Principles was issued in 1999, it was clear that there were inconsistencies between the Statement's approach promoting relevance, reliability, comparability and understandability, and SSAP 2 which identified going concern, consistency, accruals and prudence as fundamental concepts. SSAP 2 has therefore been withdrawn and replaced by FRS 18 which is consistent with the Statement of Principles.

2.2 Purpose of FRS 18

FRS 18 sets out the principles to be followed in selecting accounting policies, and the disclosures needed to help users to understand the accounting policies adopted and how they have been applied.

The overriding requirement is for accounting policies to be selected to enable the financial statements to give a true and fair view. Accounting policies should normally be chosen to comply with accounting standards and UITF Abstracts. However where in exceptional circumstances following an accounting standard or Abstract would not give a true and fair view, the standard or Abstract should be departed from to the extent necessary to give a true and fair view.

2.3 Pervasive concepts

FRS 18 identifies the going concern concept and the accruals concept as playing a pervasive role in the process of selecting accounting policies:

♦ an entity should prepare its financial statements on a going concern basis, unless the entity is being liquidated or the directors have no realistic alternative but to cease trading. In such circumstances the financial statements should not apply the going concern basis.

♦ an entity should prepare its balance sheet and profit and loss account on an accruals basis rather than a strict cash basis.

2.4 Four objectives

When choosing accounting policies, an entity should judge possible policies against the objectives of relevance, reliability, comparability and understandability. (Note how this is directly consistent with the wording of the Statement of Principles.)

2.5 Reviewing and changing accounting policies

Accounting policies should be reviewed regularly to ensure that they remain the most appropriate to the particular circumstances.

Changes in accounting policies should be accounted for as a prior period adjustment in accordance with FRS 3. This should be differentiated from changes in accounting estimates, which should be reflected in the current (and future) year's results.

For example, a company might have an accounting policy of depreciating its machines on a straight line basis over five years. A machine is bought for £10,000 with an expected scrap value after five years of £2,000. The depreciation charge for the first year is £8,000/5 = £1,600.

In the second year it is felt that although the total life of the machine remains at five years (ie, there are still four years to go), the scrap value of the machine is now only £600. This is a change in accounting estimate, not a change in accounting policy. The policy remains to depreciate the historical cost less scrap value, on a straight line basis over its useful life. There is no prior year adjustment. The depreciation charge for the second year will be:

$$\frac{\text{NBV b/f - scrap value}}{\text{Remaining life}} = \frac{£8,400 - £600}{4 \text{ years}} = £1,950$$

FRS 18 draws the distinction between estimation techniques and accounting policies. Estimation techniques are used to implement the measurement aspects of accounting policies. A change to an estimation technique should not be accounted for as a prior period adjustment, unless it represents the correction of a fundamental error, or such accounting is required by statute, accounting standard or Abstract.

2.6 Disclosures

An entity should disclose a description of all the accounting policies used for material items in the financial statements.

Where a change in accounting policy has been made the entity should disclose the particulars of the change and the reasons why it is believed that the new policy is more appropriate.

The directors should disclose any uncertainties which cast doubt on whether the entity is a going concern.

Where the statutory true and fair view override has been invoked, the entity should disclose the particulars of the matter, the reasons and the effect.

2.7 Commentary on FRS 18

FRS 18 is broadly uncontroversial. It is widely recognised that SSAP 2 was no longer tenable once the Statement of Principles had been issued. The main discussion area has been the alleged downgrading of the prudence concept. SSAP 2 identified prudence as a fundamental concept; in FRS 18 it is only part of the reliability characteristic. Some commentators believe that there will be less emphasis placed on prudent accounting in the future as a result of this downgrading. It remains to be seen whether these fears are well grounded.

2.8 Learning outcome

Given that FRS 18 was recently issued, you have now covered the learning outcome for this chapter:

Discuss emerging developments in financial reporting.

3 Relevant UITF Abstract

3.1 Abstract 4: Presentation of long-term debtors in current assets

Certain Abstracts assist companies in presenting a true and fair view when drawing up their financial statements.

Abstract 4 points out that although the CA 85 statutory format for the balance sheet splits liabilities on the face of the balance sheet between those payable within one year and those payable after more than one year, this is not true for debtors. The CA 85 requires debtors receivable after more than a year to be disclosed in a note, but they are included in current assets on the face of the balance sheet.

The UITF are concerned that readers of accounts might be misled if a large long-term receivable balance is included in the total of current assets without being highlighted. Ratios such as the current ratio might be misinterpreted.

The UITF decision is therefore that any large debtor due after more than one year must be disclosed separately on the face of the balance sheet amongst current assets.

4   Summary

The ASB's Statement of Principles sets out the conceptual framework underpinning the development of accounting standards.

After the Statement of Principles was issued, SSAP 2 was withdrawn since it was inconsistent with the Statement of Principles. FRS 18 has now been issued in place of SSAP 2. FRS 18 requires accounting policies to be chosen to meet the objectives of relevance, reliability, comparability and understandability, ie it is entirely consistent with the Statement of Principles.

Multiple choice questions *(The answers are in the final chapter of this book)*

1   Which of the following are the four qualitative characteristics of useful financial information from the ASB's Statement of Principles?

   A   Reliability, prudence, relevance, consistency

   B   Comparability, relevance, understandability, reliability

   C   Relevance, prudence, comparability, understandability

   D   Relevance, neutrality, comparability, understandability

2   Which of the following is not a chapter in the ASB's Statement of Principles?

   A   Presentation of financial information

   B   The reporting entity

   C   Accounting for group undertakings

   D   Recognition in financial statements

3   A company has previously had a policy of not charging depreciation on its freehold properties but is now to do so on the straight line basis over a period of 50 years. Which of the following statements is true?

   A   This is a change of estimation technique and should be dealt with as a prior period adjustment

   B   This is a change of estimation technique and should be dealt with in the current year

   C   This is a change of accounting policy and should be dealt with as a prior period adjustment

   D   This is a change of accounting policy and should be dealt with in the current year

CHAPTER 15

Reporting financial performance

EXAM FOCUS

FRS 3 *Reporting Financial Performance* is one of the most important and most frequently examined accounting standards. You must ensure that you are thoroughly familiar with its provisions.

After studying this chapter you should be able to incorporate the provisions of FRS 3 when preparing a profit and loss account in a form suitable for publication.

This chapter also takes the opportunity to study FRS 12 on provisions and contingencies, the Financial Reporting Standard for Smaller Entities (FRSSE) and relevant ASB discussion papers.

LEARNING OUTCOMES

There are no specific Learning Outcomes associated with this chapter.

The following topics are included

> The structure of the profit and loss account
>
> Other disclosures required by FRS 3
>
> FRS 12: Provisions, contingent liabilities and contingent assets
>
> The Financial Reporting Standard for Smaller Entities (FRSSE)
>
> Relevant ASB discussion papers

---

1   The structure of the profit and loss account

1.1   The aim of FRS 3

The aim of FRS 3 is to improve financial reporting by addressing a number of important issues. These include the following.

- The structure of the profit and loss account
- Exceptional items and extraordinary items
- The statement of total recognised gains and losses (STRGL)
- Other required disclosures

 FRS 3 requires that all statutory headings from turnover to operating profit must be analysed between amounts arising from continuing operations and amounts arising from discontinued operations. In addition, turnover and operating profit must be further analysed between amounts from existing and amounts from newly acquired operations. Only figures for turnover and operating profit need be shown on the face of the profit and loss account. All additional information, namely costs, may be relegated to a note.

The situation is summarised in Figure 1.

Figure 1 **The structure of the profit and loss account under FRS 3**

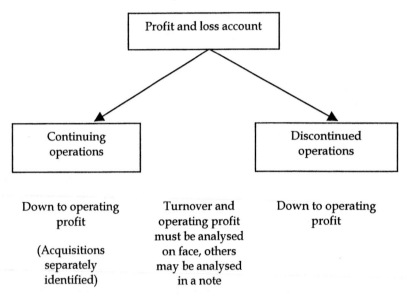

A proforma profit and loss account complying with these requirements is given below.

X LIMITED
PROFIT AND LOSS ACCOUNT FOR THE YEAR ENDED 31 OCTOBER 20X4

| | Continuing operations | | Discontinued | |
	Existing £000	Acquisition £000	operations £000	Total £000
Turnover	550	50	175	775
Cost of sales	(415)	(40)	(165)	(620)
Gross profit	135	10	10	155
Distribution costs	(35)	(4)	(8)	(47)
Administrative expenses	(50)		(7)	(57)
Operating profit	50	6	(5)	51
Profit on sale of properties	22			22
Loss on sale of discontinued operations			(10)	(10)
Profit on ordinary activities before interest	72	6	(15)	63
Interest payable				(18)
Profit on ordinary activities before taxation				45
Tax on profit on ordinary activities				(16)
[Profit before extraordinary items]				29
[Extraordinary items] (to show position only)				-
Profit for the financial year				29
Dividends				(8)
Retained profit for the financial year				21

1.2 Discontinued operations

A discontinued operation is one that meets all of the following conditions.

♦ The sale or termination must have been completed before the earlier of three months after the year end or the date the financial statements are approved. (Terminations not completed by this date may be disclosed in the notes).

♦ The former activity must have ceased permanently.

♦ The sale or termination has a material effect on the nature and focus of the entity's operations and represents a material reduction in its operating facilities resulting either from its withdrawal from a particular market (class of business or geographical), or from a material reduction in turnover in its continuing markets.

♦ The assets, liabilities, results of operations and activities are clearly distinguishable, physically, operationally and for financial reporting purposes.

1.3   *Further required disclosures*

Three exceptional items are required to be disclosed on the face of the profit and loss account.

♦ Profits or losses on the sale or termination of discontinued operations
♦ Costs of a fundamental restructuring/reorganisation
♦ Profit/loss on disposal of fixed assets

The details of other exceptional items must be disclosed in a note.

FRS 3 virtually abolishes extraordinary items.

1.4   *Example*

A&Z PLC
PROFIT AND LOSS ACCOUNT FOR THE YEAR ENDED 31 DECEMBER 20X1

	20X1
	£
Turnover	300,000
Cost of sales	(100,000)
Gross profit	200,000
Distribution costs	(40,000)
Administrative expenses	(90,000)
Operating profit	70,000

During the year the company ran down a material business operation with all activities ceasing on 26 January 20X2. The costs attributable to the closure amounted to £3,000 charged to administrative expenses. The results of the operation for 20X1 were as follows.

	20X1
	£
Turnover	32,000
Cost of sales	(15,000)
Distribution costs	(12,000)
Administrative expenses	(10,000)
Operating loss	(5,000)

In addition, the company acquired an unincorporated business which contributed £9,000 to turnover and an operating profit of £1,500. Its distribution costs and administrative expenses were £2,900 and £1,000 respectively. Cost of sales was £3,600.

Required

Prepare the profit and loss account for the year ended 31 December 20X1 for A&Z plc complying with the provisions of FRS 3.

1.5   *Approach to the example*

As soon as you see in a question that a company has closed a significant operation you must now consider whether FRS 3 applies. Remember that the question will not necessarily mention FRS 3. This means that you will need to learn the definition of a discontinued activity.

As soon as you notice a discontinuance, the easiest approach is to use a four-column layout.

Profit and loss account

	Continuing			
Existing		Acquisitions	Discontinued	Total
£		£	£	£

Remember that all we are doing here is a simple analysis. We can therefore start by identifying, from within the question, any misclassification of costs.

We can see here that costs attributable to the closure of £3,000 have been charged into administrative expenses. Under FRS 3 this will need to be extracted and separately disclosed as an exceptional item immediately after operating profit.

We can then consider the analysis required. We need to set out our four columns. Our starting point is to do the total column as normal.

Profit and loss account

	Continuing			
	Existing	Acquisitions	Discontinued	Total
	£	£	£	£
Turnover				300,000
Cost of sales				(100,000)
Gross profit				200,000
Distribution costs				(40,000)
Administrative expenses				(87,000)
Operating profit				73,000
Costs of closure				(3,000)
Profit before interest				70,000

We can then add in the information given about the discontinued activity and the acquisition.

Profit and loss account

	Continuing			
	Existing	Acquisitions	Discontinued	Total
	£	£	£	£
Turnover		9,000	32,000	300,000
Cost of sales		(3,600)	(15,000)	(100,000)
Gross profit		5,400	17,000	200,000
Distribution costs		(2,900)	(12,000)	(40,000)
Administrative expenses		(1,000)	(7,000)	(87,000)
Operating profit/loss		1,500	(2,000)	73,000
Costs of closure		-	(3,000)	(3,000)
Profit/loss before interest		1,500	(5,000)	70,000

Remember: the £3,000 closure costs must be extracted from the discontinued column as well as from the total column.

The existing operations column will now become the balancing figure.

Profit and loss account

	Continuing Existing £	Acquisitions £	Discontinued £	Total £
Turnover	259,000	9,000	32,000	300,000
Cost of sales	(81,400)	(3,600)	(15,000)	(100,000)
Gross profit	177,600	5,400	17,000	200,000
Distribution costs	(25,100)	(2,900)	(12,000)	(40,000)
Administrative expenses	(79,000)	(1,000)	(7,000)	(87,000)
Operating profit/loss	73,500	1,500	(2,000)	73,000
Costs of closure	-	-	(3,000)	(3,000)
Profit/loss before interest	73,500	1,500	(5,000)	70,000

1.6   The rationale of FRS 3

FRS 3 achieves a *clarification* of what is included in the profit figure and generally adds *completeness* of information.

The profit of £70,000 in the above example in itself is quite informative, but when we look at the analysis provided by FRS 3 we can see that the £70,000 is in fact *distorted* by a loss of £5,000 on an activity which is now discontinued.

By 'stripping out' the loss on the discontinued activity we can see that the profit on continuing activities is actually £75,000, of which £1,500 was achieved by a new acquisition.

Practice question 1 *(The answer is in the final chapter of this book)*

Sunshine

You have been given the following details about Sunshine plc for the year ending 31 December 20X4.

SUNSHINE PLC
CONSOLIDATED PROFIT AND LOSS ACCOUNT FOR YEAR ENDED 31 DECEMBER 20X4

	£m
Turnover	2,709.0
Net operating costs	2,303.2
Operating profit	405.8
Interest receivable	8.2
Profit on ordinary activities before taxation	414
Taxation	148
Profit on ordinary activities after taxation	266
Dividends	95
Retained profit	171

The company ceased production of its manufacturing product line in June 20X4, having decided to concentrate on its growing distribution and aftermarket work. The turnover of this product during the year ended 31 December 20X4 was £100 million based on market prices and expenses were £51 million.

Required

Prepare the profit and loss account for Sunshine plc for the year ended 31 December 20X4. Comparative figures for 20X3 are not required.

2 Other disclosures required by FRS 3

2.1 Statement of total recognised gains and losses (STRGL)

This is required by FRS 3 to be presented with the same prominence as the profit and loss account, balance sheet and cash flow statement as a primary statement.

A proforma is given below.

STATEMENT OF TOTAL RECOGNISED GAINS AND LOSSES FOR THE PERIOD

	£
Profit for the financial year (per the profit and loss account)	X
Items taken directly to reserves	
Unrealised surplus on revaluation of fixed assets	X
Surplus on revaluation of investment properties	X
Currency translation differences on foreign currency net investments	X
Total recognised gains and losses for the year	X
Prior period adjustments	(X)
Total gains and losses recognised since last annual report	X

The statement will include all gains and losses occurring during the period. FRS 3 requires that transactions with shareholders are to be excluded (ie dividends paid and proposed; share issues and redemptions). This is because these transactions do not represent either gains or losses.

Therefore the first figure in the statement is the profit for the financial year, ie before the deduction of dividends for the year.

Where profit or loss for the year is the only recognised gain or loss, a statement to that effect should be given immediately below the profit and loss account.

2.2 Reconciliation of movements in shareholders' funds

This is required by FRS 3 to be included in the notes to the accounts, or it may be a separate statement. What the statement aims to do is to pull together the financial performance of the entity as reflected in:

♦ the profit and loss account

♦ other movements in shareholders' funds as determined by the statement of total recognised gains and losses

♦ all other changes in shareholders' funds not recognised in either of the above, such as new share capital subscribed.

Once again, a proforma is given below.

RECONCILIATION OF MOVEMENTS IN SHAREHOLDERS' FUNDS FOR THE PERIOD

	£
Profit for the financial year	X
Dividends	(X)
	X
Other recognised gains and losses (per STRGL)	X
New share capital	X
Net addition to shareholders' funds	X
Opening shareholders' funds	X
Closing shareholders' funds	X

2.3   Example

KENNETH LTD
PROFIT AND LOSS ACCOUNT EXTRACTS FOR THE YEAR ENDED 31 DECEMBER 20X1

	£000
Profit after tax	421
Dividend	(98)
Retained profit	323

During the year the following important events took place.

♦ Assets were revalued by £105,000.
♦ £250,000 share capital was issued at par during the year.
♦ Certain stock items were written down by £21,000.
♦ Net gains of £18,000 on foreign exchange translation were recorded in reserves.
♦ Opening shareholders' funds were £2,302,000.

Required

Show how the events for the year would be shown in the statement of total recognised gains and losses and the reconciliation of movements in shareholders' funds.

2.4   Approach to the example

The key is to remember that the statement of total recognised gains and losses is a very simple statement.

The main gain or loss in the year is always the profit or loss from the profit and loss account (before dividends).

The other gains and losses from the balance sheet are limited in number.

♦ Asset revaluations
♦ Foreign exchange differences

Once you have the statement of total recognised gains and losses the only other items to include in the reconciliation of movements in shareholders' funds are:

♦ dividends
♦ new share capital.

The key is therefore to learn the formats.

*STATEMENT OF TOTAL RECOGNISED GAINS AND LOSSES FOR THE YEAR ENDED
31 DECEMBER 20X1*

	£000
Profit for the year	421
Asset revaluation	105
Foreign exchange gains	18
Total recognised gains for the year	544

The write down of the stock items will not be included in the statement as it has already been
included in the profit and loss account.

*RECONCILIATION OF MOVEMENTS IN SHAREHOLDERS' FUNDS FOR THE YEAR ENDED
31 DECEMBER 20X1*

	£000
Profit for the year	421
Dividends	(98)
	323
Other recognised gains and losses (105 +18)	123
New share capital	250
	696
Opening shareholders' funds	2,302
Closing shareholders' funds	2,998

2.5 Prior period adjustments

Prior period adjustments (also called 'prior year adjustments') are material adjustments
applicable to prior periods arising from:

♦ changes in accounting policy, or
♦ correction of fundamental errors.

They are *not* recurring adjustments or revision of estimates.

The definition is a narrow one and in practice prior period adjustments are rare.

Changes in accounting policy are permitted only if the new policy gives a fairer presentation. This
usually arises when a new accounting standard is issued or where an existing standard allows a
choice and the company switches from one option to the other (eg SSAP 13 in relation to
capitalising development costs).

Distinguish a change in accounting policy from:

♦ a change in an estimate (eg useful economic life, outcome of development project)
♦ a refinement of accounting policy (eg if business moves into a new area).

Fundamental errors are extremely rare and are so large that they destroy the true and fair view.

In an exam question, you are likely to be told if an error is fundamental.

To record a prior period adjustment proceed as follows.

♦ Restate opening balances for current year and apply new basis in preparing current year's
  accounts.

♦ Adjust comparative figures.

Calculate what amounts would have been in the opening balance sheet for the current year on the new basis. The difference in opening net assets for the current year compared to the old basis gives the prior period adjustment to:

♦ opening reserves for the current year, shown in the statement of reserves and in the statement of total recognised gains and losses

♦ opening shareholders' funds in the reconciliation of movements in shareholders' funds, and

♦ balance sheet comparatives in the current year's accounts.

2.6   Example

Leonard plc incurs considerable research and development expenditure. Its accounting policy to date has been to carry forward development expenditure where the criteria for this are met. The final accounts for the year ended 30 June 20X2, and the 20X3 draft accounts, reflect this policy and show the following.

	20X3 £000	20X2 £000
Profit after tax	4,712	3,200
Dividends	(2,500)	(1,750)
Retained profit for the financial year	2,212	1,450
Profit and loss account brought forward	23,950	22,500
	26,162	23,950

The directors have now decided to change the accounting policy to one of immediate write-off of all development expenditure as it is incurred.

The net book value of development costs included in intangible fixed assets has been as follows.

	£000
At 30 June 20X1	400
At 30 June 20X2	450
At 30 June 20X3	180

Amortisation of, and expenditure on, development has been as follows.

	Amortisation £000	Expenditure £000
Year ended 30 June 20X2	450	500
Year ended 30 June 20X3	870	600

The issued share capital of Leonard plc is £10,000,000. Leonard plc has no other recognised gains and losses.

Required

Show how the change in accounting policy will be reflected in the financial statements for the year ended 30 June 20X3.

2.7 Solution

LEONARD PLC
PROFIT AND LOSS ACCOUNT FOR THE YEAR ENDED 30 JUNE 20X3 (EXTRACT)

	20X3	20X2
	£000	*As restated £000*
Profit after tax (W1)	4,982	3,150
Dividends	(2,500)	(1,750)
Retained profit for the financial year	2,482	1,400

STATEMENT OF TOTAL RECOGNISED GAINS AND LOSSES FOR THE YEAR ENDED 30 JUNE 20X3

	20X3	20X2
	£000	*As restated £000*
Profit for the financial year	4,982	3,150
Prior period adjustment (note)	(450)	
Total recognised gains and losses since last annual report	4,532	3,150

RECONCILIATION OF MOVEMENTS IN SHAREHOLDERS' FUNDS FOR THE YEAR ENDED 30 JUNE 20X3

	20X3	20X2
	£000	*As restated £000*
Profit for the financial year	4,982	3,150
Dividends	(2,500)	(1,750)
Net addition to shareholders' funds	2,482	1,400
Opening shareholders' funds (originally £33,950,000 before a prior period adjustment of £450,000)	33,500	32,100
Closing shareholders' funds	35,982	33,500

STATEMENT OF RESERVES FOR THE YEAR ENDED 30 JUNE 20X3

	Profit and loss account *20X3* *£000*
At 30 June 20X2	
As previously stated	23,950
Prior year adjustment (W2)	(450)
As restated	23,500
Retained profit for the financial year (2,212 + 270)	2,482
At 30 June 20X3 (26,162 - 180 (W3))	25,982

Note. The prior year adjustment arises from a change of accounting policy from capitalisation of development costs to immediate write-off of expenditure as incurred.

Workings

(W1)   Profit after tax

	20X3	20X2
	£000	*As restated £000*
As previously	4,712	3,200
Add back amortisation	870	450
Deduct expenditure in year	(600)	(500)
As restated	4,982	3,150

(W2)   *Prior year adjustment (in balance sheet at 30 June 20X2)*

Adjustment is the elimination of the £450,000 asset. This gives the figure for the prior year adjustment in the statement of reserves, ie adjustment in opening balances for current year.

(W3)   *Balance sheet at 30 June 20X3*

Adjustment is £180,000 asset to be eliminated.

Practice question 2 *(The answer is in the final chapter of this book)*

Claret

Claret Ltd has an issued share capital of 2,000,000 50p ordinary shares, all of which were issued at par on incorporation.

The balance on the profit and loss account at 1 January 20X8 was £20,658,000 and the draft retained profit for 20X8 was £1,825,000. The directors had incorporated their draft decision to propose a dividend of £250,000 for the year.

At 1 January 20X8 the balance on the revaluation reserve was £83,000. On 31 December 20X8 a property was revalued to £430,000. It was purchased on 1 January 20X1 for £650,000 and is being depreciated over 20 years.

During the year the company issued 160,000 50p ordinary shares at a market price of 210p per share.

After the preparation of the draft accounts had been completed, it was discovered that the method of valuing closing stock had been incorrectly applied for the last three years resulting in the following overvaluations of stock which are considered fundamental.

	£000
At 31 December 20X6	40
At 31 December 20X7	55
At 31 December 20X8	62

Required

Prepare the following extracts from the financial statements of Claret Ltd as at 31 December 20X8:

(a)   statement of total recognised gains and losses;

(b)   note on reconciliation of shareholders' funds.

Ignore the requirement to produce comparative figures.

2.8   *Note of historical cost profits and losses*

If a company has adopted any of the alternative accounting rules as regards revaluation of assets then the reported profit figure per the profit and loss account may differ from the historical cost profit figure. If the difference is material then the financial statements must include a reconciliation statement after the statement of total recognised gains and losses or the profit and loss account. The profit figure to be reconciled is profit before tax. However, the retained profit for the year must also be restated.

The reason is that one of the key qualities of financial statements is the requirement for them to be comparable. This causes difficulties where we have a choice of accounting method (as we do, for example, with fixed assets).

The situation can be illustrated by reference to the example of fixed assets: see Figure 2.

Figure 2. Historical cost vs revaluation

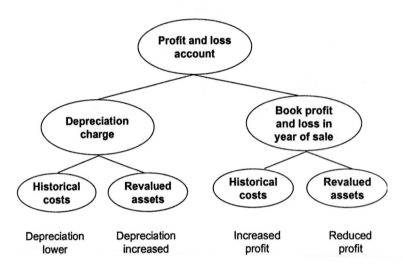

Companies who revalue their assets suffer a 'double whammy' of increased depreciation and reduced profit on sales, giving them an overall lower profit figure. The impact of this distortion is highlighted for users in the note of historical cost profits and losses.

2.9 Example

Beta Ltd reported a profit before tax of £705,000 for the year ended 31 December 20X4. During the year the following transactions in fixed assets took place:

An asset with a book value of £70,000 was revalued to £110,000. The remaining useful life is estimated to be five years.

A piece of land which was revalued by £200,000 five years ago was sold to a property developer for £1,200,000, giving a profit of £340,000.

Required

Show the note of historical cost profit for the year ended 31 December 20X4.

2.10 Approach to the example

Start with reported profit before tax.

Note of historical cost profits and losses	£000
Profit before tax per profit and loss account	705
'Excess' depreciation	8
Realisation of revaluation surplus	200
Historical cost profit before tax	913

The 'excess' deprecation is the difference between historical cost depreciation and depreciation on the revalued amount.

$$\frac{£110,000 - £70,000}{5} = £8,000 \text{ pa}$$

In this example the historical cost retained profit for the year cannot be disclosed since the necessary figures are not given in the question.

2.11   Recognition of gains and losses

Once an unrealised gain or loss is recognised in the statement of total recognised gains and losses, transfer for inclusion in the profit and loss account when it becomes realised at a later date is not allowed. For example, on the sale of an asset originally revalued any remaining revaluation reserve must be credited to the profit and loss reserve and not through the profit and loss account.

Practice question 3 *(The answer is in the final chapter of this book)*

Meld

Draft accounts for Meld plc for the year ended 30 June 20X4 include the following amounts.

	£
Turnover	472,800
Cost of sales and expenses (including interest payable of £15,000)	(376,800)
Profit before tax	96,000
Tax	(28,800)
Dividends proposed	(21,600)
Retained profit for the year	45,600

Additional information

♦ Meld plc acquired an unincorporated business during the year for £12,000. The fair value of separable net assets acquired was £9,120 and goodwill is to be carried as a permanent intangible asset. Turnover and operating expenses (included in the figures above) for this business since acquisition were £4,800 and £3,600 respectively.

♦ The directors have decided to change the company's accounting policy for development costs from one of capitalisation and amortisation to immediate write-off of all expenditure as incurred. At present, development costs are included in the draft figures as follows.

	Cost £	Amortisation £
At 1 July 20X3	34,560	20,160
Costs incurred	3,100	-
Amortisation charged	-	4,800
At 30 June 20X4	37,660	24,960

♦ In July 20X3, the company revalued fixed assets which had originally cost £19,200 to £28,800. Accumulated depreciation at the date of revaluation was £7,200. At the date of revaluation, the remaining useful economic life of these assets was five years and depreciation has been charged on the revalued amount for the year.

♦ At 1 July 20X3, capital and reserves were as follows.

	£
Ordinary share capital	240,000
Revaluation reserve (relating to freehold land)	48,000
Profit and loss account	168,000
	456,000

Required

Prepare the following for the year ended 30 June 20X4, insofar as the information given permits.

(a)   Profit and loss account
(b)   Statement of total recognised gains and losses
(c)   Note of historical cost profits and losses
(d)   Reconciliation of movements in shareholders' funds
(e)   Statement of reserves.

Note. Comparatives are not required.

3   Proposed changes to reporting financial performance

3.1   Introduction

In June 1999 the ASB issued a discussion paper 'Reporting financial performance: Proposals for change', following work carried out by the G4+1 group of accounting standard-setters.

The current position in FRS 3 is that there are two separate performance statements, the profit and loss account and the STRGL, and that they should be looked at together when interpreting an entity's performance. However, in practice, the STRGL is almost completely ignored, with all the emphasis of interpretation being placed on the profit and loss account and ratios such as EPS calculated from the profit and loss account.

3.2   The main proposals of the discussion paper

 A single performance statement should be prepared in place of the profit and loss account and STRGL. The new statement should comprise three sections:

♦   the results of operating (ie trading) activities
♦   the results of financing and other treasury activities
♦   other gains and losses.

An example of the new statement is shown below.

STATEMENT OF FINANCIAL PERFORMANCE FOR THE PERIOD

	£m	£m
Operating activities		
Revenues		775
Cost of sales		(620)
Other expenses		(104)
Operating income		51
Financing and other treasury activities		
Interest on debt	(26)	
Gains on financial instruments	8	
Financing expense		(18)
Operating and financing income before tax		33
Tax on income		(12)
Operating and financing income after tax		21

Other gains and losses

Profit on disposal of discontinued operations	3
Profit on sale of properties in continuing operations	6
Revaluation of fixed assets	4
Exchange loss on overseas net investment	(2)
Other gains and losses before tax	11
Tax on other gains and losses	(4)
Other gains and losses after tax	7
Total recognised gains and losses	28

Note that dividends are not deducted in the above statement example, contrary to what is the practice in the UK. The G4+1 group believe that dividends are an appropriation of profit, nothing to do with financial performance, so they have no place in a statement of performance. This is a valid argument, but there will have to be changes to statute in the UK before it can be implemented, since the CA 85 requires dividends paid and proposed to be shown as a deduction in the profit and loss account.

3.3   FRED 22

The ideas in the discussion paper have been developed (largely unchanged) into FRED 22: Revision of FRS 3 'Reporting financial performance'. It is still proposed that the profit and loss account and STRGL should be combined into a single statement of financial performance which reports the comprehensive income (ie the total recognised gains and losses) for the period.

Dividends for the period are excluded from the performance statement but the earnings per share, dividends per share and any prior period adjustments should be disclosed at the foot of the statement.

Detailed notes to the statement are proposed:

(a)   a reconciliation of ownership interests for the period.
(b)   a statement of movements on reserves.
(c)   a table of exceptional items reported over the last five years.

Optional notes are proposed for:

(a)   the tax effects of items in 'other gains and losses'.
(b)   a note of historical cost gains and losses.

 Clearly the ASB cannot produce an FRS based on these proposals in the immediate future, since the CA 1985 requires a profit and loss account in statutory format, including dividends payable for the period. However, the ASB is planning to try to persuade the DTI to amend company law in line with the proposals described above.

4   FRS 12: Provisions, Contingent Liabilities and Contingent Assets

4.1   Introduction

FRS 12 is a far reaching standard that explores one of the basic notions of accounting: the fundamental accounting concept of prudence. This has traditionally encouraged accountants to provide early for potential liabilities and to err on the side of caution in estimating the amounts involved.

The problem is that prudence not only allows us to make sure that the bad news gets into the accounts as soon as possible; it also allows the accounts to be manipulated. By careful use of provisions, managers can smooth results from one year to another and produce year on year good results using the release of provisions to manipulate profits.

FRS 12 was issued to prevent this manipulation and force the accounts to show a true and fair view without 'fudging'.

The objective of the standard is to ensure that:

◆ provisions and contingencies are recognised and measured consistently

◆ sufficient information is disclosed to enable a user of the accounts to understand the nature, timing and amount of any provisions and contingencies included in the accounts.

4.2 Recognition of a provision

A provision is defined as a liability where there is uncertainty over either the timing or the amount of the future expenditure. It is not necessary to know the identity of the person to whom the obligation is owed. It is acceptable to recognise a provision only when the reporting entity has a legal or constructive obligation to transfer economic benefits as a result of past events, and a reasonable estimate can be made of the amount needed to settle the obligation. A legal obligation arises by operation of the law. A constructive obligation arises from the entity's past actions, for example:

◆ A retail store that habitually refunds purchases for dissatisfied customers and could not change its policy without damaging its reputation.

◆ An entity that has caused environmental damage and is obliged to rectify this because of its published policies and previous actions, even though there may be no legal obligation for it to do so.

4.3 Guidance on specific situations

Detailed guidance is given on the following specific situations.

◆ Future operating losses – no provisions should be recognised for such losses, since there is no liability at the balance sheet date. However the assets relating to the loss-making operation may need to be reviewed for impairment under the requirements of FRS 11.

◆ Reorganisation costs – provision should only be made where the entity is demonstrably committed to the reorganisation. In the past provisions have been made on the basis of a board decision taken before the financial year end, but under FRS 12, provisions for reorganisation costs are only justifiable when a specific announcement has been made and/or the reorganisation is under way.

◆ Onerous contracts – these are contracts where the unavoidable costs of meeting the terms of the contract exceed the expected revenues (for instance, where an entity is committed to continuing the lease on a vacant property). Provision should be made for the net loss that is expected to arise.

◆ Environmental liabilities – provision should be made when the entity becomes legally or constructively obliged to rectify the damage it has caused, but the creation of environmental contamination does not in itself give rise to such an obligation.

◆ Major refurbishment programmes – a business may have to undertake a major refurbishment programme every few years in order to continue its operations, but it does not have an obligation to transfer economic benefits until each refurbishment has been completed and the related payment is due. It is therefore not acceptable to recognise a provision for such costs in the years between actual refurbishments.

The appendices to FRS 12 consider other practical examples covering decommissioning costs, warranties, expenditure on replacement of key components, self-insurance and substantial staff training programmes (eg to enable a business to deal with major legislative changes).

4.4   Measurement of a provision

The amount recognised as a provision should be the best estimate of the expenditure needed to settle the obligation existing at the balance sheet date, and provisions should be discounted whenever the effect of this is material. FRS 12 sets out guidance on appropriate methods of estimation, establishing appropriate discount rates and accounting for the amortisation of the discount in subsequent years.

Prudence can never be used to justify the creation of excessive reserves or provisions and care should be taken to avoid any effective double counting. For instance, if an estimate is based on prudent assumptions, it should not be necessary to make a further adjustment for prudence when carrying out the calculation.

In some cases, part or all of the expenditure covered by a provision may be recoverable from a third party. In these circumstances, FRS 12 requires the provision and the anticipated recovery to be accounted for as separate items unless the reporting entity no longer has any obligation for the element to be met by the third party, in which case the amounts should be offset.

4.5   Disclosure of provisions

 For each class of provision, an entity should disclose:

♦   A brief description of the nature of the obligation and the timing of the payment.

♦   The amount provided and the basis of any estimates.

♦   Details of movements during the year, showing separately additions and adjustments, amounts used in the year, amounts released unused, the amortisation of any discount and the effect of any exchange differences.

♦   Where relevant, the discount rate used.

4.6   Accounting for contingencies

FRS 12 deals with contingencies as well as provisions.

The objective of FRS 12 in relation to contingencies is to ensure that:

♦   contingencies are recognised and measured consistently

♦   sufficient information is disclosed to enable a user of the accounts to understand the nature, amount and uncertainties relating to any contingencies.

A contingency is defined as a condition that exists at the balance sheet date whose outcome will be confirmed only on the occurrence of one or more uncertain future events. Contingent losses should be recognised when there is sufficient evidence of an obligation to transfer economic benefits as a result of past events, and a reasonable estimate of the contingent loss can be made. This mirrors the requirements in respect of provisions. Where a contingent loss may be partly reduced or avoided by a matching claim or counter-claim, the two aspects should be accounted for separately. Contingent gains should only be recognised when they are virtually certain to crystallise.

The accounts should give the following disclosures for each material class of unrecognised contingency.

- ♦ The nature of the contingency
- ♦ The uncertainties expected to affect the ultimate outcome.
- ♦ An estimate of the potential financial effect.

4.7 Criticisms of the standard

As in FRS 18, it can be argued that the ASB is in danger of going beyond the elimination of a bias towards prudence and actively encouraging imprudence.

Possible losses that were known about but didn't meet FRS 12's definitions can be excluded from accounts. It is debatable whether this is in the best interests of the users of accounts.

Practice question 4 *(The answer is in the final chapter of this book)*

Hill plc

The year end of Hill plc is 31 March 20X0. Hill plc is a very diverse group. One of its consistent features is that it has a reputation as an ethical organisation. Much is made of the company's policies with regard to recycling, emission of noxious substances and making use only of renewable resources.

Many of its goods in its beauty and cosmetic range (Sophie Beauty Products) use ingredients that are sourced overseas and the company publishes full details of its environmental policies as part of its annual report.

You are the chief accountant of the group and your assistant has prepared draft accounts for the year ended 31 March 20X0. Your assistant, however, is uncertain as to the application of FRS 12 *Provisions, Contingent Liabilities and Contingent Assets* to four material items described below and has requested your advice.

Required

(a) (i) Explain why there was a need for FRS 12 to be issued on accounting for provisions in the UK. **(7 marks)**

   (ii) Explain the circumstances under which a provision should be recognised in the financial statements according to FRS 12. **(6 marks)**

(b) Explain how each of the following issues should be treated in the consolidated financial statements for the year ended 31 March 20X0.

   (i) On 12 February 20X0 the board of Hill plc decided to close down a large factory in Aylesbury. The board expects that production will be transferred to other factories. No formal plan has yet been drawn up but it is expected the closure will occur on 31 August 20X0. As at the balance sheet date this decision has not been announced to the employees or to any other interested parties. The overall costs of this closure are foreseen as £79 million. **(3 marks)**

   (ii) During last November one of the subsidiary companies moved from Spain to Solihull. It holds its buildings in Spain under an operating lease which runs until 31 March 20Y7. Annual rentals payable on the property in Spain are £8 million. Hill plc is unable to cancel the lease. It is attempting to rent out the premises at a commercial rent, but the directors have been advised that the chances of achieving this are less than 50%. **(3 marks)**

(iii)   During the year to 31 March 20X0, a customer started legal proceedings claiming one of the products from the 'Sophie Beauty' range had caused a skin complaint. The group's lawyers have advised that the chances of this action succeeding are remote.   **(3 marks)**

(iv)   The group has an overseas subsidiary 'Melinat' that is involved in mining certain minerals. These activities cause significant damage to the environment, including deforestation. The company expects to abandon the mine in eight years time. The country where the subsidiary is based has no environmental legislation obligating companies to rectify environmental damage and it is unlikely that such legislation will be enacted within the next eight years. It has been estimated that the cost of putting right the site will be £10 million if the tree re-planting were successful at the first attempt, but it will probably be necessary to have a further attempt costing an additional £5 million.   **(3 marks)**

(Total : 25 marks)

---

5   *The Financial Reporting Standard for Smaller Entities*

5.1   *Introduction*

As accounting standards get more and more complicated, it has been increasingly recognised that small companies are able to produce accounts that give a true and fair view without having to implement all the detailed requirements of accounting standards which are more aimed at larger companies.

A Financial Reporting Standard for Smaller Entities (known as the FRSSE) was therefore first issued in November 1997. Entities that fall within its scope have a choice: they can either prepare their accounts as normal by applying all the requirements of accounting standards and Abstracts in the usual way. Alternatively they can choose to apply the limited requirements of the FRSSE, in which case they are exempted from having to comply with all the other standards and Abstracts. Either means of preparing accounts is capable of showing a true and fair view.

5.2   *Scope of the FRSSE*

Entities eligible to apply the FRSSE are those that are:

(a)   small companies or groups as defined in the Companies Acts, or
(b)   entitles that would have qualified under (a) if they had been companies.

The FRSSE is therefore not applicable to large or medium-sized entities, public companies, banks, building societies, insurance companies, or companies carrying on an investment business.

5.3   *Contents of the FRSSE*

You do not have to know the detailed contents of the FRSSE, only that it is a comprehensive document containing the measurement and disclosure requirements of existing accounting standards and Abstracts that are relevant to smaller entities, in a simplified form.

For example, finance charges on a finance lease can be charged to the profit and loss account on a straight line basis, which is simpler than the actuarial method required by SSAP 21.

There are some controversial decisions. For example, small companies are exempted from FRS 1 so do not currently have to disclose a cash flow statement. The FRSSE encourages, but does not require, smaller entities to prepare a cash flow statement.

5.4   Keeping the FRSSE up to date

Every year new FRSs and new UITF Abstracts are issued, which have to be considered as to their impact on smaller entities. So every year or so, a revised FRSSE is issued which incorporates the requirements of recent standards and Abstracts if relevant. The most recent FRSSE issued at the date of writing was issued in December 2001.

5.5   Review of the FRSSE

In February 2001 the ASB issued a discussion paper 'Review of the Financial Reporting Standard for Smaller Entities'. There are no firm proposals or conclusions; instead the ASB is seeking feedback on the effectiveness of the FRSSE after its first two full years of operation.

At the time of its original issue, there were several schools of thought as to how the 'big GAAP, little GAAP' problem should be resolved. 'Big GAAP' refers to the reporting regime for large companies in the UK, principally the accounting standards and UITF Abstracts. 'Little GAAP' refers to the reporting regime for small companies; the ASB decided in the FRSSE that small companies should have the option of adopting the 'little GAAP' specified in the FRSSE's contents.

6   *Improving communication of corporate performance*

6.1   Introduction

The increase in regulatory requirements governing financial statements means that they have become longer and more complex documents. Many shareholders are put off trying to assess their investment's performance, by the size and the detail in the annual report document.

The ASB has been researching ways in which the financial statements of listed companies could be simplified for private shareholders, without unduly increasing the cost burden on companies, and issued a discussion paper in 2000: 'Year-end financial reports: improving communication'.

6.2   The ASB's proposals

(a)   Summary financial statements should become the main report for shareholders. All listed companies should have to prepare them.

(b)   The full audited financial statements should continue to be produced for those who request them and for filing purposes.

(c)   Summary financial statements should contain at least the information required by the ASB's Statement of Best Practice 'Preliminary announcements'.

(d)   Companies with a large number of smaller shareholders (eg the privatised utilities) could offer their shareholders an even simpler financial review that reported in plain language without pages of numbers. Shareholders would be sent this review unless they opted to receive full or summary financial statements.

Some changes in the law would be necessary before the above proposals could be implemented, but the ASB is aware that the DTI are currently considering revisions to the Companies Acts in the new Parliament.

7   Share-based payment

7.1   Introduction

Transactions in which companies buy goods or services from other parties (such as employees or suppliers), and pay for those items by issuing shares or share options to those other parties, are becoming increasingly common. For example, many new 'dot-com' companies do not expect to be profitable in their early years, so try to attract quality staff by offering share schemes to employees rather than high cash salaries.

There is no UK accounting standard dealing comprehensively with this topic; current practice appears to be confused and inconsistent. For example, if a company issues shares to acquire another company, everyone agrees that the shares issued (the cost of the investment) should be valued at fair value. However, if a company issues share options to an employee, no immediate cost is generally recognised. Traditionally the options are only accounted for when they are exercised, and are then treated as a normal share issue.

The ASB has long believed this to be unsatisfactory. The ASB was the driving force behind a discussion paper issued in 2000 by the G4 + 1 group of accounting standard-setters. The IASB have now picked the topic up and issued an exposure draft of a proposed International Accounting Standard in November 2002. On the same day the ASB published FRED 31 *Share-Based Payment*, containing a draft FRS based closely on the IASB proposals.

7.2   Recognition of share-based payment

We must first decide whether share-based payment should be recognised in the financial statements at all. Where share options are granted to employees at an exercise price greater than the current market price of the shares, current UK accounting practice is to recognise no cost in the employing company's financial statements. Effectively no charge is made in respect of the employee services purchased with the share options.

The ASB rejects the 'no cost therefore no charge' argument. A transaction has occurred, in that employees have provided valuable services to the entity in return for valuable shares or options, so an accounting entry is required to recognise the resources paid and received.

7.3   Definitions

A **share-based payment transaction** is a transaction in which the entity receives goods or services as consideration for equity instruments of the entity (including shares or share options), or acquires goods or services by incurring liabilities for amounts that are based on the price of the entity's shares or other equity instruments.

Share-based payment transactions may therefore be either cash-settled or equity-settled.

In a **cash-settled** transaction, the entity acquires goods or services by incurring liabilities for amounts that are based on the price (or value) of the entity's shares or other equity instruments.

In an **equity-settled** transaction, the entity receives goods or services as consideration for equity instruments of the entity (including shares or share options).

7.4   Examples

Categorise the following share-based payment transactions:

(i)   The directors of a listed company are granted share appreciation rights, under which they will be paid a cash bonus in five years time equal in value to the share price appreciation over and above UK inflation between the date of grant and exercise.

(ii)   The directors of another listed company are granted share options, under which they are given the right to subscribe to the company's shares at £5 each at any time between three years and ten years from the date of grant.

(iii)   A company is short of cash, so pays a trade creditor by issuing shares to the creditor rather than paying cash.

7.5   Solution

(i) is a cash-settled transaction. (ii) and (iii) are equity-settled transactions.

7.6   Accounting for cash-settled share-based payment transactions

An entity that engages in cash-settled transactions must measure the goods or services acquired and the liability incurred at the fair value of the liability. Until the liability is settled, it must be remeasured to fair value at each balance sheet date, with changes in fair value recognised in the profit and loss account.

If the transaction involves the receipt of services, the liability must be built up over the period of service.

For example, some share appreciation rights vest immediately, so that the employees do not have to complete any further period of service. The entity must recognise immediately the services that have been rendered and the full liability to pay for them.

Other share appreciation rights do not vest until the employees have completed a specified period of service. For example, if the share appreciation rights granted are conditional on the employees remaining in the entity's employment for the next four years and only one year's service has been completed at the balance sheet date, then only one quarter of the ultimate liability need be recognised in the balance sheet.

The fair value of the liability should be calculated at each balance sheet date using a recognised option pricing model. FRED 31 mentions the Black-Scholes model and the binomial model, but no particular model is required.

7.7   Accounting for equity-settled share-based payment transactions

When a transaction is to be settled by issuing equity rather than paying cash, FRED 31 takes the view that an equity instrument is issued on grant date, and that the fair value of that instrument on grant date will equal the fair value of the goods or services that are expected at grant date to be received.

The fair value of the goods or services received can therefore be determined:

(a)   either **directly**, ie by measuring this value if it is immediately available, for example if the goods were traded on an active market.

(b)   or **indirectly**, by reference to the fair value of the equity instruments granted. The fair value of each unit of goods or services received would be estimated as equalling the grant date fair value of the equity instrument issued divided by the number of units of goods or services expected on grant date to be received.

For goods received, the fair value amount will be recognised as an expense and as an increase in equity at the normal recognition point for such goods (ie when they have become an asset of the purchaser, normally on receipt).

For services received, the expense recognised and the increase in equity in each period will be the fair value of each unit of goods or services received, multiplied by the number of units of service actually received in the period.

7.8   *Example 1*

On 31 December 20X1 an employee of Cameron plc is granted a bonus of £10,000 payable in the form of 1,000 £1 shares with a market value of £10 each. How should this transaction be accounted for in the books of the company?

7.9   *Solution*

The shares issued have a readily determinable fair value of £10,000. At 31 December 20X1 the transaction will be recorded as:

		£	£
DR	Staff costs (expense in P/L account)	10,000	
CR	Share capital (par value)		1,000
CR	Share premium account (premium)		9,000

In this example the grant date (the date on which the parties agree to the arrangement) and the vesting date (the date when the recipient is entitled to receive what is due to him) are the same.

7.10   *Example 2*

Nush plc grants 2,000 share options to each of its 100 employees, on condition that the employee remains at the company for the next three years. The options can be exercised to buy shares in the company in five years time.

Using a recognised option pricing model, the fair value of each option at the grant date is estimated to be £2.

The company estimates that 20% of employees will leave during the next three years, and will forfeit their options. These departures are expected to be spread evenly over the period. In reality, 9 employees leave halfway through year 1, 6 employees leave halfway through year 2 and 5 employees leave halfway through year 3.

Required

Show how the share options should be accounted for at the end of years 1, 2 and 3.

7.11   *Solution*

The total fair value of options expected to be paid =

2,000 options × 100 employees × 80% staying × £2 = £320,000.

The company expects 20 employees to leave evenly over the three years, ie 6.67 employees to leave each year. In year 1 we start with 100 employees and finish with 93.33 employees, meaning an average number during the year of 96.67 employees. In year 2 we start with 93.33 and finish with 86.67, an average of 90. In year 3 we start with 86.67 and finish with 80, an average of 83.33.

The total years service expected during the three years is 96.67 + 90 + 83.33 = 270.

FRED 31 requires that we calculate a fair value of each unit of service expected to be received. The total fair value of options expected is divided by the number of units of service expected during the vesting period to give a value of:

$$\frac{£320,000}{270 \text{years}} = £1,185 \text{ per year of employee service}$$

The charge for each year can now be determined:

	£
Year 1	
[91 + (9 × 0.5) years of service] × £1,185	113,168
Year 2	
[85 + (6 × 0.5) years of service] × £1,185	104,280
Year 3	
[80 + (5 × 0.5) years of service] × £1,185	97,762

We can see that the total charge for the period is only £315,210 rather than the £320,000 expected, since in reality the leaving employees left earlier than was expected, so fewer services were received than expected.

Each year the double entry will be a charge to the profit and loss account for the cost of the share options, and an increase in equity (a credit to 'other reserves' in the balance sheet).

7.12 Commentary on the proposals

Some commentators argue that the impact of the proposals will be adverse, since many companies (including struggling e-businesses) will see an additional charge in the profit and loss account.

But the principle of recognising the cost of share-based payment is sound. There may be practical difficulties, for example in determining the fair value of share options at each balance sheet date, but the ASB is expected to move to issue an accounting standard in this area as a matter of priority.

8 Summary

This chapter has covered three important topics:

♦ FRS 3 – which added additional disclosures to the profit and loss account and required new statements to be disclosed, most notably the statement of total recognised gains and losses.

♦ FRS 12 – which tightened the rules for when provisions and contingencies should be included in the financial statements.

♦ The FRSSE – which gives smaller entities the option to prepare their financial statements under a simplified accounting regime.

Multiple choice questions *(The answer is in the final chapter of this book)*

1   The profit and loss account of a company is shown below.

	£	Item no
Turnover	115,000	(1)
Cost of sales	(96,000)	(2)
Gross profit	19,000	(3)
Distribution costs	(6,300)	(4)
Administrative expenses	(2,750)	(5)
Other operating income	1,550	(6)
Operating profit	11,500	(7)
Interest receivable	10,000	(8)
Interest payable	(10,500)	(9)
Profit on ordinary activities before taxation	11,000	(10)
Taxation	(4,000)	(11)
Profit on ordinary activities after taxation	7,000	(12)
Dividends	(3,500)	(13)
Retained profit for the financial year	3,500	(14)

Under FRS 3 which of these items must be analysed between continuing operations, acquisitions and discontinued operations?

A   (1), (2) and (3)

B   (1), (2), (3), (4), (5), (6) and (7)

C   (1) to (10)

D   (1), (3), (7), (10), (12) and (14)

2   Strachey Ltd has analysed its turnover as follows in its accounts for the years ended 31 December 20X6 and 31 December 20X7.

	20X7 £000	20X6 £000
Continuing operations	26,550	25,750
Acquisitions	7,890	7,025
	34,440	32,775
Discontinued operations	6,750	7,950
	41,190	40,725

£2,500,000 of the 20X6 turnover classified under acquisitions relates to operations that were discontinued in 20X7. No other operations were discontinued in 20X7.

How should the comparative figures relating to 20X6 appear in the accounts for the year ended 31 December 20X7?

	Continuing operations £000	*Acquisitions* £000	*Discontinued operations* £000
A	25,750	4,525	10,450
B	25,750	7,025	7,950
C	30,275	-	10,450
D	32,775	-	7,950

3   During the year ended 31 March 20X3 Woolf Ltd sells a leasehold building for £1,550,000. It was purchased on 1 July 20W0 for £100,000 but had been revalued to £1,900,000 on 31 March 20X0. Woolf Ltd depreciates leasehold buildings on a straight line basis over the life of the lease, with a full year's depreciation in the year of acquisition and none in the year of disposal. The lease expires on 30 June 20Y0.

Woolf Ltd revalues another leasehold building to £2,000,000 on 31 March 20X3. Its historical cost was £1,000,000 and accumulated depreciation on the building was £350,000.

How are these transactions reflected in the statement of total recognised gains and losses and in the profit and loss account?

	Statement of total recognised gains and losses	*Profit and loss account*
A	£1,350,000 gain	£1,510,000 profit
B	£500,000 loss	£1,510,000 profit
C	£1,350,000 gain	£30,000 profit
D	£500,000 loss	£30,000 profit

4   The following describe potential provisions.

(1)   A provision to cover refunds. The company is in the retail sector and has a reputation for a 'no questions asked' policy on refunds.

(2)   A provision to cover an onerous contract on an operating lease. The lease was on a building which the company has subsequently vacated. The lease cannot be terminated and cannot be re-let.

Following FRS 12 covering provisioning, in which of the above situations would a company be allowed to recognise a provision in their accounts?

A   Neither situation

B   Both situations

C   Situation (1) only

D   Situation (2) only

CHAPTER 16

Price level accounting

EXAM FOCUS

With the general level of inflation being low, you might think that price level accounting is not an important subject. But even when general inflation is low, the prices of particular assets, eg property, can rise or fall rapidly, so this is not an area that you can ignore.

LEARNING OUTCOMES

This chapter covers the following Learning Outcomes of the CIMA Syllabus.

> Explain the problems of profit measurement and alternative approaches to asset valuations

> Explain measures to reduce distortion in financial statements when price levels change

In order to cover these Learning Outcomes the following topics are included.

> The meaning of profit
> Current value accounting
> Accounting for the effects of changing prices
> The ASC handbook

1 The meaning of profit

1.1 Introduction

A major objective of financial accounting is to calculate the 'profit' a business has made in an accounting period. You already know that accounting standards have been developed to lay down some of the principles to be followed in this process. In an imaginary world in which inflation did not exist and the value of the unit of measurement (let us say the £ sterling) was constant, there are two ways we could calculate profit.

First of all, we could set against revenue receivable the expenses incurred in earning that revenue. That is the calculation we perform in the profit and loss account. Alternatively, we may seek to define 'income' as the increase in the value of the business during the period. In other words, we could define 'income' as the difference between the opening balance sheet and the closing balance sheet, allowing, of course, for new capital introduced and for dividends paid out.

The two definitions of profit will, if we ignore the impact of inflation, be the same, and we recognise this equality in historical cost accounting, at any rate, by introducing the retained profit of a business into the balance sheet, thus implicitly accepting that 'income equals more assets (or fewer liabilities)'.

These calculations are performed in historical cost accounting regardless of the fact that inflation and other factors influencing the value of the £ sterling distort the result.

In this chapter we shall examine some of the alternative ways of measuring income, involving various ideas as to how capital is maintained:

♦ Economic income
♦ Current value accounting
♦ Capital maintenance – money, real and operating

1.2 The work of Hicks and Fisher: economic income

Sir John Hicks, the noted economist, recognised the basic concept of income and defined personal income in 1946 as 'the maximum value which (a person) can consume during a week and still expect to be as well off at the end of the week as at the beginning'. The Sandilands Committee, which produced a report on inflation accounting in 1979, modified this definition to make it more appropriate for business profit: 'a company's profit for the year is the maximum value which the company can distribute during the year, and still expect to be as well off at the end of the year as it was at the beginning'.

These definitions imply that the measurement of income requires the measurement of capital, that *economic income equals consumption* (or distributions in the case of businesses) *plus changes in the value of capital* during the period:

$$I = C + (K_2 - K_1)$$

where C = Consumption

K_1 = Capital at beginning of period

K_2 = Capital at end of period

One possibility is to use this equation to calculate income, defining capital (in economic terms) as the present value of the cash flows arising from owning the asset.

1.3 Example

Spock purchased a space invader entertainment machine at the beginning of year 1 for £1,000. He expects to receive at annual intervals the following receipts: at the end of year 1 £400; end of year 2 £500; end of year 3 £600. At the end of year 3 he expects to sell the machine for £400.

Spock could receive a return of 10% in the next best investment.

The present value of £1 receivable at the end of a period discounted at 10% per annum is as follows:

End of year 1	0.909
End of year 2	0.826
End of year 3	0.751

Required

Calculate the economic income for each year, ignoring taxation and working to the nearest whole pound. Your answer should show that Spock's capital is maintained throughout the period and that his income is constant.

1.4   Solution

We may first compute Spock's capital in the space invader project in discounted cash flow terms at the beginning of year 1 and at the end of each of the three years:

Beginning of year 1			*End of year 1*		
		£			£
£400 × 0.909		364			
£500 × 0.826		413	£500 × 0.909		455
£1,000 × 0.751		751	£1,000 × 0.826		826
		1,528			1,281

End of year 2			*End of year 3*		
		£			£
£1,000 × 0.909		909			Nil

These calculations recognise the fact that the receipt of income at the end of a year is worth less than the same amount at the beginning of the year: assuming a 10% interest rate the 'present value' of £100 one year hence is £91, because the £91 invested at 10% will produce interest of £9.10, thus leading to an end-year value of £100.

The loss in capital suffered each year is thus:

					Loss of capital	
					Per year	*Cumulative total*
					£	£
Year 1	£1,528	–	£1,281		247	247
Year 2	£1,281	–	£909		372	619
Year 3	£909	–	£0		909	1,528

If we are to maintain the capital at £1,528, we must set aside £247 at the end of year 1, a further £372 out of year 2 and £909 from year 3. These capital sums may be reinvested and are assumed to produce 10% per annum, giving the result tabulated below:

	Receipts	*Retained to maintain capital*	*Income from project*	*Investment income*	*Economic income*
	£	£	£	£	£
Year 1	400	247	153	–	153
Year 2	500	372	128	25	153
Year 3	1,000	909	91	62	153
Year 4	–	–	–	153	153
	1,900	1,528	372	240	612

Capital is maintained at £1,528 throughout the period, and a constant income of £153 is derived from it. For year 4 and onwards the income of £153 continues in perpetuity.

1.5   Economic income versus accounting income

It is salutary to compare these results with the profits that would be shown by conventional historical cost profit and loss accounts. Annual depreciation would be £200 ((£1,000 – £400) ÷ 3) and incomes in the three years would be:

	Receipts	*Depreciation*	*'Profit'*
	£	£	£
Year 1	400	200	200
Year 2	500	200	300
Year 3	600	200	400

The effect would be to preserve money capital at £1,000 ie the £400 proceeds of sale plus £600 retained by virtue of the depreciation provisions.

The difference between the historical cost total profit of £900 and the Hicksian income of £372 is £528. This is the amount of the 'windfall' profit occurring on the purchase of the machine, when expenditure of £1,000 gave rise to a discounted capital value of £1,528.

The illustration we have been studying shows the value of Hicks' approach and also its limitations. Perhaps the greatest limitation is that we have to forecast the future cash flows and their timing, and estimate an appropriate discount rate. All of these are subjective judgements open to a possible considerable margin of error. You can also see in the worked question that we assumed that the part of the cash received retained and reinvested to preserve capital could in fact earn the stated rate of 10%.

An alternative definition of income is that offered by Irving Fisher in *The theory of interest* (1930). He defined income in terms of consumption. He regarded savings as an investment to 'help towards the cost of living in future years'. As Nicholas Kaldor pointed out in *An expenditure tax* (1955) 'if we reserved the term income for consumption we should still need another term for what would otherwise be called income; and we should still be left with the problem of how to define the latter.'

Both Hicks and Fisher require the use of a discounting approach in arriving at the present capital value of projects in hand. That implies the question of what rate to take for the calculation. Hicks suggested the use of the rate available from the next best investment available, while Fisher suggested using the market rate.

2 Current value accounting

2.1 Introduction

One major limitation in the use of the historical cost convention is that it does not include realistic values for the assets of a business. Current value accounting is an alternative which seeks to introduce such realistic asset values.

How are we to arrive at current value? There are basically two possibilities:

(a) *Replacement cost.* Replacement cost is also called current *entry* value – the value at which a replacement asset would *enter* the business.

(b) *Net realisable value.* This is the current *exit* value – the amount that would be realised as the asset *left* the business.

In general, the use of replacement cost is more practical. The advantages and disadvantages of the use of the two current values are summarised later.

In historical cost accounting (HCA) profit is calculated as the difference between cost and sales proceeds. In current value accounting (CVA) we analyse that profit into components. Here is a simple illustration.

2.2 Illustration

At 1 January 20X3 X purchased an item of stock for £10. At 30 June 20X3 its replacement cost was £15. It was sold for £26 on 31 December 20X3. Its replacement cost at that time was £19.

HCA would calculate the profit on the sale as £16 (£26 – £10).

CVA would treat the transaction as follows:

	£	£
Operating income £26 – £19		7
Holding gain		
To 30 June 20X3: £15 – £10	5	
To 31 December 20X3: £19 – £15	4	
		9
		16

The total profit is the same but its components can be seen.

In the year for which the asset was held its value rose by £9; there is a 'holding' gain of £9. This was realised at 31 December. Prudence may dictate that it is unwise to take credit for a profit until it has been realised, but it also makes sense to have available for decision-making purposes the information that the unrealised holding gain has in fact taken place.

2.3   *Current exit values (net realisable value)*

The calculation of profit using net realisable values requires us to calculate income as the difference between the opening net realisable value of net assets and their closing value on the same basis, subject of course to distributions made or fresh capital introduced.

Net realisable value could mean the break-up value of assets, but if a business is a going concern it would be more meaningful to take the net realisable value from a sale in the normal course of business. Another problem is the basis for determining the realisable value of partly completed items which might only be capable of being sold as scrap until completed. It might then be possible to consider valuing them on the basis of their net realisable value when completed, less costs to be incurred to completion.

2.4   *Current entry value accounting*

Advantages

(a)   CVA provides more information about the source of total HC profit by separating holding gains from operating profit thus improving the quality of decision-making information available to management, and indicating the extent to which dividends can be paid without reducing the real value of the business.

(b)   The inclusion of fixed assets at current values is more useful than including them at cost because a better indication of the true worth of the enterprise is given.

(c)   By quantifying holding gains, it gives the opportunity to exclude them.

Disadvantages

(a)   Subjective judgement may often be necessary in determining replacement cost, especially when fixed assets have been rendered obsolete by new products.

(b)   Data is less verifiable by auditors and others.

(c)   Judgement as to the effectiveness of management's stewardship may be difficult.

2.5 Current exit value accounting

Advantages

(a) Exit value represents the opportunity cost of holding an asset: the benefit forgone by holding it is in exit value accounting, the cash realisable by its sale.

(b) For creditors, net realisable value may give a more reliable indication of the minimum worth of a company and its liquidity.

(c) Net realisable value may provide a more realistic estimate of worth than replacement cost, and is in fact used in practice to some extent, when revaluing land and buildings for example. All monetary items are also included in the balance sheet at net realisable value.

Disadvantages

(a) Subjective judgement may be necessary for some items.
(b) It does not adhere to the going concern concept.

In spite of the advantages listed, the importance of the above two disadvantages means that current exit value accounting has little support, especially from accountants.

2.6 Current cost accounting

Another possibility is to use a mixture of economic values, entry values and exit values to derive a 'current cost' for each asset. Current cost accounting (CCA) was mandatory in the past under SSAP 16, but this standard has now been withdrawn.

3 Accounting for the effects of changing prices

3.1 Introduction

Although the practical application of current cost accounting (CCA) has proved to be unacceptable to UK commerce and industry and indeed much of the UK accounting profession, it remains in the syllabus for your examination.

3.2 Weaknesses of historical cost accounts

 It has long been apparent that accounts prepared using historical cost (HC) principles have serious weaknesses in times of inflation or other price changes.

In a balance sheet, unexpired costs of assets purchased at different times with pounds of different purchasing power are summed to produce totals which are difficult to interpret. Amounts shown for assets such as plant and machinery or stocks do not represent any measure of the current value of such assets.

In a profit and loss account, out of date historical costs are deducted from current revenues to produce a profit figure that may not be useful.

In addition, the prudence convention requires the application of an asymmetric test in determining whether or not profits or losses are to be recognised. Profits are recognised only when they have been realised, but provision is made for all foreseeable losses.

This has the result that the profit for a year includes certain gains which relate to earlier periods but have been realised during this year, while it excludes certain gains which relate to the current year but have not been realised at the end of the year. Conversely, such a profit is reduced by all foreseeable losses, whether or not they have been realised in the current period.

It is not surprising therefore, that the profit figure produced in HC accounts often proves to be useless for the purposes of decision-making that it was originally intended for. In an inflationary era it does not measure the increase in the owners' wealth during a period, nor can it be used as a guide to the maximum amount which may be distributed. When the prices of its assets are rising, a firm which distributed the profit shown by the HC accounts would be unable to replace its assets without raising additional capital.

3.3 The considerations of a new approach

If reforms are to be carried out within the traditional framework of balance sheet and profit and loss account, given that prices change over time, there are three main issues which need to be addressed:

(a) the valuation of assets and liabilities;

(b) the measurement of profit;

(c) what unit of measurement to use.

3.4 Asset valuation

We have seen that it is possible to criticise both the individual figures and the total figures shown in the balance sheet prepared under HC principles. If we wish to make the balance sheet figures more useful, it is necessary to consider the reforms which might be made.

Possible bases for valuing assets (and liabilities) may be listed under two headings:

(a) Historical cost adjusted for inflation, that is, for changes in the general purchasing power of money.

(b) Current value:

(i) replacement cost (or entry value);

(ii) net realisable value (or exit value);

(iii) economic value (or value in use or present value of future inflows); and

(iv) value to the business (or deprival value).

The Companies Act 1985 permits fixed assets (other than goodwill) and stocks to be valued at 'current cost', when the alternative accounting rules are used. Since no definition of current cost is given, both bases would be possible.

Our final candidate for current value, value to the business or deprival value, is the one which was adopted by the *Sandilands Report* and in ensuing pronouncements on this subject by the ASC. For this reason it is discussed in the following section.

3.5 Value to the business

The concept of *value to the business* was first discussed in depth by Professor JC Bonbright of Columbia Business School. He called it *value to the owner* and described it thus:

> 'The value of a property to its owner is identical in amount with the adverse value of the entire loss, direct and indirect, that the owner might expect to suffer if he were to be deprived of the property.'

In the UK the concept has been discussed and developed in the context of accounting by Professor WT Baxter of the London School of Economics. He calls it *deprival value* and Chapter 12 of his work *Accounting values and inflation* provides an excellent discussion of the concept which the Sandilands Committee described as *value to the business*.

In order to value any individual asset it is necessary to ask:

> 'If the firm were to be deprived of the asset, what sum of money would make it whole again, given that it has time to take any necessary action to minimise its loss?'

In some cases a sum of money equal to the replacement cost of the asset would be sufficient, whilst in other cases an amount equal to the net disposal proceeds or the value in use would be sufficient.

A helpful formula is:

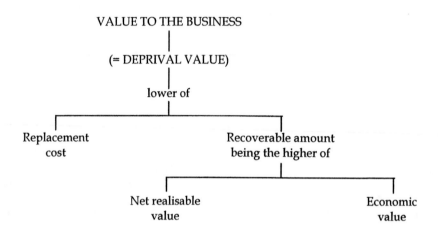

3.6 Illustrations

The best way to understand the concept is to look at a few illustrations.

		Replacement cost £	*Net realisable value* £	*Economic value* £
Asset	X	500	200	1,000
	Y	500	200	400
	Z	400	200	100

(a)   If the firm were deprived of asset X, what action would it take? As economic value is greater than replacement cost, it would purchase another asset X. Thus £500 of cash would enable the firm to replace its asset (ignoring time delays, etc.) and represents the value to the business of asset X.

(b)   Application of the formula to asset Y tells us that its value to the business is £400, the economic value. What then is the logic for this? If the firm were deprived of asset Y, would it replace it? The answer is no, for it would cost £500 to replace, and both the net realisable value and the economic value are less than this sum. While the firm has the asset it should continue to use it as economic value is greater than net realisable value but, if deprived of it, it would lose the present value of future cash flows, that is, the economic value. Value to the business in this case is therefore £400.

(c)   Our formula tells us that the value to the business of asset Z is £200, the net realisable value. In this case, if the firm owns the asset, its best course of action is to sell it, as net realisable value is greater than economic value and both are below replacement cost. If deprived of the asset, the firm would certainly not replace it; it would merely lose the opportunity to sell it for £200 and hence net realisable value is the appropriate value.

3.7   Measurement of profit

Having established a reasonable basis for measuring the value of assets, we must now consider the second problem, which is how to measure profit between the balance sheet dates. What do we mean by the term *profit*?

Again, consider the definition of income, the personal equivalent of profit, by Sir John Hicks in his work *Value and capital*:

> 'A man's income is the maximum value which he can consume during a week, and still expect to be as well-off at the end of the week as he was at the beginning.'

The major difficulty in the above definition is, of course, the meaning of the term 'well-off'. Traditionally, accountants have perceived 'well-offness' in terms of money capital and hence have measured profit by reference to money capital maintenance. Under this approach, if a firm has capital or net assets of £10,000 on 1 January 20X1 it must have capital or net assets of £10,000 on 31 December 20X1 to be as well off at the end of the period. Thus, providing there have been no injections of share capital into the firm and no dividends or withdrawals of share capital, a firm with capital of £14,000 on 31 December 20X1 would have made a profit of £4,000, ie £14,000 – £10,000, using this capital maintenance concept. The opening capital or equity shareholders' interest in money terms is used as a benchmark to determine profit.

Although this approach may be satisfactory in a period when prices are not changing, most people would agree that it is not satisfactory in a period when prices in general and/or specific prices are changing. £10,000 at the year end does not have the same value as £10,000 at the beginning of the year and therefore calculating profit is not simply a matter of subtracting £10,000 from £14,000.

3.8   Different concepts of capital maintenance

In measuring a company's capital, two different basic approaches can be identified:

(a)   *The operating capital maintenance concept.* Profit is measured after provision has been made to maintain a company's physical operating capital (operating capital is usually thought of in terms of a company's ability to produce a certain volume of goods and services).

(b)   *The financial capital maintenance concept.* This can be subdivided into:

   (i)   money financial capital maintenance – this is the approach used in HC accounts;

   (ii)   real financial capital maintenance – in this approach capital is regarded in terms of a fund of general purchasing power and profit is measured after the general purchasing power of opening shareholders' funds has been maintained.

3.9   Illustration

Consider a company financed only by equity share capital with net assets on 1 January and 31 December 20X1 of £1,000 and £1,500 respectively. There has been no change in share capital in the year.

During the year the general rate of inflation (as measured by the RPI), is 20%. The specific rate of price increase of the goods which the company buys and sells is 10%.

The profit calculated using each of the concepts described above, is as follows:

	Maintenance of		
	money financial capital £	real financial capital £	operating capital £
Net assets on 31.12.X1	1,500	1,500	1,500
Less: Net assets required on 31.12.X1 to maintain capital as at 1.1.X1			
Money financial capital	(1,000)		
Real financial capital (120% × 1,000)		(1,200)	
Operating capital (110% × 1,000)			(1,100)
Profit	500	300	400

(a)   Using money financial capital maintenance, the firm is as well-off at the end of the year with £1,000. Hence the profit is £500.

(b)   The use of real financial capital maintenance recognises that there has been a decline in the general purchasing power of money. As a result, £1,200 is needed at the end of the year to give the same command over goods and services in general as was given by £1,000 on 1 January. Here the profit or increase in well-offness is therefore only £300.

(c)   Under the third option £1,100 is required at the year-end to buy the same specific goods that £1,000 would have bought on 1 January 20X1. In this case the profit is therefore £400. As we shall see, the application of this concept becomes rather complex where a firm buys a number of different assets subject to different rates of price change. It also gives rise to difficulties where the firm is financed not only by equity capital but also by borrowings and other monetary liabilities.

In the above example, the profit shown using the maintenance of operating capital is greater than that shown using real financial capital maintenance. It should be appreciated that this is not always the case but depends on the relationship between, on the one hand, the price increases or decreases of specific assets which the firm purchases and, on the other hand, the change in the general level of prices.

3.10   The unit of measurement

The problem here is the manner in which the results are reported. Should they be stated in terms of historic 'nominal' £s, ie at the date of the transaction, or should the figures be adjusted to a value reflecting a common 'purchasing power' £ (often the current £)?

Long term trends, in particular, can be distorted by the comparison of figures stated in terms of historic £s.

3.11 The different systems of accounting

Depending upon the choice of valuation of assets, profit measures and units of measurement, four systems of accounting can be defined:

Asset valuation	Profit measurement (capital maintained)	Unit of measurement	System
HC	Money financial	Nominal £	HISTORIC COST ACCOUNTING (HCA)
HC	Real financial	Current £	CURRENT PURCHASING POWER (CPP)
Value to the business	Operating or real financial	Nominal £	CURRENT COST ACCOUNTING (CCA) (2 versions)

The two versions of CCA are those that were recommended by the ASC in their publication *Accounting for the effects of changing prices: a handbook*. This is still the latest official publication on this topic but is non-mandatory.

4 The ASC handbook

4.1 Introduction

The ASC's suggested solution to the price level accounting debate is that companies should disclose information about the current year's result and financial position on the basis of:

(a)   CC valuation:
(b)   either the operating or financial capital maintenance concept; and
(c)   the nominal pound as the unit of measurement.

The choice of capital maintenance concepts depends on the nature of the company's business and on its perception of the users of its accounts. Manufacturing companies are likely to select operating capital maintenance since they have an identifiable operating capital.

Financial capital maintenance is more suitable for companies in which asset value increases are viewed as an alternative to trading as a means of generating profits. It is particularly suitable for companies which, by the very nature of their business, do not have an easily definable operating capital to maintain, or for companies that do not have the maintenance of their operating capital as an objective. Some companies involved in unique or discontinuous ventures, such as those engaged in the extraction or construction industries or in commodity trading, may find it difficult if not impossible to define their operating capital: commodity traders commonly would show little or no profit if they charged profit with the replacement cost of their dealing assets since their aim is to achieve holding gains. Other companies deemed to be 'value-based' (such as insurers, property companies, investment trusts or other similar long term investment entities) would encounter similar difficulties.

A company that is seeking to measure the 'real' return on its shareholders' capital will do this by comparing its capital at the end of the period with opening shareholders' invested capital restated in terms of constant purchasing power. In this way the company will show its shareholders whether it has succeeded not only in preserving their initial investment but in increasing it. Alternatively, where the company's aim is to demonstrate its capacity to continue in existence by ensuring that at the end of the accounting period it is as capable of producing a similar quantity of goods and services as it was at the beginning, profit would be regarded as the surplus remaining only after its operating capital had been maintained.

Before we proceed to examine profit measurement based on real financial capital maintenance and the maintenance of operating capital in more detail, we must re-examine the concept of holding gains.

4.2   Holding gains and operating gains

Most companies hold fixed assets and stocks. The opportunity cost of using these assets usually bears little relationship to their historical cost, but may be determined by reference to their 'value to the business' at the date of consumption. As we have seen earlier, for a company which uses its resources profitably, value to the business will usually be the replacement cost of the asset.

Recognising this, it is possible to divide the HC profit, that is, the profit based on money financial capital maintenance, into two elements:

(a)   current cost (CC) profit (or operating gains) = sales revenue less replacement cost of assets consumed; and

(b)   holding gains = replacement cost of assets consumed less historical cost of those assets.

Holding gains are sometimes described as cost savings or revaluation surpluses. They may be thought of as the cost savings made by buying assets and holding them until the date of sale or usage (during which period the asset prices change) as opposed to merely buying at the date of sale or usage. There may, of course, be holding losses as well as holding gains.

4.3   Illustration

You have already come across the idea of holding and operating gains in the context of CVA. Another simple illustration will help to explain the distinction. Let us suppose that Pinker Ltd, a £100 equity financed company, buys one item of stock for £100 on 1 January 20X1. It holds the stock until 31 January 20X1 and sells it for £150 when the replacement cost is £120.

This HC profit of £50 for January may be analysed as follows.

Analysis of profit for January 20X1

		£	£
CC profit (or operating gain)			
Sales revenue		150	
Less:	Replacement cost of stock sold	120	
			30
Holding gain			
Replacement cost of stock sold		120	
Less:	Historical cost	100	
			20
HC profit			50

Thus the CC profit is presumed to occur instantaneously and the difference between CC and HC is shown separately.

It may be argued that, for many companies, such a division of profit is artificial and that it should not be used to appraise decisions on operations or asset holding policy. After all, for most companies any gains or losses on asset holdings are not avoidable but are as much a part of operations as the difference between sales revenue and replacement costs. In spite of this limitation, such a dichotomy is a feature of CCA, and we shall now see how the treatment of the holding gains or losses depends upon whether profit is measured by reference to the maintenance of general purchasing power or specific purchasing power.

4.4 Holding gains under real financial capital maintenance

If real financial capital maintenance is adopted as a benchmark for measuring profit, it is necessary to divide the holding gains into two elements, a real element and a fictitious element. The real element measures the extent to which the price of the specific asset has appreciated to a greater extent than the rise in the general level of prices. The fictitious element measures the extent to which the price of the specific asset has merely kept up with the change in the general level of prices.

If for simplicity we assume a rate of inflation of 5% for the month of January 20X1, the holding gain of Pinker Ltd may be analysed.

Analysis of holding gain

	£	£
Real element		
Replacement cost at date of sale	120	
Less: Historical cost adjusted by general index		
(100 × 1.05)	105	
		15
Fictitious element		
Historical cost adjusted by general index – as above	105	
Less: Historical cost	100	
		5
Total holding gain		20

Using the real financial capital maintenance benchmark, the real holding gain is a part of the total profit for January whilst the fictitious element is most certainly not. Thus on this basis a profit and loss account would appear as follows:

Analysis of profit for January 20X1 using real financial capital maintenance

	£	£
Current cost profit		
Sales revenue	150	
Less: Current cost of sales	120	
		30
Real holding gain		15
Total profit		45

If the profit of £45 were to be distributed, a summarised balance sheet on 31 January 20X1 would take the following form:

Summarised balance sheet on 31 January 20X1

	£		£
Cash (150 – 45)	105	Share capital	100
		Inflation adjustment (5% × 100)	5
	105		105

The general purchasing power or real capital of the opening shareholders has been maintained. £105 gives the same general purchasing power on 31 January 20X1 as did £100 on 1 January 20X1.

4.5 Holding gains and the maintenance of specific purchasing power

Opponents of the use of real financial capital maintenance would point out that, although the use of the above approach results in the maintenance of the general purchasing power of the equity shareholders, it does not in this case result in the maintenance of the specific purchasing power of the company (or operating capital). In order to replace the items of stock which cost £100 on 1 January, the company requires £120, that is, the replacement cost, on 31 January. Advocates of the measurement of profit by reference to maintenance of specific purchasing power would argue that no part of the holding gain should be described as profit. The holding gain is a capital adjustment which must be retained to continue operations in the same line of business. It should therefore be credited to some such account as a 'capital maintenance reserve' (or 'current cost reserve' (CCR) as it has come to be called).

Following this approach, our profit and loss account for Pinker Ltd would merely include the CC profit.

Pinker Ltd
Profit and loss account for January 20X1
(Using maintenance of operating capital)

	£
Sales revenue	150
Less: Current cost of sales	120
CC operating profit	30

If this profit were to be paid out as a dividend, the balance sheet on 31 January 20X1 would appear as follows:

Balance sheet on 31 January 20X1

	£		£
Cash (150 – 30)	120	Share capital	100
		Current cost reserve (holding gain)	20
	120		120

Providing there are no further price rises during the time lag between the use of the stock and its replacement, the company is able to continue operations at the same level by purchasing a replacement item of stock at a cost of £120.

By charging depreciation based upon current replacement costs, rather than historical costs, of fixed assets, and excluding holding gains from profit, the use of this concept of capital maintenance again attempts to enable the company automatically to continue at the same level of operations.

Practice question 1 (The answer is in the final chapter of this book)

Appledore plc

Appledore plc buys 100 widgets in January 20X0 for £12 each and makes the following sales during 20X0.

	Number sold	Selling price £	Replacement cost at date of sale £
March	50	20	13
August	30	25	15

The replacement cost at 31 December 20X0 was £20 per widget.

Required

(a)   Produce the HC trading account and the CC trading account for 20X0.

(b)   Analyse the 'holding' gains made during the year, including any unrealised holding gains.

4.6   Learning outcomes

You have now covered both the learning outcomes for this chapter:

> Explain the problems of profit measurement and alternative approaches to asset valuations.

> Explain measures to reduce distortion in financial statements when price levels change.

5   Summary

This chapter has covered the basic principles behind the various income and profit measurement methods, incorporating different asset valuations and ideas of capital maintenance.

Be sure you appreciate the differences between the two CCA versions:

Operating capital maintenance version

♦   maintains the ability of the business to *produce* a certain level of goods and services, by taking account of *specific* price changes in assets used.

Real financial capital maintenance

♦   maintains the ability of the shareholders to purchase the same level of goods and services, by taking account of general price changes.

The detailed computations for the preparation of accounts under CCA and CPP are not examinable.

Multiple choice questions *(The answers are in the final chapter of this book)*

1   On 1 April 20X1 a business purchased an item of stock costing £20,000. It was sold for £30,000 on 1 October 20X1, at which time its replacement cost was £24,000. At 31 March 20X2 the item's replacement cost was £27,000.

What is the holding gain on this item of stock for the year ending 31 March 20X2?

A   £3,000

B   £4,000

C   £6,000

D   £10,000

2   A business has an asset which originally cost £10,000 on 1 January 20X2. At the balance sheet date of 31 March 20X2 the asset could be sold for £14,000 or used within the business earning a present value of cash flows of £15,000. If the asset were to be replaced at 31 March 20X2 it would cost £13,000.

What is the asset's value to the business at 31 March 20X2?

A   £10,000

B   £13,000

C   £14,000

D   £15,000

3   A company has net assets of £100,000 at 1 January 20X2 and net assets of £120,000 at 31 December 20X2. There has been no change in share capital in the period.

During the year the general level of inflation was 3% but the price of the specific goods that the company buys and sells increased by 5%.

What is the profit for the year using the concepts of real financial capital maintenance and operating capital maintenance?

	Real financial capital maintenance £	Operating capital maintenance £
A	£3,600	£6,000
B	£17,000	£6,000
C	£17,000	£15,000
D	£3,600	£15,000

CHAPTER 17

Accounting for tangible fixed assets

EXAM FOCUS

FRS 15 *Tangible fixed assets* is the main Standard covered in this chapter. It is unlikely to be the subject of a question on its own, but FRS 15 and the other two Standards covered (SSAP 19 *Accounting for investment properties* and SSAP 4 *Accounting for government grants*) are all likely to contribute to the answer to both computational and non-computational questions.

LEARNING OUTCOMES

This chapter covers the following Learning Outcome of the CIMA Syllabus.

> Explain the problems of profit measurement and alternative approaches to asset valuations

In order to cover this Learning Outcome the following topics are included.

> FRS 15: Tangible fixed assets
> SSAP 19: Accounting for investment properties
> SSAP 4: Accounting for government grants

---

1 FRS 15: Tangible fixed assets

1.1 Introduction

FRS 15 **Tangible fixed assets** is a largely straightforward FRS regulating the initial measurement, valuation and depreciation of all tangible fixed assets other than investment properties (to which SSAP 19 applies – see later). FRS 15's role is to codify existing good practice. You will have studied FRS 15 in Paper 6 but its provisions remain relevant for Paper 7. Your need for detailed study of this chapter depends on how much you remember from Paper 6.

1.2 Definitions

♦ Tangible fixed assets

Assets that have physical substance and are held for use in the production or supply of goods or services, for rental to others, or for administrative purposes on a continuing basis in the reporting entity's activities.

♦ Depreciation

The measure of the cost or revalued amount of the economic benefits of the tangible fixed asset that have been consumed during the period.

Consumption includes the wearing out, using up or other reduction in the useful economic life of a tangible fixed asset whether arising from use, effluxion of time or obsolescence through either changes in technology or changes in demand for the goods and services produced by the asset.

1.3 Initial measurement

Initial measurement of the asset (whether acquired or self-constructed) should be at its **cost**.

Cost should include all costs directly attributable to bringing the asset into working condition for its intended use. Cost can include finance costs – see 1.4.

If the carrying amount of a tangible fixed asset exceeds its recoverable amount (defined as the higher of net realisable value and value in use) it should be written down to its recoverable amount.

1.4 Capitalising finance costs

Finance costs directly attributable to the construction of a tangible fixed asset may be capitalised as part of the cost of the asset. Such capitalisation is optional.

Conditions:

♦ Finance costs may only be capitalised if the entity adopts a policy of capitalising them. If such a policy is adopted, all qualifying finance costs must be capitalised.

♦ Finance costs capitalised in a period must not exceed finance costs incurred in the period.

♦ Capitalisation should **begin** when:

- finance costs are being incurred; and
- expenditure for the asset is being incurred; and
- work has begun on the asset or on getting it ready for use

♦ Capitalisation should **cease** when:

- substantially all the activities necessary to get the asset ready for use are complete

♦ Capitalisation should be suspended if work on the asset is interrupted for an extended period.

Disclosures when finance costs are capitalised:

♦ Accounting policy adopted
♦ Finance costs included in the cost of the asset
♦ Finance costs capitalised in the period
♦ Finance costs recognised in the profit and loss account in the period
♦ Capitalisation rate used

1.5 Subsequent expenditure

Subsequent expenditure should be capitalised if it enhances the economic benefits of the asset in excess of its previously assessed standard of performance. Otherwise, subsequent expenditure that helps to maintain the asset's standard of performance (eg, routine repairs and maintenance) should be charged to the profit and loss account as it is incurred.

1.6 Valuation

Revaluation of tangible fixed assets is allowed if a policy of revaluation is adopted. Just as with the capitalisation of interest, revaluation is optional rather than mandatory.

Conditions:

♦ All assets of the same class must be revalued. For example, if certain land and buildings were to be revalued, this would not require the revaluation of plant and machinery, but would require the revaluation of all land and buildings held.

♦ Once revalued, the carrying amount in each balance sheet must be current value.

This requirement is met for properties, according to FRS 15, by a full valuation every five years and an interim valuation in year 3. Interim valuations should be carried out in years 1, 2 and 4 if it is likely there has been a material change in value.

Alternatively, for non-specialised properties, a rolling revaluation may be undertaken, with (say) one fifth of properties valued each year, with interim valuations of the remainder when it is likely that values have changed materially.

♦ A qualified valuer must be used for a full valuation. If an internal valuer is used, the valuation must be reviewed by a qualified external valuer.

♦ The basis of valuation should be:

- non-specialised properties: existing use value, with open market value shown by note if materially different

- specialised properties: depreciated replacement cost

- assets other than landed property: open market value

1.7   *Reporting valuation gains and losses*

♦ Gains

- Show in the statement of total recognised gains and losses (STRGL) unless they reverse previous losses recognised in the profit and loss account, when they can be taken to the profit and loss account

♦ Losses

- Losses caused by consumption of economic benefits – show in profit and loss account

- Other losses – show in STRGL until the carrying amount reaches depreciated historical cost, then the excess balance thereafter in the profit and loss account. (If the recoverable amount exceeds the revalued amount, then the excess loss can be recognised in the STRGL to the extent that recoverable amount exceeds revalued amount.)

♦ In reporting gains and losses, material revaluation gains and losses on individual assets in a class of assets should **not** be offset

1.8   *Example*

A non-specialised property cost £1 million and has a useful life of 10 years and no residual value. It is depreciated on a straight-line basis and revalued annually. The entity has a policy of calculating depreciation based on the opening book amount. At the end of years 1 and 2 the asset has existing use values of £1,080,000 and £700,000 respectively. At the end of year 2, the recoverable amount of the asset is £760,000 and its depreciated historical cost is £800,000. There is no obvious consumption of economic benefits in year 2, other than that accounted for through the depreciation charge.

Show the calculation of the carrying values at the end of years 1 and 2, indicating the gains and losses recognised and where they will be reported.

1.9 Solution

	Year 1 £000	Year 2 £000
Opening book amount	1,000	1,080
Depreciation	(100)	(120)
Adjusted book amount	900	960
Revaluation gain (loss)		
- recognised in the STRGL	180	(220)
- recognised in the profit and loss account	-	(40)
Closing book amount	1,080	700

Explanatory notes

1 **In Year 1**, after depreciation of £100,000 a revaluation gain of £180,000 is recognised in the statement of total recognised gains and losses.

2 **In Year 2**, after a depreciation charge of £120,000, the revaluation loss on the property is £260,000. According to FRS 15, where there is not a clear consumption of economic benefits, revaluation losses should be recognised in the statement of total recognised gains and losses until the carrying amount reaches the asset's depreciated historical cost. Therefore, the fall in value from the adjusted book amount (£960,000) to depreciated historical cost (£800,000) of £160,000 is recognised in the statement of total recognised gains and losses.

The rest of the revaluation loss, £100,000 (ie the fall in value from depreciated historical cost (£800,000) to the revalued amount (£700,000)), should be recognised in the profit and loss account, unless it can be demonstrated that recoverable amount is greater than the revalued amount. In this case, recoverable amount of £760,000 is greater than the revalued amount of £700,000 by £60,000. Therefore £60,000 of the revaluation loss is recognised in the statement of total recognised gains and losses, rather than the profit and loss account – giving rise to a total revaluation loss of £220,000 (£60,000 + £160,000) that is recognised in the statement of total recognised gains and losses. The remaining loss (representing the fall in value from depreciated historical cost of £800,000 to recoverable amount of £760,000) of £40,000 is recognised in the profit and loss account.

3 As the remaining useful economic life of the asset is nine years, the depreciation charge in year 2 is 1/9th of the opening book amount (£1,080,000/9 = £120,000).

1.10 Gains and losses on disposal

Gains and losses on disposal of tangible fixed assets are shown in the profit and loss account and are calculated as the difference between proceeds and carrying amount.

1.11 Depreciation

The depreciable amount (cost or valuation, less residual value) of a tangible fixed asset should be allocated on a systematic basis over its useful economic life. The depreciation method used should reflect as fairly as possible the pattern in which the asset's economic benefits are consumed.

The following factors need to be considered when determining the useful economic life, residual value and depreciation method of an asset:

♦ Expected usage, assessed by reference to expected capacity or physical output
♦ Expected physical deterioration through use or the passage of time
♦ Economic or technological obsolescence
♦ Legal or similar limits on use, such as the expiry dates of related leases

FRS 15 mentions the straight-line and reducing balance methods but does not stipulate a particular method. It is up to the directors to choose the fairest method possible.

 A change from one method of depreciation to another should only be made if the new method will give a fairer presentation of the results and financial position. Such a change does not constitute a change of accounting policy.

The carrying amount of the asset is depreciated using the revised method over the remaining useful life, beginning in the period in which the change is made.

Where the tangible fixed asset comprises two or more major components with different useful economic lives, each component should be accounted for separately for depreciation purposes and depreciated over its individual useful economic life.

1.12   Review of useful economic life and residual value

There should be an **annual** review of the useful economic life and, if material, of the residual value of the assets. Any change should be reflected in future depreciation charges.

1.13   Disclosures

The following information should be disclosed separately in the financial statements for each class of tangible fixed assets:

♦   the depreciation methods used;

♦   the useful economic lives or the depreciation rates used;

♦   total depreciation charge for the period;

♦   where material, the financial effect of a change during the period in either the estimate of useful economic lives or the estimate of residual values;

♦   the cost or revalued amount at the beginning of the financial period and at the balance sheet date;

♦   the cumulative amount of provisions for depreciation or impairment at the beginning of the financial period and at the balance sheet date;

♦   a reconciliation of the movements, separately disclosing additions, disposals, revaluations, transfers, depreciation, impairment losses, and reversals of past impairment losses written back in the financial period;

♦   the net carrying amount at the beginning of the financial period and at the balance sheet date; and

♦   where there has been a change in the depreciation method used, the effect, if material, should be disclosed in the period of change. The reason for the change should also be disclosed.

For each class of revalued assets, the following should be disclosed:

♦   the name and qualifications of the valuer(s) or the valuer's organisation and a description of its nature;

♦   the basis or bases of valuation (including whether notional directly attributable acquisition costs have been included or expected selling costs deducted);

♦   the date and amounts of the valuations;

♦   where historical cost records are available, the carrying amount that would have been included in the financial statements had the tangible fixed assets been carried at historical cost less depreciation;

♦   whether the person(s) carrying out the valuation is (are) internal or external to the entity.

1.14 Publication of FRED 29

In May 2002 the ASB issued FRED 29 as part of the project to align UK accounting with international standards. FRED 29 proposes that FRS 15 should be replaced by two separate FRSs, one dealing with 'Property, plant and equipment' (ie tangible fixed assets in general) and the other dealing with 'Borrowing costs' (ie the capitalisation of borrowing costs into the cost of fixed assets).

Few changes in UK accounting are proposed. Both the capitalisation of borrowing costs and the revaluation of tangible fixed assets will be optional, as is the case currently. However there are some differences:

♦ FRS 15 requires revaluation to *current value*, whereas FRED 29 proposes revaluation to *fair value*, where a policy of revaluations is adopted. FRS 15 defines 'current value' as the value to the business (the deprival value), while the 'fair value' in FRED 29 will normally be the market value.

♦ FRS 15 requires a revaluation loss that exceeds an existing revaluation surplus to be recognised in the STRGL to the extent that the recoverable amount exceeds the revalued amount (ie there is no impairment). FRED 29 proposes that such a revaluation loss should be charged to the profit and loss account.

The differences between FRS 15 and FRED 29 are ones of fine detail. In nearly all respects, current UK practice is maintained in the new proposed standards.

2 SSAP 19: Accounting for investment properties

2.1 Definition

An investment property is an interest in land and/or completed buildings which is held for its investment potential, any rental income being negotiated at arm's length.

Property owned by a company and occupied for its own purposes, or let to and occupied by another group company, is not an investment property.

2.2 Accounting treatment

Investment properties should not be depreciated. Instead, they are revalued annually at their open market value, gains and losses being taken to an investment revaluation reserve and included in the statement of total recognised gains and losses (STRGL). If a deficit is expected to be permanent, it should be charged to the profit and loss account.

As an exception to the general rule of non-depreciation, leased investment properties with an unexpired term of twenty years or less must be depreciated over their remaining lives in the normal way.

2.3 Commentary on SSAP 19

SSAP 19 recognises that the economic substance of holding investment properties is different from other tangible fixed assets. Usually tangible fixed assets are owned in order to be consumed within the business, therefore FRS 15 requires them to be shown in the balance sheet at the amount of the cost/revalued amount which has not yet been consumed, since this is what users are most interested in.

However, investment properties are not held to be consumed, but instead for their investment potential. Depreciation (as a measure of consumption) is irrelevant; what users are most interested in is the market value, so this is the balance sheet valuation required by SSAP 19.

3   SSAP 4: Accounting for government grants

3.1   Definition

Government includes central, local and international government and their agencies.

3.2   Accounting treatment

Revenue grants (grants received to help pay for revenue expenditure)

Revenue grants are recognised in the period in which the related expenditure is recognised.

Capital grants (grants received to help pay for fixed assets)

Capital grants could be recognised in several ways including:

♦   Crediting the grant to the asset account concerned, leading to a reduction in annual depreciation charges

♦   Crediting the grant to a deferred income account, released to the credit of profit and loss account in step with depreciation

♦   Credit to profit and loss account on receipt

♦   Credit to a non-distributable reserve

SSAP 4 allows only the first two of these, since they comply with the accruals concept. The adoption of the first would contravene the Companies Act requirement that fixed assets should initially be stated at cost, so cannot be used by companies.

The second method is acceptable in all circumstances, so is generally recommended.

4   Relevant UITF Abstracts

4.1   Abstract 5: Transfers from current assets to fixed assets

Consider the scenario where a property is being held for intended sale (so is included in current assets) but the decision is taken instead to hold the property long-term as an investment property (so it must be reclassified as a fixed asset). The question arises as to the appropriate value at which to transfer the property from current assets to fixed assets.

If the property had fallen in value, the temptation might be to transfer it at its book value, and then charge the write-down in value against the investment revaluation reserve, thus avoiding charging the profit and loss account.

The UITF decision is that such accounting is inappropriate. The current asset accounting rules must be applied up to the date of management's change of intent. The transfer should be made at the lower of cost and net realisable value at the transfer date, so any write-down in value before this date must be charged to the profit and loss account in line with the normal accounting for current assets.

4.2   Abstract 29: Website development costs

Many companies incur significant costs in developing their company website, including planning costs, infrastructure costs, design costs and content costs. How should these costs be accounted for?

The UITF decision is that planning costs do not in themselves give rise to future benefits, so they should be written off as incurred.

The other categories of costs should be capitalised as an asset if the relationship between the expenditure and the future economic benefits is sufficiently certain.

Website development costs are not 'development expenditure' coming within the scope of SSAP 13. They would be capitalised as tangible fixed assets and subject to the rules of FRS 15.

4.3 Learning outcome

You have now covered the learning outcome for this chapter:

> Explain the problems of profit measurement and alternative approaches to asset valuations in the context of accounting for tangible fixed assets

5 Summary

The vital points to pick up from this chapter are:

♦ Role of depreciation as a means of measuring consumption rather than an attempt to value fixed assets

♦ Rules governing capitalisation of interest

♦ Rules governing revaluation

♦ Changing from one depreciation method to another

♦ Reviews of asset lives and residual value

♦ Accounting treatment of investment properties, and reasons why a different accounting treatment is required from normal tangible fixed assets

♦ Accounting treatment of government grants, especially capital grants

---

Multiple choice questions *(The answers are in the final chapter of this book)*

1   A firm buys a fixed asset at the beginning of 20X1 for £1,000. The estimated useful life is ten years, with a scrap value of zero. The firm uses the straight line method of depreciation. During 20X4 the estimated useful life is shortened to a total of eight years.

The appropriate depreciation charge for 20X5 is:

A   £100

B   £125

C   £140

D   £150

2   Upton Ltd makes up its financial statements to 31 December each year. On 1 January 20X0 it bought a machine with a useful life of ten years for £200,000 and started to depreciate it at 15% per annum on the reducing balance basis. On 31 December 20X3 the accumulated depreciation was £95,600 and the net book value £104,400. During 20X4 the company changed the basis of depreciation to straight line.

What is the correct accounting treatment to be adopted in the financial statements of Upton Ltd for the year ended 31 December 20X4?

A	Depreciation charge (£10,440)	Prior period adjustment	Nil
B	Depreciation charge (£17,400)	Prior period adjustment	Nil
C	Depreciation charge (£20,000)	Prior period adjustment	£15,600
D	Depreciation charge (£20,000)	Extraordinary item	£15,600

The following information relates to questions 3 and 4.

Lankaland purchased freehold land and buildings on 1 July 20W3 for £380,000 including £80,000 for the land. The building had been depreciated at the rate of 4% per annum on cost for each of the ten years to 30 June 20X3. The property was professionally revalued at £800,000 including £200,000 for the land on 1 July 20X3, and recorded in the books. At 1 July 20X3 it was estimated that the building had a remaining useful life of twenty years and a residual value of £100,000 at the end of that period.

3   What is the surplus on revaluation on 1 July 20X3?

A   £420,000

B   £540,000

C   £572,000

D   £620,000

4   What is the net book value of the freehold land and buildings on 30 June 20X4?

A   £760,000

B   £765,000

C   £770,000

D   £775,000

CHAPTER 18

Intangibles

EXAM FOCUS

Accounting for goodwill was a controversial and highly examinable topic when UK practice was out of line with international practice. Now that FRS 10 has brought the UK back in line, the topic is no longer so important. This chapter also covers SSAP 13 and FRS 11.

LEARNING OUTCOMES

This chapter covers the following Learning Outcome of the CIMA Syllabus.

> Explain the problems of profit measurement and alternative approaches to asset valuations

In order to cover this Learning Outcome the following topics are included.

> FRS 10: Goodwill and intangible assets
> SSAP 13: Accounting for research and development
> FRS 11: Impairment of fixed assets and goodwill

1 FRS 10: Goodwill and intangible assets

1.1 Introduction

Accounting for goodwill has had a long and chequered history. The original accounting standard was SSAP 22 which recommended that purchased goodwill should be immediately eliminated against reserves, while permitting goodwill to be capitalised and amortised as an alternative accounting treatment.

SSAP 22 was unsatisfactory for two reasons:

(a)   it permitted a choice of accounting treatment, thus not promoting comparability

(b)   the recommended treatment (immediate elimination) was prohibited by International Accounting Standards, therefore the UK was out of step with international practice.

In 1997 SSAP 22 was withdrawn and FRS 10 was issued in its place. FRS 10 is more consistent with international practice and also deals generally with all intangible assets, not just goodwill.

1.2 Definitions

Purchased goodwill is the difference between the cost of an acquired entity and the aggregate of the fair values of that entity's identifiable assets and liabilities.

Non-purchased goodwill is any other goodwill. At any time, the value of a business is likely to be different to the aggregate of the fair values of the net assets of the business. However the value of non-purchased (or inherent) goodwill is uncertain since no purchase transaction has taken place to confirm its value.

Intangible assets are non-financial fixed assets that do not have physical substance but are identifiable and are controlled by the entity through custody or legal rights.

1.3 Examples

Goodwill can be either positive or negative. Consider the following examples:

(a) A plc pays £100,000 to acquire 80% of B plc, whose net assets have a fair value of £110,000 at the acquisition date. Calculate the purchased goodwill.

(b) C plc issues 100,000 £1 shares, each with a fair value of £1.20, to acquire 70% of D plc, whose net assets have a book value of £200,000 and a fair value of £250,000. Calculate the purchased goodwill.

(c) E plc has received an offer of £100,000 for all of its equity share capital, at a time when it believes its net assets have a fair value of £80,000. Estimate the inherent goodwill.

1.4 Solutions

(a) Positive purchased goodwill = £100,000 – (80% × £110,000) = £12,000
(b) Negative purchased goodwill = £120,000 – (70% × £250,000) = £55,000
(c) Inherent goodwill = £100,000 – £80,000 = £20,000

1.5 Accounting for goodwill

(a) *Inherent goodwill*

Inherent goodwill should not be recognised in the balance sheet, due to the subjectivity required to value it. It should be ignored.

(b) *Positive purchased goodwill*

Positive purchased goodwill should be recognised as an intangible fixed asset and amortised through the profit and loss account over its useful economic life.

There is a rebuttable presumption that the useful life does not exceed 20 years from the date of acquisition. However it is possible for goodwill to have a life greater than 20 years, or even an indefinite life.

If a useful life of more than 20 years is used, annual impairment reviews must be carried out on the goodwill balance (in accordance with FRS 11 – see later) to demonstrate the durability of the acquired business.

No residual value may be placed on goodwill in calculating the annual amortisation charge. The straight line method of amortisation should normally be used.

(c) *Negative purchased goodwill*

If an acquisition appears to give rise to negative goodwill, first the fair values of the net assets acquired should be checked carefully to ensure that they have not been overstated. Negative goodwill remaining after this check should be recognised and separately disclosed on the face of the balance sheet, immediately below the goodwill heading. A subtotal should show the net total of positive and negative goodwill.

Negative goodwill up to the fair values of the non-monetary assets acquired should be recognised in the profit and loss account in the periods in which the non-monetary assets are recovered, whether through depreciation or sale.

Any negative goodwill in excess of the fair values of the non-monetary assets acquired should be recognised in the profit and loss account in the periods expected to benefit. It would be rare for any excess negative goodwill to arise in this way.

1.6   Example

On 1 January 20X2 XY plc acquired 100% of the share capital of CD plc for £200,000, at which date the summarised balance sheet of CD plc was as follows:

	£
Fixed assets (useful life 10 years)	150,000
Stocks	50,000
Other current assets	30,000
Current liabilities	(20,000)
	210,000

Calculate the credit to the consolidated profit and loss account of XY plc in respect of negative goodwill for the year ended 31 December 20X2.

1.7   Solution

Negative goodwill	= £200,000 – £210,000	= £10,000
Total non-monetary assets acquired	= £150,000 + £50,000	= £200,000

Non-monetary assets recovered in 20X2

	£
Depreciation (£150,000 ÷ 10)	15,000
+ stock sold	50,000
	65,000

$\therefore$ credit for negative goodwill $= \dfrac{65}{200} \times £10,000 = £3,250$

1.8   Accounting for other intangible assets

(a)   *Internally generated intangible assets*

Internally developed intangible assets should be capitalised only where they have a readily ascertainable market value.

(b)   *Purchased intangible assets*

An intangible asset purchased separately from a business should be capitalised at its cost.

An intangible asset acquired as part of the acquisition of a business should be capitalised separately from goodwill if its value can be measured reliably on initial recognition. Otherwise it should be subsumed into the amount of the purchase price paid for goodwill.

Once capitalised, the requirements for amortising intangible assets are the same as for goodwill: they should be amortised over their useful lives, which are assumed to be 20 years or less. If a longer, or even indefinite, life is used, then annual impairment reviews are required.

1.9 Abstract 27: Revision to estimates of the useful economic life of goodwill and intangible assets

FRS 10 contains a rebuttable presumption that the useful lives of purchased goodwill and intangible assets are 20 years or less. The UITF has considered the situation where originally an entity rebutted the presumption (eg believing that the goodwill had an indefinite life) but for the current period no longer wishes to do so. Is this a change in accounting policy (requiring a prior period adjustment) or a change in useful life (accounted for prospectively, not requiring a prior period adjustment)?

The UITF decision is that a decision not to rebut the presumption is **not** a change of accounting policy. It is a change in the estimate of the useful life of the goodwill or intangible asset concerned.

2 SSAP 13: Accounting for research and development

2.1 Introduction

FRS 10 applies to intangible assets in general (including patents, copyrights, brands, know-how, etc) but not to research and development costs, for which a specific accounting standard, SSAP 13, has been developed.

It has proved extremely difficult to standardise the accounting treatment of research and development (R and D) expenditure. This has been because this is an area where two fundamental accounting concepts, those of 'accruals' and of 'prudence' come into head-on conflict. From one point of view, R and D expenditure is incurred for the future development of business, with a view to decreasing future costs or increasing future revenue, so the 'accruals' concept would therefore have R and D expenditure which leads to reduced costs or increased sales carried forward and written off over all the accounting periods which benefit from that expenditure.

The contrary argument holds that it is effectively impossible to judge at any date which R and D expenditure will lead to future benefits, since such a large proportion of such expenditure proves totally abortive, or else turns out to have less than the anticipated future benefit. The 'prudence' concept is then invoked to justify the full write-off of all such expenditure in the year in which it is incurred. The accounting problem is then: which of the two concepts should have precedence?

SSAP 13 gives guidance regarding the appropriate accounting treatment for R and D expenditure, and sets out disclosure requirements.

2.2 Definitions

Research and development activity is distinguished from non-research based activity by the presence or absence of an appreciable element of innovation.

The SSAP classifies R and D expenditure in the following broad categories:

(a) *Pure (or basic) research*: original investigation undertaken in order to gain new scientific or technical knowledge and understanding. Basic research is not primarily directed towards any specific practical aim or application;

(b) *Applied research*: original investigation undertaken in order to gain new scientific or technical knowledge and directed towards a specific practical aim or objective;

(c) *Development*: use of scientific or technical knowledge in order to produce new or substantially improved materials, devices, products, processes, systems or services prior to the commencement of commercial production.

Research and development expenditure as defined by SSAP 13 does *not* include expenditure incurred in locating and exploiting oil, gas and mineral deposits in the extractive industries (but development of new surveying methods and techniques as an integral part of research on geological phenomena is classified as R and D).

2.3   *Examples*

SSAP 13 cites various examples of activities normally included and those normally excluded from R and D.

Normally included

(a)   Experimental, theoretical or other work aimed at the discovery of new knowledge, or the advancement of existing knowledge;

(b)   searching for applications of that knowledge;

(c)   formulation and design of possible applications for such work;

(d)   testing in search for, or evaluation of, product, service or process alternatives;

(e)   design, construction and testing of pre-production prototypes and models and development batches;

(f)   design of products, services, processes or systems involving new technology or substantially improving those already produced or installed;

(g)   construction and operation of pilot plants.

Normally excluded

(a)   Testing and analysis either of equipment or product for purposes of quality or quantity control;

(b)   periodic alterations to existing products, services or processes even though these may represent some improvement;

(c)   operational research not tied to a specific research and development activity;

(d)   cost of corrective action in connection with break-downs during commercial production;

(e)   legal and administrative work in connection with patent applications, records and litigation and the sale or licensing of patents;

(f)   activity, including design and construction engineering, relating to the construction, relocation, rearrangement or start-up of facilities or equipment other than facilities or equipment whose sole use is for a particular research and development project;

(g)   market research.

2.4   *Accounting treatment of fixed assets used in R and D*

The cost of fixed assets acquired or constructed in order to provide facilities for research and development activities over a number of accounting periods should be capitalised and written off over their useful life. Depreciation will be calculated in accordance with FRS 15 and such depreciation may itself form part of development expenditure covered below which will be carried forward to later periods.

2.5   *Other expenditure*

Expenditure on pure and applied research (other than on fixed assets) should be written off through the profit and loss account in the year of expenditure. This is based on the premise that expenditure incurred on pure and applied research can be regarded as part of a continuing operation required to maintain a company's business and its competitive position. In general, one particular period rather than another will not be expected to benefit and therefore it is appropriate that these costs should be written off as they are incurred.

Regarding development expenditure, the Standard argues that the development of new and improved products is, however, distinguishable from pure and applied research. Expenditure on such development is normally undertaken with a reasonable expectation of specific commercial success and of future benefits arising from the work, either from increased revenue and related profits or from reduced costs. On these grounds it may be argued that such expenditure should be deferred to be matched against the future revenue.

In general, SSAP 13 requires that development expenditure should also be written off in the year of expenditure. However, it permits the deferral of such expenditure, to the extent that its recovery can reasonably be regarded as assured, if all the following circumstances apply:

(a)   There is a clearly defined project.

(b)   The related expenditure is separately identifiable.

(c)   The outcome of such a project has been assessed with reasonable certainty as to:

      (i)   its technical feasibility, and

      (ii)   its ultimate commercial viability considered in the light of factors such as likely market conditions (including competing products), public opinion, consumer and environmental legislation.

(d)   The aggregate of the deferred development costs, any further development costs, and related production, selling and administration costs is reasonably expected to be exceeded by related future sales or other revenues.

(e)   Adequate resources exist, or are reasonably expected to be available, to enable the project to be completed and to provide any consequential increases in working capital.

2.6   Illustration

The Ansi Company is midway through development of a new sweet, the 'Tasstea'.

Cash expenditure on development so far has amounted to £164,000 and work has involved the use of a simulator machine for a period of 6 months. The machine cost £40,000 and has a three-year life, and a residual value of £4,000.

Although the project is both technically feasible and commercially viable, further work is required before production can commence. This work is estimated to involve cash expenditure of £27,000 and will require another three months' use of the simulator.

Once production of the new sweet starts, total variable production costs will be 6p per sweet plus 3p packaging plus annual fixed costs of £280,000 including provision for machinery costs. Sales are expected to be 2,000,000 units per month at 12p each, but in order to obtain this level, heavy television advertising of £750,000 is required in the first six months. Demand will remain at the 2 million level for two and a half years and production will then cease.

Adequate resources exist to enable completion of the programme outlined above. Advise whether the development costs to date can be capitalised under SSAP 13.

2.7   Solution

Calculation of future revenues and costs

Selling price per unit		12p
Production cost per unit	6p	
Packaging cost per unit	3p	
		9p
Contribution per unit		3p

	£	£
Contribution per month 3p × 2m = £60,000		
Total contribution £60,000 × 30 months		1,800,000
Fixed costs £280,000 × 2½ yrs		700,000
Advertising		750,000
Future development costs	27,000	
Add: Depreciation on machine (3 months)	3,000	
		30,000
Total costs		1,480,000
Surplus of future revenues over future costs		£320,000

Development costs to date

	£
Cash expenditure	164,000
Add: Depreciation on machine	6,000
Total costs to date	170,000

As this figure of £170,000 is adequately covered by the £320,000 surplus of future revenues over future costs the £170,000 may be deferred until production commences, and then amortised over the two and a half year production period. If the total costs to date had exceeded the surplus of future revenues over future costs then that excess would be written off immediately as irrecoverable.

2.8   Amortisation

Amortisation of deferred development costs should commence with the commercial production of the product or process, and should be allocated on a systematic basis to each accounting period over which the product or process is expected to be sold or used.

Deferred development expenditure should be reviewed at the end of each accounting period and written off to the extent that it is deemed irrecoverable.

In the above example, suppose that the production and sale of the Tasstea commenced in April 20X4. The amortisation of the by then £200,000 development costs (£170,000 + £30,000) would thus begin in the accounts to 31 December 20X4. The notes to the balance sheet would show:

		20X4	£000 20X5	20X6
Intangible fixed assets				
Development costs				
Costs	– b/f	170	200	200
	– additions	30	–	–
	– c/f	200	200	200
Amortisation	– b/f	–	60	140
	– charge (W)	60	80	60
	– c/f	60	140	200
Net book value		140	60	–

WORKING

As sales are expected to arise evenly, amortisation will be pro-rata over 30 months, commencing in April 20X4:

$$20X4 \text{ charge} = 9/30 \times £200,000 \quad = £60,000$$
$$20X5 \text{ charge} = 12/30 \times £200,000 \quad = £80,000 \text{ etc}$$

2.9 Disclosure requirements of SSAP 13

(a) The accounting policy on R and D expenditure should be stated and explained.

(b) The total amount of R and D expenditure charged in the profit and loss account should be disclosed, analysed between the current year's expenditure and amounts amortised from deferred expenditure (see below).

(c) Movements on deferred development expenditure and the amount carried forward at the beginning and end of the period should be disclosed.

(d) Deferred development expenditure should be disclosed under intangible fixed assets in the balance sheet.

Note

The disclosure requirement (b) outlined above applies only to companies that are:

(a) (i) public limited companies;
    (ii) special category companies (eg, banks or insurance companies); or
    (iii) holding companies with a PLC or special category company as a subsidiary;

or

(b) exceed the criteria, multiplied by 10, for defining a medium-sized company (S248 CA 1985).

All the other requirements of SSAP 13 apply to all financial statements intended to give a true and fair view.

3 FRS 11: Impairment of fixed assets and goodwill

3.1 Introduction

We have already met impairment in two places in this text:

(a) FRS 15 requires tangible fixed assets to be written down to their recoverable amount when the carrying amount exceeds the recoverable amount.

(b) FRS 10 requires annual impairment reviews to be carried out whenever a useful life of more than 20 years is selected for goodwill and intangible assets.

The purpose of FRS 11 is to standardise the accounting treatment of impairment, so that impairment losses are recognised on a consistent basis.

3.2 Definitions

Impairment is the reduction in the recoverable amount of a fixed asset or goodwill below its carrying amount.

Recoverable amount is the higher of net realisable value and value in use.

Net realisable value is the amount at which an asset could be disposed of, less any direct selling costs.

Value in use is the present value of the future cash flows arising from an asset's continued use, including those resulting from its ultimate disposal.

3.3   Example

A machine has a net book value of £5,000 in the draft balance sheet as at 31 December 20X3. It could be sold now for £4,000, or retained in the business where it is expected to earn cash inflows of £1,800 pa for each of the next three years after which it will expire worthless. Current interest rates are 10% pa.

Assess whether the machine is impaired at 31 December 20X3.

3.4   Solution

Current book value (= carrying amount) = £5,000

Compare this with the recoverable amount, ie the higher of NRV and value in use.

NRV = £4,000

$$\text{Value in use} = \frac{£1,800}{1.1} + \frac{£1,800}{(1.1)^2} + \frac{£1,800}{(1.1)^3} = £4,476$$

∴ Recoverable amount = £4,476

∴ the machine has a book value of £5,000 but a recoverable amount of only £4,476. It is impaired and should be written down to £4,476 in the balance sheet. An impairment loss of £5,000 – £4,476 = £524 must be recognised.

3.5   Accounting for impairment losses

Impairment losses must be recognised in the profit and loss account, unless they arise on a previously revalued fixed asset. Impairment losses on revalued fixed assets are recognised in the STRGL until the carrying amount of the asset falls below depreciated historical cost (unless the impairment is clearly caused by a consumption of economic benefits, in which case the loss is recognised in the profit and loss account).

Impairments below depreciated historical cost are recognised in the profit and loss account.

3.6   When an impairment review is required

It is not necessary to carry out a test for impairment of all fixed assets and goodwill every year; that would be unnecessarily expensive. Instead, FRS 11 requires that fixed assets and goodwill need only be reviewed for impairment if there is some indication that impairment has occurred.

FRS 15 and FRS 10 contain additional requirements:

♦   FRS 15 requires an annual impairment review whenever the useful life of a tangible fixed asset has been chosen as greater than 50 years.

♦   FRS 10 requires an annual impairment review whenever the useful life of goodwill or an intangible asset has been chosen as greater than 20 years.

3.7   Indicators of impairment

Examples of indications that an impairment may have occurred are as follows:

♦   a current period operating loss or net cash outflow from operating activities

♦   a significant decline in a fixed asset's market value during the period

♦   obsolescence or physical damage to a fixed asset

♦   a significant adverse change in the business or the market in which the fixed asset or goodwill is involved

♦   a management commitment to undertake a significant reorganisation

♦   a major loss of key employees, or

♦   a significant increase in market interest rates

3.8   *Income-generating units*

Where possible, individual fixed assets should be tested for impairment. However, it is possible that cash flows do not arise from a single asset, in which case impairment should be measured for the smallest group of assets that produces a largely independent income stream. This group of assets is called an income-generating unit.

In principle, all the operating assets and liabilities of the reporting entity should be allocated to the various income streams earned by the entity. Certain assets may have to be apportioned across the units on a systematic basis.

3.9   *Example*

ABC plc has three independent income streams X, Y and Z with net assets directly attributable to each of £2m, £3m and £5m. In addition there are central head office net assets with a carrying value of £200,000. The head office provides benefits to each unit in proportion to their net assets.

Determine the total net assets of each income-generating unit for the purposes of an impairment review.

3.10   *Solution*

| | Income-generating unit | | | |
| | X | Y | Z | Total |
	£000	£000	£000	£000
Directly attributable net assets	2,000	3,000	5,000	10,000
Head office net assets				
apportioned to the units	40	60	100	200
Total net assets	2,040	3,060	5,100	10,200

If there was an indication that Unit X might have become impaired, the net assets of £2.04m would be compared with the recoverable amount of Unit X.

If there is no reasonable basis on which to apportion the central net assets between the units, then they should be excluded from the impairment tests on the individual units, but a further impairment test must be carried out on the combined business.

For example, using the figures above, if it is not possible to allocate the head office assets between the units, but there are still indications that Unit X might be impaired, an impairment review is first carried out on Unit X to compare its carrying value of £2m with the recoverable amount. Then an additional review must be carried out to compare the total carrying amount of £10.2m with the recoverable amount of the whole business.

3.11   *Allocation of impairment losses between income-generating units*

To the extent that the carrying amount of an income-generating unit exceeds its recoverable amount, that unit is impaired. In the absence of specific instructions, the impairment loss should be allocated:

(a)   first, to any goodwill in the unit
(b)   next, to any capitalised intangible asset in the unit
(c)   finally, to the tangible assets in the unit (normally on a pro rata basis)

In this allocation, no intangible asset with a readily ascertainable market value should be written down below its net realisable value. Similarly, no tangible asset with a reliably measured net realisable value should be written down below its net realisable value.

3.12   Example

An income-generating unit comprising a factory and associated purchased goodwill has become impaired due to the entry of a more efficient competitor. The draft carrying amounts of the net assets of the unit (before any impairment calculation) are as follows:

	£m
Goodwill	5
Patent (with no market value)	3
Land and buildings	20
Plant and machinery	2
	30

The recoverable amount of the unit has been calculated as £19m. Show how the impairment loss should be allocated.

3.13   Solution

The impairment loss is £30m – £19m = £11m.

This is first allocated to the goodwill, then to the patent, leaving £11m – £5m – £3m = £3m to be allocated pro rata to the tangible fixed assets. The allocation is as follows:

	Before £m	Impairment loss £m	After £m
Goodwill	5	(5)	–
Patent	3	(3)	–
Land and buildings ($\frac{20}{22} \times 3$)	20	(2.7)	17.3
Plant and machinery ($\frac{2}{22} \times 3$)	2	(0.3)	1.7
	30	(11)	19

3.14   Disclosure requirements

In the profit and loss account, impairment losses should be included within operating profit as part of the appropriate statutory headings.

In the notes to the balance sheet, the impairment loss should be included within accumulated historical cost depreciation; the cost of the asset should not be reduced. For revalued assets held at market value, the impairment loss should be included within the revalued carrying amount.

3.15   Learning outcome

You have now covered the following learning outcome:

> Explain the problems of profit measurement and alternative approaches to asset valuations

in the context of accounting for intangible assets.

4 Summary

This chapter has covered three key accounting standards:

♦ FRS 10: Goodwill and intangible assets
♦ SSAP 13: Accounting for research and development
♦ FRS 11: Impairment of fixed assets and goodwill

Any of these could form a large part of an exam question.

Multiple choice questions *(The answers are in the final chapter of this book)*

1   Dodgy Ltd has a property which is currently stated at a revalued net book value of £253,000.

Due to a slump in property prices the value of the property is currently only £180,000.

The historical cost net book value of the property is £207,000.

How should the above impairment in value be reflected in the financial statements in accordance with FRS 11?

	Profit and loss account	*Statement of total recognised gains and losses*
A	Dr £73,000	Cr £46,000
B	Dr £27,000	Dr £46,000
C	Dr £73,000	-
D	-	Dr £73,000

2   On 1 April 20X6 Brook plc established a new research and development unit to acquire scientific knowledge about the use of synthetic chemicals for pain relief. The following expenditures were incurred during the year ended 31 March 20X7.

(1)   Purchase of building for £400,000. The building is to be depreciated on a straight line basis at the rate of 4% per annum on cost.

(2)   Wages and salaries of research staff £2,355,000.

(3)   Scientific equipment costing £60,000 to be depreciated using a reducing balance rate of 50% per annum.

How much of the above research and development expenditure should be written off in the year ended 31 March 20X7?

A   £2,355,000

B   £2,385,000

C   £2,401,000

D   £2,415,000

3   Both FRS 10 and the *Companies Act 1985* deal with accounting for goodwill.

A difference between them is that FRS 10:

A   prohibits the capitalisation of non-purchased goodwill

B   allows purchased goodwill to be amortised over the period of its effective life

C   allows goodwill to have an indefinite life

D   prohibits the revaluation of goodwill

4   Rook Ltd purchased the net assets of a business for £100,000. On the date of purchase the books of the acquired business showed the following assets.

	£	
Goodwill	8,000	(fair value £12,000)
Separable net assets		
Patents	7,000	(fair value £10,000)
Plant	60,000	(fair value £55,000)
Net current assets	15,000	

Under the provisions of FRS 10 the goodwill arising on this purchase was:

A   £8,000

B   £12,000

C   £18,000

D   £20,000

CHAPTER 19

Taxation in company accounts

EXAM FOCUS

Accounting for tax has been a controversial topic in recent years, with FRS 16 on current tax and FRS 19 on deferred tax both being recently issued. You can expect the examiner to be interested in your understanding of these recent accounting standards.

LEARNING OUTCOMES

This chapter covers the following Learning Outcome of the CIMA Syllabus.

> Discuss emerging developments in financial reporting

In order to cover this Learning Outcome the following topics are included.

> SSAP 5: Accounting for value added tax
> FRS 16: Current tax
> Deferred tax
> Bases for providing for deferred tax
> FRS 19: Deferred tax

---

1 SSAP 5: Accounting for value added tax

1.1 Introduction

SSAP 5 is an uncontroversial standard which explains whether amounts in the financial statements should be presented inclusive or exclusive of attributable VAT.

VAT is collected by businesses on behalf of the government. VAT is incurred by a business within the price paid for supplies purchased (an input tax) and levied by the business when it charges for goods sold to its customers (an output tax). The difference between the amount levied and the amount incurred is paid quarterly to HM Customs and Excise. The current rate is $17^1/2\%$. The eventual payer is the consumer who stands at the end of the manufacturing and distribution chain.

1.2 Illustration

If goods are purchased for cash for £100 + VAT, then the accounting entries will be:

	£	£
Dr Purchases (exclusive of VAT)	100	
Dr VAT	17.50	
Cr Cash		117.50

If the goods are then sold for cash for £300 + VAT, the accounting entries will be:

	£	£
Dr Cash	352.50	
Cr Sales (exclusive of VAT)		300
Cr VAT		52.50

Thus the amounts shown for revenue and costs are not affected by VAT. But the net amount (£35) collected for value added tax by the business and owed to Customs and Excise is shown in the VAT account.

VAT account

	£		£
Input tax on purchases	17.50	Output tax on sales	52.50
Balance due to HM Customs and Excise	35.00		
	52.50		52.50
Cash paid	35.00	Balance b/f	35.00
	35.00		35.00

1.3 The standard

SSAP 5 is short and simple. The standard consists of two short paragraphs which are reproduced below, followed by a little necessary explanation.

(a) *Turnover* – Turnover shown in the profit and loss account should exclude VAT on taxable outputs. If it is desired to show also the gross turnover, the VAT relevant to that turnover should be shown as a deduction in arriving at the turnover exclusive of VAT.

(b) *Irrecoverable VAT* – Irrecoverable VAT allocable to fixed assets and to other items disclosed separately in published accounts should be included in their cost where practicable and material.

1.4 Explanation

(a) *Turnover* – Since the trader who is registered for VAT is merely acting as a tax collector by adding VAT to his prices and then paying it over to HM Customs and Excise, it is reasonable and correct to exclude the VAT from turnover.

(b) *Irrecoverable VAT* – When a trader actually bears VAT it is again reasonable and correct that capital and revenue items affected should include that VAT. Cases in which a trader is unable to offset VAT suffered on his purchases are:

    (i)   when the trader is not registered for VAT;

    (ii)   when the trader is carrying on a trade involving 'exempt' activities in whole or part (an exempt trader does not charge VAT on his sales but is not allowed to obtain a refund on VAT suffered on his purchases);

    (iii)   where the legislation specifies that VAT on certain goods is non-deductible. Examples are the purchase of motor cars and business entertaining expenses.

1.5 Example

A trader who is registered for VAT purchases a new car for £10,000 + VAT at 17.5%. The car will be scrapped after five years when worthless. How will the car be shown in the financial statements after one year of ownership?

1.6 Solution

VAT on the purchase of cars is irrecoverable, so the cost of the car is shown in the balance sheet at £10,000 × 1.175 = £11,750. The depreciation for the first year will be £11,750 ÷ 5 = £2,350.

So the net book value in the balance sheet is £11,750 – £2,350 = £9,400, and the depreciation charged in the profit and loss account is £2,350.

2 FRS 16: Current tax

2.1 Introduction

The current tax for a company is the amount of corporation tax estimated to be payable in respect of the taxable profit for the year, along with adjustments to estimates in respect of previous periods.

Now that advance corporation tax (ACT) has been abolished in the UK, FRS 16 explains how amounts should be presented in the financial statements concerning current tax. We start with a simple revision of the principles of corporation tax.

2.2 Corporation tax

Companies pay corporation tax on their profits. The current rate of corporation tax is 30% normally but companies with 'small' profits pay corporation tax at 19% only. In examination questions you will normally be told the rate, and often the amount, of corporation tax.

It is obvious that the corporation tax charge cannot be calculated until after the profit figure has been found. When preparing a profit and loss account, provision must be made for the corporation tax payable on those profits.

2.3 Illustration 1

A company makes an operating profit before taxation of £300,000. Corporation tax is estimated at £105,000. (The corporation tax charge is not 30% of the accounting profit before tax, since accounting profits are adjusted to calculate the taxable profit before tax.)

Profit and loss account (extract) for the year

	£
Profit on ordinary activities before taxation	300,000
Tax on profit on ordinary activities	
Corporation tax based on the profit of the year @ 30%	105,000
Profit on ordinary activities after taxation	195,000

Corporation tax account

	£		£
Balance c/f	105,000	Profit and loss	105,000
	105,000		105,000
		Balance b/f	105,000

The balance on the corporation tax account is carried forward and will appear on the balance sheet under the 'creditors within one year' heading. The full description given in the profit and loss account above is required either on the face of the profit and loss account as shown, or in the notes to the accounts.

2.4 Due dates for payment

Companies with large profits are required to pay their corporation tax due by quarterly equal instalments. For other companies, corporation tax is payable nine months after the end of the company's accounting period. In the profit and loss account above, being (say) to 31 December 20X1, the corporation tax we have identified will be payable on 1 October 20X2. In the statutory accounts the amount of £105,000 will be included in:

'Creditors: amounts falling due within one year'

and within that heading it will be included under the description:

'Other creditors, including taxation and social security'.

2.5 Adjustments relating to prior years

When the provision for corporation tax is made in the accounts, it is only an estimate of the actual liability which will eventually be agreed with HM Inspectors of Taxes. Any difference between the original estimate and the actual figure will be adjusted in the next year's provision. If material this figure will be shown separately.

2.6 Illustration 1, continued

In 20X2 the company pays £99,000 corporation tax on the 20X1 profit on 1 October (not the £105,000 as estimated). The profit for the year 20X2 is £400,000 and corporation tax is estimated at £132,000.

Profit and loss account (extract) 20X2

	£	£
Profit on ordinary activities before taxation		400,000
Tax on profit on ordinary activities		
Corporation tax based on the profit of the year @ 30%	132,000	
Adjustment for overprovision in previous year	(6,000)	
		(126,000)
Profit on ordinary activities after taxation		274,000

Corporation tax account

	£		£
1.10.X2 Bank	99,000	1.1.X2 Balance b/f	105,000
31.12.X2 Profit and loss overprovision	6,000	31.12.X2 Profit and loss	132,000
31.12.X2 Balance c/f	132,000		
	237,000		237,000
		1.1.X3 Balance b/f	132,000

2.7 Dividends received and paid

When a UK company receives a dividend from another UK company, this dividend is paid out of profits on which corporation tax has already been paid. This income in the hands of the recipient company is therefore fully taxed and no further tax is payable on it.

The question arises as to whether dividends received and paid should be shown in the profit and loss account inclusive or exclusive of attributable tax credits.

A *tax credit* is given under UK tax legislation to the recipient of a dividend from a UK company, to discharge or reduce the recipient's liability to tax on the dividend.

For example, if an investor receives a cash dividend of £900 when tax credits are available at a rate of $\frac{1}{9}$th of the cash dividend, then the gross amount of the dividend (called the 'franked investment income') would be £1,000.

Should the company receiving this dividend show it at £900 or £1,000? Should the company paying this dividend show it at £900 or £1,000?

 FRS 16 states that dividends receivable and payable should be shown **excluding** attributable tax credits. Both the paying and the receiving company should show this dividend at £900 in the profit and loss account.

2.8   Interest and other amounts received and paid

When a company makes certain payments, eg. debenture interest or royalty payments, it is required to deduct income tax (at 20% for interest payments) from these payments, paying the net amount to the payee, and the tax deducted to the Inland Revenue. For example, if company A Limited pays £10,000 debenture interest gross, it will pay:

	£
To the payee	8,000
To the Revenue	2,000
	10,000

This is, of course, very similar to what a company does when it pays salaries; it pays the net amount to the employee and the tax is paid to the Revenue under PAYE. Similarly, if a company receives these types of income, the paying company will have deducted income tax from the payment and paid it to the Revenue, so that the receiving company only receives the net amount.

Note that the paying company is simply acting as a *collector* of the tax which it then pays to the Revenue. Consider again the analogy with PAYE. When the company pays this tax to the Revenue it is not paying part of its own liability; it is simply collecting that tax on behalf of the Revenue. The tax it pays over is the liability of the employee. It is exactly the same with the tax deducted by the company when making these payments. In the example above, when A Limited pays £2,000 income tax to the Revenue, it is not paying part of its own liability but the liability of those who receive the payments.

2.9   Accounting entries

FRS 16 is framed in terms of withholding tax.

A *withholding tax* is tax on dividends or other income that is deducted by the payer of the income and paid to the tax authorities wholly on behalf of the recipient.

 FRS 16 states that all interest and other amounts payable or receivable should be shown *including* withholding taxes.

Therefore amounts paid and received as interest or royalties are grossed up by the amount of the tax deducted, and shown in the profit and loss account at their *gross* amount. Income tax on payments made is debited to the appropriate expense account and then credited to the income tax account to record the liability to the Inland Revenue. Income tax on amounts received is credited to the appropriate revenue account, and debited to the income tax account, thus reducing the credit balance to be paid over to the Revenue.

2.10   Illustration

Exe plc pays debenture interest of £50,000 gross and receives a royalty of £40,000 gross. Assume for simplicity that income tax is deducted from both amounts at 20%. Each amount is shown gross in the profit and loss account and the income tax suffered on the royalty is set off against tax deducted from the debenture interest when payment is made to the Inland Revenue.

Debenture interest			
	£		£
Cash	40,000	Profit and loss	50,000
Income tax (20%)	10,000		
	50,000		50,000

Royalties received

	£			£
Profit and loss	40,000	Cash		32,000
		Income tax (20%)		8,000
	40,000			40,000

Income tax

	£		£
Royalties	8,000	Debenture interest	10,000
Cash paid	2,000		
	10,000		10,000

2.11 Disclosure summary

The purpose of FRS 16 is to standardise the treatment of current taxation in company accounts, so to summarise this section we will concentrate on the taxation disclosures in the profit and loss account and the balance sheet.

(a) *Profit and loss account*

			£
(i)	*Income*		
	Dividends received from UK companies (net ie, not grossed up for tax credits)		X
	Interest and royalties received (gross up for income tax deducted)		X
(ii)	*Expenditure*		
	Debenture interest paid (grossed up for income tax deducted)		X
	Tax on profits on ordinary activities (Note)		X

Note: Tax on profits on ordinary activities

	£
Corporation tax on ordinary activities @ 30%	X
Under/(over) provision in previous year	X/(X)
	X

(b) *Balance sheet*

	£
Creditors: amounts falling due within one year	
Proposed dividend (not grossed up for tax credits)	X
Other creditors including taxation and social security	
Income tax due to Revenue (difference between IT deducted from debenture interest paid and IT suffered on royalty income)	X
Corporation tax payable (this year's CT charge)	X

Practice question 1 *(The answer is in the final chapter of this book)*

Rubislaw plc

Rubislaw plc was formed in 20X0. During the year to 31 December 20X3 the following payments of tax were made:

	£
Corporation tax – accounting period ended 31.12.X2	69,000
Income tax	5,000

At 1.1.X3 the balance on the taxation account was £76,500, made up as follows:

	£
Corporation tax – accounting period ended 31.12.X2	74,000
Income tax	2,500

The company has in issue £200,000 10% debentures. Interest is paid by the company on 30 June and 31 December each year.

The company received the following income during the year to 31.12.X3.

	£
Dividend (received on 15 December 20X3)	800
Debenture interest	2,250

The profit for tax purposes was estimated at £150,000.

The company proposed a dividend of £30,000.

The corporation tax rate is 30%.

Income tax is deducted from interest payments and receipts at a rate of 20%.

Required

Disclose how the above should be presented in the profit and loss account for the year ended 31 December 20X3 and in the balance sheet as at that date, in a form suitable for presentation to the members of Rubislaw plc.

---

3   Deferred tax

3.1   Introduction

Deferred tax can crop up as a question in its own right in the examination. Alternatively, you may have to deal with deferred tax as one element of a question on published accounts. The standard accounting for deferred tax has changed recently with the issue of FRS 19 in December 2000.

3.2   Accounting profits and taxable profits

 The amount of current taxation payable on the profits of a particular period may bear little relationship to the reported profit before tax appearing in the published accounts. The difference comes from two main sources: permanent differences and timing differences.

Permanent differences arise where items taken into account for the purpose of the financial accounts are disallowable or non-taxable for tax purposes. An example might be disallowable entertaining expenses. This is a permanent difference because no tax relief will ever be received for such expenditure, even though it is quite properly deducted as an expense when computing accounting profits.

Timing differences arise when certain types of income and expenditure are recognised in different periods for the purpose of financial accounts on the one hand and taxation on the other.

3.3   An example of timing differences

An example of a timing difference is that depreciation charges appear in the financial accounts, but are not allowed as an expense for tax purposes. Instead, *capital allowances* reduce taxable profits. Over the lifetime of a fixed asset total depreciation charges will equal (roughly) total capital allowances. However, in any particular accounting period the two amounts will differ — a timing difference.

The common feature of timing differences, which distinguishes them from permanent differences, is simply this: timing differences *originate* in one period and are capable of *reversal* in later periods.

Deferred taxation is a system of dealing with the distortions caused by timing differences. It is not concerned at all with permanent differences. The objective of deferred taxation is to ensure that the tax charge shown in the profit and loss account is not out of line with the amount of profit earned.

Without deferred taxation, the tax charge in the profit and loss account would be based on the actual current liability payable to the Inland Revenue. This would have the following effects.

♦ In a year when tax allowances (eg capital allowances) are high compared to the expenditure shown in the accounts (eg depreciation) our tax liability will be *lower* than our reported profits would suggest.

♦ In a year when capital allowances fall short of depreciation charges our tax liability will be *higher* than our reported profits would suggest.

To overcome this problem, the tax charge shown in the profit and loss account is not simply the tax liability agreed with the Inland Revenue. Instead, it is this liability adjusted − up or down − by an amount reflecting the value of timing differences.

3.4 Example

A company makes a profit of £100,000 (after depreciation but before taxation) each year. The company buys an asset in Year 1 costing £40,000 and claims a 25% writing down allowance on the reducing balance basis each year.

Depreciation policy is to write off the cost of the asset over five years on a straight line basis. The rate of corporation tax is 30%.

Show the company's tax liability for each of the years from Year 1 to Year 6.

3.5 Solution

A tabular layout is needed.

	Year 1 £	Year 2 £	Year 3 £	Year 4 £	Year 5 £	Year 6 £
Profit before tax	100,000	100,000	100,000	100,000	100,000	100,000
Add back depreciation	8,000	8,000	8,000	8,000	8,000	
	108,000	108,000	108,000	108,000	108,000	100,000
Less capital allowances	(10,000)	(7,500)	(5,625)	(4,218)	(3,164)	(2,373)
Taxable profit	98,000	100,500	102,375	103,782	104,836	97,627
Tax at 30%	29,400	30,150	30,712	31,135	31,451	29,288

We can see from this that the tax liability is not the same as 'profit before tax × corporation tax rate' (£100,000 × 30% = £30,000).

♦ In Year 1 the liability is less than this: we have deferred some tax by virtue of generous capital allowances exceeding the depreciation charge.

♦ In Years 2 to 5 the liability is greater than £30,000: the originating timing difference reverses.

This example shows the accounting problem very clearly. The company's operating performance is identical in each of the six years, and yet its tax liability differs from one year to the next. Deferred tax is designed to remove this kind of distortion.

4   Bases for providing for deferred tax

4.1   Possible approaches

Three possible approaches have been suggested to deal with the problem of timing differences: nil provision, full provision and partial provision.

Nil provision, as the name suggests, means that we simply ignore the problem. In the example above, the tax charge shown in our profit and loss account each year would simply be the liability payable to the Inland Revenue. We would resign ourselves to the distortions caused by timing differences.

Full provision means that we adjust our tax liability in respect of every timing difference we can identify. The tax charge reported in the profit and loss account is this adjusted liability.

Partial provision is the middle course. We provide for deferred tax on timing differences *only if their reversal in later years is probable.* Where a timing difference is likely to persist for some time into the future we ignore it.

This is summarised in Figure 1.

Figure 1. Alternative approaches to timing differences

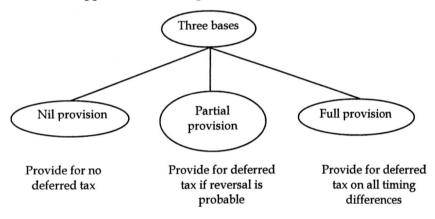

4.2   Example: full provision basis

Peter Ltd was incorporated on 1 April 20X1. In the year ended 31 March 20X2 the company made a profit before tax of £100,000 (after charging depreciation of £10,000) and made the following capital additions.

Plant	£48,000
Motor vehicles	£12,000

Corporation tax is chargeable at the rate of 30%, and writing down allowances are available at 25%.

Required

Compute the following

(a)   The corporation tax payable for the year ended 31 March 20X2.

(b)   The deferred tax charge for the year on the basis that full provision is made for all originating timing differences, showing also the relevant extracts from the financial statements.

4.3 Approach to the example

Start with the accounting profit, then add back the depreciation and deduct the capital allowance to find the taxable profit.

	£
Reported profit	100,000
Add back depreciation	10,000
	110,000
Less capital allowance (48,000 + 12,000) × 25%	(15,000)
Taxable profit	95,000

Remember that tax payable is calculated on taxable profit not accounting profit. Tax payable is therefore £95,000 × 30% = £28,500.

To calculate the amount of tax deferred, you need first of all to identify the timing difference by comparing accumulated depreciation to cumulative capital allowances.

	£
Depreciation	10,000
Capital allowance	(15,000)
Originating timing difference	(5,000)

To calculate the amount of tax deferred simply apply the current tax rate to the timing difference. Tax deferred is therefore £5,000 × 30% = £1,500.

You will then need to make a provision for deferred tax. The double entry is as follows.

Debit   Taxation charge (profit and loss)

Credit   Provision for deferred tax (shown in the balance sheet under 'Provisions for liabilities and charges')

This leads to the following extracts from the accounts.

EXTRACT FROM BALANCE SHEET

	£
Provisions for liabilities and charges	
Deferred tax	1,500

EXTRACT FROM PROFIT AND LOSS ACCOUNT	£	£
Profit before tax		100,000
Taxation		
UK corporation tax at 30%	28,500	
Deferred tax	1,500	
		30,000
Profit after tax		70,000

5 FRS 19: Deferred tax

5.1 Introduction

The previous accounting standard, SSAP 15, required the partial provision basis for calculating deferred tax. However this had two main disadvantages:

(a)   it relies on forecasts of the future to determine which timing differences will reverse, so is subjective

(b)   it is contrary to the International Accounting Standard on deferred tax which requires full provision.

In December 2000 the ASB therefore brought the UK into line with international practice by issuing FRS 19 which requires the full provision basis for calculating deferred tax.

5.2   The requirements of FRS 19

Deferred tax must be recognised in full on the following sorts of timing differences:

♦   accelerated capital allowances (as seen earlier, where the capital allowances granted against taxable profits exceeds the depreciation charge made against accounting profits)

♦   accruals for pension costs that will be deductible for tax purposes only when paid

♦   elimination of unrealised intragroup profits on consolidation

♦   unrelieved tax losses

♦   other short-term timing differences (those that originate in one period and are expected to reverse in the following period).

Deferred tax should not be recognised when:

♦   a fixed asset is revalued without there being any commitment to sell the asset, or
♦   the gain on sale of an asset is rolled over into replacement assets.

5.3   Discounting and deferred tax

Deferred tax is calculated to take account of future reversals of accumulated timing differences, so the question arises as to whether the future reversals should be discounted to their present values. FRS 19 is slightly unsatisfactory in that it permits but does not require a policy of discounting deferred tax assets and liabilities.

5.4   Tax rate to be used

Deferred tax should be calculated using the average tax rates that are expected to apply in the periods in which the timing differences are expected to reverse, based on tax rates that have been enacted by the balance sheet date.

Usually, future tax rates will not be known, so the current rate of tax is used as the best estimate of the future rate in force when the reversal occurs.

5.5   Learning outcome

You have now covered the following learning outcome insofar as it relates to the accounting for tax.

Discuss emerging developments in financial reporting.

6   Summary

SSAP 5 deals with the accounting for VAT. Turnover should be shown in the profit and loss account exclusive of VAT. All costs should be shown exclusive of recoverable VAT but inclusive of irrecoverable VAT.

FRS 16 deals with current tax. All dividends, interest and other amounts payable or receivable should be shown in the profit and loss account at amounts

♦   including withholding taxes, but
♦   excluding attributable tax credits

This means that dividends received and paid are shown at the actual cash amount received or paid, while interest received and paid is grossed up for any income tax deducted.

FRS 19 deals with deferred tax. Deferred tax is required to be calculated under the full provision basis. This is easier to calculate than the partial provision basis which was required by the old SSAP 15, so FRS 19 should be welcomed by students and teachers.

Multiple choice questions *(The answers are in the final chapter of this book)*

1   The following information relating to taxation appears in the records of Stapley plc.

	£
Balance on corporation tax account on 1 January 20X2	187,500
Corporation tax paid in 20X2 in respect of the year ended 31 December 20X1	194,300
Estimated corporation tax for the year ended 31 December 20X2	137,600

The corporation tax liability on 31 December 20X2 is:

A   £194,300
B   £187,500
C   £137,600
D   £130,800

2   The following information relates to the tax matters of Easton Ltd for the year ended 30 September 20X5.

	£
Estimated corporation tax for the year ended 30 September 20X5	189,000
Debenture interest received (gross)	23,000

Assume a rate of income tax of 20%.

What is the amount to be included in 'Creditors: amounts falling due within one year' in respect of the tax liability on 30 September 20X5?

A   £183,250
B   £184,400
C   £189,000
D   £193,600

3   A company received and paid the following net amounts during the six months ended 30 June 20X8.

	Net receipt	Net payment
Royalties	£8,000	
Debenture interest		£32,000

Assume a rate of income tax of 20%.

The amounts for royalties received and debenture interest paid to be shown in the half year's profit and loss account for the six months ended 30 June are:

	Royalties received	*Debenture interest paid*
A	£8,000	£32,000
B	£8,000	£40,000
C	£10,000	£32,000
D	£10,000	£40,000

4   Which of the following is an example of a permanent difference for deferred tax purposes?

A   Accelerated capital allowances
B   Interest received and paid
C   Entertaining expenses
D   Pension costs

CHAPTER 20

Pensions

EXAM FOCUS

Accounting for pension costs is another area where UK practice found itself out of line with international practice, so the ASB has recently issued FRS 17 to bring the UK more in line. Since FRS 17 is recent, the examiner will be keen to test it soon.

LEARNING OUTCOMES

This chapter covers the following Learning Outcome of the CIMA Syllabus.

Explain the recognition and valuation issues concerned with pension schemes and the treatment of actuarial deficits and surpluses

In order to cover this Learning Outcome the following topics are included.

Types of pension scheme
Accounting for defined contribution schemes
Accounting for defined benefit schemes

1 Types of pension scheme

1.1 Introduction

Over the past 40 years there has been a huge increase in the number and importance of pension schemes in the UK:

♦ very many employers offer pension scheme membership to their employees as part of the remuneration package offered

♦ the Government is keen to encourage individuals to have their own pension arrangements rather than rely on the State scheme, therefore tax benefits are offered

♦ as a category, pension schemes own a large proportion of the issued share capital of all public companies

The cost of pension provision to companies has increased accordingly. In November 2000 the ASB issued FRS 17 *Retirement benefits* to regulate accounting in this area.

1.2 Two sorts of scheme

There are two sorts of pension scheme available:

(a) In a **defined contribution scheme**, an employer pays regular contributions into the scheme which are fixed as an amount or as a percentage of pay. On retirement, the size of the member's benefits depends on the size of the fund which has accumulated to that date. This will depend on the size of the amounts paid in, and the investment returns achieved by the scheme managers.

(b)   In a **defined benefit scheme**, the scheme rules define the benefits payable, independently of the contributions paid in. The size of the benefits payable is not directly related to the investment performance of the scheme assets.

1.3   Examples

(a)   H plc operates a pension scheme where 5% of an employee's gross pay is deducted and paid to the scheme, along with an 8% contribution paid by the company. No promise is made as to the size of pension to be paid; this depends on the size of the fund of assets accumulated at the date of retirement.

(b)   I plc operates a pension scheme where the same 5% and 8% of gross pay are currently paid to the scheme respectively by the employee and employer. On retirement, the scheme promises to pay a pension calculated as

$$\frac{\text{Number of years worked}}{60} \times \text{Salary at retirement date}$$

For example, an employee who has worked 20 years for the company and retires when earning £45,000 pa would receive an annual pension of $\frac{20}{60} \times £45,000 = £15,000$ pa from the scheme.

What type of pension scheme are (a) and (b) above?

1.4   Solution

(a)   H plc has a defined contribution scheme.
(b)   I plc has a defined benefit scheme.

1.5   Funded and unfunded schemes

In a **funded scheme**, the employer pays the contributions to an external pension fund which is legally separate from the employer. If the employer company is wound up, the pension scheme assets are still secure for the employees.

In an **unfunded scheme**, there is no separate fund of assets. The employer pays the pensions due, directly out of the company's assets. This is much less secure for the employees; if the company is wound up, the employees' pension rights are just one of many liabilities to be settled out of the available assets.

1.6   Funding and accounting

A final distinction to be made is between funding a scheme and the accounting cost of contributing to a scheme. Funding relates to the actual transfer of assets from the employer company to the scheme. For example, a company might pay £1m cash to a scheme every other year. Each year in the profit and loss account must be shown the expense of pension provision; this accounting charge must comply with the accruals concept, so a regular amount must be charged each year. For example, the company paying £1m every second year might decide on an appropriate accounting cost of £0.5m pa.

2   Accounting for defined contribution schemes

2.1   Introduction

Accounting for a defined contribution scheme is simple, since the employer company has no further liability after paying the agreed contributions payable to the scheme.

2.2   Profit and loss account

The pension cost for a period is equal to the contributions payable to the scheme for the period.

2.3   Balance sheet

A prepayment or accrual might arise if the employer company has made too large or too small payments to the scheme. These will be shown in current assets or current liabilities in the normal way.

3   Accounting for defined benefit schemes

3.1   Introduction

This is more complicated, since estimates of the future will be required, concerning future investment returns, future salary increases, deaths before retirement etc. The professional advice of an actuary is required to advise on such matters. The actuary will recommend a contribution rate to be applied now to build up sufficient assets to meet the future liabilities of the scheme.

In practice, an actuary usually carries out a full actuarial valuation every three years to ensure that the scheme's assets are sufficient and to identify any shortfall or surplus of assets.

3.2   Measuring the assets of defined benefit schemes

Defined benefit scheme assets should be measured at fair value, so that:

♦   quoted securities should be at mid-market value
♦   unquoted securities should be at estimated fair value
♦   property should be at open market value

3.3   Measuring the liabilities of defined benefit schemes

The scheme liabilities comprise the benefits promised under the formal terms of the scheme, plus any constructive obligations for further benefits that the employer cannot avoid.

The scheme liabilities should be measured using an actuarial basis, ie estimating the future cash flows arising under the actuarial assumptions and then discounting these cash flows at an appropriate discount rate.

3.4   Accounting for the surplus or shortfall

The excess/shortfall in the value of the assets over the present value of the liabilities is the actuarial surplus/deficit in the scheme. The employer and actuary will consult on whether and how to clear the surplus or deficit.

The employer should recognise a surplus as an asset in his balance sheet to the extent that he will benefit from reduced contributions in the future or refunds from the scheme.

The employer should recognise a deficit as a liability in his balance sheet to the extent that it reflects a legal or constructive obligation.

The asset or liability arising should be shown on the face of the balance sheet separately from any sundry prepayments or accruals arising from the timing of the payments of contributions to the scheme.

3.5 *Illustration of disclosure of pension asset*

FRS 17 requires any defined benefit asset or liability to be shown on the face of the balance sheet after all other assets and liabilities, for example as follows:

X plc
Balance sheet as at 31 December 20X2

	£m	£m
Fixed assets		X
Current assets	X	
Creditors: amounts falling due within one year	(X)	
Net current assets		X
Total assets less current liabilities		X
Creditors: amounts falling due after more than one year		(X)
Net assets excluding pension asset		X
Pension asset		X
Net assets including pension asset		X
Capital and reserves		X

3.6 *Recognition in the performance statements*

The pension costs and credits for the period must be recognised in the profit and loss account and the STRGL. Let us first consider the categories of expenses and income that must be recognised:

Expenses

(a) Current service cost – the increase in the present value of the scheme liabilities expected to arise from employee service in the current period

(b) Past service cost – the increase in the present value of the scheme liabilities related to employee service in prior periods arising in the current period (for example, due to improved benefits offered)

(c) Interest cost – the expected increase during the period in the present value of the scheme liabilities because the benefits are one period closer to settlement.

Income

(a) Expected return on assets – the average rate of return (including both income and change in fair value) expected over the life of the obligation on the actual assets held by the scheme. This return should be based on long-term expectations and should be reasonably stable, and will be chosen on the advice of actuaries.

Items that could be expenses or income

(a) Actuarial gains and losses – changes in actuarial deficits or surpluses that arise due to actual events not coinciding with previous actuarial assumptions (experience gains and losses), or changes in actuarial assumptions

(b) Gains or losses on settlements and curtailments – pension obligations can be settled (eg, an employee is paid a cash sum to transfer out to another scheme) or curtailed (eg, reducing the benefits that employees will be paid).

FRS 17 requires that each of the above items should be shown in the performance statements according to the substance of the item.

3.7 The profit and loss account

In the profit and loss account:

(a) the current service cost and the past service cost are charged as an expense against operating profit

(b) the interest cost is netted off against the expected return on assets and the net charge or credit is shown as a finance cost adjacent to other interest receivable or payable.

3.8 The statement of total recognised gains and losses

Actuarial gains and losses are of the nature of revaluation items, so they are recognised in the STRGL (like on revaluation of tangible fixed assets).

3.9 Settlements and curtailments

Normal settlements and curtailments (eg, employees retiring early or transferring out of the scheme) are allowed for in the actuarial assumptions, so any gains or losses arising are actuarial gains and losses.

However some settlements and curtailments arise from a specific decision of the employer (eg, to close down a particular operation). Gains or losses arising from such events are part of the employer's operating results for the period.

3.10 Example

Anouska plc operates a defined benefit pension scheme for its employees. On 1 January 20X1 the pension fund assets had a fair value of £2m but there was a deficit on the fund of £100,000. The expected return on plan assets for the year was 10% and the appropriate rate for discounting the liabilities was 8%.

During 20X1 there were no material settlements or curtailments, but the following totals are relevant for the year:

	£000
Contributions paid to the scheme	300
Benefits paid by the scheme to pensioners	260
Current service cost	270

At 31 December 20X1 the pension fund assets had a fair value of £2.1m but the deficit had increased to £200,000.

You are required to explain how the amounts in respect of the pension scheme should be reported in the financial statements of Anouska plc at 31 December 20X1.

3.11 Solution

First we must reconcile the movements on the assets and liabilities of the pension fund during the year. The balancing figure in each column is the actuarial gain or loss arising in the year.

	Assets £000	Liabilities £000
Balance b/f, 1 January 20X1	2,000	2,100
Expected return (10% × 2,000)	200	
Interest cost (8% × 2,100)		168
Current service cost		270
Benefits paid out	(260)	(260)
Contributions paid in	300	
Gain/loss (balancing figure)	(140)	22
Balance c/f, 31 December 20X1	2,100	2,300

There is a loss on the assets of £140,000 and a loss on the liabilities of £22,000, ie a total actuarial loss of £162,000.

The financial statements at 31 December 20X1 will include the following amounts:

♦ the balance sheet will include the pension liability of £200,000 as at the balance sheet date.

♦ the profit and loss account will include an operating expense of £270,000 for the current service cost, and a net £32,000 finance credit for the net of the £200,000 expected return on assets and £168,000 interest charge on the liabilities.

♦ the STRGL will include the £162,000 actuarial loss arising in the year.

3.12 Disclosures

FRS 17 requires the following disclosures

(a)   For defined contribution schemes

    (i)   the nature of the scheme (ie, defined contribution)
    (ii)   the pension cost for the period
    (iii)   any outstanding or prepaid contributions at the balance sheet date

(b)   For defined benefit schemes

    (i)   the nature of the scheme (ie, defined benefit)

    (ii)   the date of the most recent full actuarial valuation

    (iii)   the contributions made in respect of the accounting period

    (iv)   special disclosures for closed schemes (closed to new members)

    (v)   the main financial assumptions used (eg, rate of salary increase)

    (vi)   the fair value and expected return on assets, split between equities, bonds and other

    (vii)   analysis of amounts included in the profit and loss account

    (viii) analysis of amounts included in the STRGL

    (ix)   historical record for the current period and previous four periods of amounts recognised in the STRGL

    (x)   analysis of the movements in the surplus/deficit in the scheme over the period

For example, the analysis required for this last point for Anouska plc would look as follows:

	£000
Deficit in scheme at start of the year	(100)
Current service cost	(270)
Contributions paid to the scheme	300
Finance income arising in the year (200 – 168)	32
Actuarial loss arising in the year (140 + 22)	(162)
Deficit in scheme at end of the year	(200)

3.13 Implementation of FRS 17

When FRS 17 was issued in 2000, it introduced significant changes to the accounting for pension costs in the accounts of UK companies, so a long period was permitted before it became mandatory. Full adoption was necessary for accounting periods ending on or after 22 June 2003.

As that date approached, it seemed unwise to force implementation with FRS 17 in 2003, when compliance with the relevant international standard (IAS 19) would be required in 2005. There are significant differences between FRS 17 and IAS 19 as it is currently drafted. In particular, FRS 17 requires the immediate recognition of actuarial gains and losses in the STRGL, while IAS 19 requires actuarial gains or losses to be recognised over a number of years in the profit and loss account once they have exceeded a corridor limit.

The ASB continues to believe that the FRS 17 approach is preferable, and hopes to convince the IASB to issue a revised IAS 19 along the lines of FRS 17 before 2005.

Regardless of whether they are successful in convincing the IASB, or not, in November 2002 the ASB revised FRS 17 to defer the full implementation date. Although earlier adoption is encouraged, full implementation is now required for accounting periods beginning on or after 1 January 2005.

3.14 Learning outcome

You have now covered the following learning outcome:

Explain the recognition and valuation issues concerned with pension schemes and the treatment of actuarial deficits and surpluses

4 Summary

FRS 17 is a recent standard dealing with the accounting for pension costs and other retirement benefits. Items must be shown in the balance sheet, profit and loss account and STRGL according to the substance of each individual item.

Multiple choice questions *(The answers are in the final chapter of this book)*

1   The employees of Denver Ltd receive a pension on retirement based upon a formula which involves the number of years worked and the employee's final salary at the date of retirement. The employees pay 4% of their gross salary into the pension scheme each month and the employer contributes 7% of gross salary.

       The employees of Vegas Ltd also contribute 4% of their gross salary into the company pension scheme and the employer contributes 9%. The pension received on retirement by each employee depends upon the size of the investment fund which has accumulated at the date of retirement.

What type of pension scheme is being run by Denver Ltd and Vegas Ltd?

	Denver Ltd	*Vegas Ltd*
A	Funded	Unfunded
B	Unfunded	Funded
C	Defined benefit	Defined contribution
D	Defined contribution	Defined benefit

2   Which of the following elements of the pension cost to a company would not appear in the profit and loss account?

A   Past service cost

B   Expected return on assets

C   Current service cost

D   Actuarial losses

CHAPTER 21

Reporting the substance of transactions

EXAM FOCUS

As part of the reliability characteristic, the Statement of Principles requires transactions to be accounted for in accordance with their substance. This requirement is then amplified in FRS 5. A whole question could be set on your understanding of this principle.

LEARNING OUTCOMES

This chapter covers the following Learning Outcome of the CIMA Syllabus.

Discuss the principle of Substance over Form to a range of transactions

In order to cover this Learning Outcome the following topics are included.

The principle of substance over form
FRS 5: Reporting the substance of transactions
Application notes of FRS 5

1 The principle of substance over form

1.1 Introduction

The principle of substance over form is first seen in the ASB's Statement of Principles, which identifies reliability as a desirable characteristic of financial information. Information is reliable when it represents faithfully what it purports to represent ie, transactions and events must be accounted for and presented in accordance with their substance and economic reality and not merely their legal form.

1.2 Example

X plc sells goods on sale or return. At the balance sheet date goods costing £1,000 to X plc have been provisionally sold for £1,500, but the purchaser still has the right to return the goods without penalty. This right expires in one month's time.

How should these goods be shown in the financial statements at the balance sheet date?

1.3 Solution

The economic substance is that no genuine sale has yet occurred, because the 'purchaser' can still return the goods. Therefore no sale should be recognised yet; the goods should be shown as stock at their cost of £1,000.

2 FRS 5: Reporting the substance of transactions

2.1 Introduction

FRS 5 was issued to give detailed guidance on the application of the substance over form principle. The standard contains advice on:

(a)   how to determine the substance of a transaction
(b)   whether any resulting assets and liabilities should be included on the balance sheet
(c)   disclosures
(d)   application to specific examples (in Application Notes at the end of the FRS)

2.2 Definitions

FRS 5 repeats the definitions of assets and liabilities from the Statement of Principles:

Assets are rights or other access to future economic benefits controlled by an entity as a result of past transactions or events.

Liabilities are an entity's obligations to transfer economic benefits as a result of past transactions or events.

2.3 Determining the substance of a transaction

The key step in determining the substance of any transaction is to identify whether it has given rise to new assets or liabilities of the entity, and whether it has increased or decreased the entity's existing assets or liabilities.

In the example above of the company selling goods on sale or return, as at the balance sheet date no valid debtor can be recognised for the provisional sale of £1,500. Since no new asset or liability has been creased by the provisional sale, the substance is that nothing has happened, so the goods should remain in stock at their cost of £1,000.

FRS 5 has been criticised for taking an unashamedly balance-sheet-oriented view of substance, rather than considering what should appear in the profit and loss account. Substance is defined in terms of the impact on assets and liabilities in the balance sheet.

2.4 Recognition in the balance sheet

Once identified, an asset or liability should be included in the balance sheet provided that:

(a)   there is sufficient evidence that the asset or liability exists, and
(b)   the asset or liability can be measured at a monetary amount with sufficient reliability

This requirement is consistent with Chapter 5 of the Statement of Principles, but again since the Statement of Principles is non-mandatory, the rule needs to be repeated in a mandatory standard.

2.5 Example

Should the following be shown as assets in the balance sheet?

(a)   internally generated goodwill
(b)   employees
(c)   advertising expenditure

2.6 Solution

(a) The measurement of non-purchased goodwill is too subjective to enable it to be shown as an asset.

(b) Normally, employees are paid a wage or salary which is written off to the profit and loss account, and no further asset is recognised. However in particular circumstances there is an argument for recognising employees on the balance sheet. For example, if a football club paid a transfer fee of £4m to sign a footballer on a four year contract, it would be possible to capitalise the employee and write his services off over the four year period.

(c) Prepaid advertising could certainly be shown on the balance sheet as any other prepayment, if the advertising had not yet started. Once the campaign had started, the costs should probably be written off as incurred, since there is no guarantee of future economic benefits.

2.7 Linked presentation

A special 'linked presentation' should be used to present non-recourse finance arrangements where the finance will be repaid only from benefits generated by the specific item. This presentation shows, on the face of the balance sheet, the finance deducted from the gross amount of the item that it finances. For example, if a bank transfers title to a portfolio of debts of £10m in exchange for non-returnable proceeds of £9m plus a further sum (calculated as £1m less bad debts less a finance charge) depending on whether and when the debtors pay, then the linked presentation would show this portfolio on the face of the balance sheet amongst debtors:

	£m	£m
Debts subject to financing arrangements		
Portfolio of debts	10	
Less: non-returnable amounts received	(9)	
		1

Such a presentation shows that the bank retains risks and benefits relating to the full £10m of debts, but that the amount of expected future benefit from the portfolio is £1m.

2.8 Offset

In general, assets and liabilities should not be offset ie, presented as a single net item in the balance sheet. Debit and credit entries should only be offset where they do not constitute separate assets and liabilities. For example, a company might both sell items to and purchase items from the same company, and settle their monthly balance due to/from each other on a net settlement basis. In such a case, it would be wrong to show both a debtor and a creditor in respect of trading balances at the balance sheet date; one net balance should be shown as a debtor or creditor as appropriate.

2.9 Quasi-subsidiaries

A quasi-subsidiary of an entity is a company, trust or other vehicle that, while not fulfilling the definition of a subsidiary, is controlled by the reporting entity and gives rise to benefits no different in substance from if the vehicle were a subsidiary.

In keeping with the substance over form principle, quasi-subsidiaries should be accounted for as though they were subsidiaries, so they should normally be consolidated into the consolidated financial statements.

2.10 Disclosures

Disclosures for all transactions should be sufficient to enable the user of the financial statements to understand the commercial effect.

3   Application notes of FRS 5

3.1   Introduction

FRS 5 contains six application notes explaining how the principles of the standard should be applied in the specific circumstances of:

(a)   consignment stock
(b)   sale and repurchase agreements
(c)   factoring of debts
(d)   securitised assets
(e)   loan transfers
(f)   Private Finance Initiative and similar contracts

A seventh application note dealing with revenue recognition has been issued in draft form. The ASB is currently considering the comments received in respect of this draft.

3.2   Consignment stock

Consignment stock is stock held by one party (the dealer) but legally owned by another (the manufacturer), on terms that give the dealer the right to sell the stock in the normal course of its business or, at its option, to return it unsold to the owner.

Such an arrangement is common in the motor trade. A car manufacturer will 'lend' cars to a dealer. The dealer is only invoiced for the cars when he actually sells them to the public.

A similar situation might exist in the book publishing business. The publisher would pay for the books to be printed, and then deliver them to booksellers. The bookseller would be invoiced for the books that they sell and would return the others at no penalty to the publisher.

The accounting will depend on which party has the stock as an asset at the balance sheet date ie, the right to control the asset and enjoy future benefits from it.

In the simple examples described above, the manufacturer still retains the risks and rewards of the goods, so the consignment stock should remain in the balance sheet of the manufacturer.

But what if the price paid by the dealer increases over the period that he holds the stock, and there are stiff penalties imposed if the dealer decides to return any stock unsold? In such cases the dealer is exposed to the risks and rewards of the goods, so they should appear in his balance sheet. Where stock is in substance an asset of the dealer, the stock should be recognised in the dealer's balance sheet, together with a corresponding liability to the manufacturer.

You must consider the details given in each situation, and decide which party to the agreement should show the asset in his balance sheet.

3.3   Sale and repurchase agreements

Sale and repurchase agreements are arrangements under which assets are sold by one party to another on terms that provide for the seller to repurchase the asset in certain circumstances.

For example, a house-builder may decide to sell some of the land that it owns to a bank for £10m. The house-builder has the right to repurchase the land at any time over the next five years for £10m plus interest at 10% pa up to the date of repurchase.

The substance of this arrangement is that of a secured loan offered by the bank, rather than a sale. The house-builder should continue to recognise the land as an asset in its balance sheet, and should show the £10m received as a loan liability.

Again, you must read the details carefully to see if the benefits and risks of ownership have been passed to the buyer (a genuine sale) or whether they have been retained by the 'seller' (a secured loan).

3.4   *Factoring of debts*

Factoring of debts is a common method for small companies to raise finance on the strength of their accounts receivable. Specified debts are transferred to the factor, and the factor then offers a credit facility permitting the seller to draw up to a fixed percentage of the face value of the debts transferred.

Again, the question is whether the seller has validly sold the debts (in which case they should not appear in the seller's balance sheet), or whether the seller should continue to show the factored debts as an asset, with a corresponding liability for the proceeds received from the factor.

The key criterion is whether the risks and rewards of the debtors have been transferred to the factor. Where the seller has no further benefits and risks (eg, the factor will bear the cost of bad debts arising), then derecognition of the debts from the seller's balance sheet is appropriate. However, where the seller must repay the advance from the factor regardless of whether the debtors have paid or not, the substance is one of a secured loan, with the risks of the debtors not having been passed to the factor.

The linked presentation described earlier will be appropriate if the seller's downside exposure to loss is limited to a fixed monetary amount.

3.5   *Securitised assets*

Securitisation involves the transfer of a specific block of assets to a special purpose vehicle in return for an immediate cash payment. The vehicle finances the transfer by the issue of debt, normally tradeable loan notes.

In the UK it has been common for banks and building societies to securitise their household mortgages or hire purchase loans.

Once again, the analysis is similar to the factoring of debts. If the assets have been validly sold, they should be excluded from the seller's balance sheet. If the seller retains the risks and rewards of ownership, the assets should be maintained within assets, with the proceeds received being shown as a liability.

3.6   *Loan transfers*

An interest-bearing loan may be transferred by the lender to an entity which is not a special purpose vehicle. Loans cannot be 'sold' in the same way as tangible assets, however the rights receivable under a loan can be assigned to a new third party which has the same effect.

The principles of accounting for loan transfers are exactly the same as for securitised assets above.

3.7   *Private Finance Initiative and similar contracts*

Private Finance Initiative (PFI) contracts were introduced by the previous UK Conservative government. Under a PFI contract, the private sector is responsible for supplying services that traditionally have been provided by the public sector. For example, a private sector operator might build a road bridge and would then be permitted to charge users to cross the bridge for a ten year period. The advantage to the government is that no public funds are used to construct the asset in the first place. The advantage to the operator is the prospect of making a profit over the whole period of the contract.

The question to address is whether the asset built under the contract should be shown on the operator's balance sheet. FRS 5 requires that the property element of a PFI contract should be accounted for as a lease under SSAP 21 in the usual way. If the lease is a finance lease then it should be shown on the lessee's balance sheet.

If it is not possible to split the contract into property and service elements, then the general principles of FRS 5 should be applied. As ever, the asset should be recorded in the balance sheet of the party who is exposed to the risks and rewards of ownership.

3.8 Learning outcome

You have now covered the learning outcome for this chapter.

Discuss the principle of Substance over Form to a range of transactions

4 Revenue recognition

4.1 Introduction

Revenue is defined (in IAS 18) as the gross inflow of economic benefits during the period arising in the course of the ordinary activities of an enterprise when those inflows result in increases in equity, other than increases relating to contributions from equity participants.

The main example of revenue is sales revenue: if a company sells goods for £1,000 it will recognise £1,000 of sales revenue at the top of the profit and loss account.

Revenue recognition is concerned with deciding the point in time at which revenue should be recorded in the financial statements (or the period of time over which it should be recorded).

This is an accounting topic for which no UK accounting standard has been issued to date, despite its importance. The ASB issued a discussion paper 'Revenue Recognition' in 2001 but has now decided that a separate FRS on this topic is inappropriate. Instead, in February 2003, the ASB issued a draft application note to be added to FRS 5. Let us first consider the accounting principles involved.

4.2 The Statement of Principles

Revenue recognition is briefly mentioned in the ASB's Statement of Principles, as part of the general recognition criteria. Any element of financial statements (including gains) should be recognised if:

♦ sufficient evidence exists that a new asset or liability has been created, and
♦ the new asset or liability can be measured reliably.

The Statement of Principles is therefore promoting an unashamedly balance sheet-oriented view of revenue recognition. As long as a sale has resulted in a new asset of £1,000 (debtor or cash), then the sales revenue should be recognised.

4.3 The draft application note

The draft application note issued in 2003 builds on the Statement of Principles and is not intended to change UK accounting practice. Instead it offers guidance on how best practice should be applied.

4.4   Basic principles of revenue recognition

Revenue should be recognised by entities at the point at which their performance entitles them to recognise either:

♦ an increase in assets (eg a debtor), or

♦ a decrease in liabilities (eg no longer having a liability for repayment of a receipt of payment in advance of performance).

Revenue should be measured at the fair value of the consideration receivable, taking into account where material the time value of money.

Turnover is defined as the revenue arising from operating activities. Thus, for example, a sale of fixed assets will give rise to revenue, but this should not be reported as turnover. The profit or loss on sales of fixed assets will be reported separately in the profit and loss account.

4.5   Recognition of turnover in long-term contracts

SSAP 9 deals with the accounting for long-term contracts, and this new application note does not amend SSAP 9. However, SSAP 9 is silent on some matters. The application note states that the amounts recognised by a seller in respect of a long-term contract should represent the stage of completion of its contractual obligations. This proportion will not necessarily correspond with the proportion of expenditure incurred to date in comparison to total expenditure. Similarly, the receipt of a stage payment does not in itself justify the recognition of turnover.

4.6   Sales with rights of return

Some contractual arrangements contain terms allowing customers to return goods that they have purchased and to be refunded what they have paid.

The seller's recognition of its right to be paid and its obligation to make refunds to its customers are linked. Thus, turnover recognised should be net of the sales value of estimated returns.

It is possible that the seller's historical experience of comparable sales will enable him to estimate reliably the expected value of returns. In this case the deduction from turnover in respect of returns can be properly calculated as less than the maximum potential obligation.

In an extreme case, where no reasonable estimate of returns can be made, the seller can recognise no turnover from the 'sale' since all the risks of the related goods remain with the seller.

4.7   Acting as a principal or as an agent

A seller may act on his own account when making sales to customers, in which case he is acting as a principal. Alternatively, he may act as an intermediary, earning a commission in return for arranging the sale on behalf of a third party. In such cases he is acting as an agent.

Where the seller acts as a principal, he should report turnover based on the gross amount receivable under the contractual arrangement.

Where the seller acts as an agent, he should report turnover only to the extent of the commission receivable under the contractual arrangement. The gross value of sales throughput is encouraged to be disclosed as additional information.

5 Summary

The Statement of Principles requires that transactions should be accounted for in the financial statements according to their economic substance rather than their legal form. FRS 5 provides guidance on how this principle should be applied in practice.

The ASB has issued draft guidance on the recognition of revenue in UK financial statements. This is planned to be developed into a new application note to accompany FRS 5.

Multiple choice questions *(The answers are in the final chapter of this book)*

1   A company sells some of its goods on a sale or return basis. During the year ending 31 March 20X2 goods costing £54,000 had been sent to customers on this basis. At the year end 10% of these goods had yet to be accepted by customers. The company operates on a gross profit margin of 20%.

How much profit should appear in the profit and loss account for these sales for the year ending 31 March 20X2 and what figure for stock of these goods should appear in the balance sheet at that date?

	Profit	Stock value
A	£9,720	Nil
B	£9,720	£5,400
C	£12,150	£5,400
D	£13,500	Nil

2   A quasi-subsidiary company is:

A   A company in which more than 50% of the shares are owned but the investor does not have control of the company

B   A company which does not fulfil the definition of a subsidiary but is controlled by the investor

C   A company in which the investor has a participating interest but not control

D   A company in which the investor has significant influence but not control

3   A property company sells some land to a bank for £2 million on 1 January 20X2. The land originally cost £600,000 and has a book value of £1 million. The company has the right to repurchase the land at any time over the next year at a price of £2.2 million. The property company will require the use of the land within the next 12 months.

What figure will appear in the profit and loss account for this transaction for the year ending 31 December 20X2?

A   No figure

B   £1,000,000 income

C   £1,400,000 income

D   £200,000 expense

CHAPTER 22

Financial instruments

EXAM FOCUS

Accounting for financial instruments is a complex topic, soon to be progressed when Standards based on the ASB's December 2000 Consultation Paper and FRED 30 are published. You should be prepared for a fairly basic computational element included in a question, or a non-computational question discussing risk in general.

LEARNING OUTCOMES

This chapter covers the following Learning Outcome of the CIMA Syllabus.

> Explain the difference between liabilities and shareholders' funds, and allocate finance costs appropriately

In order to cover this Learning Outcome the following topics are included.

> FRS 4: Capital instruments
> FRS 13: Derivatives and other financial instruments – disclosures
> Proposals contained in FRED 23 and FRED 30

---

1 FRS 4: Capital instruments

1.1 Introduction

The objectives of FRS 4 are to ensure that:

♦ there is a clear distinction between debt, non-equity shares and equity shares in the balance sheet

♦ costs of debt and shares are dealt with in a manner appropriate to their classification

♦ costs of redeemable instruments are spread over accounting periods equitably

♦ financial statements give adequate disclosures on these matters

1.2 Key definitions of FRS 4

Capital instruments	All instruments issued as a means of raising finance. For example, all shares, debentures and loan stocks would qualify as capital instruments.
Debt	Capital instruments classed as liabilities
Equity shares	Shares other than non-equity shares
Finance costs	The difference between the net proceeds of an instrument and the total payments which the issuer may be required to make
Net proceeds	The fair value of the consideration received on the issue of an instrument net of direct issue costs
Non-equity shares	Redeemable shares or shares where dividend or participation in winding up is limited. For example, all preference shares would qualify as non-equity shares.
Shareholders' funds	Called-up share capital plus all reserves (excluding minority interests)
Term of instrument	The period from the date of issue of an instrument to its expiry/redemption/cancellation date. If options exist, use the earliest date of exercise

1.3   Key requirements of FRS 4

All capital instruments should be classified as either liabilities, shareholders' funds, or minority interests.

Classify capital instruments (other than shares) as liabilities if they contain an obligation to transfer economic benefits.

Instruments that do not contain an obligation to transfer economic benefits should be reported within shareholders' funds.

The balance sheet formats in the Companies Act specify that share capital of all kinds – ordinary and preferred – should be shown in the line 'called up share capital'. Therefore all shares must be shown amongst share capital on the balance sheet.

Analyse capital instruments (normally on the face of the balance sheet) as follows.

Item	*Analysed between*	
Shareholders' funds	Equity	Non-equity
Minority interests in subsidiaries	Equity interests	Non-equity interests
Liabilities	Convertible	Non-convertible

FRS 4 requirements mean that accounts will show, for both shareholders' funds and minority interest, an analysis between equity and non-equity elements. The effect is that users of accounts have their attention drawn to non-equity sources of capital and can therefore easily make their own adjustments to treat such sources of capital as debt if they so wish.

FRS 4 requires the legal form of capital instruments to be reported. Many users of accounts would regard, for example, redeemable preference shares as much more like debt than shareholders' funds. This is because they have the dual aspect of repayment or redemption and also a fixed prior charge on income.

However, FRS 4 requires such items to be reflected in shareholders' funds since this is a disclosure requirement of CA 1985.

There is a further distinction between preference shares and debt in that debt interest has to be paid in all circumstances whereas preference dividends may only be paid if there are distributable profits available; the same distinction applies as regards the redemption or repayment.

1.4   Finance costs for debt

Recognise debt liabilities initially at their net proceeds.

Allocate the finance costs of debt over their term so as to give a constant rate of charge on the outstanding debt.

Where cash paid is not equal to the finance charge for a period, the difference is normally added to or subtracted from the debt carrying value (include in accruals if payable next period).

Calculate the finance costs of non-equity shares (eg redeemable preference shares) on the same basis but classify these costs as 'dividends' in the profit and loss account.

1.5   Example

Bonds with a nominal value of £200,000 were issued at £157,763. The coupon rate is 4% paid at each year-end whilst the effective interest rate is 9.5%. Redemption is at par in five years. Issue costs are immaterial.

Required

Show the liability outstanding at the end of years 1 to 5.

1.6   Solution

Period	Amount borrowed £	Interest (at 9.5%) £	Repaid £	Interest rolled up £	Liability £
Year 1	157,763	14,988	(8,000)	6,988	164,751
Year 2	164,751	15,651	(8,000)	7,651	172,402
Year 3	172,402	16,378	(8,000)	8,378	180,780
Year 4	180,780	17,174	(8,000)	9,174	189,954
Year 5	189,954	18,046	(8,000)	10,046	200,000

The redemption is for £200,000 at the end of Year 5 leaving a nil liability.

1.7   Repurchase of debt

Gains and losses arising on the repurchase or early settlement of debt should be recognised in the profit and loss account when the repurchase or early settlement is made.

The gain or loss arises where the repurchase price is not equal to the carrying value at repurchase.

1.8   Maturity of debt

Disclose an analysis showing when debt will mature.

Determine the maturity by referring to the earliest date on which the lender can demand payment.

1.9   Shares and warrants

Recognise shares initially at the net proceeds of issue. (Note that equity shares issued on a business combination accounted for as a merger are exempt from this requirement.)

Calculate the finance costs of non-equity shares (eg redeemable preference shares) on the same basis as debt but classify these costs as 'dividends'.

1.10   Example

100,000 8% £1 preference shares are issued at a premium of 60% on 1 January 20X1. Issue costs are £2,237. Redemption is at 100% premium on 31 December 20X5. Implicit return rate is 9.5%.

Required

Show the balance sheet value for the preference shares at the end of years 1 to 5.

1.11   Solution

	£
Full value of consideration (100,000 × 160%)	160,000
Issue costs	(2,237)
Net proceeds	157,763

Period	Balance b/f	Finance charge (at 9.5%)	Dividend paid	Charge rolled up	Balance c/f
	£	£	£	£	£
Year 1	157,763	14,988	(8,000)	6,988	164,751
Year 2	164,751	15,651	(8,000)	7,651	172,402
Year 3	172,402	16,378	(8,000)	8,378	180,780
Year 4	180,780	17,174	(8,000)	9,174	189,954
Year 5	189,954	18,046	(8,000)	10,046	200,000

There is a nil balance sheet value at the end of Year 5 once the shares have been redeemed for £200,000.

On issue			£	£
Dr	Cash		157,763	
	Cr	Preference share capital		100,000
	Cr	Share premium		57,763

Example of annual entry – Year 1			£	£
Dr	Profit and loss account		14,988	
	Cr	Cash		8,000
	Cr	Non-distributable reserve		6,988

1.12 Warrants

A warrant is an instrument that requires a company to issue shares to the holder. Warrants are separately traded on the stock market. The net proceeds from the issue of warrants should be credited direct to shareholders' funds.

When a warrant is exercised, value of share = warrant proceeds on exercise plus any amount previously recognised for the warrant.

When a warrant lapses unexercised, the warrant issue proceeds should be shown as a gain in the statement of total recognised gains and losses.

1.13 Scrip dividend

Where shareholders may elect to receive shares in lieu of a cash dividend, the value of the shares in lieu of cash dividend is deemed to be the amount receivable if the cash alternative had been chosen.

1.14 Convertible instruments

Conversion should not be anticipated. Treat convertible debt as a liability until it is actually converted. Calculate finance costs on the assumption of no conversion.

State the amount of convertible debt separately from other debt (normally on the face of the balance sheet).

On conversion, the amount credited for shares issued is the carrying value of the debt at the conversion date. No gain or loss should be recognised on conversion.

1.15 Example

On 1 January 20X1 company M issued £750,000 2% convertible bonds at £98. Issue costs were £10,000. There is a redemption option at a premium at any time from the end of year 3. The total redemption value would be £915,325. 40% of the bond holders take this option at the end of year 3. The remainder convert in 20X5 at 30 £1 shares per £100 of stock. The implicit interest rate is 10%.

Required

Show the liability outstanding at the end of years 1 to 5.

1.16   *Solution*

On issue		£	£
Dr	Cash (750 × 98%) – 10	725,000	
	Cr Bond		725,000

Years 1-3

Period	Amount borrowed	Interest (at 10%)	Repaid	Interest rolled up	Liability
	£	£	£	£	£
20X1	725,000	72,500	(15,000)	57,500	782,500
20X2	782,500	78,250	(15,000)	63,250	845,750
20X3	845,750	84,575	(15,000)	69,575	915,325

At end of Year 3

		£	£
Dr	Bond (915,325 × 40%)	366,130	
	Cr Cash		366,130

Years 4 – 5

Period	Amount borrowed	Interest (at 10%)	Repaid	Interest rolled up	Liability
	£	£	£	£	£
20X4	549,195*	54,919	(9,000)*	45,919	595,114
20X5	595,114	59,511	(9,000)	50,511	645,625
	* 915,325 × 60%		* 15,000 × 60%		

On conversion		£	£
Dr	Bond	645,625	
	Cr Share capital (W)		135,000
	Cr Share premium account (balance)		510,625

Working

$$750,000 \times 60\% \times \frac{30}{100} = 135,000 \text{ £1 ords}$$

1.17   *Learning outcome*

You have now covered the learning outcome for this chapter

> Explain the difference between liabilities and shareholders' funds, and allocate finance costs appropriately.

2   FRS 13: Derivatives and other financial instruments - disclosures

2.1   *Introduction*

The objective of FRS 13 is to ensure that entities within its scope disclose in their financial statements information to enable users to assess:

(a)   The risk profile of the entity for the main financial risks that arise in connection with financial instruments.

(b)   The significance of financial instruments in relation to the financial position, performance and cashflows of the entity.

FRS 13 is in three parts A, B and C. Parts B and C deal with banks and other financial institutions, so we concentrate on Part A only, which applies to ordinary commercial entities. Only listed companies need to comply with FRS 13.

2.2 Definitions

Derivative: a financial instrument that derives its value from the price or value of an 'underlying item'. Underlying items include equities, bonds, commodities, interest rates, exchange rates and stock market and other indices.

Examples of derivatives include forward contracts, forward rate agreements, futures contracts, swaps, options and combinations of these.

Financial instrument: any contract that gives rise to both a financial asset of one entity and a financial liability or equity instrument of another entity.

A *financial asset* is any asset that is:

♦   cash

♦   a contractual right to receive cash or another financial asset from another entity

♦   a contractual right to exchange financial instruments with another entity under conditions that are potentially favourable, or

♦   an equity instrument of another entity.

A *financial liability* is any liability that is a contractual obligation:

♦   to deliver cash or another financial asset to another entity, or

♦   to exchange financial instruments with another entity under conditions that are potentially unfavourable.

An *equity instrument* is any contract that evidences an ownership interest in an entity, ie a residual interest in the assets of the entity after deducting all of its liabilities.

2.3 Risk profile

There are various possible risk factors affecting financial instruments. These are:

♦   Credit risk – the risk of default by another party

♦   Liquidity risk – the risk that an entity will have difficulty in raising funds to meet commitments (also known as funding risk)

♦   Cash flow risk – the risk of fluctuations in future cash flows

♦   Market price risk – the risk that future changes in market prices may change the value, or the burden, of a financial instrument.

Market price risk consists of three main components:

-   interest rate risk: the risk of fluctuation in the value of a financial instrument because of changes in market interest rates

-   currency risk: the risk of fluctuation in the value of a financial instrument because of changes in foreign exchange rates

-   other market price risk, including risk from fluctuations in commodity prices and share prices

2.4   Disclosure requirements of FRS 13

The disclosure requirements call for both *narrative disclosures* and *numerical disclosures* for all financial assets and liabilities except:

♦ Interests in subsidiaries, associates and joint ventures
♦ Employee share schemes
♦ Pension scheme assets and liabilities
♦ Leases
♦ Equity shares issued by the entity

2.5   Narrative disclosures

♦ Explanation of the role that financial instruments have had during the period in creating or changing the risks faced by the entity, including details of any significant change since the previous period

♦ Details of the impact of the risk factors listed above on the financial instruments

♦ Explanation of the objectives, policies and strategies of the entity as regards financial instruments

♦ Details of hedging transactions

♦ Commentary on the numerical disclosures, stating how they reflect the objectives, policies and strategies of the entity

2.6   Numerical disclosures

♦ Interest rate risk disclosures

Analysis of financial liabilities according to interest rates:

- fixed rates, with disclosure of the weighted average rate

- floating rates, with disclosure of the benchmark rate by reference to which the floating rate is determined

– nil interest rate

Analysis as above for financial assets also, if material

♦ Currency risk disclosures

Analysis of net monetary assets and liabilities held in each currency

♦ Liquidity disclosures

Details of due dates of all financial liabilities:

- in one year or less, or on demand
- in more than one year but not more than two years
- in more than two years but not more than five years
- in more than five years

Details of undrawn committed borrowing facilities with expiry dates:

- in one year or less
- in more than one year but not more than two years
- in more than two years

♦ Fair value disclosures

For each appropriate category of financial asset and liability:

Disclose either:

- the aggregate fair value and carrying amount at the balance sheet date

or

- the aggregate fair value of items with a positive fair value and the aggregate fair value of items with a negative fair value, with carrying amounts for each case.

2.7 Illustrative disclosures

FRS 13 contains a specimen set of disclosures in an appendix. These are reproduced in a simplified form below. They are intended to represent the kind of disclosures a smaller company might have to make.

Narrative disclosures

The Group's financial instruments, other than derivatives, comprise borrowings, some cash and liquid resources, and various items, such as trade debtors, trade creditors etc, that arise directly from its operations. The main purpose of these financial instruments is to raise finance for the Group's operations.

The Group also enters into derivatives transactions (principally interest rate swaps and forward foreign currency contracts). The purpose of such transactions is to manage the interest rate and currency risks arising from the Group's operations and its sources of finance.

It is, and has been throughout the period under review, the Group's policy that no trading in financial instruments shall be undertaken.

The main risks arising from the Group's financial instruments are interest rate risk, liquidity risk and foreign currency risk. The Board reviews and agrees policies for managing each of these risks and they are summarised below. These policies have remained unchanged since the beginning of 20X0.

Interest rate risk

The Group finances its operations through a mixture of retained profits and bank borrowings. The Group borrows in the desired currencies at both fixed and floating rates of interest and then uses interest rate swaps to generate the desired interest profile and to manage the Group's exposure to interest rate fluctuations. The Group's policy is to keep between 50% and 65% of its borrowings at fixed rates of interest. At the year end, 62% of the Group's borrowings were at fixed rates after taking account of interest rate swaps.

Liquidity risk

As regards liquidity, the Group's policy has throughout the year been that, to ensure continuity of funding, at least 50% of its borrowings should mature in more than five years. At the year end 57% of the Group's borrowings were due to mature in more than five years.

Short term flexibility is achieved by overdraft facilities.

Foreign currency risk

The Group has one significant overseas subsidiary – Foreign – which operates in the USA and whose revenues and expenses are denominated exclusively in US dollars. In order to protect the Group's sterling balance sheet from the movements in the US dollar/sterling exchange rate, the Group finances its net investment in this subsidiary by means of US dollar borrowings.

About one-third of the sales of the Group's UK businesses are to customers in continental Europe. These sales are priced in sterling but invoiced in the currencies of the customers involved. The Group's policy is to eliminate all currency exposures on sales at the time of sales through forward currency contracts. All the other sales of the UK businesses are denominated in sterling.

Numerical information

Interest rate risk profile of financial assets and financial liabilities

Financial assets

The Group has no financial assets, other than short-term debtors and an immaterial amount of cash at bank.

Financial liabilities

After taking into account the various interest rate swaps and forward foreign currency contracts entered into by the Group, the interest rate profile of the Group's financial liabilities at 31 December 20X1 was:

Currency	Total	Floating rate financial liabilities	Fixed rate financial liabilities	Financial liabilities on which no interest is paid
	£ millions	£ millions	£ millions	£ millions
Sterling	415	150	250	15
US dollar	200	80	120	-
Total	615	230	370	15

	Fixed rate financial liabilities		Financial liabilities on which no interest is paid
Currency	Weighted average interest rate	Weighted average period for which rate is fixed	Weighted average period until maturity
	%	Years	Years
Sterling	10	5	1.4
US dollar	7	8	-
Total	-	6	1.4

The floating rate financial liabilities comprise:

♦ sterling denominated bank borrowings and overdrafts that bear interest at rates based on the six month LIBOR, and

♦ US dollar denominated bank borrowings that bear interest at rates based on the US Prime rate.

Currency exposures

As at 31 December 20X1, after taking into account the effects of forward foreign exchange contracts the Group had no currency exposures.

Maturity of financial liabilities

The maturity profile of the Group's financial liabilities at 31 December 20X1 was as follows:

	£m
In one year or less, or on demand	200
In more than one year but not more than two years	15
In more than two years but not more than five years	60
In more than five years	340
	615

Borrowing facilities

The Group has various undrawn committed borrowing facilities. The facilities available at 31 December 20X1 in respect of which all conditions precedent had been met were as follows:

	£m
Expiring in one year or less	40
Expiring in more than one year but not more than two years	7
Expiring in more than two years	3
	50

Fair values of financial assets and financial liabilities

Set out below is a comparison by category of book values and fair values of the Group's financial assets and liabilities as at 31 December 20X1.

	Book value £ millions	Fair value £ millions
Primary financial instruments held or issued to finance the Group's operations:		
Short-term financial liabilities and current portion of long-term borrowings	(215)	(223)
Long-term borrowings	(400)	(370)
Financial assets	7	8
Derivative financial instruments held to manage the interest rate and currency profile:		
Interest rate swaps	-	15
Forward foreign currency contracts	-	(5)

The fair values of the interest rate swaps, forward foreign currency contracts and sterling denominated long-term fixed rate debt with a carrying amount of £250 million have been determined by reference to prices available from the markets on which the instruments involved are traded. All the other fair values shown above have been calculated by discounting cash flows at prevailing interest rates.

Market price risk

The Group's exposure to market price risk comprises interest rate and currency risk exposures. It monitors these exposures primarily through a process known as sensitivity analysis. This involves estimating the effect on profit before tax over various periods of a range of possible changes in interest rates and exchange rates. The sensitivity analysis model used for this purpose makes no assumptions about any interrelationships between such rates or about the way in which such changes may affect the economies involved. As a consequence, figures derived from the Group's sensitivity analysis model should be used in conjunction with other information about the Group's risk profile.

The Group's policy towards currency risk is to eliminate all exposures that will impact on reported profit as soon as they arise. This is reflected in the sensitivity analysis, which estimates that five and ten percentage point increases in the value of sterling against all other currencies would have had minimal impact on profit before tax.

On the other hand, the Group's policy is to accept a degree of interest rate risk as long as the effects of various changes in rates remain within certain prescribed ranges. On the basis of the Group's analysis, it is estimated that a rise of one percentage point in all interest rates would have reduced 20X1 profit before tax by approximately 1.5% and that a three percentage point increase would have reduced such profits by 4.2%. This is well within the ranges that the Group regards as acceptable.

2.8   Further developments

FRS 13 deals only with disclosure. The more difficult matter of measurement of financial instruments is still to be dealt with. In December 2000 the ASB published a Consultation Paper "Financial Instruments and Similar Items" developed by a joint working group composed of standard-setters from thirteen countries plus the International Accounting Standards Committee.

The objective is to produce an internationally agreed standard on the recognition and measurement of financial instruments. The main proposals in the Consultation Paper are:

♦ All financial instruments held should be measured at fair value – that is, market value or its equivalent

♦ All gains and losses arising on changes in fair value should be recognised in the profit and loss account

2.9   Hedge accounting

For accounting purposes, hedging means designating one or more hedging instruments so that their change in fair value is an offset, in whole or in part, to the change in fair value or cash flows of a hedged item. The purpose is to reduce some or all of the risk associated with the hedged item.

You have already seen a specific example of hedging in SSAP 20, where an overseas investment was hedged by borrowings taken out in foreign currency. Movements in the value of the investment were covered (hedged) by movements in the value of the foreign loan.

When looking at financial instruments, we are concerned with hedge accounting in general. For example, a holder of fixed rate debt might be worried that interest rates in general will rise, leading to a loss in value of his debt investment. He could hedge his position by himself issuing fixed rate debt.

2.10   FRED 23: Financial instruments: hedge accounting

In May 2002 the ASB issued FRED 23 which is based on the equivalent international standard, IAS 39. The objective is to limit the use of hedge accounting only to circumstances when it is appropriate. The relationship between the hedging instrument and the hedged item must have been designated as a hedge from the outset, and the hedge must actually be effective. If the hedging relationship does not satisfy these conditions (clearly defined, measurable and effective), then hedge accounting must not be used.

2.11 FRED 30: Financial instruments: disclosure and presentation; recognition and measurement

In June 2002 the ASB issued FRED 30 as its latest proposed thinking on accounting for financial instruments. In order to smooth the UK's transition to listed companies having to follow IASs from 2005, FRED 30 contains two draft FRSs:

♦ The first FRS 'Financial instruments: disclosure and presentation' would replace FRS 4 and FRS 13 covering the disclosure issues described earlier.

♦ The second FRS 'Financial instruments: measurement' would cover the recognition and measurement issues currently dealt with by IAS 39 but not in any UK standard.

Adopting these two new FRSs would involve significant changes to aspects of current UK accounting some of which would require changes to UK statute. Consider the following examples:

(a) The CA 1985 requires the issuer of shares to classify all shares as 'share capital' on the balance sheet. All payments made to shareholders are currently classified as 'dividends' on the profit and loss account.

FRED 30 proposes that the issuer of capital instruments should classify them in accordance with the substance of the contractual arrangements involved. Normal ordinary shares would continue to be shown as equity on the balance sheet. However, redeemable preference shares which are in substance liabilities would be shown as liabilities on the balance sheet.

Payments to holders of equity instruments will be treated as dividends (although no longer reported in the profit and loss account, since dividends are an appropriation of profit rather than a measure of financial performance). Payments to holders of all other instruments (including preference shares reported in liabilities) will be treated as an interest expense in the profit and loss account.

(b) FRS 4 currently requires convertible debt to be classified as a liability. FRED 30 proposes that convertible debt should be split into two components, an equity element reported as equity and a liability element reported in liabilities.

(c) FRED 30 proposes that the UK should adopt the disclosure requirements of IAS 32 rather than the more detailed requirements of FRS 13. This should be popular since many preparers of UK accounts believe that FRS 13 is unnecessarily extensive.

(d) The CA 1985 requires assets to be measured using either the historical cost accounting rules or the alternative accounting rules. The ASB is pressing for a third set of rules to be permitted, the fair value accounting rules. This would then allow financial assets to be measured in the balance sheet at fair value when required by IAS 39.

The UK government is intending to have amended the Companies Acts before 1 January 2004 to enable the adoption of IASs by listed companies to proceed in accordance with the presently planned time frame.

3 Summary

The most examinable aspects of financial instruments are:

♦ The distinction between debt, equity shares and non-equity shares in FRS 4
♦ Discussion of the FRS 13 disclosures concerning risk factors affecting financial instruments
♦ The proposal that in future most financial assets should be measured in the balance sheet at fair value

Multiple choice questions *(The answers are in the final chapter of this book)*

1   A company issues 4% bonds with a nominal value of £500,000 for £394,408 on 1 January 20X0.   Redemption is at par in five years time and the effective rate of interest of the bonds is 9.5%.

What figure would FRS 4 require to appear in the balance sheet at 31 December 20X2 for these bonds and in the profit and loss account for the year ending 31 December 20X2?

	Balance sheet £	Profit and loss account £
A	451,951	20,000
B	451,951	40,946
C	500,000	20,000
D	500,000	47,500

2   On 1 January 20X0 a company issues £500,000 4% convertible debentures at £95 with issue costs of £8,000.   The debentures can be converted into ordinary shares or redeemed at a total value of £523,358 on 31 December 20X2.   The conversion rate is 40 £1 ordinary shares per £100 of debentures.   The effective rate of interest is 8% per annum.

On 31 December 20X2 30% of shareholders redeemed the debentures and the remainder converted them to ordinary shares.

What is the double entry for the transactions on 31 December 20X2?

A	Debit	Debentures	£500,000	
	Credit	Cash		£150,000
	Credit	Share capital		£350,000
B	Debit	Debentures	£500,000	
	Credit	Cash		£150,000
	Credit	Share capital		£140,000
	Credit	Share premium		£210,000
C	Debit	Debentures	£523,358	
	Credit	Cash		£157,007
	Credit	Share capital		£366,351
D	Debit	Debentures	£523,358	
	Credit	Cash		£157,007
	Credit	Share capital		£146,540
	Credit	Share premium		£219,811

CHAPTER 23

Leasing

EXAM FOCUS

Accounting for leases and hire purchase transactions is regularly examined since it contains both calculations as well as the discussion of accounting principles. Be prepared for questions on this area.

LEARNING OUTCOMES

There is no specific Learning Outcome associated with this chapter.

The following topics are included in this chapter.

> Types of extended credit agreement
> Accounting for finance leases
> Treatment of finance leases in the lessor's accounts
> Operating leases
> Disclosure requirements of SSAP 21

---

1 The accounting problem of leasing

1.1 Introduction

Prior to SSAP 21, fixed assets were accounted for according to the legal form of the transaction under which their use was acquired.

If fixed assets were purchased for cash, the purchaser would record the acquisition of the fixed assets in his balance sheet. If a loan was raised and fixed assets were acquired with the proceeds, the purchaser would record the acquisition of the fixed assets and the loan liability in his balance sheet. However, if the use of a fixed asset was acquired under a lease, the lessee would not record the fixed asset or the corresponding obligation to the lessor in his balance sheet. This complies with the legal form of a lease, since the lessor owns the asset and at no time does title to the asset pass to the lessee.

The practice therefore grew for companies to be keen to acquire new fixed assets under leases rather than borrowing to buy the assets. Leased assets and the obligation to the lessor were not recognised on the lessee's balance sheet, despite the lessee having signed a contract agreeing to pay annual amounts to the lessor over the period of the lease. The omission of the lease obligation from the lessee's balance sheet meant that the lessee could report a much lower gearing ratio. Prospective investors in the company would believe that the company was less risky than was in fact the case. The company could raise fresh borrowings at a lower interest rate than would be charged if the true situation was known.

The purpose of SSAP 21 is to ensure that transactions that are *in substance* the same, even if not *in legal form*, are treated in the same way in the financial accounts of a business. For example, if it is believed that the contractual obligations entered into in a finance lease are in substance the same as those involved in borrowing funds to acquire an asset, then the same accounting methods should be used to record each of these ways of acquiring the use of fixed assets.

1.2 Types of extended credit

Credit sale – involves a contract of sale with payment by instalments. Ownership of the goods passes on delivery by the supplier, and a binding debt is created which cannot be avoided by returning the goods.

Hire purchase – goods are supplied on hire to customers until, on fulfilment of certain conditions (usually the payment of an agreed number of instalments), the customer becomes entitled to purchase the asset (usually for a nominal amount). Legal title passes to the customer at this point.

Lease – SSAP 21 distinguishes between two types of lease, finance and operating:

A *finance lease* is a lease that transfers substantially all the risks and rewards of ownership of an asset to the lessee. It should be presumed that such a transfer of risks and rewards occurs if at the inception of a lease the present value of the minimum lease payments, including any initial payment, amounts to substantially all (normally 90% or more) of the fair value of the leased asset. The present value should be calculated by using the interest rate implicit in the lease. If the fair value of the asset is not determinable, an estimate thereof should be used.

An *operating lease* is a lease other than a finance lease.

The **minimum lease payments** are the minimum payments that the lessee has contracted to pay the lessor under the terms of the lease.

1.3 Substance over form

Although each of the above types of agreement is different in its legal form, SSAP 21 recognises that they could be very similar in substance.

1.4 Credit sale/finance leases

It can be seen that a finance lease is similar in substance to the ownership of an asset, financed by a loan repayable by instalments over the period of the lease. The lessee would normally have sole use of the asset and would be responsible for its maintenance, repair and insurance even though legal title to the asset remains with the lessor.

Thus SSAP 21 requires that finance leases (or equivalent agreements) are capitalised in the lessee's balance sheet by including both the

- value of the asset in fixed assets; and
- the outstanding lease commitment in creditors.

The profit and loss account is charged with depreciation on the asset and an appropriate share of the finance charge each year.

The lessor will account for future amounts receivable under finance leases as a debtor, which are then allocated to the profit and loss account over the term of the lease.

1.5   Operating lease

An operating lease is effectively a short-term rental agreement, with no option to purchase the goods. The supplier retains title throughout, and usually undertakes to keep them in good working order. The domestic rental of a television or video recorder would generally constitute such an agreement.

In this case, it is the lessor that records the asset as a fixed asset and depreciates it. Rental is recognised on a straight-line basis in both the lessee's and the lessor's books over the lease term.

1.6   Hire purchase

Hire purchase agreements could fall into either of these categories, depending upon the terms of the agreement, and SSAP 21 requires that they are accounted for accordingly. It is more common that they are treated as a finance lease. A difference may be that the hire purchase seller takes credit not only for finance income, but also for gross profit on the actual sale of the asset.

2   Accounting for finance leases

2.1   Capitalisation of finance leases and off balance sheet gearing

Where finance leases are not reflected in the lessee's balance sheet as described above, the economic resources and the level of future obligations of the business are understated. In this situation, the leasing of assets under finance leases becomes a form of 'off balance sheet gearing'.

Without capitalisation, the profit and loss account is only charged with the lease payments. This charge does not reflect the use of the asset, especially where there is a secondary term to the lease at nominal rental. For example, if the lease term for an asset stipulated four annual rentals of £5,000 followed by six annual rentals of £1, simply charging the rental paid against income would not adequately match the revenues (which would, other things being equal, stay constant over the 10 years) with the costs associated with those revenues.

A similar problem arises in lessor accounting – how to match the lease rentals receivable over the period of the agreement to the cost of generating rentals.

2.2   Capitalisation of finance leases in the lessee's accounts

The two critical questions to be answered are:

(a)   At what value should the asset be capitalised?
(b)   What finance charge should be made in the profit and loss account?

2.3   The capitalised value in the balance sheet

At the start of the lease, the sum to be recorded both as an asset and as a liability should be the present value of the minimum lease payments, derived by discounting them at the interest rate implicit in the lease.

In practice in the case of a finance lease the fair value of the asset will often be a sufficiently close approximation to the present value of the minimum lease payments and may in these circumstances be substituted for it.

2.4   *The finance charge*

The excess of the minimum lease payments over the initial capitalised value represents the finance charge. The total finance charge should be allocated to accounting periods during the lease term so as to produce a constant periodic rate of charge on the remaining balance of the obligation for each accounting period (ie, the actuarial method), or a reasonable approximation thereto.

2.5   *Example*

A lessee enters into a lease on 1 January 20X1 for an item of plant. The following details are relevant:

Fair value of asset	£10,000
Residual value	Nil after five years
Lease terms	£2,500 pa in advance for five years, the first rental payable on 1.1.X1

Required

Show how this transaction would be recorded in the ledger accounts of the lessee for the first two years, and show also how the transaction would be reflected in the profit and loss account and balance sheet over the five years.

2.6   *Solution*

Firstly, we must calculate the rate of interest implicit in the lease.

Amount effectively loaned	£10,000 less first instalment £2,500 = £7,500
Period of loan	Four years (last instalment is on first day of year 5)
Total loan repayments	£10,000 (four years × £2,500)
Annuity factor	$\dfrac{£7,500}{£2,500} = 3$ (over four years)

From discount tables, the implicit rate of interest = 12.6%.

The total finance charge is the total amount paid less the fair value of the asset, ie $(5 \times £2,500) - £10,000 = £2,500$.

The finance charge will be apportioned as follows:

Year	Average amount outstanding £	Interest @ 12.6% £	Repayment on 1 January following £
1	7,500	945	2,500
2	5,945	749	2,500
3	4,194	528	2,500
4	2,222	278	2,500
5	–	–	–
		2,500	

The annual depreciation charge will be:

$$\dfrac{£10,000}{5} = £2,000 \text{ pa}$$

The ledger entry at the beginning of the lease will be:

			£	£
Dr	Leased assets		10,000	
	Cr	Obligation under finance leases		10,000

being the recording of the 'purchase' of an asset under a finance lease at its fair value and the assumption of a liability.

Thereafter the entries in the leased asset account and the depreciation account will be exactly the same as for a purchased asset. The entries in the leasing obligation account will be as follows:

Obligation under finance leases account

		£			£
1.1.X1	Cash	2,500	1.1.X1	Leased asset	10,000
31.12.X1	Balance c/f	8,445	31.12.X1	Interest expense	945
		10,945			10,945
1.1.X2	Cash	2,500	1.1.X2	Balance b/f	8,445
31.12.X2	Balance c/f	6,694	31.12.X2	Interest expense (8,445 – 2,500) × 12.6%	749
		9,194			9,194
			1.1.X3	Balance b/f	6,694

The charges to the profit and loss account over the period of the lease are:

Year	1	2	3	4	5	Total
	£	£	£	£	£	£
Depreciation	2,000	2,000	2,000	2,000	2,000	10,000
Interest	945	749	528	278	–	2,500
	2,945	2,749	2,528	2,278	2,000	12,500

The balance sheets would reflect the net book value of the asset and the outstanding principal of the loan together with the accrued interest for the year which will be paid on the first day of the next period.

Balance sheets

Year	1	2	3	4	5
	£	£	£	£	£
Fixed assets					
Leased plant					
Cost	10,000	10,000	10,000	10,000	10,000
Accumulated dep'n	2,000	4,000	6,000	8,000	10,000
Net book value	8,000	6,000	4,000	2,000	–
Creditors: amounts falling due within one year					
Obligations under finance leases:					
Principal	1,555	1,751	1,972	2,222	–
Accrued interest	945	749	528	278	–
	2,500	2,500	2,500	2,500	–

Creditors: amounts falling due after more than one year Obligations under finance leases (principal only)	5,945	4,194	2,222	–	–
	8,445	6,694	4,722	2,500	–

Obligations under finance leases have been split between the current portion (payable within 12 months of the balance sheet date) and the long-term portion.

The accounting treatment adopted for hire purchase contracts is very similar to the above. SSAP 21 requires that 'those hire purchase contracts which are of a financing nature should be accounted for on a basis similar to that set out for finance leases'.

2.7 Other methods of allocation of the finance charge

SSAP 21 requires the use of the actuarial method (or a reasonable approximation) to allocate the interest charge to accounting periods. Two of the possible methods are:

♦ sum of the digits; and
♦ straight line.

Under the sum of the digits method the total interest charge of £2,500 will be allocated to accounting periods as follows:

Year			£
1	$\dfrac{4}{4+3+2+1}$	$\dfrac{4}{10} \times £2,500$	1,000
2	$\dfrac{3}{4+3+2+1}$	$\dfrac{3}{10} \times £2,500$	750
3	$\dfrac{2}{4+3+2+1}$	$\dfrac{2}{10} \times £2,500$	500
4	$\dfrac{1}{4+3+2+1}$	$\dfrac{1}{10} \times £2,500$	250
			2,500

Under the straight-line method, the amount of interest allocated to each of the first four years would be £625 (£2,500/4).

The results of the three methods of interest allocation may be compared as follows:

Year	Actuarial £	Sum of digits £	Straight line £
1	945	1,000	625
2	749	750	625
3	528	500	625
4	278	250	625
	2,500	2,500	2,500

In general, and in exams, the sum of the digits may be a suitable approximation to the actuarial method if the implicit rate of interest is unknown. The straight-line method, however, is not usually a reasonable approximation and should not be used except, in practice, in the case of 'small' leases.

2.8   Non annual payments

So far we have looked at leases in which the rental payments are made annually. Frequently, rentals may be made monthly, quarterly or half yearly. In these cases the same principles apply except that when allocating interest we need to allocate it to the periods of the lease using the implicit rate of interest for the quarter, half year, etc. (or the sum of the digits as appropriate).

2.9   Current and long-term liabilities

In the example the current portion of the obligation is the payment to be made on the next day, and the long-term portion is the balance of the obligation. This is only the case where the lease has annual payments which are made on the first day of the accounting period.

In general the current portion is made up of:

♦   the capital to be repaid within 12 months; plus

♦   any interest accrued but not yet paid;

and the long-term portion is made up of:

♦   the capital to be repaid after more than 12 months.

3   Treatment of finance leases in the lessor's accounts

3.1   Introduction

Where a lessor enters a finance lease or hire purchase contract of similar nature, although he may retain legal title to the asset, he passes the risks and rewards of ownership to the lessee in return for a stream of future lease payments. Under SSAP 21, amounts receivable under finance leases are treated as debtors, termed the net investment in finance leases.

The net investment in a lease comprises:

(a)   the minimum lease payments;

The *minimum lease payments* are the minimum payments over the remaining part of the lease term (excluding charges for services and taxes to be paid by the lessor) and any residual amounts guaranteed by the lessee or by an independent third party.

plus

(b)   any unguaranteed residual value;

Unguaranteed residual value is that portion of the residual value of the leased asset (estimated at the inception of the lease), the realisation of which by the lessor is not assured or is guaranteed solely by a party related to the lessor.

less

(c)   gross earnings allocated to future periods.

Gross earnings comprise the lessor's gross finance income over the lease term, representing the difference between his gross investment in the lease (the total of the minimum lease payments and any unguaranteed residual value accruing to the lessor) and the cost of the leased asset.

3.2   *Allocation of the finance charge*

Many leases are arranged because the lessor can utilise capital allowances which the lessee, were he to purchase, could not. The benefit of the capital allowance to the lessor may be accelerated cash flow. The allowance received early in the lease is 'repaid' by way of the tax charge on rentals as the lease term progresses.

This benefit not only makes finance leases cheaper to fund, it also significantly alters the pattern of the lessor's funding costs, with a heavy bias towards the earlier periods in the lease term.

Recognising this, SSAP 21 requires:

> 'The total gross earnings under a finance lease should normally be allocated to accounting periods to give a constant periodic rate of return on the lessor's **net cash investment** in the lease in each period. In arriving at the constant periodic rate of return, a reasonable approximation may be made.'

The apportionment of gross earnings over the period of the lease to give a constant periodic rate of return on the net cash investment recognises all significant **cash flows** which affect a lease. The net cash investment in a lease at a point in time is the amount of funds invested in a lease by the lessor, and usually comprises the cost of the asset minus rentals received, tax effects and residual values.

This after tax method was originally developed under a corporation tax system with high tax rates and high first year allowances. Now that first year allowances have been abolished, the allocation of earnings using after tax methods will tend to be similar to that using before tax methods.

The mechanics of the actuarial method after tax are somewhat complex and are dealt with in the guidance notes to SSAP 21. It is not considered necessary for you to study this method in detail. It is important though, that you appreciate that this method, despite its apparent complexity, is just another way of allocating the same total finance income to the different accounting periods. The difference is that in the allocation it takes account of all the cashflows associated with the lease.

In the case of a hire purchase contract, SSAP 21 suggests that the use of the pre-tax actuarial method based on the **net investment** may be a suitable approximate method for the hire purchase seller to use to recognise finance income. In the case of a hire purchase seller, the cash flows are not distorted by the tax treatment since the seller does not get capital allowances.

3.3   *The accounting entries*

In order to illustrate the accounting entries in the books of the lessor, we shall consider the previous example where for simplicity we shall allocate the gross earnings using the pre-tax actuarial method – ie the same as that used for the lessee.

The initial accounting entry in the lessor's books will be:

		£	£
Dr	Investment in finance leases	10,000	
	Cr Cash		10,000

being investment of £10,000 in a finance lease over 5 years.

The entries in the investment in finance leases account over the first two years will then be as follows.

Debtor – net investment in finance leases

		£			£
1.1.X1	Cash	10,000	1.1.X1	Cash	2,500
31.12.X1	Finance income	945	31.12.X1	Balance c/f	8,445
		10,945			10,945
1.1.X2	Balance b/f	8,445	1.1.X2	Cash	2,500
31.12.X2	Finance income	749	31.12.X2	Balance c/f	6,694
		9,194			9,194
1.1.X3	Balance b/f	6,694			

3.4 Hire purchase – seller's books

For dealers financing their own operations, credit is normally taken over the period of the contract for both gross profit and finance charge. The same basis of taking profit may be applied to both *gross profit* and *interest*, or they may be treated separately, applying a different basis to each (eg equal instalment method to the gross profit, and sum of digits method to the finance charge).

Where the amounts involved are immaterial, credit is sometimes taken immediately for the whole of the gross profit, the finance charge being spread over the period of the contract.

It must be appreciated that there are many ways of apportioning both gross profit and finance charges. These are very similar to those used for the lessee. Examination questions may specify a particular method. If not, you are free to choose the simplest method.

3.5 Illustration

Ace Floggers Ltd sells a certain type of machine for cash and also on hire-purchase terms. The cost of the machine is £1,790 – and it has a cash selling price of £2,350. The hire-purchase terms for this machine require an initial deposit of £235, followed by 12 monthly instalments of £200 each. The company, which prepares accounts to 31 March each year, entered into an agreement with a hirer on 1 January 20X6 and it was agreed that the instalments should fall due on the first day of each month starting from 1 February 20X6. Let us assume that Ace Floggers Ltd wishes to take credit for the trading profit on an equal-instalment basis. We will deal with the finance charge using the sum of the digits method.

The situation can be summarised as follows.

	£
Cost	1,790
Gross profit	560
	2,350
Deposit	(235)
	2,115
Finance charge	285
12 instalments of £200 each	2,400

3.6 Gross profit – equal instalment

The gross profit of £560 must be spread over the 12 month contract. Thus the company will take credit for (3/12 × £560) £140 in the accounts to 31 March 20X6 and (9/12 × £560) £420 in the accounts to 31 March 20X7.

3.7 Finance charge – sum of digits

In the first three months of the contract the finance charge credited would be

$$\frac{12+11+10}{78} \times £285 \quad = £121$$

leaving $\frac{45}{78} \times £285$ = £164 to be credited in the year to 31 March 20X7.

3.8 Presentation in the accounts

In the above example we calculated the amount of income to be credited in the accounts; you may be required to calculate a company's profit for the year in that way. However, a common practice is to credit to the trading account the total hire-purchase sales for the year, and to make a provision for the profit (gross profit and interest) which remains unearned at the year end. For balance sheet purposes this provision is deducted from the balances outstanding on hire-purchase debtors.

If we were to apply this method to the above illustration under the various bases, the trading account for the year to 31 March 20X6 would appear as follows.

	£
Hire purchase sales	2,635
Cost of sales	1,790
	845
Less: provision for unearned profit (W)	584
	261

Working

Provision for unearned profit

	£
Gross profit (9/12 × £560)	420
Finance charge (45/78 × £285)	164
	584

4 Operating leases

An operating lease is a lease other than a finance lease, under which there is no suggestion that the risks and rewards of ownership are transferred from the lessor to the lessee. A business may lease a photocopier or fax machine under this type of lease.

Thus the asset is treated as a fixed asset in the books of the lessor and the rental is treated as income for the lessor and as expense for the lessee. Thus the treatment of operating leases may be summarised as follows:

(a)   The rental under an operating lease should be charged on a straight-line basis over the lease term.

(b)   An asset held for use in operating leases by a lessor should be recorded as a fixed asset and depreciated over its useful life.

(c)   Rental income from an operating lease should be recognised on a straight-line basis over the period of the lease.

5   Disclosure requirements of SSAP 21

5.1   Disclosure requirements by lessees

The disclosures required by SSAP 21 are complex. The principal disclosures for lessees are in respect of:

♦   assets held under finance leases;
♦   maturity of the obligations;
♦   charges in the profit and loss account; and
♦   commitments under operating leases.

The first two can be illustrated using the earlier example at the end of Year 2:

♦   **Assets held under finance leases**

   The net book value of fixed assets of £X includes an amount of £6,000 in respect of assets held under finance leases.

♦   **Obligations under finance leases**

   The minimum lease payments to which the company is committed fall due as follows:

	£	£
Under one year		2,500
Over one year		
In the 2nd to 5th years inclusive	5,000	
Over 5 years	–	
		5,000
		7,500
Amount representing future financing charges (2,500 – 945 – 749)		806
Obligations under finance leases		6,694

The other required disclosures are illustrated below:

♦   **Profit is stated after charging:**

	£
Depreciation of owned assets	X
Depreciation of assets held under finance leases and hire purchase contracts	X
Interest payable – bank loans and overdrafts	X
Finance charges payable – finance leases and hire purchase contracts	X
Hire of plant and machinery – operating leases	X
Hire of other assets – operating leases	X

♦   **Operating lease commitments**

   At 31 December 20X7 the company had annual commitments under non-cancellable operating leases as set out below.

	20X7 Land and buildings £000	Other £000	20X6 Land and buildings £000	Other £000
Operating leases which expire				
within one year	X	X	X	X
in the second to fifth years	X	X	X	X
inclusive over five years	X	X	X	X
	X	X	X	X

5.2 Disclosure requirements by lessors

(a) *Net investment* – The net investment in finance leases and hire purchase contracts at each balance sheet date should be disclosed.

(b) *Operating lease assets* – The gross amount of assets held for use in operating leases and the related accumulated depreciation charges, should be disclosed.

(c) *Accounting policies* – The policy adopted for operating leases and finance leases and in detail, the policy for accounting for finance lease income should be disclosed.

(d) *Rentals receivable* – The aggregate rentals receivable in respect of an accounting period in relation to (i) finance leases and (ii) operating leases should be disclosed.

(e) *Assets for letting under finance leases* – The cost of assets acquired in the period for the purpose of letting under finance leases should be disclosed.

Practice question 1 *(The answer is in the final chapter of this book)*

Flash

On 1 October 20X3 Flash plc entered into a non-cancellable agreement, whereby Flash plc would lease a new rocket booster. The terms of the agreement were that Flash plc would pay 26 rentals of £3,000 quarterly in advance commencing on 1 October 20X3, and that after this initial period Flash plc could continue, at its option to use the rocket booster for a nominal rental which is not material. The cash price of this asset would have been £61,570 and the asset has a useful life of 10 years. Flash plc considers this lease to be a finance lease and charges a full year's depreciation in the year of purchase of an asset. The rate of interest implicit in the lease is 2% per quarter.

On 1 July 20X2 Flash plc entered into another non-cancellable agreement to lease a Zarkov rocket for a period of 10 years at a rental of £5,000 half-yearly to be paid in advance commencing on 1 July 20X2. Flash plc considers this lease to be an operating lease.

Required

Show how these transactions would be reflected in the financial statements (excluding the cashflow statement) for the year ended 31 December 20X3.

Ignore comparative figures and make all computations to the nearest £.

---

6 Proposed changes in lease accounting

6.1 Introduction

In December 1999 the ASB issued a discussion paper 'Leases: implementation of a new approach' based on a position paper developed by the G4+1 group of accounting standard-setters.

The key proposal is that the current arbitrary distinction between operating and finance leases is unsatisfactory, and that the usefulness of financial statements would be improved if a single accounting method could be applied to **all** leases.

6.2 *Proposals in the 1999 discussion paper*

(a) All material leases give rise to assets and liabilities for lessees, which must be recognised on the lessee's balance sheet. At the beginning of the lease, lessees should record the fair value of the rights and obligations that are conveyed by the lease. The fair value of the rights obtained by a lease will normally be the present value of the minimum lease payments. After the lease has been recognised, it should be accounted for similarly to how finance leases are accounted for under SSAP 21.

(b) The lessor should show two separate assets on his balance sheet:

    (i)   amount receivable from the lessee (under debtors)

    (ii)   an interest in the residual value of the asset (under fixed assets).

This treatment recognises that the substance of the two amounts is quite different. The amount receivable from the lessee will be the mirror image of the amount shown in the lessee's balance sheet as the obligation due to the lessor.

6.3 *Conclusion*

The proposal that the distinction between operating leases and finance leases should be abolished is a good idea, since it would end the artificial manipulation of lease conditions to fulfil one definition or the other. However, many lessees' gearing ratio would increase if the proposals were implemented, so they may not be popular in practice.

7 *Summary*

SSAP 21 is an important contribution in the development of Accounting Standards since it represents the application of commercial substance as the solution to one form of off-balance sheet finance. The important matters which you must appreciate are:

(a) the problem of legal form accounting;

(b) the distinction between a finance lease and an operating lease;

(c) the capitalisation of finance leases in the lessee's books and the recognition of the obligation;

(d) the allocation of interest (and gross profits where applicable) in both the lessor's and lessee's books;

(e) the disclosures required by SSAP 21.

Multiple choice questions *(The answers are in the final chapter of this book)*

1   Henry acquired a lorry on hire purchase. The details were as follows.

Date of acquisition	1 January 20X8
Cash price	£20,000
Deposit	£5,000
Quarterly repayments	12 @ £1,800

The charge for interest is to be spread over the three year period on the sum of the digits basis. The repayments are made on the last day of each quarter.

How much interest would be allocated to the fifth quarterly repayment?

A   £700

B   £677

C   £550

D   £423

2   On 1 January 20X7 Melon plc bought a machine on hire purchase. The terms of the contract were as follows.

	£
Cash price	18,000
Deposit	(6,000)
	12,000
Interest (9% for two years)	2,160
Balance – payable in two annual instalments commencing 31 December 20X7	14,160

The rate of interest implicit in the contract is approximately 12%.

Applying the provisions of SSAP 21 *Accounting for leases and hire purchase contracts* the finance charge in the profit and loss account for the year ended 31 December 20X7 is:

A   £1,080

B   £1,440

C   £1,620

D   £2,160

3   Alpha plc enters into a lease with Omega Ltd of an aircraft which had a fair value of £240,000 at the inception of the lease. The terms of the lease require Alpha plc to pay ten annual rentals of £36,000 in arrears. Alpha plc is totally responsible for the maintenance of the aircraft which has a useful life of approximately fifteen years.

The present value of the ten annual rentals of £36,000 discounted at the interest rate implicit in the lease is £220,000.

Applying the provisions of SSAP 21 *Accounting for leases and hire purchase contracts* to this lease, the fixed assets of Alpha plc will increase by:

A   Nil

B   £220,000

C   £240,000

D   £358,040

CHAPTER 24

International issues

EXAM FOCUS

As commercial activity is increasingly carried out on a global scale, issues of international harmonisation of accounting policies assume greater urgency. The areas covered in this chapter are highly topical and you must expect to encounter them in exam questions.

This chapter also looks at the ASB's project to move UK accounting standards ever closer to international accounting standards.

LEARNING OUTCOMES

This chapter covers the following Learning Outcomes of the CIMA Syllabus.

> Identify the influences on financial reporting of cultural differences across the world
> Identify major differences between UK GAAP, IASs and US GAAP
> Prepare and interpret international comparisons

In order to cover these Learning Outcomes the following topics are included.

> Advantages of international harmonisation
> Obstacles to international harmonisation
> International accounting standards
> The ASB convergence project

1 Advantages of international harmonisation

1.1 Advantages to companies

 Multinational companies recognise that international harmonisation of accounting practices brings better access to foreign investor funds, as international accounting standards may be the basis for a listing on stock markets worldwide.

Appraisal of foreign enterprises for acquisitions and mergers would be more straightforward.

The consolidation exercise would be easier where foreign subsidiaries and associated companies are involved.

Staff could be more mobile between different countries.

Internal communication and comparison of results would be improved, aiding management control.

1.2 Advantages to investors

Consistency of treatment over international borders would increase the comparability of financial results of different companies.

This would improve the understandability of accounts, which in turn improves investment decisions when comparing the results of companies operating in different countries.

1.3 Other advantages

To tax authorities, standardisation would improve their ability to calculate tax liabilities of investors, including multinationals who receive income from overseas sources.

The 'big four' accountancy firms would benefit if accounting standards were harmonised across the world since employees could be moved between different countries with fewer problems arising.

2 Obstacles to international harmonisation

2.1 Different legal systems

Countries have enacted different amounts of detailed legislation on accounting.

For example, prior to the issue of the EC Directives, accounting requirements in the UK differed substantially from those in France.

2.2 Different capital financing systems

Types of business organisation and their financing differ internationally. It follows that if financiers and owners differ then the primary users of accounting information will also differ.

For example, the rule makers in the US and the UK regard the existing and potential investors as the primary users. However in Germany and Japan the banks are important owners of companies as well as providers of debt finance. They are able to appoint directors and obtain information beyond that included in the published annual report.

Where there are fewer outsider shareholders external reporting has been largely for the purposes of government, eg tax authorities or controllers of the economy.

2.3 Taxation regulations

In some countries the tax rules are the accounting rules.

For example, in the UK, depreciation charges may differ from the capital allowance but in some countries the accounting depreciation is the same as the equivalent of the capital allowance for tax purposes.

2.4 The size and competence of the accounting and auditing profession

The lack of a substantial body of private investors and public companies in some countries means that the need for and status of the auditors is much less than in the US or UK. Also there is an impact on the type of accounting that is or could be practised. Without a strong profession there is a limit on the extent to which national accounting standards can be developed.

2.5 Environmental and cultural factors

These include the following.

♦ Educational standards, which can be an important factor in developing countries.

♦ Political factors where there is central control over the accounting and reporting system.

♦ Cultural factors where, for example, cultures that tend towards secrecy are unlikely to adopt full disclosure in their financial reporting practices. Religion may also have an impact eg, Islamic law forbids the charging of interest, so debt finance will be unavailable.

2.6 Learning outcome

You have now covered the first learning outcome for this chapter:

Identify the influences on financial reporting of cultural differences across the world

3   International accounting standards

3.1   The role of IASs in the UK

 UK Financial Reporting Standards are formulated with due regard to international developments.

The International Accounting Standards Board (IASB) develops International Accounting Standards (IASs) in a similar way to the ASB issuing FRSs in the UK. The Accounting Standards Board supports the IASB in its aim to harmonise international financial reporting.

Each FRS contains a section explaining how it relates to the IAS dealing with the same topic.

In most cases compliance with an FRS automatically ensures compliance with the relevant IAS.

For UK companies, where the requirements of a UK accounting standard and an IAS differ, the current requirement is that the relevant UK accounting standard should be followed. However this is set to change for listed companies from 2005, as explained below.

The ASB has planned its agenda to include many of the issues that are the subjects of IASB standards.

This allows the ASB to develop its views through consultation with the financial community so that it can exert an influence on the development of IASs.

3.2   Example

Abroad Ltd is a 100% owned subsidiary of Home plc, a UK based company. Abroad Ltd is located in a foreign country and was purchased on 1 November 20X5. The financial statements of Abroad Ltd are drawn up in accordance with the local accounting regulations. The following translated profit and loss account related to Abroad Ltd for the year ended 31 October 20X6.

ABROAD LTD
PROFIT AND LOSS ACCOUNT FOR THE YEAR ENDED 31 OCTOBER 20X6

	£000	£000
Turnover		8,900
Cost of sales		(7,094)
		1,806
Sales and distribution cost	(633)	
Motor lorry depreciation	(32)	
Administration and finance costs	(541)	
Interest received	161	
Interest paid	(172)	
		(1,217)
Profit before taxation		589
Taxation: Corporation tax	(20)	
Deferred taxation	(68)	
		(88)
Profit after taxation		501
Extraordinary profit	103	
Less taxation	(33)	
		70
Profit after tax and extraordinary items		571
Dividends paid and proposed		(52)
Retained profit for the year		519

The following notes are relevant to the above profit and loss account.

(a)   The extraordinary profit comprises the following elements. The company had withdrawn from a contract to develop property. As a result, it was felt that there were costs to be incurred of £50,000 before taxation relief (32%). Additionally the company had made profits on the sale of a factory. This factory had not been used for production purposes for several years. The profit on the sale of the factory was calculated using depreciated historical cost of £85,000. The carrying value in the accounting records after a recent revaluation was £180,000. The tax charge provided for on this transaction was £49,000 under the law of the overseas country.

(b)   Abroad Ltd has overprovided for deferred taxation by an amount of £12,000.

(c)   The closing stock of Abroad Ltd includes stock of £2 million held on consignment from suppliers. The main terms of the consignment agreement, which can be terminated by either side, are such that Abroad Ltd can return any or all of the stock to the supplier without any penalty and the price paid to the supplier when goods are sold will depend upon the current price list of the supplier. The opening stock held on consignment from the same supplier was £1.25 million. No other accounting entries had been made regarding this stock.

(d)   Abroad Ltd had issued £2 million of 8% debenture stock on 1 November 20X5. This stock is repayable on 31 October 20X9 and costs of £12,000 were incurred. The issue costs and interest paid for the year were both included in the interest paid figure of £172,000 in Abroad Ltd's profit and loss account.

The auditors of Home plc have been asked to make the necessary adjustments to the financial statements in order to ensure that they comply with the UK Accounting Standards and the Companies Acts.

Required

Prepare a revised profit and loss account for the year ended 31 October 20X6 for Abroad Ltd in accordance with UK Accounting Standards and the Companies Acts.

3.3   Solution

ABROAD LTD - PROFIT AND LOSS ACCOUNT FOR THE YEAR ENDED 31 OCTOBER 20X6

	Notes	£000	£000
Turnover – continuing operations			8,900
Cost of sales	2		(7,844)
Gross profit			1,056
Distribution costs		665	
Administrative expenses		541	
			(1,206)
Operating loss			(150)
Provision for cost of withdrawal from property development		(50)	
Profit on disposal of tangible fixed assets	3	58	
			8
			(142)
Interest receivable		161	
Interest payable	4	(163)	
			(2)
Loss on ordinary activities before taxation			(144)
Taxation on ordinary activities	5		(109)
Loss on ordinary activities after taxation			(253)
Dividends paid and proposed			(52)
Retained loss for the year			(305)

Tutorial notes

1   Note the need to use the Companies Act format

2   Apply FRS 5 to the consignment stock

3   The extraordinary items must be separated, recalculated and shown as exceptional per FRS 3

4   Apply FRS 4 to the issue costs

5   Adjust deferred tax charge as instructed.

Workings (all workings in £000)

1   *Cost of sales*

Balance in profit and loss account	7,094
Add consignment stock at 31 October 20X6	2,000
Less consignment stock at 31 October 20X5	(1,250)
	7,844

FRS 5 *Reporting the Substance of Transactions* requires the above treatment of the consignment stock of Abroad Ltd. It is likely that a prior year adjustment would be made if this accounting practice had occurred in the previous year.

2   *Exceptional items*

Provision for cost of withdrawal from property development	50
Sale of factory – sale proceeds (103 + 50 + 85)	238
Less: carrying value	(180)
Profit on disposal	58

3   *Issue costs*

Year	Total cost – P&L a/c	Interest	Issue costs
1	163	160	3
2	163	160	3
3	163	160	3
4	163	160	3
	652	640	12

A straight line method of writing off issue costs has been adopted on the grounds of materiality.

4   *Taxation*

Tax charge in profit and loss account

Current charge	88
Decrease in deferred tax provision	(12)
Tax on 'extraordinary items' (49 – 16)	33
	(109)

Practice question 1 *(The answer is in the final chapter of this book)*

Orlando

(a) Discuss the potential benefits of greater harmonisation of international accounting policies and disclosure requirements, and comment on the obstacles hindering its progress.

(b) (i) Explain why you think each of the adjustments has been made in the statement below for Orlando group reconciling UK to US GAAP as at 31 May 20X5.

Income statement reconciliation

	£m
Net profit per UK GAAP	100
US GAAP Adjustments (assumed net of tax)	
Capitalised interest amortised	(5)
Elimination of results prior to merger	(190)
Acquisition accounting – additional depreciation	(200)
and amortisation of goodwill	——
Estimated reported loss as adjusted to accord with US GAAP	(295)
	——

(ii) Explain whether the equity as reported per UK GAAP will be increased or decreased when reconciled to the equity as adjusted to accord with US GAAP for the items in (b)(i).

(iii) Explain the effect on the equity of a proposed final dividend which under US GAAP has to be included in the year in which the directors propose to pay the dividends.

3.4 Differences between UK GAAP, IASs and US GAAP

The ASB has acted in recent years to eliminate many of the differences between UK Generally Accepted Accounting Principles (GAAP) and other international requirements. However, the table below illustrates some of the major differences that still remain.

	UK GAAP	IASs	US GAAP
Goodwill	Capitalise and amortise. Maximum life normally 20 years, but can be indefinite	Capitalise and amortise. Maximum life normally 20 years. Cannot be indefinite	Capitalise but do not amortise, subject to an annual impairment test.
Development costs	If criteria are met, either write off immediately, or capitalise	If criteria are met, must capitalise	Must be written off immediately
Tangible fixed assets	Carry at cost or valuation	Carry at cost or valuation	Carry at cost. Revaluation not permitted
Borrowing costs	Capitalisation is optional	Capitalisation is optional	Compulsory if criteria are met. Otherwise prohibited
Dividends	Must provide for proposed dividends, even if not declared until after the balance sheet date	Do not provide for dividends declared after the balance sheet date	Do not provide for dividends declared after the balance sheet date

3.5   Learning outcome

You have now covered the final learning outcomes for this chapter:

> Identify major differences between UK GAAP, IASs and US GAAP.
> Prepare and interpret international comparisons

4   The ASB convergence project

4.1   Introduction

 The European Union Council of Ministers decided in 2002 that, with effect from 1 January 2005, all listed companies in the EU must prepare their consolidated financial statements in accordance with adopted international accounting standards (effectively IASs and IFRSs, although the EU reserves the right to amend standards before adopting them. Hopefully this right will never be used). It is up to the UK government to decide whether individual (ie non-group) financial statements and the financial statements of unlisted companies should also have to comply with international standards. Consultations are currently proceeding on this point.

The ASB is hoping for a 'phased transition' under which UK standards are gradually amended in line with IASs between now and 2005. To that end, the ASB issued 7 FREDs in May 2002, proposing amendments to existing UK standards to bring them more in line with IASs.

FREDs 23, 24, 26 and 29 are covered in the relevant chapter of this text. FREDs 25, 27 and 28 are covered below, as is the topic of discounting which the ASB is considering together with the IASB.

For each FRED below, we give a brief summary of the current UK standard before commenting on the proposals of the FRED.

4.2   FRED 25: Related party disclosures

Current standard: FRS 8: related party disclosures

FRS 8 states that a true and fair view can only be given if financial statements disclose the details of the possibility that the financial results may have been affected by transactions with related parties.

Parties are defined as related if:

♦ one has direct or indirect control of the other, or

♦ they are subject to common control from the same source, or

♦ one influences the other to the extent that the other might not at all times pursue its own interests, or

♦ they are subject to influence from the same source, to the extent that one has subordinated its own separate interests.

FRS 8 requires the disclosure of:

♦ material transactions undertaken with a related party

♦ the name of the party controlling the reporting entity (whether or not any transactions have taken place between the reporting entity and this controlling entity)

No disclosure is required in consolidated financial statements of transactions and balances eliminated on consolidation.

No disclosure is required in the financial statements of subsidiaries, of transactions with other entities in the group, as long as the subsidiary is 90% or more owned within the group.

Proposed standard: FRED 25

In May 2002 the ASB issued FRED 25 as part of the project to align UK accounting with international standards. FRED 25 is based on a revised IAS expected to be published soon.

There are some changes in the detail of required disclosures if the UK moves from FRS 8 to FRED 25:

♦ FRED 25 does not require the names of transacting related parties to be disclosed (required by FRS 8).

♦ The exemption for subsidiaries' disclosures is only available to wholly-owned subsidiaries (FRS 8 exempts 90%-owned subsidiaries).

However the main thrust of FRED 25 is broadly equivalent to FRS 8, and few problems are envisaged in moving to a new standard based on FRED 25.

4.3   FRED 27: Events after the balance sheet date

Current standard: SSAP 17: Accounting for post balance sheet events

Post balance sheet events are events which occur between the balance sheet date and the date on which the financial statements are approved by the board of directors. SSAP 17 splits up post balance sheet events into two categories:

♦ adjusting events, which provide additional evidence of conditions existing at the balance sheet date

♦ non-adjusting events, which concern conditions arising after the balance sheet date.

Certain events (eg proposed dividends receivable and payable and transfers to reserves) occur after the balance sheet date but are treated as adjusting events under traditional UK accounting.

SSAP 17 requires that the amounts included in the financial statements should be changed if

♦ an adjusting event occurs, or

♦ application of the going concern concept is no longer appropriate

SSAP 17 requires that disclosure in a note to the accounts is necessary if

♦ a non-adjusting event occurs, or

♦ window-dressing has taken place at the balance sheet date

SSAP 17 also requires all financial statements to state the date on which they were approved by the board of directors.

An appendix to SSAP 17 contains the statement that, in exceptional circumstances, it may be necessary on the grounds of prudence to reclassify a non-adjusting event as adjusting, but no examples of this are provided.

Proposed standard: FRED 27

In May 2002 the ASB issued FRED 27 as part of the project to align UK accounting with international standards. FRED 27 is based on a revised IAS expected to be published soon.

FRED 27 contains an important amendment to the definition of adjusting events in SSAP 17. Although the definition looks the same (those events that provide evidence of conditions that existed at the balance sheet date), there is no longer the extension to the definition to cover items customarily included (proposed dividends, changes in tax rates and dividends receivable).

In particular, if dividends to holders of equity instruments are declared after the balance sheet date, then there is no obligation complying with the FRS 12 definition of a liability as at the balance sheet date, so proposed ordinary dividends are no longer to be shown in the current liabilities in the balance sheet if they were declared after the balance sheet date (the usual situation).

Although this new requirement appears technically sound, there is a problem in that the Companies Act formats currently require all dividends paid and proposed to be included in the profit and loss account. Thus a change in the law will be required before the FRED 27 proposals can be implemented; the ASB has asked the DTI to consider just such a change in the law.

FRED 27 also drops the idea of reclassifying non-adjusting events as adjusting events to comply with the prudence concept.

The FRS based on FRED 27 will be some time in coming, since the UK government must first amend the CA 85 accounting rules and formats in line with the revised requirements.

4.4   Publication of FRED 28

Current standard: SSAP 9: Stocks and long-term contracts

SSAP 9 deals with two linked topics:

♦   stocks other than long-term contracts

♦   long-term contracts.

The first of these is the 'normal' stocks appearing as a current asset in the balance sheet, including goods purchased for resale, raw materials, partly-completed products and finished goods. Such stocks should be stated in the balance sheet at the lower of cost and net realisable value.

'Cost' comprises all expenditure which has been incurred in the normal course of business in bringing the product or service to its present location and condition. Where the actual costs of the units in closing stock are not known, management must choose a method such as FIFO or average cost to provide a fair approximation to the actual cost of the items in stock.

'Net realisable value' is the estimated selling price, less all further costs to completion and all costs to be incurred in selling the items.

Long-term contracts should be assessed on a contract by contract basis and the relevant turnover and costs should be recognised in the profit and loss account as contract activity progresses.

Once the profitable outcome of a contract can be foreseen with reasonable certainty, attributable profit can be recognised in the profit and loss account. If a contract is expected to make a loss, the full amount of the loss must be recognised as soon as it is foreseen.

The balance sheet contains several entries in respect of long-term contracts:

♦ the cost incurred to date, less amounts transferred to cost of sales, is included in stocks.

♦ the amount by which recognised turnover exceeds payments made on account is included in debtors

♦ any excess payments made on account are included in creditors

♦ a provision for foreseeable losses should be included in provisions

Proposed standard: FRED 28

In May 2002 the ASB issued FRED 28 as part of the project to align UK accounting with international standards. Since IASs deal with the topics of stocks and long-term contracts in two different standards, it is proposed to withdraw SSAP 9 and replace it with two new FRSs, 'Inventories' dealing with stocks other than long-term contracts, and 'Construction and service contracts' dealing with long-term contracts.

Inventories

The normal rule from SSAP 9 continues: inventories should be measured at the lower of cost and net realisable value. Items that are not interchangeable should be costed at their individual unit costs. Items that are interchangeable should be costed using either FIFO or the weighted average cost method.

Construction and service contracts

SSAP 9 requires attributable profits on long-term contracts to be 'prudently calculated' once the outcome of a contract can be assessed with 'reasonable certainty'. FRED 28 requires recognition of contract revenue and contract costs once the outcome of a contract can be 'estimated reliably'. In stressing reliability rather than prudence, FRED 28 is more in keeping with FRS 18 and the Statement of Principles.

In practice the net effect on the profit and loss account and the balance sheet of the FRED 28 rules for long-term contracts rather than the SSAP 9 rules is expected to be minimal.

4.5   Discounting

Introduction

An example of a topic that the ASB is examining alongside other international standard-setters is discounting. No official guidance currently exists, so that for example a receivable of £1m in one week's time and another receivable of £1m in ten years' time would both be shown in a balance sheet at £1m. Should there be a requirement for long-term payables and receivables to be discounted to their fair values?

ASB work to date

In 1997 the ASB issued a Working Paper 'Discounting in Financial Reporting' to stimulate debate on this topic. The ASB decided in the Working Paper that it did not propose to develop an FRS dealing with discounting. Instead each FRS would contain individual requirements appropriate to discounting in that area. For example, FRS 19 permits but does not require discounting when calculating deferred tax assets and liabilities, whereas the relevant IAS does not permit discounting when calculating deferred tax balances.

Future developments

There is clearly still some work to be done in this area. The IASB has disbanded the previous IASC project that was working on this topic, so no international standard is expected in the near future. Thus, the ASB is expected to place this topic on the back burner while it concentrates on other areas of higher priority.

5   *Summary*

International harmonisation of accounting practices is a laudable objective, towards which great progress has been made in recent years. In fact, IASs have become so popular that the future of domestic standard-setting is being questioned. Perhaps all countries should give up their own accounting standards and simply adopt IASs. It remains to be seen whether such a development is practical.

Multiple choice questions (The answers are in the final chapter of this book)

1   Abba Ltd is a wholly-owned subsidiary of Beatle Ltd. Abba Ltd operates in the country of Galvania and its accounts are drawn up according to local accounting rules. On this basis the reported profit after tax is £143,000.

On analysis of the profit and loss account the following is discovered:

(a)   Deferred tax has been provided for on the partial provision basis. Provision was made in the year for £15,000 and the unprovided amount totals £12,000.

(b)   A profit has been recorded on the sale of a property for £120,000. The property had originally cost £80,000 and had a net book value of £98,000. A profit of £40,000 was included in the profit and loss account.

(c)   Research costs of £16,000 have been capitalised in the balance sheet.

What would be the profit after tax for the year under UK GAAP?

A   £94,000

B   £97,000

C   £114,000

D   £137,000

2   Which of the following statements is correct?

A   Under UK GAAP, IASs and US GAAP capitalisation of borrowing costs when constructing one's own fixed assets is optional.

B   Under UK GAAP, IASs and US GAAP revaluation of fixed assets is allowed.

C   Under UK GAAP and IASs the maximum useful life for goodwill is normally 20 years but under US GAAP goodwill may be retained indefinitely subject to an impairment test.

D   Under UK GAAP and IASs development costs may be written off or capitalised but under US GAAP they must be capitalised.

CHAPTER 25

Environmental and social reporting

EXAM FOCUS

Environmental reporting, social reporting and human resource accounting are all fashionable topics that the examiner may wish to examine. There is generally no legal framework for such reporting, so the company is free to present the information in any form it wishes.

LEARNING OUTCOMES

This chapter covers the following Learning Outcomes of the CIMA Syllabus.

> Explain how financial information concerning the interaction of a business with the natural environment can be communicated in the published accounts
>
> Identify those environmental issues which should be disclosed
>
> Explain the process of measuring, recording and disclosing the effect of exchanges between a business and its sociological environment – human resource accounting

In order to cover these Learning Outcomes the following topics are included.

> Environmental reporting
> Issues in environmental accounting
> Social reporting

---

1 Environmental reporting

1.1 Introduction

Environmental reporting is the communication of information, in the published annual report or elsewhere, on the effect that the activities of the business have on the natural environment.

Traditionally, such reporting has been voluntary. More recently a debate has started on whether environmental reporting should be made mandatory. In the Netherlands and New Zealand, for example, legislation on environmental reporting has been introduced. The voluntary European Eco-Management and Audit Scheme (EMAS) requires that environmental statements should be produced, as does International Standard ISO 14001 (though it is not specified that they are made publicly available).

1.2 Existing regulation

You should already be familiar with the concept of an Operating and Financial Review. The ASB has issued a non-mandatory statement of best practice (revised in January 2003) recommending that listed companies and other large entities should contain information in the annual report concerning:

- a description of the business, its objectives and strategy
- an operating review explaining the performance achieved
- a financial review explaining the capital structure and the treasury policy

The statement recommends that where a business has objectives in the area of corporate responsibility, these should be stated in the OFR. Similarly it might be appropriate to discuss risks relating to environmental issues in the 'operating' section of the OFR.

However the ASB's statement on the OFR is non-mandatory, so we have to look instead at accounting standards to provide any mandatory regulation on environmental issues.

Where environmental liabilities fall within the scope of FRS 12, ie there is a legal or constructive obligation as a result of a past event, then the rules contained in FRS 12 must be applied. But the act of contaminating the environment does not in itself create an obligation to repair the damage.

1.3 Possible forms of report

There are two possible forms of environmental report:

(a) a section within the published annual report. For example all the disclosures that a company wishes to make could be included within the Operating and Financial Review

(b) a separate environmental report, either published as a stand-alone paper document, or simply posted on the company's website.

1.4 Examples of disclosure

The Body Shop International plc is a company which prides itself on its commitment to social and ethical issues. In its Annual Report and Accounts 2000 it contained the following mission statement:

Body Shop Mission Statement

- To dedicate our business to the pursuit of social and environmental change

- To creatively balance the financial and human needs of our stakeholders: employees, franchisees, customers, suppliers and shareholders

- To courageously ensure that our business is ecologically sustainable: meeting the needs of the present without compromising the future

- To meaningfully contribute to local, national and international communities in which we trade, by adopting a code of conduct which ensures care, honesty, fairness and respect

- To passionately campaign for the protection of the environment, human and civil rights, and against animal testing within the cosmetics and toiletries industry

- To tirelessly work to narrow the gap between principle and practice, whilst making fun, passion and care part of our daily lives

---

Most large companies make some sort of comment on environmental matters in their Annual Report, in the directors' report, chairman's report, Operating and Financial Review, or elsewhere. But the most comprehensive disclosure of environmental matters is usually in a separate environmental report. This will typically contain the following contents:

- Introduction from the Chief Executive.

- Background information about the organisation.

- The organisation's Environmental Policy.

- The organisation's overall position with regard to the environment (frequently broken down into smaller business units for large organisations).

- Progress made towards specific targets established in previous reports.

- Setting of new targets or actions to improve the organisation's environmental performance in the future.

Organisations that have committed themselves to produce annual environmental reports will have to collect new data each year to show their progress achieved. This will produce an ongoing pressure to improve their environmental performance.

For example, Corus Group plc (formed in 1999 from the old British Steel) published a 44 page environmental report in 2000 describing the Group's environmental performance during 1999 and detailing targets for improvements. As well as a number of case studies, the report's contents were:

- Introducing Corus
- Message from the Chairman
- Sustainability and other key issues
- Corporate environmental policy
- Environmental targets
- Approach to environmental management
- Environmental protection costs
- Operational performance
- Product development
- Corus in the community
- Validation
- Glossary

The most relevant sections to your studies are the 'Corporate environmental policy' and the 'Environmental targets' which are reproduced below.

Corporate environmental policy

Corus Group plc considers care for the environment to be essential, both in terms of our duty to society and to ensure the continuity of our business. We are committed to protecting the environment by minimising the impact of our operations and our products through the adoption of sustainable practices and through continuous improvement in environmental performance and control.

Our objectives are to:

- meet the requirements of all relevant legislation and agreements, in all countries and regions in which we operate

- implement effective environmental management systems and to ensure the environmental awareness of our workforce, while encouraging every employee to act in an environmentally responsible manner

- improve the environmental performance of our processes by reducing emissions, minimising waste and controlling noise

- contribute to sustainable development by using energy and raw materials more efficiently, thus optimising our use of natural resources

♦ evaluate the environmental impacts associated with the manufacture and use of our products and by-products, and to research and develop new technologies for improvements

♦ help customers understand the environmental effects of our products throughout their life cycle

♦ promote the recovery, recycling and reuse of our products

♦ encourage suppliers and contractors to maintain sound environmental practices

♦ respect the general environment and wildlife habitats in and around our sites and, where appropriate, progressively improve their visual amenity

♦ respond to the concerns of local communities and other interested parties on environmental issues

♦ co-operate with government and regulatory authorities in the development of cost-effective legislation

♦ audit environmental performance and report progress on policy objectives on a regular basis

We put our environmental policy into practice as follows:

♦ Compliance with legislation and other agreements, such as covenants, is achieved through effective environmental management systems, for example ISO 14001 or equivalent, within each business unit. Any temporary, inadvertent, non-compliance is corrected as soon as possible. Where adequate regulations do not exist, we adopt and apply internal standards that reflect our commitment to the environment.

♦ Concern for the environment is integral to our organisation. We believe that protection of the environment is the responsibility of everybody and expect all employees, contractors and visitors to behave in an environmentally responsible manner. Appropriate and effective education and training on environmental matters are provided at all levels within the Group.

♦ Product stewardship is vital to sustainability. In this respect, we focus on the environmental aspects of our products throughout their life cycle; optimising our use of natural resources by minimising inputs of raw materials and energy. Through research and development and the application of life-cycle assessment (LCA) techniques, we demonstrate a sustainable approach by developing cleaner techniques for the manufacture, use, application, recovery and recycling of our products and by-products.

♦ Our aim is to continuously improve the environmental performance of our processes and products, within the constraints of our financial position. This includes reducing emissions to air and water, minimising solid waste arisings and controlling noise to acceptable levels. Performance is monitored and targets are set, where appropriate. We take into account the expectations of the public, modern management practices and the latest scientific knowledge and technology. Due consideration is given to local wildlife habitats and to the visual appearance of our sites.

♦ We communicate widely, internally and externally, about environmental issues and also respond to any concerns which may arise. This includes our employees; local communities; local authorities; non-governmental organisations; financial institutions; schools, colleges and other educational establishments; industry groups at national and international level; and shareholders.

♦ We aim to ensure that environmental legislation and agreements achieve their objectives in the most cost-effective manner. We therefore support governments and regulatory authorities by providing expertise and assistance in the development of legislation, where appropriate.

♦ To assess progress on improving environmental performance and in meeting policy objectives, internal audits, led by a central audit manager, are carried out as necessary. These audits are an effective means of transferring best practice and knowledge between different business units and sites.

♦ Through supply chain management, including auditing where appropriate, we encourage suppliers and contractors to behave in a responsible manner and to maintain sound environmental practices.

♦ Where future planning and investments are concerned, we endeavour to adopt processes that are not only economic but also have a minimum impact on the environment. All newly installed plant and equipment will be capable of meeting, as a minimum, the applicable up-to-date national and international standards.

Environmental targets

Our targets are to:

♦ achieve 95% certification to ISO 14001 for all Corus European manufacturing operations by the end of 2002

♦ audit all major suppliers and contractors by the end of 2002 and set improvement targets for those not meeting ISO 14001 or equivalent standards

♦ undertake appropriate risk assessments for any potentially contaminated land at all European sites under Corus ownership by the end of 2001

♦ reduce emissions of perfluoro-carbons from the primary aluminium production process by 50%, compared to 1990, by the end of 2005

♦ reduce total energy consumption in the UK by 10% by 2010, compared to 1997, and to become one of the world's top steelmakers and primary aluminium producers in terms of energy use in the Netherlands by 2012

♦ fully evaluate the potential for the suppression of dioxin emissions from the iron ore sintering process by the end of 2001

♦ quantify the emissions associated with our transportation of materials and people by the end of 2001

♦ reduce waste to landfill by 10% from 1999 levels by the end of 2002

♦ increase the amount of steel packaging waste recycled in the UK by 20%, compared to 1999 levels, by the end of 2001

♦ install, where necessary, enhanced incoming scrap and product radiation detection equipment at all steelmaking sites by the end of 2002

♦ identify and assess, where necessary, our contribution to ambient air concentrations of fine dust particles (PM10s) and evaluate options for improvement by the end of 2003.

1.5   Learning outcome

You have now covered the first learning outcome for this chapter:

> Explain how financial information concerning the interaction of a business with the natural environment can be communicated in the published accounts

2 Issues in environmental accounting

2.1 Terminology

Environmental costs include environmental measures and environmental losses:

♦ *Environmental measures* are the costs of conserving resources and the costs of preventing, reducing or repairing damage to the natural environment

♦ *Environmental losses* are costs which bring no benefit to the business (eg, fines imposed for noxious emissions)

2.2 Accounting for environmental costs

There is no accounting standard that deals specifically with environmental costs, so you must apply existing UK GAAP as normal. The biggest problem is likely to centre around provisions for future costs, where FRS 12 applies.

2.3 Example

AB plc causes contamination while operating in a country where there is no environmental legislation. However, the company has a widely published environmental policy in which it undertakes to clean up all contamination that it causes. The company is committed to honouring this published policy.

Should a provision be recognised for the cost of the clean-up?

2.4 Solution

The company has a constructive obligation as a result of a past event (the contamination), so should set up a provision for the best estimate of the costs of the clean-up.

2.5 Learning outcome

You have now covered the second learning outcome for this chapter:

Identify those environmental issues which should be disclosed

3 Social reporting

3.1 Terminology

Social reporting is the communication of information, in the published annual report or elsewhere, on the effect that the activities of the business have on the sociological environment (ie, on society as a whole).

A business will interact with society in a number of ways:

(a) it employs human resources in the form of its employees and pays them wages

(b) it might damage the local environment (eg, emit smoke into the air) which decreases the enjoyment of local people

(c) it produces outputs (ie, goods for sale) which can increase or decrease the enjoyment of local people. For example, hearing aids might benefit the elderly, while loud car audio systems might be a nuisance to them.

3.2   *Preparing social accounts and social reports*

Academics have proposed that a social income statement and a social balance sheet should be prepared, disclosing the benefits and costs of the company's activities on society. However this is unlikely to be practical due to the necessary subjectivity involved in measuring the items involved.

Instead, social reporting has followed the same path as environmental reporting already described, with a social report prepared, either as part of the annual report, or in a stand-alone document. In some companies the social report is combined with the environmental report as an overall ethical report.

3.3   *Typical contents of a social report*

A social report might contain

♦   information on the company's relationship with each of its categories of stakeholders (eg, facilities offered to customers, wages and salaries paid to employees, involvement in the local community)

♦   information on the company's accountability to society (eg, noise levels, accident rates, number of disabled employees)

♦   information concerning targets for ethical standards and ecological sustainability

You will be aware that some of these items are already required to be disclosed in a statutory set of accounts, for example the number of employees and their aggregate remuneration must be disclosed in a note, while the total of political and charitable contributions (if more than £200) must be disclosed in the directors' report.

3.4   *Human resource accounting*

Human resource accounting is the process of recognising, measuring and disclosing the human resources (ie, the employees) of a business in the financial statements. It is one component of social accounting.

Under human resource accounting, the human resources of the business are capitalised as an intangible fixed asset and then amortised over the period during which the business expects to derive benefit from them.

The question arises as to whether human resources are assets that can be recognised. Remember the rules of the Statement of Principles:

(a)   an asset is defined as rights or other access to future economic benefits controlled by an entity as a result of past transactions or events

(b)   an asset should be recognised if there is sufficient evidence that it exists and it can be measured at a monetary amount with sufficient reliability.

In the real world it is probably uncertain whether the employer can *control* the benefits from an employee's service. An employee could always go sick or refuse to turn up for work, in which case the employer has no control over the flow of benefits.

Some large football clubs recognise their players on the balance sheet, but otherwise human resource accounting is rarely seen in practice.

3.5   *Learning outcome*

You have now covered the final learning outcome for this chapter:

> Explain the process of measuring, recording and disclosing the effect of exchanges between a business and its sociological environment – human resource accounting.

4   Summary

Environmental and social reporting is an evolving topic, following the growing public interest in protecting the environment and promoting high ethical standards.

Those companies that do produce environmental reports and social reports generally do so as stand-alone documents (in paper or on the company website) rather than as part of the published annual report.

Multiple choice question (The answer is in the final chapter of this book)

1   A company has two foreign subsidiary companies, Ferndale Ltd and Fernbank Ltd.

The country in which Ferndale Ltd operates has just passed a new law requiring environmentally sound adjustments to factory emissions. Ferndale Ltd has four such factories and the cost of the adjustments is estimated as £20,000 per factory.

Fernbank Ltd operates in a country where there is no environmental legislation, however the company has always, in the past, cleaned up any contamination that it has caused. Fernbank Ltd is well known in this country for this policy. The estimated cost of cleaning up contamination caused to date by Fernbank Ltd is £100,000.

What provision should there be in the consolidated balance sheet for environmental costs?

A   None

B   £80,000

C   £100,000

D   £180,000

CHAPTER 26

Ratio analysis

EXAM FOCUS

The analysis of financial statements represents 20% of the syllabus. That means that a question based on this chapter (and to a lesser extent based on the next two chapters on earnings per share and segmental reporting) should be expected in most examinations.

LEARNING OUTCOMES

This chapter covers the following Learning Outcomes of the CIMA Syllabus.

> Evaluate financial statements and prepare a concise report on the results of the analysis
>
> Identify the limitations of analysis based on financial statements
>
> Explain the weaknesses of the financial report which reduce its effectiveness in communicating meaningful information to users.
>
> Prepare and interpret inter-firm comparisons

In order to cover these Learning Outcomes the following topics are included.

> Introduction to interpretation of accounts
> Profitability ratios
> Liquidity ratios
> Gearing ratios
> Investors' ratios
> Influences on ratios
> Interpretation technique

---

1 Introduction to interpretation of accounts

1.1 Users and their information needs

A useful start in the interpretation of accounts is to establish which classes of people have an interest in the messages conveyed by accounts. In other words, we try to ascertain who are the users of accounts and what information they need.

Shareholders and potential investors are primarily concerned with receiving an adequate return on their investment, but it must at least provide security and liquidity.

Creditors are concerned with the security of their debt or loan and therefore evaluate the company's liquidity to determine the amount and period of credit they consider prudent.

Management are concerned with the trend and level of profits, since this is the main measure of their success. Salaries may be linked to profits.

Bank managers and financial institutions, employees, professional advisors to investors, financial journalists and commentators are interested in liquidity, profit potential, or ownership of a company.

 This is summarised in Figure 1 below. The ratios listed in Figure 1 will all be discussed in this chapter.

Figure 1   Users and their information needs

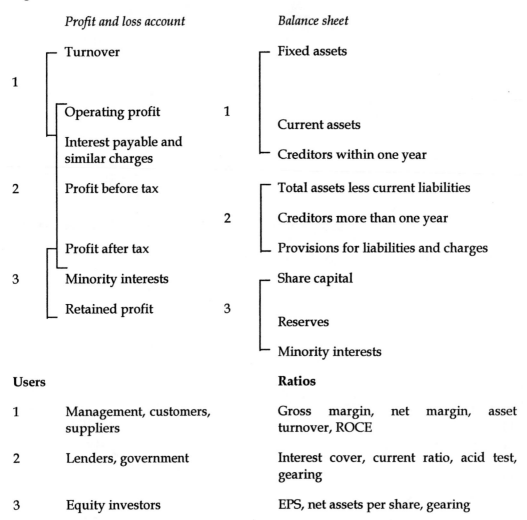

	Profit and loss account		*Balance sheet*	
1	Turnover		Fixed assets	
	Operating profit	1		
			Current assets	
	Interest payable and similar charges		Creditors within one year	
2	Profit before tax		Total assets less current liabilities	
		2	Creditors more than one year	
	Profit after tax		Provisions for liabilities and charges	
3	Minority interests		Share capital	
	Retained profit	3	Reserves	
			Minority interests	

Users		**Ratios**
1	Management, customers, suppliers	Gross margin, net margin, asset turnover, ROCE
2	Lenders, government	Interest cover, current ratio, acid test, gearing
3	Equity investors	EPS, net assets per share, gearing

All users require information on liquidity and cash flow.

1.2   Accounting ratios

A vital tool in the interpretation of accounts is the use of ratio analysis. We will be looking in detail at the main ratios in the course of this chapter. Table 1 below provides a summary that you can use for reference.

Table 1 The main accounting ratios

Ratio	Calculation
Profitability	
Return on capital employed	$\dfrac{\text{Profit before interest payable and tax}}{\text{Capital employed}} \times 100\%$ where capital employed = total assets less current liabilities
Profit margin on sales	$\dfrac{\text{Profit before interest payable and tax}}{\text{Turnover}} \times 100\%$
Asset turnover	$\dfrac{\text{Turnover}}{\text{Capital employed}}$
Fixed asset turnover	$\dfrac{\text{Turnover}}{\text{Fixed assets}}$
Gross margin	$\dfrac{\text{Gross profit}}{\text{Turnover}} \times 100\%$
Working capital turnover	$\dfrac{\text{Turnover}}{\text{Net current assets}}$
Liquidity and use of assets	
Current ratio	$\dfrac{\text{Current assets}}{\text{Current liabilities}}$
Quick ratio	$\dfrac{\text{Current assets} - \text{stock}}{\text{Current liabilities}}$
Stock turnover	$\dfrac{\text{Cost of sales}}{\text{Stock}}$
Debtors collection period	$\dfrac{\text{Trade debtors}}{\text{Credit sales}} \times 365 \text{ days}$
Debtor turnover	$\dfrac{\text{Credit sales}}{\text{Trade debtors}}$
Creditors payment period	$\dfrac{\text{Trade creditors}}{\text{Purchases}} \times 365 \text{ days}$
Gearing	
Gearing ratio	$\dfrac{\text{Loans and preference share capital}}{\text{Capital employed}} \times 100\%$
Debt/Equity	$\dfrac{\text{Loans and preference share capital}}{\text{Ordinary shareholders' funds}} \times 100\%$
Interest cover	$\dfrac{\text{Profit before interest payable and tax}}{\text{Interest payable}}$

Ratio	Calculation
Investors' ratios	
Earnings per share	$\dfrac{\text{Profit after tax and minority interests} - \text{preference dividends}}{\text{Number of ordinary shares in issue}}$
Earnings yield	$\dfrac{\text{Earnings per share}}{\text{Current market price per share}} \times 100\%$
Dividend yield	$\dfrac{\text{Dividend per share}}{\text{Current market price per share}} \times 100\%$
Dividend cover	$\dfrac{\text{Earnings per share}}{\text{Dividend per share}}$
Price/earnings ratio	$\dfrac{\text{Current market price per share}}{\text{Earnings per share}}$
Net assets per share	$\dfrac{\text{Net assets (shareholders' funds)}}{\text{Number of shares}}$

1.3   Benefits and limitations of ratios

Ratios are a tool to assist analysis. They help to focus attention systematically on important areas and summarise information in an understandable form. They assist in identifying trends and relationships.

Ratios must always be considered in relation to other information, for example:

♦ previous performance
♦ budgeted performance (for management use)
♦ competitors/industry average.

Ratios are not predictive if they are based on historical information (they ignore future action by management). They may be distorted by differences in accounting policies.

Finally, comparisons between different types of business are difficult because of differing resource structures and market characteristics.

Ratios are not the only tool used in interpretation of accounts.

♦ Absolute comparisons can provide information without computing ratios, eg comparing a balance sheet between this year and last.

♦ Background information supplied about the nature of the business may help to explain changes or trends.

2   Profitability ratios

2.1   Introduction

These ratios are used as a basis for assessing management effectiveness in generating profits from the resources under their control.

Return on capital employed (ROCE) measures the return achieved by management from assets which they control, before payments to providers of financing for those assets (ie lenders and shareholders). Usually year-end capital employed is used to compute this ratio.

ROCE can be sub-divided into profit margin and asset turnover.

Profit margin	×	Asset turnover	=	ROCE
$\dfrac{\text{PBIT}}{\text{Turnover}}$	×	$\dfrac{\text{Turnover}}{\text{Capital employed}}$	=	$\dfrac{\text{PBIT}}{\text{Capital employed}}$

PBIT = profit before interest and taxation.

Profit margin is often seen as an indication of the quality of products or services supplied (top-of-range products usually have higher margins). Asset turnover is often seen as a measure of how intensively the assets are worked.

A trade-off may exist between margin and asset turnover.

♦   Low-margin businesses (eg food retailers) usually have a high asset turnover.

♦   Capital-intensive manufacturing industries usually have relatively low asset turnover but higher margins (eg electrical equipment manufacturers).

2.2   Example

Below are extracts from the most recent draft accounts of Radioactive Communications plc and Pineapple Distributors plc. Radioactive Communications plc provides telecommunications services. Pineapple Distributors plc markets and distributes fresh produce.

Radioactive Communications Plc
Consolidated profit and loss account for the year ended 31 March 20X2

	£m
Turnover	3,176.2
Trading profit	726.9
Associated undertakings	22.3
Exceptional loss	(70.3)
Interest receivable	23.6
Interest payable	(59.0)
Profit on ordinary activities before taxation	643.5
Taxation	(134.1)
Profit on ordinary activities after taxation	509.4
Minority interests	(185.7)
Profit for the financial year	323.7

Consolidated balance sheet at 31 March 20X2

	£m	£m
Total assets less current liabilities		3,831.7
Creditors: amounts falling due after more than one year	795.7	
Provisions for liabilities and charges		
Deferred taxation	105.4	
Other provisions	58.2	
		959.3
Net assets		2,872.4

Capital and reserves

Called up share capital	539.6
Share premium account	303.1
Associated undertakings	41.7
Profit and loss account	1,479.0
	2,363.4
Minority interests	509.0
	2,872.4

At 31 March 20X2 short-term bank loans and overdrafts were £69.9 million.

Pineapple Distributors Plc
Consolidated profit and loss account for the year ended 31 March 20X2

	£000
Turnover	625,049
Cost of sales	(538,664)
Gross profit	86,385
Administrative expenses	(67,267)
Profit before interest	19,118
Interest receivable	9,212
Interest payable	(6,116)
Profit before exceptional items	22,214
Exceptional loss	(1,839)
Profit on ordinary items before taxation	20,375
Taxation	(5,966)
Profit on ordinary activities after taxation	14,409
Minority interests	(117)
Profit for the financial year	14,292

Consolidated balance sheet at 31 March 20X2

	£000
Total assets less current liabilities	128,227
Creditors: amounts falling due after more than one year	(31,851)
Provisions for liabilities and charges	(6,314)
Net assets	90,062
Capital and reserves	
Called up share capital	3,577
Share premium account	12,040
Other reserves	180
Profit and loss account	68,792
	84,589
Minority interests	5,473
	90,062

At 31 March 20X2 short-term bank loans and overdrafts amounted to £23,178,000.

Required

Calculate ROCE, net profit margin and asset turnover for both companies.

2.3 Solution

ROCE

$$\frac{\text{PBIT}}{\text{Capital employed}} = \frac{\text{PBIT}}{\text{Turnover}} \times \frac{\text{Turnover}}{\text{Capital employed}}$$

Total assets - Current liabilities = Capital + Reserves + Long-term liabilities

Radioactive Communications plc

ROCE	$\frac{643.5+59.0}{2,872.4+959.3} \times 100\%$	=	18.33%
Net profit margin	$\frac{643.5+59.0}{3,176.2} \times 100\%$	=	22.11%
Asset turnover	$\frac{3,176.2}{2,872.4+959.3}$	=	0.83 times

Pineapple Distributors plc

ROCE	$\frac{20,375+6,116}{128,227} \times 100\%$	=	20.66%
Net profit margin	$\frac{20,375+6,116}{625,049} \times 100\%$	=	4.24%
Asset turnover	$\frac{625,049}{128,227}$	=	4.87 times

Net profit margin × Asset turnover = ROCE

Radioactive Communications plc	22.11%	×	0.83	=	18.33%
Pineapple Distributors plc	4.24%	×	4.87	=	20.66%

Tutorial note. When calculating ROCE, short-term bank loans and overdrafts may be included in capital employed. If short-term borrowings were taken into account the ROCE for both companies would be as follows:

Radioactive Communications plc

$$\frac{643.5+59.0}{2,872.4+959.3+69.9} \times 100\% = \quad 18.0\%$$

Pineapple Distributors plc

$$\frac{20,375+6,116}{128,227+23,178} \times 100\% = \quad 17.5\%$$

3 Liquidity ratios

3.1 Introduction

Liquidity ratios are used to assess a company's ability to raise cash to meet payments when due.

Note the following limitations of liquidity ratios.

♦ Some current assets (eg stocks) may not be readily convertible into cash, other than at a large discount.

♦ As the quick ratio omits stocks, it is a more useful ratio but is subject to distortions. For example, retailers have few debtors and utilise cash from sales quickly, but finance their stocks from trade creditors. Hence, their quick ratios are usually low.

A cash flow statement is often more useful than the balance sheet when analysing liquidity.

3.2 Example

Big Ron Plc
Group cash flow statement for the year ended 31 December 20X7

Notes		£000	£000
(1)	Net cash inflow from operating activities		926
	Returns on investments and servicing of finance		
	Finance charge element of finance lease rentals paid	(45)	
	Interest received	130	
	Interest paid	(120)	
	Dividends paid to minority shareholders	(25)	
			(60)
	Taxation		(98)
	Capital expenditure		
	Cash paid to acquire tangible fixed assets	(307)	
	Cash proceeds on sale of freehold site	900	
	Cash proceeds on sale of other tangible fixed assets	70	
			663
(4)	*Acquisitions and disposals*		
	Net cash acquired with subsidiary		215
	Equity dividends paid		(600)
	Financing		
	Capital element of finance lease rentals paid	(40)	
	Proceeds of issue of bonds	280	
	Redemption of 15% loan notes	(800)	
			(560)
	Increase in cash		486

Notes to the cash flow statement

(1) *Reconciliation of operating profit to net cash inflow from operating activities*

	£000
Operating profit	329
Depreciation	588
Decrease in stocks	1
Increase in debtors	(45)
Increase in creditors	53
Net cash inflow from operating activities	926

(2)   *Reconciliation of net cash flow to movement in net debt (Note 3)*

	£000	£000
Increase in cash in the period	486	
Cash inflow from decrease in debt and increase in lease financing	560	
Change in net debt resulting from cash flows		1,046
New finance leases		(900)
Translation difference		221
Change in net debt		367
Net debt at 1 January 20X7		(1,471)
Net debt at 31 December 20X7		(1,104)

(3)   *Analysis of changes in debt*

	At 1 January 20X7	Cash flows	Other non-cash changes	Exchange movement	At 31 December 20X7
	£000	£000	£000	£000	£000
Cash at bank and in hand	197	(98)		221	320
Bank overdrafts	(732)	584			(148)
		486			
Debt due after one year	(936)	520			(416)
		40	(900)		(860)
		560			
Total	(1,471)	1,046	(900)	221	(1,104)

(4)   *Acquisition of subsidiary undertaking — Vehicle plc*

	£000
Net assets acquired (31 December 20X7)	
Tangible fixed assets	272
Stocks	80
Debtors	53
Cash	215
Creditors	(73)
	547
Consideration	
Issue of equity shares	400
Deferred consideration	147
	547

The sale and leaseback of the freeholds was entered into on 1 January 20X7. Zero coupon bonds were issued during the year at a discount of £220,000.

Required

Critically appraise the methods of financing and cash generation used by the company in the year, and explain their implications on future cash flows.

3.3   Solution

Overall strategy. The company has undertaken a major re-structuring of its financing during the year with the primary goal of reducing short-term and high coupon borrowings. The company has also kept a high level of dividend payout in order to maintain stock market ratings.

Methods of cash generation and financing. The necessary financing for the restructuring has been raised as follows.

(a)   Sale and leaseback

The company has raised £900,000 by entering into a sale and leaseback arrangement on one of its major freehold properties. The lease is clearly for a substantial term given the level of rentals and the accounting as a finance lease, and thus the operations of the business will not be affected.

The arrangement will result in a cash outflow of £85,000 per annum in future periods for rentals.

(b)   Acquisition of subsidiary undertaking

Big Ron plc acquired during the year a highly cash-rich subsidiary, Vehicle plc. The method of financing this acquisition was chosen to entail no cash outflows in the current period and represents an inexpensive source of financing.

The consideration comprised a share issue and an element of deferred consideration. The latter component will possibly entail future cash outflows of more than the £147,000 recorded in the financial statements if the £147,000 represents a discounted present value.

(c)   Issue of zero coupon bond

£280,000 was raised by the issue of a zero coupon bond. In the short run this will be beneficial as no interest payments will be required. In the longer term, the bond will entail a major cash repayment of £500,000 which must be budgeted for.

(d)   Foreign exchange gains

Owing to foreign subsidiaries (accounted for using the temporal method) holding substantial cash balances, relative falls in the value of sterling have resulted in substantial gains to the company. These gains represent the increase in the sterling value of the subsidiaries' cash balances although they do not represent actual cash flow.

Currency gains cannot be relied on to recur and the holdings of cash in subsidiaries abroad should be monitored to avoid future exchange losses.

Effect of usage of cash generated. The company has largely repaid its overdrafts, and has redeemed the bulk of its 15% loan notes. These repayments have substantial cash flow benefits by removing substantial interest payments at high rates. The nature of the finance raised has resulted in a lower fixed return burden allowing the payment of a high level of dividends. The restructuring overall is likely to have a substantial beneficial effect on Big Ron plc's share price.

3.4   Use of assets

A number of ratios are used to assess management effectiveness in controlling the business. These include:

♦   stock turnover rate
♦   debtors collection period (or debtors turnover)
♦   creditors payment period.

The calculation of these ratios is detailed in Table 1. Note that, if possible, you should use the *average* of opening and closing stocks, debtors and creditors in computing the ratios. If the opening balance sheet is not given, you will not be able to calculate the average figures and should use year-end figures instead.

Together, these ratios give an indication of whether a business is able to generate cash as fast as it uses it.

4   Gearing ratios

The term 'gearing' refers to the extent to which a business is dependent on fixed-return capital (eg loans, preference shares), as opposed to equity capital (ordinary shares and reserves).

Gearing ratios indicate the degree of risk attached to the company and the sensitivity of earnings and dividends to changes in profitability and activity level.

Preference share capital is usually counted as part of debt rather than equity since it carries the right to a fixed rate of dividend which is payable before the ordinary shareholders have any right to a dividend.

Highly geared businesses – those using a large proportion of fixed-return capital – have greater risk of insolvency but returns to shareholders will grow proportionately more in highly geared businesses if profits are growing.

Low gearing provides scope to increase borrowings when potentially profitable projects are available. Companies with low gearing can usually borrow more easily.

Interest cover indicates the ability of a company to pay interest out of profits generated. Low interest cover indicates to shareholders that their dividends are at risk (because most profits are eaten up by interest payments) and that the company may have difficulty financing its debts if its profits fall. Interest cover of less than two is usually considered unsatisfactory.

Practice question 1 *(The answer is in the final chapter of this book)*

Witton

The following information has been extracted from the accounts of Witton Way Ltd.

Profit and loss account for the year to 30 April 20X6

	20X6	20X5
	£000	£000
Turnover (all credit sales)	11,500	7,650
Less cost of sales	(9,430)	(5,800)
Gross profit	2,070	1,850
Other expenses	(170)	(150)
Loan interest	(350)	(50)
Profit before taxation	1,550	1,650
Taxation	(550)	(600)
Profit after taxation	1,000	1,050
Dividends (all ordinary shares)	(300)	(300)
Retained profits	700	750

Balance sheet as at 30 April 20X6

	20X6 £000	20X5 £000
Fixed assets		
Tangible assets	11,350	10,050
Current assets		
Stocks	2,450	1,500
Trade debtors	3,800	1,200
Cash	50	900
	6,300	3,600
Creditors: amounts falling due within one year	(2,700)	(2,400)
Net current assets	3,600	1,200
Total assets less current liabilities	14,950	11,250
Creditors: amounts falling due after more than one year		
Loans and other borrowings	(3,350)	(350)
	11,600	10,900
Capital and reserves		
Called up share capital	5,900	5,900
Profit and loss account	5,700	5,000
	11,600	10,900

Note

During the year to 30 April 20X6, the company tried to stimulate sales by reducing the selling price of its products and by offering more generous credit terms to its customers.

Required

(a)   Calculate six accounting ratios, specifying the basis of your calculations, for each of the two years to 30 April 20X5 and 20X6 which will enable you to examine the company's progress during 20X6.

(b)   From the information available to you, including the ratios calculated in part (a) of the question, comment upon the company's results for the year to 30 April 20X6 under the heads of 'profitability', 'liquidity', 'efficiency' and 'shareholders' interests'.

(c)   List the additional information which would have been useful to you in formulating your comments in (b) above.

5   Investors' ratios

5.1   User focus

For equity investors, return on investment comprises a combination of dividend income and capital growth.

Investors' ratios help to establish the characteristics of ordinary shares in different companies.

♦   Earnings per share is important to those looking for capital growth
♦   Dividend yield, dividend cover and dividends per share are useful to income seekers.

Ideally, investors should use forecast information when making investment decisions (eg forecast earnings, dividends and net asset values). This is because the value of investments depends primarily on *future* returns.

In practice, investors usually only have historical figures representing recent performance and need to draw conclusions on this basis.

5.2   *Dividend yield*

Dividend yield is calculated as follows.

$$\text{Dividend yield} = \frac{\text{Dividend per share}}{\text{Current market price per share}} \times 100\%$$

The ratio measures dividend policy rather than performance.

Note that a high dividend yield based on the most recent dividends and current share price may arise because the share price has fallen in anticipation of a future dividend cut.

Rapidly growing companies may have low dividend yields based on historical dividends, especially if the current share price reflects anticipated future growth in earnings and dividends.

5.3   *Earnings per share*

The calculation of basic EPS is as follows.

$$\text{EPS} = \frac{\text{Profit available for ordinary dividends}}{\text{Number of ordinary shares in issue}}$$

The calculation of EPS is looked at in more detail in the next chapter.

5.4   *Dividend cover*

Dividend cover is calculated as follows.

$$\text{Dividend cover} = \frac{\text{Earnings per share}}{\text{Dividend per share}}$$

This ratio shows how many times a company could have paid its current dividend from available earnings, ie it indicates how secure dividends are. Dividend cover of less than 2 is usually considered inadequate.

Investors may be attracted to companies with relatively high dividend yield but if dividend cover is low, this indicates that dividends are at greater risk of being cut, and that the high yield is because the share price already reflects an anticipated cut in dividends.

5.5   *Price-earnings ratio (P/E ratio)*

The P/E ratio is calculated as follows.

$$\text{P/E ratio} = \frac{\text{Current market price per share}}{\text{Earnings per share}}$$

The ratio is used to indicate whether shares appear expensive or cheap in terms of how many years of current earnings investors are prepared to pay for.

If calculated on historical earnings, a high P/E ratio usually indicates that investors expect significant future earnings growth and hence are prepared to pay a large multiple of historical earnings. Low P/E ratios usually indicate that investors consider growth prospects to be poor.

If a P/E ratio is based on forecast EPS, relatively expensive shares (ie with high P/E ratios) will not be attractive to shareholders.

5.6 Net assets per share (NAPS)

NAPS is calculated as follows.

$$\text{NAPS} = \frac{\text{Net assets (shareholders' funds)}}{\text{Number of shares in issue}}$$

NAPS is usually less significant than other investors' ratios because investors are not usually able to realise the assets. However, if NAPS is greater than the share price, this may indicate that the company should be broken up (eg through demergers).

The ratio is most relevant to asset-based businesses (eg property investment companies and investment trusts), where asset values are more significant to overall net worth.

As investment properties are revalued annually (and valuations usually reflect expected future rentals), current values are reflected in the balance sheets of property investment companies. The relationship between net asset values and the market price of the shares represents for them the equivalent of the price-earnings ratio for other types of business.

NAPS is of little relevance in a 'people business' such as public relations or advertising as the tangible asset base is likely to be negligible. Such companies should be considered from the point of view of earnings generated by its staff, who are not reported as assets in the balance sheet.

The ratio is also subject to distortions as asset values in the balance sheet may not reflect current values to the business.

6 Influences on ratios

6.1 Business factors

Ratios may change over time or differ between companies because of the nature of the business or management actions.

The type of business affects the nature of assets employed and returns earned.

- Manufacturing industries: capital intensive, therefore relatively low asset turnover.
- Service industries: principal resource is people, therefore asset turnover relatively high.
- Builder: stocks and work in progress high, therefore stock turnover relatively low.
- Supermarket: perishable stocks, therefore stock turnover high.

Other business factors that may affect ratios include the following.

- Acquisition or disposal of a subsidiary during the year.

- Management actions (eg price discounting to increase market share) or changes in nature of business (eg diversification or divestment).

- Fund raising near year-end.

- The nature of the business (eg highly seasonal, fashionable, high technology).

- Quality of management. Better managed businesses are likely to be more profitable and have better working capital management than businesses where management is weak.

- The state of the economy and market conditions. If the market or the economy in general is depressed, this is likely to affect companies adversely and make most or all of their ratios appear worse. The impact may differ between market sectors.

6.2   Impact of accounting policies

Accounting policies can significantly affect the view presented by accounts, and ratios computed, without affecting a business's core ability to generate profits and cash.   Some examples are given in Table 2.

Table 2 The effect of accounting policies on ratios

Effect on	*EPS*	*ROCE*	*Gearing*
Revaluation of fixed assets v inclusion at historical cost	Reduced	Reduced	Reduced
Credit grants received to deferred income v credit grants received against cost of fixed asset	No effect	Reduced	Increased
Apply foreign currency hedging provisions (where sterling depreciates against foreign currency)	Increased	Reduced	Reduced

The potential impact is especially important where:

♦   accounting standards permit a choice
♦   judgement is needed in making accounting estimates
♦   there is no accounting standard (eg revenue recognition).

The effects of selected accounting standards are shown in Table 3.

Table 3 The effect of accounting standards on ratios

Accounting standard	*Choice*	*Judgement*
SSAP 9		Definition of long-term contract.
SSAP 13	Development costs meeting criteria may be written off as incurred or deferred.	
SSAP 20	Foreign equity investments financed by foreign borrowings may be translated at closing rate or historic rate.	Foreign enterprises – closing rate v temporal method.
SSAP 21		Finance lease v operating lease.
FRS 15	Tangible fixed assets may be revalued or kept at historical cost.	Useful life of fixed assets.

7   Interpretation technique

7.1   Analysing the question requirement

An interpretation question may present you with a specific requirement (eg 'Comment on business factors affecting the company's performance', 'discuss whether it is feasible to...') or with a general requirement ('Report to an individual investor commenting on the company's performance and strategy').

If the requirement is specific, use key phrases from the requirement ('Business factors...', 'Feasibility...') as headings in your answer.

If the requirement is general, plan to include general headings.

7.2   Calculation of ratios

If the requirement includes 'key/principal analytical ratios':

♦   present these as an Appendix, showing your calculations.   This is especially important where there are different ways of calculating a ratio, eg the gearing ratio.

♦ try to direct your answer at the reader (eg an investor: EPS, NAPS, dividend cover), and/or the scenario (eg significant investment in finance leases: interest cover, gearing).

Note that most readers are concerned with ROCE, gearing, liquidity.

Go for variety (eg balance sheet ratio, profit and loss ratio, ratios linking both, eg ROCE).

If the scenario presents ratios, look for and calculate obvious omissions, if any (eg EPS, gearing).

Do not dwell on **calculating** ratios at the expense of interpretation.

7.3   Interpretation

Perform an analytical review of the financial statements. This can often tell you more, more quickly, than calculating ratios (and does not depend on selecting the correct ratios).

In the balance sheet, consider the following issues.

♦ Fixed assets: revaluations? significant additions – expansion, how financed?
♦ Working capital: in line with turnover, cost of sales?
♦ Loans: repaid – how? (shares issued?)
♦ Share capital: share issues – why? (repay debt, finance acquisition, expansion?)
♦ Reserves: anything interesting?

In the profit and loss account, consider the following issues.

♦ Sales growth v profit growth.
♦ Interest (relate to debt, economic factors).
♦ Dividends (trend, level, cover).

Note that you may need to indicate further information needed for fuller analysis. Here are some ideas.

♦ Additional information needed for specific ratios (eg share price for price/earnings ratio)
♦ Segmental analysis
♦ Industry averages
♦ Changes in management policy (eg relating to stockholding or credit terms given)
♦ Reasons for specific changes not explained by information given

Finally, check that your answer

♦ covers all aspects of the requirements (eg assumptions, further information)

♦ considers both business factors and accounting policies (although the emphasis may not be equal).

Most marks in the exam are likely to be for specific, relevant comments rather than solely for computations.

Practice question 2 *(The answer is in the final chapter of this book)*

Big Brother

Big Brother Group plc serves the growing market for electronic security systems and equipment. The group accounts for the year ended 31 December 20X8 are summarised below.

Profit and loss accounts	20X8	20X7
	£000	£000
Turnover	51,882	43,217
Cost of sales	(21,705)	(18,221)
Gross profit	30,177	24,996
Expenses	(17,020)	(14,235)
Operating profit	13,157	10,761
Interest payable	(4,695)	(3,574)
Profit before tax	8,462	7,187
Taxation	(1,671)	(1,714)
Profit after tax	6,791	5,473
Minority interest	(1,400)	(980)
Profit for the year	5,391	4,493
Dividends	(700)	(600)
Retained profit	4,691	3,893
Reserves brought forward	4,669	776
Reserves carried forward	9,360	4,669

Balance sheets	20X8		20X7	
	£000	£000	£000	£000
Tangible fixed assets		62,247		51,457
Current assets				
Stocks	8,159		7,181	
Debtors	10,021		8,715	
Cash	3,609		1,924	
	21,789		17,820	
Creditors: amounts falling due within one year	(15,215)		(12,615)	
Net current assets		6,574		5,205
Total assets less current liabilities		68,821		56,662
Creditors: amounts falling due after more than one year				
Loans		(30,105)		(27,419)
Accruals and deferred income				
Rentals in advance		(8,261)		(4,357)
		30,455		24,886
Capital and reserves				
Called up share capital (see note)		10,000		10,000
Share premium account		3,000		3,000
Profit and loss account		9,360		4,669
		22,360		17,669
Minority interest		8,095		7,217
		30,455		24,886

Note   Called up share capital

Authorised	£000
40,000,000 Ordinary shares of 50p each	20,000
10,000,000 6% Preference shares of £1 each	10,000
	30,000

Issued (all fully paid)	
10,000,000 Ordinary shares of 50p each	5,000
5,000,000 6% Preference shares of £1 each	5,000
	10,000

The directors have asked for your comments about the profitability, liquidity and solvency of the group and have provided you with the following typical industry statistics which have been independently assimilated from the statutory accounts of companies in the security systems and equipment sector. The industry statistics have been calculated on the basis that accruals and deferred income are included within 'creditors: amounts falling due within one year', that preference shares are treated as debt and that the minority interest are treated as equity.

Gross profit margin	50%
Net profit margin (based on operating profit)	25%
Current ratio	1.20
Quick ratio	0.90
Gearing (debt divided by total capital employed)	50%
Stock turnover (based on year end stocks and cost of sales)	3.5
Debtors turnover (based on year end debtors and net sales)	5.0
Return on capital employed (profit before interest and tax divided by total capital employed)	17%

Required

In your capacity as a financial advisor write a report for submission to the directors of Big Brother Group plc.

7.4 Learning outcomes

You have now covered all the learning outcomes for this chapter:

Evaluate financial statements and prepare a concise report on the results of the analysis

Identify the limitations of analysis based on financial statements

Explain the weaknesses of the financial report which reduce its effectiveness in communicating meaningful information to users

Prepare and interpret inter-firm comparisons

8   Summary

Ratio analysis is not the only technique used in interpretation of accounts. However, in most examination questions in this area there will be a large number of marks available for computing and commenting on ratios. It is helpful in structuring your solution if you analyse the ratios into appropriate categories: profitability, liquidity and use of assets, gearing and investors' ratios.

Multiple choice questions *(The answers are in the final chapter of this book)*

1   The following are extracts from the financial statements of Lamas Ltd for the year ended 31 December 20X2.

Balance sheet		Profit and loss account	
	£		£
Issued share capital	2,000	Operating profit	795
Reserves	1,000	Less debenture interest	(120)
	3,000		675
12% debenture stock 20X8	1,000		
	4,000		

What is the return on long-term funds?

A   22.5%

B   19.9%

C   16.9%

D   16.6%

2   Welwyn Ltd buys and sells a single product. The following is an extract from its balance sheet at 31 December 20X7.

	20X7 £000	20X6 £000
Stocks	50	40
Debtors	16	24

Sales and purchases during 20X7 were £200,000 and £120,000 respectively. 20% of sales were for cash.

What were the average debtors' collection period and gross profit percentage for the year ended 31 December 20X7?

	Average debtors' collection period	Gross profit percentage
A	37 days	35%
B	37 days	45%
C	46 days	35%
D	46 days	45%

3   The asset turnover of Taplow Ltd is 110% of that of Stoke Ltd.

The return on capital employed by Taplow Ltd is 80% of that of Stoke Ltd.

Taplow Ltd's profit margin expressed as a percentage of that of Stoke Ltd is:

A   73%

B   88%

C   95%

D   138%

4   The share capital of Woosnam plc comprises ordinary shares only. Its price/earnings ratio and dividend cover are 6 and 3 respectively.

Its dividend yield is:

A   4.4%

B   5.5%

C   6.1%

D   12.6%

CHAPTER 27

Earnings per share

EXAM FOCUS

Earnings per share is the key measure of a company's financial performance from the shareholders' point of view. FRS 14 standardises how the statistic should be measured in a number of complex situations. This topic will be regularly examined.

LEARNING OUTCOMES

This chapter covers the following Learning Outcome of the CIMA Syllabus.

Evaluate financial statements and prepare a concise report on the results of the analysis

In order to cover this Learning Outcome the following topics are included.

FRS 14: Earnings per share
Diluted earnings per share

1 FRS 14: Earnings per share

1.1 Introduction

 The basic EPS calculation is simply $\dfrac{\text{Earnings for year}}{\text{Shares in issue}}$.

Here 'earnings' means group profit after tax, less minority interests and preference dividends; and 'shares' means the weighted average number of ordinary shares outstanding during the period.

FRS 14 requires public companies to disclose their basic EPS on the face of the profit and loss account for the year (even if the EPS is negative, ie a loss per share).

1.2 Example

GERARD PLC
DRAFT PROFIT AND LOSS ACCOUNT FOR THE YEAR ENDED 31 DECEMBER 20X4

	£'000	£'000
Profit before tax		5,060
Taxation		(2,300)
Profit after tax		2,760
Transfer to reserves	230	
Dividends		
Paid – preference interim dividend	276	
Paid – ordinary interim dividend	368	
Proposed – preference final dividend	276	
Proposed – ordinary final dividend	460	1,610
Retained profit		1,150

On 1 January 20X4 the issued share capital of Gerard plc was 9,200,000 6% preference shares of £1 each and 8,280,000 ordinary shares of £1 each.

Required

Calculate the earnings per share (EPS) in respect of the year ended 31 December 20X4 on the basis that there was no change in the issued share capital of the company during the year ended 31 December 20X4.

1.3 Approach

Take the number of ordinary shares and put them beneath the line.

$$\overline{8,280,000}$$

The amount of earnings generated by the ordinary shares (ie exclude the preference dividend) goes above the line.

$$\frac{£2,760,000 - £276,000 - £276,000}{8,280,000} = 26.7p$$

The basic EPS for the year is therefore 26.7p.

1.4 Issue of shares at full market price

In the example of Gerard plc, suppose that the company had issued 3,312,000 new shares at their full market value on 30 June 20X4. This would have had an impact on the earnings. We would need to reflect this in the earnings per share working by recognising the impact on the earnings using a weighted average number of shares.

Date	Actual number of shares	Fraction of year	Total
1 January 20X4	8,280,000	$\frac{6}{12}$	4,140,000
30 June 20X4	11,592,000 (W1)	$\frac{6}{12}$	5,796,000
Number of shares in EPS calculation			9,936,000

(W1) New number of shares

Original number	8,280,000
New issue	3,312,000
New number	11,592,000

The earnings per share for 20X4 would now be calculated as:

$$\frac{£2,760,000 - £276,000 - £276,000}{9,936,000} = 22.2p$$

1.5 Bonus issue of shares

Suppose now that the company made no issue of shares at full price but instead made a bonus issue on 1 October 20X4 of one ordinary share for every four shares in issue at 30 September 20X4.

A bonus issue causes no impact on earnings, therefore EPS can be calculated based on the new number of shares.

8,280,000 × ¼ =	2,070,000 extra shares
Original number of shares	8,280,000
New number of shares	10,350,000

The earnings per share for 20X4 would now be calculated as:

$$\frac{£2,208,000}{10,350,000} = \qquad 21.3p$$

1.6   When a rights issue takes place

Suppose now that Gerard's only share issue in 20X4 was a rights issue of £1 ordinary shares on 1 October 20X4 in the proportion of one for every five shares held at a price of £1.20. The middle market price for the shares on the last day of quotation cum rights was £1.80 per share.

 When a rights issue takes place shares are issued at less than full market price. We treat this as a combination of a bonus issue and an issue at full market price. We will therefore need to calculate the rights issue bonus fraction by using share prices.

Rights issue bonus fraction $= \dfrac{\text{Actual cum rights price}}{\text{Theoretical ex rights price}}$

Actual cum rights price   =   Price of share with rights attached immediately before rights issue.

Theoretical ex rights price   =   Expected share price immediately after rights issue (weighted average of actual cum rights price and exercise price of rights issue shares).

Use a table for full computation of the number of shares, as follows.

Date	Actual number of shares	Fraction of year	Rights issue bonus fraction	Total

In the present case, we have a rights issue made in the proportion of one for every five shares held, (ie for every five shares previously owned you now own six).

Rights issue bonus fraction

	£	£
5 shares at	1.80	9.00
1 share at	1.20	1.20
6 shares		10.20

Expected price after rights issue $= \dfrac{£10.20}{6} = £1.70$

Therefore rights issue bonus fraction $= \dfrac{£1.80}{£1.70}$

Date	Actual number of shares	Fraction of year	Rights issue bonus fraction	Total
1 January 20X4	8,280,000	$\frac{9}{12}$	$\frac{1.80}{1.70}$	6,575,294
1 October 20X4	9,936,000 (W1)	$\frac{3}{12}$		2,484,000
Number of shares to be used in EPS calculation				9,059,294

$$EPS = \frac{£2,208,000}{9,059,294} = 24.4p$$

Workings

(W1)   New number of shares

$8,280,000 \times 1 \div 5$	=	1,656,000 extra shares
New number of shares	=	$8,280,000 + 1,656,000 = 9,936,000$

2   Diluted earnings per share

2.1   Introduction

Equity share capital may change in future owing to circumstances which exist now. The diluted EPS (DEPS) attempts to alert shareholders to the potential impact on the current EPS if the dilutive *potential* ordinary shares in issue were to become actual ordinary shares in issue.

FRS 14 requires the DEPS to be disclosed as well as the basic EPS whenever such potential ordinary shares exist.

2.2   Potential ordinary shares

Examples of potential ordinary shares are:

♦   Convertible debt or convertible preference shares in issue
♦   Options granted to subscribe for new shares (eg, share warrants)

2.3   Calculating the DEPS

To deal with this, adjust the basic earnings and the number of shares assuming that the convertibles, options etc had converted to equity shares on the first day of the accounting period, or on the date of issue of the convertibles, options etc if later. The DEPS shows the effect of the worst possible dilution.

The diluted earnings per share is then calculated as follows.

$$\frac{\text{Earnings} + \text{notional extra earnings}}{\text{Number of shares} + \text{notional extra shares}}$$

Continuing with the example of Gerard plc we can calculate the diluted EPS on the basis that the company made no new issue of shares during the year ended 31 December 20X4, but on that date it had in issue £2,300,000 10% convertible loan stock 20X6 to 20X9. Assume a corporation tax rate of 50%.

This loan stock will be convertible into ordinary £1 shares as follows.

20X6	90 £1 shares for £100 nominal value loan stock
20X7	85 £1 shares for £100 nominal value loan stock
20X8	80 £1 shares for £100 nominal value loan stock
20X9	75 £1 shares for £100 nominal loan stock

If this loan stock was converted to shares the impact on earnings would be as follows.

	£	£
Basic earnings		2,208,000
Add notional interest saved ($£2,300,000 \times 10\%$)	230,000	
Less tax relief $£230,000 \times 50\%$	(115,000)	
		115,000
Revised earnings		2,323,000
Number of shares if loan converted		
Basic number of shares		8,280,000
Notional extra shares under the most dilution possible $2,300,000 \times \frac{90}{100}$		2,070,000
Revised number of shares		10,350,000

$$\text{DEPS} = \frac{£2,323,000}{10,350,000} = 22.4 \text{ p}$$

2.4   DEPS and options outstanding

Now assume that the company made no issue of shares during the year ended 31 December 20X4, but on that date there were outstanding options to purchase 920,000 ordinary £1 shares at £1.70 per share. The average fair value of ordinary shares during the year was £1.80.

		£
Earnings		2,208,000
Number of shares		
Basic		8,280,000
Options (W1)		51,111
		8,331,111

The DEPS is therefore $\dfrac{£2,208,000}{8,331,111} = 26.5p$

Working

(W1) Number of shares at option price

Options $= 920,000 \times £1.70$

              $= £1,564,000$

At fair value: $\dfrac{£1,564,000}{£1.80} = 868,889$

Number issued free = 920,000 – 868,889 = 51,111.

Where there are several categories of potential ordinary shares, FRS 14 requires that they should be taken into account in the calculation of DEPS in their order of dilution (ie, greatest dilution first). This ensures that the worst possible DEPS figure emerges.

2.5   Example

Calculate the diluted EPS as per FRS 14 given the following information.

X plc – Accounting data for year ended 31 May 20X3

Net profit after tax and minority interest	£18,160,000
Ordinary shares of £1 (fully paid)	£40,000,000
Average fair value for year of ordinary shares	£1.50

♦ Share options have been granted to directors giving them the right to subscribe for ordinary shares between 20X4 and 20X8 at £1.20 per share. The options outstanding at 31 May 20X3 were 2,000,000 in number

♦ The company has £20 million of 6% convertible loan stock in issue. The terms of conversion of the loan stock per £200 nominal value of loan stock at the date of issue (1 May 20X2) were as follows.

Conversion date	Number of shares
31 May 20X3	24
31 May 20X4	23
31 May 20X5	22

No loan stock has as yet been converted. The loan stock had been issued at a discount of 1% and the company has complied with FRS 4 *Capital Instruments* as regards the treatment of the discount.

♦ There are 1,600,000 convertible preference shares in issue. The cumulative dividend is 10p per share and each preference share can convert into two ordinary shares. The preference shares can be converted in 20X5.

♦ Assume a corporation tax rate of 33%.

2.6 Solution

We need first of all to decide on the order of the dilutive elements.

Reason for dilution	Notional extra earnings £000	Notional extra shares 000	Marginal EPS	Ranking
Options	Nil	400 (W1)	$\dfrac{\text{nil}}{400,000}$ = nil	1 most dilutive
Convertible loan stock	804 (W2) ⎫	2,300 (W3)	$\dfrac{1,004}{2,300}$ = 43.6p	3 least dilutive
Discount (20m × 1%)	200 ⎭ 1,004			
Convertible preference shares	160 (W4)	3,200 (W5)	$\dfrac{160}{3,200}$ = 5p	2 second most dilutive

Workings

(W1) Number of options at option price 2,000,000 × £1.20 = £2,400,000
Number assumed at fair value £2,400,000 ÷ £1.50 = 1,600,000
Number issued free = 2,000,000 – 1,600,000 = 400,000

(W2) Loan stock – notional extra earnings

	£
Loan stock interest saved (£20,000,000 × 6%)	1,200,000
Less: Tax 33%	(396,000)
	804,000

(W3) Loan stock – notional extra shares

20,000 × 23/200   2,300,000

Beware of using out of date information. 31 May 20X3 has passed and no loan stock has yet been converted. 31 May 20X4 is the next worst case date.

(W4) Convertible preference shares – notional extra earnings

Preference dividend saved (1,600,000 × 10p) =   £160,000

Remember no tax impact!

(W5) Convertible preference shares – notional extra shares

£1,600,000 × 2/1   3,200,000

Diluted EPS calculation

	Earnings £000	Shares £000	EPS	
Basic	18,000	40,000	45p	dilutive
Options	Nil	400		
	18,000	40,400	44.55p	
Convertible preference shares	160	3,200		dilutive
	18,160	43,600	41.65p	
Convertible loan stock	804			anti-dilutive
Discount	200	2,300		
	19,164	45,900	41.75p	

When the convertible loan stock is taken into account, the DEPS moves from 41.65p to 41.75p ie, it improves. The DEPS per FRS 14 is the worst possible dilution figure, so we conclude that the DEPS is 41.65p.

2.7   FRED 26: Earnings per share

In May 2002 the ASB issued FRED 26 as part of the project to align UK accounting with international standards. FRED 26 is based on a revised IAS expected to be published soon.

There are some changes in the detail of required disclosures if the UK moves from FRS 14 to FRED 26:

♦   FRED 26 proposes that basic and diluted EPS should be disclosed on the face of the profit and loss account, both for net profit or loss for the period *and* for profit or loss from continuing operations.

♦   Basic and diluted EPS for discontinued operations (if reported) may be shown either on the face of the profit and loss account or in a note.

♦   Additional EPS amounts can only be disclosed by way of note.

Few problems are anticipated for UK companies in moving from FRS 14 to a standard based on FRED 26.

2.8   Learning outcome

You have now covered the learning outcome for this chapter

Evaluate financial statements and prepare a concise report on the results of the analysis

insofar as the evaluation concerns earnings per share.

3   Summary

You must be able to calculate the basic EPS when the share capital in issue changes during the period, and also the diluted EPS when there are dilutive potential ordinary shares in issue.

Multiple choice questions *(The answers are in the final chapter of this book)*

1   A company has profits after tax for the year ending 30 June 20X2 of £77,540. At 1 July 20X1 the company had 600,000 shares in issue and on 30 September made a 1 for 6 rights issue at an issue price of £1.15. On that date the market value of the company's shares was £1.50. The published earnings per share for the year ending 30 June 20X1 was 10.8 pence.

What figures should appear in the profit and loss account for the year ending 30 June 20X2 for earnings per share?

	30 June 20X2	30 June 20X1
A	11.4 pence	10.8 pence
B	11.5 pence	10.4 pence
C	11.6 pence	11.2 pence
D	11.4 pence	10.4 pence

2   At 30 June 20X2 Juniper Ltd has £800,000 of 50 pence ordinary shares in issue and £200,000 of 5% convertible debentures. The terms of the debentures are that they can be converted into 50 pence ordinary shares as follows:

30 June 20X5	120	50 pence ordinary shares for £100 of debentures
30 June 20X6	115	50 pence ordinary shares for £100 of debentures
30 June 20X7	110	50 pence ordinary shares for £100 of debentures

In the year ending 30 June 20X2 Juniper Ltd had a retained profit of £548,000 after paying an ordinary dividend of £102,000. Corporation tax is at the rate of 30%.

What is the basic earnings per share and diluted earnings per share?

	Basic EPS	Diluted EPS
A	34.3 pence	35.3 pence
B	40.6 pence	35.7 pence
C	34.3 pence	36.1 pence
D	81.3 pence	63.2 pence

3   Wimble Ltd has 1 million £1 ordinary shares in issue as well as 400,000 £1 6% preference shares at the balance sheet date of 31 March 20X2. At that date there were options outstanding to purchase a further 200,000 ordinary shares at a price of £1.50. The average fair value of the ordinary shares during the year was £1.90. Wimble Ltd made a profit after tax of £232,000 during the year.

What is the basic earnings per share and the diluted earnings per share for the year?

	Basic EPS	Diluted EPS
A	20.8 pence	17.3 pence
B	20.8 pence	20.0 pence
C	23.2 pence	17.3 pence
D	23.2 pence	20.0 pence

CHAPTER 28

Segmental reporting

EXAM FOCUS

The objective of financial statements is to provide useful information. If a company operates in different businesses or different geographical areas, it will be useful to disclose the split of the results for the different segments.

LEARNING OUTCOMES

This chapter covers the following Learning Outcome of the CIMA Syllabus.

> Prepare and interpret segmental analysis

In order to cover this Learning Outcome the following topics are included.

> SSAP 25: Segmental reporting
> Illustration of SSAP 25 disclosures

1 SSAP 25: Segmental reporting

1.1 The need for a Standard

Many enterprises carry on several classes of business or operate in several geographical areas, with different rates of profitability, different opportunities for growth and different degrees of risk. Segmental information will therefore provide users of financial statements with more information about the company's past performance and future prospects.

1.2 Scope

SSAP 25 *Segmental reporting* applies to all financial statements intended to give a true and fair view. However the disclosure requirements which go further than statutory requirements only apply to an entity that:

(a) is a public limited company or a holding company that has a public limited company as a subsidiary; or

(b) is a banking or insurance company; or

(c) exceeds the criteria, multiplied in each case by 10, for defining a medium-sized company under S248 CA 1985.

Where, in the opinion of the directors, the disclosure of any information required by this Accounting Standard would be seriously prejudicial to the interests of the company, that information need not be disclosed, but the fact that any such information has not been disclosed must be stated.

Before looking at its detail, we will first consider the overall impact of the standard.

1.3 Overview of SSAP 25

The additional disclosures required by SSAP 25 are designed to reveal significant information which might otherwise be hidden by the aggregation process of presenting a single profit and loss account and balance sheet for a business.

Consider a business with three segments as follows:

	£000		
Segment	*A*	*B*	*C*
Operating profits	100	200	(250)

Disclosing the three figures individually is obviously much more revealing than just disclosing an overall profit of £50,000.

1.4 Segmental ROCE

The standard requires turnover, result and net assets to be disclosed for each class of business and geographical segment; this means that segmental ROCE can be calculated.

The analysis of this key ratio is one of the main benefits to users offered by compliance with SSAP 25.

1.5 Definitions

A *class of business* is a distinguishable component of an enterprise that provides a separate product or service or a separate group of related products or services.

A *geographical segment* is a geographical area comprising an individual country or group of countries in which an enterprise operates, or to which it supplies products or services.

Common costs are costs that relate to more than one segment.

1.6 How segments should be identified

The directors should determine whether the company has carried on business of two or more classes or has supplied markets that differ substantially from each other. In identifying separate reportable segments, the directors should have regard to the overall purpose of presenting segmental information and the need of the user of the financial statements to be informed where a company carries on operations in different classes of business or in different geographical areas that:

(a)   earn a return on investment that is out of line with the remainder of the business;

(b)   are subject to different degrees of risk; or

(c)   have experienced different rates of growth; or

(d)   have different potentials for future development.

The definition of the segments should be reviewed annually and re-defined when appropriate. Where a change is made, the reason for it and its nature and effect should be disclosed. The previous year's figures should be restated to reflect the change.

1.7 Disclosure required for each class of business and each geographical segment

(a)   *Turnover*, distinguishing between:

(i)   turnover derived from external customers; and

(ii)   turnover derived from other segments.

Note that segmental information should be given in terms of the geographical origin of the turnover, rather than the destination. So we are principally showing the geographical segments *from which* the segments were supplied, rather than the segments *to which* they were supplied. Turnover split by destination need only be disclosed if this is materially different from turnover split by source.

(b) *Segment result*, before accounting for taxation, minority interests and extraordinary items and normally before taking account of interest.

(c) *Segment net assets*, normally being the non-interest-bearing operating net assets.

In addition, the disclosure required by FRS 9 for associated companies should also be analysed segmentally, ie. share of the company's profits, net assets, etc. if associated companies account for at least 20% of the group's total result or total net assets.

The total of the information disclosed by segment should agree with the related figure in the financial statements. If it does not, the company should provide a reconciliation between the two figures.

Comparative figures for the previous accounting period should be provided. If, however, on the first occasion on which a company provides a segmental report the necessary information is not readily available, comparative figures need not be provided.

1.8   Problems

One problem is that directors can choose to opt out by claiming that disclosure is 'unfairly prejudicial'.

Segment identification is also fraught with problems, being highly subjective.

Allocation of costs between segments is another difficulty. Although common costs can be deducted from the total of segment results, some arbitrary allocation of costs is likely to be necessary.

2   Illustration of SSAP 25 disclosures

2.1   Illustration

The disclosures required by SSAP 25 are illustrated below, ignoring the comparative figures for the previous year.

Analysis by classes of business

	Industry A £m	Industry B £m	Other industries £m	Total £m
TURNOVER				
Total sales	33	42	26	101
Inter-segment sales	(4)	–	(12)	(16)
Sales to third parties	29	42	14	85
PROFIT BEFORE TAX				
Segment profit	3	4.5	1.8	9.3
Common costs				(0.3)
Operating profit				9.0
Net interest				(0.4)
				8.6
Share of associates' profit before tax				2.4
Group profit before tax				11.0
NET ASSETS				
Segment net assets	17.6	24	19.4	61
Unallocated assets				3
				64
Share of associates' net assets				19
Total net assets				83

Analysis by geographical areas

	United Kingdom £m	Far East £m	Other £m	Group £m
TURNOVER				
Total sales	67	23	12	102
Inter-segment sales	(8)	(9)	–	(17)
Sales to third parties	59	14	12	85
PROFIT BEFORE TAX				
Segment profit	6.5	1.8	1.0	9.3
Common costs				(0.3)
Operating profit				9.0
Net interest				(0.4)
				8.6
Share of associates' profit before tax				2.4
Group profit before tax				11.0
NET ASSETS				
Segment net assets	41	16	4	61
Unallocated assets				3
				64
Share of associates' net assets				19
Total net assets				83

2.2 Learning outcome

You have now covered the final learning outcome for this syllabus

Prepare and interpret segmental analysis

3 Summary

Where an enterprise carries out different classes of business or operates in different geographical areas, SSAP 25 requires disclosures of turnover, profit before tax and net assets, broken down by each segment. If the directors believe that the disclosures would be seriously prejudicial, they do not have to be made.

Multiple choice question *(The answer is in the final chapter of this book)*

1 Which of the following is not a requirement of SSAP 25?

    A   Common costs should be allocated to relevant segments

    B   The directors are responsible for determining the segments to be reported

    C   Segmental disclosure must be given by all public companies unless this would be seriously prejudicial

    D   The directors need not disclose the segmental information if it may be detrimental to the company

CHAPTER 29

Solutions to practice questions

Chapter 1 solutions

1   Puffin (I)

CONSOLIDATED BALANCE SHEET AS AT 31 DECEMBER 20X1

	£000
Fixed assets	
Intangible assets (W3)	50
Tangible assets (146 + 35)	181
Current assets (24 + 15)	39
	270
Creditors: amounts falling due within one year (30 + 10)	(40)
	230
Capital and reserves	
Share capital	100
Profit and loss account	130
	230

Workings

(W1)   *Group structure*

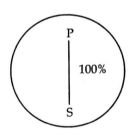

(W2)   *Net assets of Seagull Ltd*

	At date of acquisition £000	At balance sheet date £000
Share capital	40	40
Reserves	-	-
	40	40

(W3)   *Goodwill*

	£000
Purchase consideration	90
For 100% of net assets acquired	(40)
Goodwill	50

2   Puffin (II)

CONSOLIDATED BALANCE SHEET AS AT 31 DECEMBER 20X1

	£000
Fixed assets	
Intangible assets (W3)	58
Tangible assets (146 + 35)	181
Current assets (24 + 15)	39
	——
	278
Creditors: amounts falling due within one year (30 + 10)	(40)
	——
	238
	——
Capital and reserves	
Share capital	100
Profit and loss account	130
	——
	230
Minority interest (W4)	8
	——
	238
	——

Workings

(W1)   *Group structure*

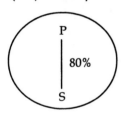

(W2)   *Net assets of Seagull Ltd*

	At date of acquisition £000	At balance sheet date £000
Share capital	40	40
Reserves	-	-
	——	——
	40	40
	——	——

(W3)   *Goodwill*

	£000
Purchase consideration	90
For 80% of net assets acquired [40] (W2)	(32)
	——
Goodwill	58
	——

(W4)   *Minority interests*

20% of net assets at balance sheet date [40] (W2)	8
	——

3   Pluto

CONSOLIDATED BALANCE SHEET AS AT 31 DECEMBER 20X8

	£000
Fixed assets	
Intangible assets (W3)	27.5
Tangible assets (120 + 150)	270
Current assets (40 + 50)	90
	387.5
Creditors: amounts due within one year (40 + 30)	(70)
	317.5
Capital and reserves	
Share capital	100
Profit and loss account (W5)	175
	275
Minority interest (W4)	42.5
	317.5

Workings

(W1)   *Group structure*

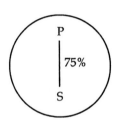

(W2)   *Net assets – Snoopy Ltd*

	At date of acquisition £000	At balance sheet date £000
£1 shares	100	100
Profit and loss	50	70
	150	170

(W3)   *Goodwill*

	£000
Purchase consideration	140
For 75% of net assets acquired (150)	(112.5)
Goodwill	27.5

(W4)   *Minority interest*

25% of net assets at balance sheet date (170)	42.5

(W5) *Group profit and loss account*

100% Pluto Ltd   160

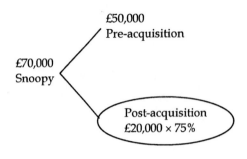

£50,000
Pre-acquisition

£70,000
Snoopy

Post-acquisition
£20,000 × 75%   15
                                                                                             ―――
                                                                                             175
                                                                                             ―――

4   Top Dog

TOP DOG GROUP BALANCE SHEET AS AT 31 DECEMBER 20X8

	£	£
Fixed assets		
Intangible fixed assets (W3)		2,000
Other fixed assets		96,700
		98,700
Current assets	181,900	
Creditors: amounts falling due within one year	(86,600)	
		95,300
		194,000
Capital and reserves		
Called up share capital		100,000
Profit and loss account (W4)		94,000
		194,000

Workings

(W1)   *Group structure*

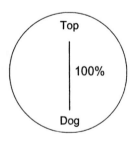

Top

100%

Dog

(W2)   *Dog – Net assets*

	At date of acquisition £	At balance sheet date £
£1 shares	40,000	40,000
Profit and loss account	6,000	25,000
Net assets	46,000	65,000

(W3) *Goodwill*

	£
Purchase consideration	48,000
For 100% of net assets acquired	(46,000)
Goodwill	2,000

(W4) *Group profit and loss account*

	£
100% Top	75,000

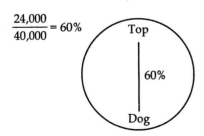

	£
	19,000
	94,000

5   Top Dog (MI)

TOP DOG GROUP BALANCE SHEET AS AT 31 DECEMBER 20X8

	£	£
Fixed assets		
Intangible assets (W3)		14,400
Tangible assets		96,700
		111,100
Current assets	181,900	
Creditors: amounts falling due within one year	(86,600)	
		95,300
		206,400
Capital and reserves		
£1 ordinary share capital		100,000
Profit and loss account (W5)		80,400
		180,400
Minority interest (W4)		26,000
		206,400

Workings

(W1) *Group structure*

$$\frac{24,000}{40,000} = 60\%$$

(W2)   Dog – Net assets

	At date of acquisition £	At balance sheet date £
Share capital	40,000	40,000
Profit and loss account	16,000	25,000
Net assets	56,000	65,000

(W3)   Goodwill

	£
Purchase consideration	48,000
For 60% of net assets acquired (£56,000)	(33,600)
Goodwill	14,400

(W4)   Minority interests

	£
40% (£65,000)	26,000

(W5)   Profit and loss account

	£
100% Top	75,000

Dog £25,000

Pre-acquisition £16,000

£9,000 × 60% Post-acquisition   5,400

	£
Group profit and loss account	80,400

Multiple choice answers

1   C

Consolidated reserves	£000
Vaynor plc	90
Weeton Ltd ((40 + 10) × 100%)	50
Yarlet Ltd ((70 – 30) × 80%)	32
	172

2   C

Goodwill	£	£
Cost of investment		300,000
Net assets acquired		
Share capital	200,000	
Profit and loss	36,000	
Group share 75% ×	236,000	(177,000)
		123,000

3   D

	£000
Cost of investment	
Cash	1,000
Shares at fair value (300 × 3)	900
Less share of fair value of net tangible assets acquired (75% × 1,000)	(750)
Goodwill	1,150

4   C

Control is established by reference to voting shares.

Chapter 2 solutions

1   Dublin

CONSOLIDATED BALANCE SHEET AS AT 31 DECEMBER 20X9

	£
Fixed assets	
Intangible (W3)	1,600
Tangible (100,000 + 60,000)	160,000
	161,600
Current assets (215,000 + 50,000)	265,000
Creditors: amounts due under one year	(170,000)
(150,000 + 20,000)	
	256,600
Capital and reserves	
Called up share capital	190,000
Profit and loss account (W5)	30,600
	220,600
Minority interest (W4)	36,000
	256,600

Workings

(W1)   *Group structure*

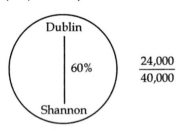

$$\text{Dublin} \quad 60\% \quad \frac{24,000}{40,000}$$

Shannon

(W2)   *Net assets – Shannon*

	At the date of acquisition £	At the balance sheet date £
Share capital	40,000	40,000
Profit and loss account	40,000	50,000
	80,000	90,000

(W3)   *Goodwill*

	£
Purchase consideration	50,000
For 60% net assets acquired (80,000)	(48,000)
Goodwill	2,000

In consolidated balance sheet: £2,000 × 4/5 = £1,600

(W4)   *Minority interest*

40% (90,000)	£36,000

(W5)   *Group reserves*

	£
100% Dublin	25,000

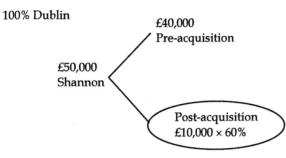

£50,000
Shannon

£40,000
Pre-acquisition

Post-acquisition
£10,000 × 60%

	£
	6,000
Less goodwill amortised $\dfrac{2,000}{5}$	(400)
	30,600

2   P and S

(W1)   *Group structure*

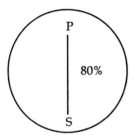

(W2)   *Net assets − S*

	At the date of acquisition £	At the balance sheet date £
Share capital	10,000	10,000
Profit and loss account	20,000	65,000
	30,000	75,000

(W3)   *Goodwill*

Not required for this example.

(W4)   *Minority interest*

	£
20% (75,000)	15,000
Less unrealised profit in stock (W5)	(600)
	14,400

(W5)   *Unrealised profit in stock*

Step 1   How much profit is unrealised?

£6,000 × ½   =   £3,000

Step 2   Who is selling to whom?

S Ltd is selling to P Ltd. Therefore the profit is recorded in the subsidiary company's accounts and the adjustment required is to credit group stock with £3,000, while debiting group profit and loss account with £2,400 (80%) and minority interests with £600 (20%).

(W6) *Group profit and loss account*

	£
100% P Ltd	100,000

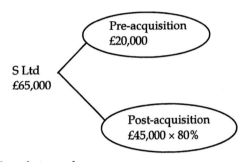

Post-acquisition £45,000 × 80%	36,000
Less unrealised profit in stock	(2,400)
	133,600

In the consolidated balance sheet remember to take £3,000 off group stock.

3 Christian

(W1) *Group structure*

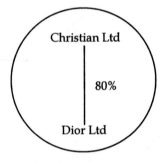

Also a 30% preference share holding

(W2) *Net assets of Dior Ltd*

	At date of acquisition £	At balance sheet date £
Share capital	10,000	10,000
Profit and loss	25,000	40,000
Net assets attributable to ordinary shareholders	35,000	50,000
Preference shares	20,000	20,000
Net assets attributable to preference shareholders	20,000	20,000

(W3) *Goodwill*

	£
Purchase consideration (total)	40,000
For 80% of net assets (£35,000) attributable to ordinary shareholders	(28,000)
For 30% of net assets (£20,000) attributable to preference shareholders	(6,000)
Goodwill	6,000

(W4) *Minority interest*

	£
20% of net assets (£50,000) attributable to ordinary shareholders	10,000
70% of net assets (£20,000) attributable to preference shareholders	14,000
	24,000

4   Hewey

CONSOLIDATED BALANCE SHEET AS AT 30 APRIL 20X8

	£000	£000
Fixed assets		
Intangible assets (W4)		19.8
Tangible assets		
Freehold property (86 + 55 – 40 – 15)	86.0	
Plant and machinery (272 + 168 – 100 – 148)	292.0	
		378.0
		397.8
Current assets		
Stock (111 + 65 - 4)	172.0	
Debtors (30 + 15 - 10)	35.0	
Cash (19 + 2 + 4)	25.0	
	232.0	
Creditors: amounts falling due within one year		
Trade creditors (35 + 22 - 6)	51.0	
Taxation (50 + 30)	80.0	
Proposed dividends		
Hewey	15.0	
Minority interest	2.6	
	148.6	
Net current assets		83.4
Total assets less current liabilities		481.2
Capital and reserves		
Called up share capital		300.0
Share premium		20.0
General reserve (W6)		64.0
Profit and loss account (W6)		56.0
		440.0
Minority interest (W5)		41.2
		481.2

Workings

(W1)   *Group structure*

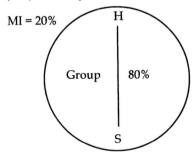

Preference shares	
Hewey	50%
Minority interest	50%
	100%

(W2)   Dividends

	£
S plc has a proposed dividend of £10,000 which includes the preference dividend	10,000
Preference dividend = 10% × £20,000	(2,000)
∴ Ordinary dividend	8,000

Receivable by Hewey

		£
50% preference dividend	(£2,000)	1,000
80% ordinary dividend	(£8,000)	6,400
		7,400

Get Hewey's accounts up to date	
Dr debtors	7,400
Cr profit and loss account	7,400

(W3)   S – Net assets

	At date of acquisition £000	At balance sheet date £000
£1 shares	100	100
Share premium	10	10
General reserve	20	15
Profit and loss account	30	35
Net assets attributable to ordinary shareholders	160	160
Preference shares	20	20
	180	180

(W4)   Goodwill

	£000
Purchase consideration (150 + 10)	160
For 80% of net assets acquired (attributable to ordinary shareholders) (160)	(128)
50% of net assets acquired (attributable to preference shareholders) (20)	(10)
Goodwill	22

At 30 April 20X8 one year's worth (ie 10%) would have been written off to the profit and loss account leaving nine years (ie 90% × £22,000 = £19,800).

(W5)   Minority interest

	£000
20% minority interest in balance sheet net assets (attributable to ordinary shareholders) (160)	32.0
50% minority interests in balance sheet assets (attributable to preference shareholders) (20)	10.0
	42.0
Less unrealised profit in stock (W7)	(0.8)
	41.2

(W6) *Group reserves*

	£000
General reserve	
	68.0

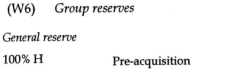
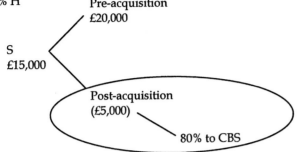

100% H

Pre-acquisition £20,000

S £15,000

Post-acquisition (£5,000)   80% to CBS   (4.0)

	‾‾‾‾
Group general reserve	64.0
	‾‾‾‾

Group profit and loss account

	£000
100% H + dividend receivable	57.4

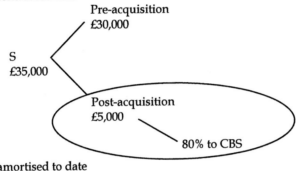

Pre-acquisition £30,000

S £35,000

Post-acquisition £5,000   80% to CBS

	4.0
Less goodwill amortised to date	(2.2)
Less unrealised profit in stock (W7)	(3.2)
	‾‾‾‾
	56.0
	‾‾‾‾

(W7) *Unrealised profit in stock*

$$£20,000 \times \frac{25}{125} = £4,000$$

The profit appears in S's accounts (because sales are from S to Hewey). Therefore the adjustment is as follows.

Debit	Group profit and loss	£3,200
Debit	Minority interest	£800
Credit	Group stock	£4,000

(Tutorial note

Exclude inter-co debt

Write back any cash in transit

Inter-co dividend consolidates out, ie H's debtor dividend receivable cancels against creditor in subsidiary (proposed dividend). If not a wholly owned subsidiary it will not be a complete cancellation and therefore you are left with a minority interest in proposed dividend.)

5 Hugh

CONSOLIDATED BALANCE SHEET AS AT 31 DECEMBER 20X7

	£	£
Fixed assets		
Intangible (7,250 (W4) - 725)		6,525
Tangible		
Freehold land		217,000
Plant		79,600
		303,125
Current assets		
Stock (130,000 + 59,400 - 3,200 (W6))	186,200	
Debtors	159,000	
Bank	60,000	
	405,200	
Creditors: amounts due within one year	(76,000)	
		329,200
		632,325
Capital and reserves		
Share capital		400,000
Profit and loss account (W7)		164,325
		564,325
Minority interest (W5)		68,000
		632,325

Workings

(W1)   *Group structure*

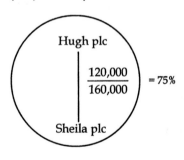

(W2)   *Net assets*

	At the date of acquisition £	At the balance sheet date £
Share capital	160,000	160,000
Profit and loss	101,000 (W3)	112,000
	261,000	272,000

(W3)   *Profit and loss as at 1 July 20X7*

Balance b/f (112,000 - 22,000)	90,000
In year (22,000 × 6/12)	11,000
Balance at date of acquisition	101,000

(W4) *Goodwill*

	£
Purchase consideration	203,000
For 75% of net assets acquired (261,000)	(195,750)
Goodwill	7,250

(W5) *Minority interest*

25% (272,000)	68,000

(W6) *Unrealised profit in stock*

$$16,000 \times \frac{25}{125} \quad = \quad 3,200$$

Hugh sells to Sheila, so the profit is in Hugh's accounts.

Debit Group profit and loss account	3,200
Credit Group stock	3,200

(W7) *Group profit and loss*

	£
100% Hugh	160,000

Post-acquisition £11,000 × 75%	8,250
Less unrealised profit in stock	(3,200)
Less goodwill amortised ($\frac{7,250}{5}$ = 1,450 × 6/12)	(725)
	164,325

Multiple choice answers

1   D

	£	£
Mabbutt Ltd		
Cost of investment		35,000
Less Share of net assets acquired		
Share capital	15,000	
Profit and loss account	21,000	
	36,000 × ⅔	(24,000)
Goodwill		11,000
Amortisation to date ($\frac{4}{10}$)		(4,400)
Balance c/f		6,600

Waddle Ltd

Cost of investment		20,000
Less Share of net assets acquired		
Share capital	20,000	
Profit and loss account	16,000	
	36,000 × 75%	(27,000)
Negative goodwill		(7,000)
Recovered ($\frac{3}{10}$)		2,100
Balance c/f		(4,900)

2   B

	£000
Ho plc	750
Add dividend receivable (60% × 100)	60
Su Ltd – Ho plc's share of post acquisition retained profit (60% (700 – 300))	240
	1,050

3   C

	£m
Net assets of Newlyn plc	25
Net assets of Dollin Ltd	20
Less PURP	(2)
	43

4   C

	£
Minority interests	
Preference shares (50% × 100,000)	50,000
Ordinary shares (25% × (200,000 + 60,000))	65,000
	115,000
Consolidated reserves	
Lynton Ltd	500,000
Pinner Ltd (75% × (60,000 – 24,000))	27,000
	527,000

Chapter 3 solutions

1   Haley

CONSOLIDATED BALANCE SHEET OF HALEY PLC AS AT 31 DECEMBER 20X9

	£000
Fixed assets	
Tangible assets	400
Interest in associated undertaking (30% × 160)	48
	448
Net current assets	505
	953
Total assets less current liabilities	953
Creditors: amounts falling due after more than one year	(150)
	803
Capital and reserves	
Called up share capital	250
Profit and loss account (W5)	469
	719
Minority interests (W4)	84
	803

Workings

(W1)   *Group structure*

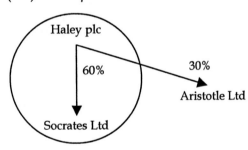

(W2)   *Net assets*

SOCRATES LTD

	At date of acquisition £000	At balance sheet date £000
Share capital	30	30
Profit and loss	70	180
	100	210

ARISTOTLE LTD

	At date of acquisition £000	At balance sheet date £000
Share capital	60	60
Profit and loss	30	100
	90	160

(W3)   *Goodwill/premium*

	Socrates Ltd £000	Aristotle Ltd £000
Cost of investment	75	30
Share of net assets acquired (60% × 100 (W2))/(30% × 90 (W2))	(60)	(27)
	15	3

(W4)   *Minority interests*

	£000
Socrates Ltd (40% × 210)	84

(W5)   *Profit and loss account*

	£000
Haley plc	400
Socrates Ltd (60% × 110 (W2))	66
Aristotle Ltd (30% × 70 (W2))	21
Goodwill fully amortised (W3)	(15)
Premium fully amortised (W3)	(3)
	469

Multiple choice answers

1   B

	£
Cost of investment in Edberg Ltd	6,660
Less share of net assets acquired at fair value (30% × 20,000)	(6,000)
Goodwill acquired	660

Investment in Edberg Ltd at 31 December 20X9

	£
Share of net assets (30% × (22,000 + 2,000))	7,200
Goodwill on acquisition ($660 \times \frac{6}{10}$)	396
	7,596

2   C

	£
Minority interest (40% × 30,000)	12,000

	£
Share of net assets of associate (40% × 30,000)	12,000
Goodwill on acquisition (32,000 – (40% × 30,000))	20,000
Investment in associate	32,000

Consolidated reserves

	£
Beed plc	20,000
Transformer plc (60% × 20,000)	12,000
Berlin plc (no post-acquisition profits)	-
	32,000

3   D

	£
Net assets of Eve Ltd	310,000
Add revaluation of land	10,000
Less unrealised profit (6,000 × 10%)	(600)
	319,400
Group share (30%)	95,820
Goodwill on acquisition (55,000 − (30% × 170,000))	4,000
	99,820

4   B

	£
Share of net assets (40% × 450,000)	180,000
Less unamortised negative goodwill (20,000 × $\frac{9}{10}$)	(18,000)
	162,000
Cost of investment	150,000
Less share of FV of NA acquired (40% × (300,000 + 125,000))	(170,000)
Negative goodwill	(20,000)

Chapter 4 solutions

1   Humphrey

CONSOLIDATED PROFIT AND LOSS ACCOUNT FOR THE YEAR ENDED 30 SEPTEMBER 20X5

	£000
Turnover (1,100 + 400 - 100)	1,400
Cost of sales (balance)	(742)
Gross profit (500 + 160 - 2)	658
Distribution costs (60 + 50)	(110)
Administrative expenses (65 + 55)	(120)
Operating profit	428
Investment income (20 - 16) + 5	9
Interest (25 + 6)	(31)
Profit on ordinary activities before tax	406
Taxation (160 + 24)	(184)
Profit on ordinary activities after tax	222
Minority interest (W3) (20% × 30,000)	(6)
Profit attributable to members of Humphrey plc	216
Dividends	(100)
Retained profit for the year	116
Retained profit at 1 October 20X4 (W3)	110
Retained profit at 30 September 20X5	226

Workings

(W1)   *Group structure*

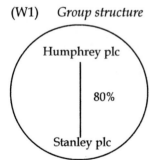

(W2)   *Minority interest*

	£000
20% × 30,000 profit after tax in question	6

(W3)   *Reserves brought forward*

	£000
Humphrey plc	90
Stanley plc (80% × (30 - 5))	20
	110

(W4)   *Inter-company dividend*

Check consistency between companies.

	£000
Payable by Stanley plc	20
Receivable by Humphrey plc (80% × 20)	16

2   King

CONSOLIDATED PROFIT AND LOSS ACCOUNT FOR THE YEAR ENDED 30 SEPTEMBER 20X9

	£000	£000
Turnover (800 + 430 - 80)		1,150
Cost of sales and expenses (balance)		(734)
Operating profit (250 + 175 - 9)		416
Income from interest in associated undertaking (160 × 25%)		40
Profit on ordinary activities before taxation		456
Tax on profit on ordinary activities		
Group (80 + 45)	125	
Share of tax of associated undertaking (60 × 25%)	15	
		(140)
Profit on ordinary activities after taxation		316
Minority interests (W2)		(26)
Profit for the financial year attributable to the members of King Ltd		290
Dividends (proposed)		(70)
Retained profit for the financial year		220
Retained profit brought forward (W3)		546
Retained profit carried forward		766

Workings

(W1)   *Group structure*

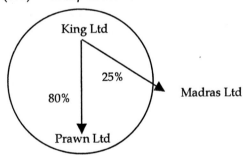

(W2)   *Minority interests*

	£000
Prawn Ltd 130,000 × 20%	26

(W3)   *Retained profit brought forward*

	£000
King Ltd	600
Prawn Ltd (80% (320 - 260))	48
Madras Ltd (25% (540 - 340))	50
Goodwill (90 + 62) fully amortised	(152)
	546

3   High

CONSOLIDATED PROFIT AND LOSS ACCOUNT FOR YEAR ENDED 31 MARCH 20X3

	£
Turnover (274,500 + 181,250 - 37,500)	418,250
Cost of sales (balance)	(176,200)
Gross profit (148,020 + 94,730 - 700)	242,050
Distribution costs (67,315 + 42,885)	(110,200)
Administration expenses (25,555 + 17,295)	(42,850)
Operating profit	89,000
Investment income (250 + 100)	350
Profit on ordinary activities before tax	89,350
Taxation (29,000 + 15,100)	(44,100)
Profit on ordinary activities after tax	45,250
Minority interests (W2)	(4,100)
Profit attributable to members of High plc	41,150
Transfers to reserves (6,000 + 80% × 5,000)	(10,000)
Dividends (3,000 + 5,000)	(8,000)
Retained profit	23,150
Retained profit brought forward (W4)	36,800
Retained profit carried forward	59,950

Workings

(W1)   *Group structure*

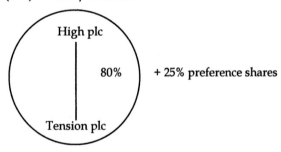

+ 25% preference shares

(W2)   *Minority interest*

	£
Profits attributable to preference shareholders 600 × 75%	450
Profits attributable to ordinary shareholders (19,550 – 600) × 20%	3,790
Less unrealised profit in stock (W3)	(140)
	4,100

(W3)   *Unrealised profit in stock*

Profits made by the subsidiary (because Tension sells to High) therefore minority interest is debited as follows:

700 × 20% = £140

(W4)   *Retained profit brought forward*

	£
100% High	28,000

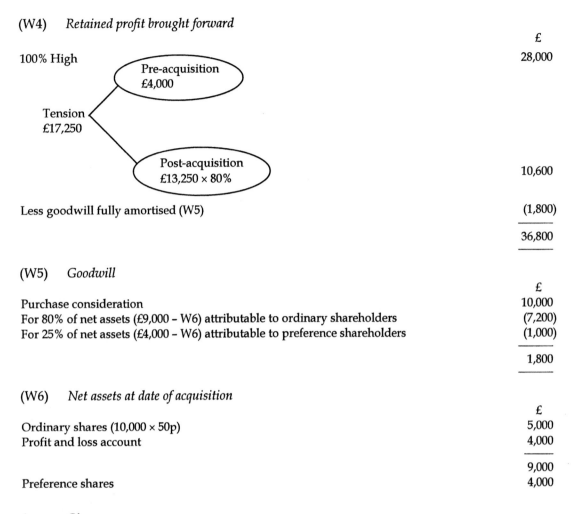

Less goodwill fully amortised (W5)	(1,800)
	36,800

(W5)   *Goodwill*

	£
Purchase consideration	10,000
For 80% of net assets (£9,000 – W6) attributable to ordinary shareholders	(7,200)
For 25% of net assets (£4,000 – W6) attributable to preference shareholders	(1,000)
	1,800

(W6)   *Net assets at date of acquisition*

	£
Ordinary shares (10,000 × 50p)	5,000
Profit and loss account	4,000
	9,000
Preference shares	4,000

4   Simon

CONSOLIDATED PROFIT AND LOSS ACCOUNT FOR THE YEAR ENDED 31 DECEMBER 20X4

	£
Turnover (W1)	7,825,000
Cost of sales (W1)	(6,455,000)
Gross profit	1,370,000
Distribution costs and administrative expenses	(810,000)
Operating profit	560,000
Interest payable and similar charges	(10,000)
Profit on ordinary activities before taxation	550,000
Tax on profit on ordinary activities	(237,500)
Profit on ordinary activities after taxation	312,500
Minority interests (W2)	(13,000)
Profit for the financial year attributable to the members of Simon plc	299,500
Dividends	(50,000)
Retained profit for the financial year	249,500

Statement of reserves

	£
Profit and loss account brought forward (W3)	1,735,675
Retained profit for the year	249,500
Profit and loss account carried forward (W6)	1,985,175

Workings

(W1) Turnover and cost of sales	Simon	Butterworth	Tolley (9/12)	Total
	£000	£000	£000	£000
Turnover	5,100	2,050	720	
Less Intra-group	(45)			
	5,055	2,050	720	7,825
Cost of sales	4,210	1,750	540	
		(45)		
	4,210	1,705	540	6,455

(W2) Minority shareholders' interest

	£
Butterworth Ltd £20,000 × 20%	4,000
Tolley Ltd £30,000 × 40% × 9/12	9,000
	13,000

(W3) Group reserves brought forward

	£		£
Simon plc			1,528,475
Butterworth Ltd at 1 January 20X4	469,000		
At acquisition	210,000		
Post-acquisition	259,000	× 80%	207,200
			1,735,675

(W4) Goodwill arising on Tolley Ltd

	£
Cost	402,000
Share of net assets acquired 60% × (£100,000 + £382,500 (W5))	(289,500)
	112,500

(W5) Pre-acquisition profits of Tolley Ltd

	£
At 1 January 20X4	375,000
To 31 March 20X4 (3/12 × £30,000)	7,500
	382,500

(W6) Proof of profit and loss account carried forward

	£
Simon plc	1,756,475
Butterworth Ltd (80% × (£479,000 - £210,000))	215,200
Tolley Ltd (60% × (£30,000 × 9/12))	13,500
	1,985,175

Multiple choice answers

1   A

      Minority interest   =   460,000 + 120,000 – 60,000

                                  =   £520,000

2   C

	Walcot plc £m	Ufton plc £m	Adjustment £m	Consolidated £m
Cost of sales	(11)	(10)	3)	
			)	(19)
PURP	(1)		)	

3   C

	£
Parent company profit	80,000
Subsidiary	
Share of preference dividend (125,000 × 8%) = 10,000 × 40%	4,000
Share of profit attributable to equity (75% × (70,000 – 10,000))	45,000
	129,000

Chapter 5 solutions

1   Hut

CONSOLIDATED BALANCE SHEET AS AT 31 DECEMBER 20X8

	£	£
Fixed assets		
Intangible (£69,400 (W3) × 90%)		62,460
Tangible		
Freehold (£80,000 + £72,000 + £18,000 (W2))		170,000
Plant at cost (120,000 + 80,000)	200,000	
Accumulated depreciation (48,000 + 22,400)	(70,400)	
		129,600
		362,060
Current assets		
Stock (£112,000 + £74,400 - £3,200 (W5))	183,200	
Debtors (£104,000 + £84,000)	188,000	
Bank (£41,000 + £8,000)	49,000	
	420,200	
Creditors: amounts falling due within one year		
(£52,000 + £24,000)	(76,000)	
Net current assets		344,200
		706,260
Capital and reserves		
Called up share capital		400,000
Profit and loss account (W6)		248,260
		648,260
Minority interests (W4)		58,000
		706,260

Workings

(W1)   *Group structure*

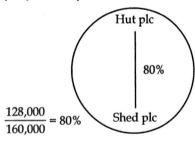

$$\frac{128,000}{160,000} = 80\%$$

(W2)   *Net assets − Shed*

	At date of acquisition £	At balance sheet date £
Share capital	160,000	160,000
Profit and loss account	(11,000)	112,000
Net assets at book value	149,000	272,000
Adjust to fair value (90,000 – 72,000)	18,000	18,000
Net assets at fair value	167,000	290,000

(W3) *Goodwill*

	£
Purchase consideration	203,000
For 80% (167,000)	(133,600)
Goodwill	69,400

(W4) *Minority interest*

	£
20% (290,000)	58,000

(W5) *Unrealised profit in stock*

	£
£16,000 × $\frac{25}{125}$ =	3,200

(W6) *Group profit and loss account*

	£
100% Hut	160,000

	£
Post-acquisition £123,000 × 80%	98,400
Less unrealised profit in stock	(3,200)
Less goodwill amortised (£69,400 × 10%)	(6,940)
Group profit and loss	248,260

Shed £112,000

(£11,000) Pre-acquisition

Multiple choice answers

1   B

All the others are prohibited by FRS 7.

2   B

Where provision has been made by the company to be acquired, and costs would be incurred whether or not acquisition went ahead, a provision should be included.

3   D

All are assets or liabilities that existed on which a fair value must be placed.

4   D

	£m
Cost of investment	12
Less share of net assets acquired	(7)
	5

Chapter 6 solutions

1 **A plc**

(a) (W1) and (W2) are as before. (W4) is as follows.

(W4) **Purchase consideration**

(i)			
1.2m × 3/2	=	1.8m new shares in A plc issued	
1.8m × £3	=	£5.4m	

(ii)			
1.2m × 2/3	=	0.8m new shares issued	
0.8m × £3	=	£2.4m	

We can now slot this into (W3)

(W3) **Goodwill**

	(i) £000	(ii) £000
Purchase consideration	5,400	2,400
For 96% of Z's net assets at fair value	(3,360)	(3,360)
	2,040	(960)

(W5) is a standard minority interest working.

(W5) **Minority interest**

4% of net assets (£3.5m)	£140,000

(W6) Group reserves is the standard working.

(W6) **Group reserves**

	(i) £000	(ii) £000
A's reserves (100%)		
Revaluation reserve	600	600
Profit and loss account	1,650	1,650

Z's reserves are all pre-acquisition.

We will then need two extra workings to calculate the new share capital of A plc and the share premium on the new issue.

(W7) **Share capital**

	(i) £000	(ii) £000
Existing share capital of A	3,600	3,600
Issued	1,800	800
New share capital	5,400	4,400

(W8) **Share premium**

	(i) £000	(ii) £000
Face value	1,800	800
Issue price	(5,400)	(2,400)
Share premium	3,600	1,600

(As this combination meets the section 131 merger relief requirements we could credit the share premium to a merger reserve.)

We are now in a position to consolidate in the usual way.

(a)   CONSOLIDATED BALANCE SHEETS

	(i) £000	(ii) £000
Fixed assets		
Goodwill (W3)	2,040	(960)
Land and buildings	3,250	3,250
Plant and fixtures and fittings	3,500	3,500
Vehicles	1,770	1,770
	10,560	7,560
Current assets		
Stock and WIP	1,090	1,090
Debtors	890	890
Other assets	650	650
	2,630	2,630
Creditors	(1,800)	(1,800)
Net current assets	830	830
Total assets less current liabilities	11,390	8,390
Capital and reserves		
Share capital (W7)	5,400	4,400
Share premium (W8)	3,600	1,600
Revaluation reserve (W6)	600	600
Profit and loss account (W6)	1,650	1,650
	11,250	8,250
Minority interest (W5)	140	140
	11,390	8,390

We are then in a position to do the same example using the merger method.

Merger adjustment	(i) £000	(ii) £000
Nominal value of subsidiaries' shares obtained in a share swap	1,200	1,200
Less nominal value of new shares issued	(1,800)	(800)
Merger adjustment	(600)	400

This can then be taken to reserves.

	(i) £000	(ii) £000
Profit and loss account		
100% A plc	1,650	1,650
96% Z plc	1,776	1,776
	3,426	3,426
Merger adjustment	(600)	400
	2,826	3,826

We are now in a position to prepare a merger method consolidated balance sheet.

(b)   Merger method

	(i) £000	(ii) £000
Net assets	8,950	8,950
	——	——
Share capital	5,400	4,400
Revaluation reserve	600	600
Profit and loss account	2,826	3,826
Minority interest	124	124
	——	——
	8,950	8,950
	——	——

2   Coll

(a)

(i)   BALANCE SHEET OF COLL PLC

	£000
Net assets	5,000
Investment in Tiree plc	6,000
	——
	11,000
	——
Share capital	2,000
Merger reserve	5,000
Profit and loss account	4,000
	——
	11,000
	——

(ii)   CONSOLIDATED BALANCE SHEET OF COLL GROUP

	£000
Goodwill (6,000 – 4,600)	1,400
Other net assets (5,000 + 4,600)	9,600
	——
	11,000
	——
Share capital	2,000
Merger reserve	5,000
Profit and loss account	4,000
	——
	11,000
	——

(b)

(i)   BALANCE SHEET OF COLL PLC

	£000
Net assets	5,000
Investment in Tiree plc	1,000
	——
	6,000
	——
Share capital	2,000
Profit and loss account	4,000
	——
	6,000
	——

(ii)   *CONSOLIDATED BALANCE SHEET OF COLL GROUP*

	£000
Net assets (5,000 + 4,000)	9,000
Share capital	2,000
Profit and loss account (4,000 + 3,000)	7,000
	9,000

(c)

(i)   If the consideration consists of 800,000 shares, a merger difference — a credit of £200,000 — arises which will be treated as a capital reserve in the consolidated balance sheet.

CONSOLIDATED BALANCE SHEET OF COLL GROUP

	£000
Net assets	9,000
Share capital	1,800
Capital reserve	200
Profit and loss account	7,000
	9,000

(ii)   If the consideration consists of 1,200,000 shares, a merger difference — a debit of £200,000 — arises. This will be eliminated by capitalising (ie reducing) the reserves of Tiree plc.

	£000
Net assets	9,000
Share capital	2,200
Profit and loss account (4,000 + 3,000 - 200)	6,800
	9,000

Multiple choice answers

1   B

The final acquisition qualifies for merger relief and therefore no share premium is created.

	Premium £
1,000 × £1	1,000
1,500 × £2	3,000
	4,000

2   B

The premium is recognised on the first acquisition only (on the second acquisition Green owns 90% of Blue and hence CA85 merger relief applies).

Share premium	=	500,000 × 30p
	=	£150,000

3   A

Acquisition accounting – Jenson Ltd only as there are no post acquisition profits of Ferrari Ltd.

Merger accounting	£
Jenson Ltd	750,000
Group share of Ferrari Ltd (95% × 320,000)	304,000
	1,054,000

Chapter 7 solutions

1   H group

CONSOLIDATED BALANCE SHEET AS AT 31 DECEMBER 20X8

	£
Sundry net assets [145,000 + 70,000 + 75,000]	290,000
Share capital	120,000
Profit and loss reserve (W5)	111,250
	231,250
Minority interest (W4)	58,750
	290,000

Workings

(1)   **Group structure**

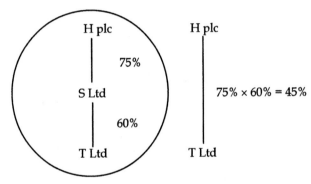

Despite the fact that H plc *owns* less than 50% of the shares in T Ltd, T Ltd is still a subsidiary owing to the *control* that S Ltd has in T Ltd.

(2)   **Net assets**

	At date of acquisition £	At balance sheet date £
Net assets – S Ltd		
Share capital	70,000	70,000
Reserves	10,000	50,000
	80,000	120,000
Net assets - T Ltd		
Share capital	40,000	40,000
Reserves	12,000	35,000
	52,000	75,000

(3)   **Goodwill**

	£
Goodwill – S Ltd	
Purchase consideration	65,000
For 75% of net assets acquired (£80,000)	(60,000)
Goodwill	5,000

Goodwill — T Ltd

	£
Purchase consideration 75% [£50,000]	37,500
For 45% of net assets acquired (£52,000)	(23,400)
Goodwill	14,100

(4)　Minority interest

	£
S Ltd 25% [£120,000]	30,000
Less 25% [£50,000] (S Ltd's investment in T)	(12,500)
	17,500
T Ltd 55% [£75,000]	41,250
Total	58,750

(5)　Group reserves

	£
Profit and loss reserve 100% H plc	90,000

£50,000 S Ltd:
- Pre-acquisition £10,000
- Post-acquisition £40,000 × 75% → 30,000

T Ltd £35,000:
- Pre-acquisition £12,000
- Post-acquisition £23,000 × 45% → 10,350

Less goodwill fully amortised (£5,000 + £14,100)	(19,100)
	111,250

2　Gucci

CONSOLIDATED BALANCE SHEET AT 31 DECEMBER 20X9

	£	£
Tangible fixed assets		18,000
Current assets		
Stocks	8,000	
Debtors	10,250	
Cash at bank and in hand	500	
	18,750	
Creditors: amounts falling due within one year		
Bank loans and overdrafts	1,900	
Trade creditors	6,300	
Proposed dividends		
To minority shareholders	1,150	
To Gucci Ltd shareholders	2,000	
	11,350	
Net current assets		7,400
Total assets less current liabilities		25,400

Creditors: amounts falling due after more than one year
10% debenture loans	(2,500)
	22,900

Capital and reserves
Called up share capital (£1 shares)	1,000
Profit and loss account (W5)	16,700
	17,700
Minority interests (W4)	5,200
	22,900

Workings

(1)   Group structure

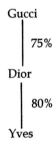

Gucci

75%

Dior

80%

Yves

Gucci's effective holding in Yves = 75% × 80% = 60%

Minority interest = 40%

(2)   Net assets

Dior Ltd

	At date of acquisition		At balance sheet date
	£	£	£
Share capital	5,000		5,000
Share premium	2,500		2,500
	7,500		7,500
Profit and loss	1,000	2,800	
Dividend receivable (80% × 2,000)		1,600	
			4,400
	8,500		11,900

Yves Ltd

Share capital	1,000		1,000
Profit and loss	3,000		6,750
	4,000		7,750

(3)   Goodwill on Dior

	£
Cost of shares	6,500
Net assets acquired (75% × £8,500)	(6,375)
	125

Goodwill on Yves

	£
Cost of shares (75% × £3,500)	2,625
Net assets acquired (60% × £4,000)	(2,400)
	225

(4)   Minority interest

	£	£
Dior Ltd (25% × £11,900)	2,975	
Cost of investment in Yves (25% × £3,500)	(875)	
		2,100
Yves Ltd (40% × £7,750)		3,100
		5,200

(5)   Profit and loss account

	£
Gucci Ltd	12,000
Dividend receivable (75% × £3,000)	2,250
Proposed dividend	(2,000)
Goodwill fully amortised (125 + 225)	(350)
	11,900
Dior Ltd [75% × (£4,400 - £1,000)]	2,550
Yves Ltd [60% × (£6,750 - £3,000)]	2,250
	16,700

3   Pace

Workings

(W1)   Group structure

Note that shares in Slow Ltd have a nominal value of 75p each.

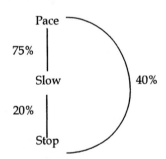

Effective interest

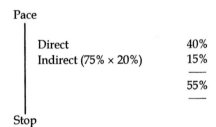

Direct	40%
Indirect (75% × 20%)	15%
	55%

Note that Stop will be treated as a subsidiary by Pace Ltd because of the overall control exercised if Pace votes its own 40% and directs the votes of Slow's 20%.

(W2)   Net assets — Slow

	At date of acquisition £	At balance sheet date £
Share capital	420,000	420,000
Other reserves	-	70,000
Profit and loss account	35,000	17,500
	455,000	507,500

Net assets — Stop

	At date of acquisition £	At balance sheet date £
Share capital	175,000	175,000
Profit and loss account	(35,000)	(17,500)
	140,000	157,500

Note that the date of acquisition of Stop is the date the ultimate parent gains control.

(W3)   Goodwill — Slow

	£
Purchase consideration	367,500
For 75% of net assets acquired (£455,000)	(341,250)
Goodwill	26,250

Goodwill — Stop

	£
Purchase consideration:	
Direct	49,000
Indirect 75% (£24,500)	18,375
Total	67,375
For 55% of net assets acquired (£140,000)	(77,000)
	(9,625)

(W4)   Minority interests

	£
Slow	
25% (£507,500)	126,875
Less 25% (£24,500)	(6,125)
Stop 45% (£157,500)	70,875
Total minority interest	191,625

(W5)   Profit and loss account

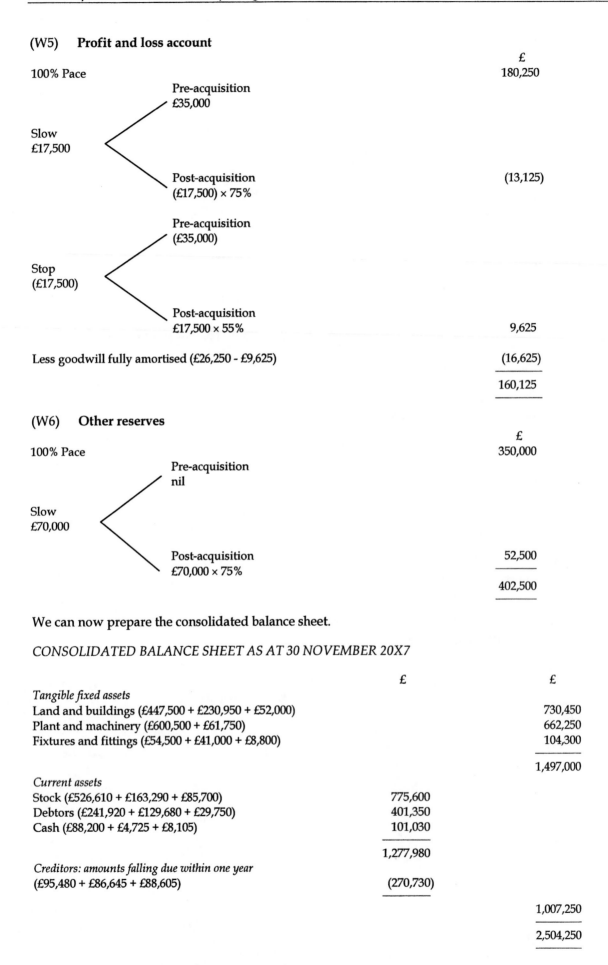

	£
100% Pace	180,250

Slow £17,500
— Pre-acquisition £35,000
— Post-acquisition (£17,500) × 75% → (13,125)

Stop (£17,500)
— Pre-acquisition (£35,000)
— Post-acquisition £17,500 × 55% → 9,625

Less goodwill fully amortised (£26,250 - £9,625)	(16,625)
	160,125

(W6)   Other reserves

	£
100% Pace	350,000

Slow £70,000
— Pre-acquisition nil
— Post-acquisition £70,000 × 75% → 52,500

	52,500
	402,500

We can now prepare the consolidated balance sheet.

CONSOLIDATED BALANCE SHEET AS AT 30 NOVEMBER 20X7

	£	£
Tangible fixed assets		
Land and buildings (£447,500 + £230,950 + £52,000)		730,450
Plant and machinery (£600,500 + £61,750)		662,250
Fixtures and fittings (£54,500 + £41,000 + £8,800)		104,300
		1,497,000
Current assets		
Stock (£526,610 + £163,290 + £85,700)	775,600	
Debtors (£241,920 + £129,680 + £29,750)	401,350	
Cash (£88,200 + £4,725 + £8,105)	101,030	
	1,277,980	
Creditors: amounts falling due within one year		
(£95,480 + £86,645 + £88,605)	(270,730)	
		1,007,250
		2,504,250

Capital and reserves

£1 shares	1,750,000
Other reserves (W6)	402,500
Profit and loss account (W5)	160,125
	2,312,625
Minority interests (W4)	191,625
	2,504,250

4   Lamb

CONSOLIDATED PROFIT AND LOSS ACCOUNT FOR THE YEAR ENDED 30 JUNE 20X7

	£
Turnover (197,000 + 100,000 + 128,000)	425,000
Cost of sales and expenses (96,600 + 52,000 + 78,000)	(226,600)
Operating profit	198,400
Profit on sale of properties	14,000
Profit on ordinary activities before taxation	212,400
Tax on profit on ordinary activities (40,000 + 17,000 + 14,000)	(71,000)
Profit on ordinary activities after taxation	141,400
Minority interests (W2)	(36,720)
Profit for the financial year attributable to members of Lamb Ltd	104,680
Dividends	(30,000)
Retained profit for the financial year	74,680
Retained profit brought forward (W3)	85,280
Retained profit carried forward (W4)	159,960

Workings

(1)   **Group structure**

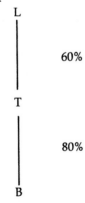

Effective interest of L in B	= 60% × 80%	= 48%
Effective minority interest in B	= 100 - 48	= 52%

(2)   Minority interest

		£	£
T	Profit after tax	39,000	
	Profit on property	14,000	
Less	Dividend from B	(8,000)	
		45,000	
		× 40%	18,000
B	£36,000 × 52%		18,720
			36,720

(3)   Retained profit brought forward

		£
L		120,000
T	60% × (70,000 - 24,000)	27,600
B	48% × (52,000 - 36,000)	7,680
Goodwill fully amortised (28,000 + 42,000)		(70,000)
		85,280

(4)   Retained profit carried forward

		£	£
L			160,000
T	Per question	93,000	
Add	Gain on sale of properties	14,000	
		107,000	
Less	Pre-acquisition	(24,000)	
		83,000 × 60%	49,800
B	48% × (78,000 - 36,000)		20,160
Goodwill fully amortised		(70,000)
			159,960

Multiple choice answers

1   A

	£	£
Goodwill on purchase of Petra Ltd		
Cost	240,000	
Share of net assets (60% × 380,000)	(228,000)	
Goodwill	12,000	
Less amortisation (12,000/3 × 2)	(8,000)	
		4,000
Goodwill on purchase of Empus Ltd		
Cost (60% × 100,000)	60,000	
Share of net assets (36% × 150,000)	(54,000)	
Goodwill	6,000	
Less amortisation (6,000/3)	(2,000)	
		4,000
		8,000

2   A

	£	£
Goodwill in B Ltd		
Cost	1,200	
Net assets acquired (75% × 1,400)	1,050	
		150
Goodwill in C Ltd		
Cost (75% × 840)	630	
Net assets acquired (60% × 1,000)	600	
		30
		180

	£
Consolidated reserves	
A Ltd	2,200
B Ltd (75% × (1,240 – 400))	630
C Ltd (60% × (450 – 200))	150
Less goodwill	(180)
	2,800

3   D

	£
Minority interest	
E Ltd (20% × 340,000)	68,000
F Ltd (52% × 300,000)	156,000
	224,000

4   C

	%
Minority interest in J Ltd	
Direct minority	15
Indirect minority (40% × 60%)	24
	39

Chapter 8 solutions

1   Dolland

CONSOLIDATED BALANCE SHEET AS AT 31 DECEMBER 20X7

	£
Tangible fixed assets	868,200
Net current assets (W6)	288,440
	1,156,640
Capital and reserves	
Called up share capital — £1 ordinary shares	500,000
Profit and loss account (W5)	463,650
	963,650
Minority interests (W4)	192,990
	1,156,640

Workings

(1)   Group structure

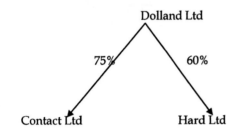

(2)   Net assets

Hard Ltd

	At date of acquisition £	At balance sheet date £
Share capital	100,000	100,000
Profit and loss account (50,600 - 15,000)	31,000	35,600
	131,000	135,600

Contact Ltd

	1 January 20X0 Acquisition £	1 January 20X2 Acquisition £	Balance sheet date £
Share capital	200,000	200,000	200,000
Profit and loss account (365,000 - 10,000)	110,000	212,000	355,000
	310,000	412,000	555,000

(3)   Goodwill

Contact Ltd

	£	£
Cost of shares	195,000	65,000
Less Net assets acquired		
(60% × £310,000 (W2))	(186,000)	
(15% × £412,000 (W2))		(61,800)
	9,000	3,200
Amortised to date	(9,000)	(3,200)
Balance carried forward	-	-

Hard Ltd

	£
Cost of shares	84,000
Less Net assets acquired (60% × £131,000 (W2))	(78,600)
	5,400
Amortised to date	(5,400)
Balance carried forward	-

(4)   Minority interest

	£
Contact Ltd (25% × £555,000 (W2))	138,750
Hard Ltd (40% × £135,600 (W2))	54,240
	192,990

(5)   Profit and loss account

	£
Dolland Ltd	318,540
Proposed dividend	(25,000)
Dividends receivable from – Contact Ltd	7,500
– Hard Ltd	9,000
Share of Contact Ltd (60% × £245,000 (W2))	147,000
(15% × £143,000 (W2))	21,450
Share of Hard Ltd (60% × £4,600 (W2))	2,760
Less Goodwill amortised to date (£12,200 + £5,400) (W3))	(17,600)
	463,650

(6)   Net current assets

	£
From balance sheets (106,540 + 165,000 + 50,400)	321,940
Dividends: Dolland	(25,000)
Contact	(2,500)
Hard	(6,000)
	288,440

2   Harrods

CONSOLIDATED BALANCE SHEET AT 30 JUNE 20X5

	£	£
Fixed assets		
Goodwill (W4)		1,707
Tangible assets (25.5 + 22.2)		47,700
Interests in associated undertakings (W7)		5,520
		54,927
Current assets		
Stocks (11,150 + 4,300 - 900)	14,550	
Debtors (5,200 + 120 - 1,200 + 1,100)	5,220	
Cash at bank and in hand	1,500	
	21,270	
Creditors: amounts falling due within one year		
Bank loans and overdrafts	2,500	
Creditors (2,100 + 2,200 - 1,200)	3,100	
Proposed dividend: parent undertaking	3,500	
Proposed dividend: minority interest	120	
	9,220	
Net current assets		12,050
Total assets less current liabilities		66,977
Creditors: amounts falling due after more than one year		
Debenture loans		(4,000)
		62,977
Capital and reserves		
Called up share capital: £1 ordinary shares		20,000
Profit and loss account (W6)		41,157
		61,157
Minority interests (W5)		1,820
		62,977

Workings

(1)   Group structure

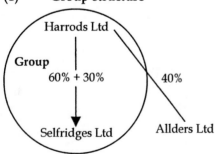

(2)   Net assets working

Selfridges Ltd	At date of acquisition		At balance
	30.6.20X1	*1.11.20X4*	*sheet date*
	£	£	£
Share capital	10,000	10,000	10,000
Profit and loss (6,400 + 1,800)	2,500	7,400 (W3)	8,200
	12,500	17,400	18,200

Allders Ltd	*At date of acquisition*	*At balance sheet date*
	£	£
Share capital	5,000	5,000
Profit and loss (1,800 + 600)	1,500	2,400
Revaluation reserve	1,000	1,000
	7,500	8,400

(3)   Selfridges profit and loss account at 1 November 20X4

	£	£
Balance brought forward		6,400
Retained profit for the year	1,800	
Add back proposed dividend	1,200	
Profit after tax	3,000	
1 July 20X4 to 31 October 20X4 (× 4/12)		1,000
Balance at 1 November 20X4		7,400

(4)   Goodwill/premium

	Selfridges Ltd		Allders Ltd
	£	£	£
Cost of acquisition	10,000	5,450	5,700
Share of net assets acquired			
60% × £12,500 (W2)	(7,500)		
30% × £17,400 (W2)		(5,220)	
40% × £7,500			(3,000)
	2,500	230	2,700
Amortisation (4/10; 1/10; 2/10)	(1,000)	(23)	(540)
Balance carried forward	1,500	207	2,160

(5)   Minority interests

Selfridges Ltd (10% × 18,200)	£1,820

(6)   Profit and loss reserve

	£	£
Harrods Ltd		38,400
Dividends receivable from:		
Selfridges Ltd (90% × £1,200)		1,080
Allders Ltd (40% × £300)		120
		39,600
Selfridges Ltd 30% (8,200 - 7,400) (W3)	240	
60% (8,200 - 2,500) (W2)	3,420	
		3,660
Allders Ltd 40% (2,400 - 1,500) (W2)		360
Stock — provision for unrealised profit		(900)
Goodwill amortisation (W4) (1,000 + 23)		(1,023)
Premium amortisation (W4)		(540)
		41,157

(7)   Share of net assets at 30 June 20X5

	£
40% × (7,400 + 1,000)	3,360
Goodwill not yet amortised	2,160
	5,520

Multiple choice answers

1   C

	£
60% × 100,000	60,000
20% × 120,000	24,000
	84,000

Aggregate the 10% acquisition into the 50% acquisition because control was not achieved until 31 December 20X6 (FRS 2). Intention to acquire control is not relevant.

2   B

	£
Cost of investment	15,000
Add share of net liabilities acquired (50% × 25,696)	12,848
	27,848

3   A

	£
Cost (50 + 350)	400,000
Net assets acquired (70% × (400 + 100))	(350,000)
	50,000

Chapter 9 solutions

1   Aston

Accounting entries			£	£
25 October 20X1	Debit	Purchases (W1)	25,627	
	Credit	Creditors		25,627
16 November 20X1	Debit	Creditors	25,627	
	Debit	Profit and loss account		
		- other operating expense	684	
	Credit	Cash (W2)		26,311

The goods will remain in stock at the year end at £25,627.

Workings

(1) SwK 286,000 ÷ 11.16 = £25,627

(2) SwK 286,000 ÷ 10.87 = £26,311

2   Moye

Accounting entries			£	£
25 October 20X1	Debit	Purchases (W1)	25,627	
	Credit	Creditors		25,627
31 December 20X1	Debit	Profit and loss account		
		– other operating expense	326	
	Credit	Creditors (W2)		326

The goods will remain in stock at the year end at £25,627.

Workings

	£
(1) SwK 286,000 ÷ 11.16 =	25,627
(2) SwK 286,000 ÷ 11.02 =	25,953
	326

3   Warrilow

Accounting entries			£000	£000
29 November 20X1	Debit	Cash (W1)	1,000	
	Credit	Creditors		1,000
31 December 20X1	Debit	Creditors	85	
	Credit	Profit and loss account - other interest receivable and similar income		85

Workings

	£000
(1) S Fr 2,217,000 ÷ 2.217 =	1,000
(2) S Fr 2,217,000 ÷ 2.424 =	915
	85

(4)   Karpal

	Situation 1 £	Situation 2 £	Situation 3 £
(Charged) credited to profit and loss account	(746)	-	2,586
Credited to reserves	-	793	4,293

Multiple choice answers

1   B

			£
Debtor at 1 October 20X2	$50,000/1.6	=	31,250
Debtor at 31 December 20X2	$50,000/1.7	=	29,412
Exchange loss			1,838

2   B

			£
US creditor	@ 1 Feb	$64,000/1.5	42,667
	@ 31 Mar	$64,000/1.7	37,647
Exchange gain			5,020
Euro debtor	@ 1 Feb	€40,000/1.6	25,000
	@ 15 Mar	€40,000/1.7	23,529
Exchange loss			1,471

Net exchange gain = 5,020 – 1,471 = £3,549

3   B

		£	£
Loss on loan	$200,000/1.5	133,333	
	$200,000/1.3	153,846	
			20,513
Gain on investment	€300,000/1.5	200,000	
	€300,000/1.4	214,286	
Offset in reserves			(14,286)
Loss in profit and loss			6,227

Chapter 10 solutions

1   Gobbo CRM

(W1)   Unchanged

(W1A) Translation

	Sly Inc $	Rate	Sly Inc £
Sundry other assets	12,900	3	4,300
	12,900		4,300
Share capital	4,000	4	1,000
Profit and loss account			
Pre-acquisition	2,000	4	500
Post-acquisition	6,900	Balance	2,800
	12,900		4,300

(W3)   Goodwill — unchanged

(W4)   Minority interest

20% of net assets at balance sheet date (£4,300)	£860

(W5)   Group profit and loss account

	£
100% Gobbo	-
80% Post-acquisition of Sly (2,800)	2,240
	2,240

CONSOLIDATED BALANCE SHEET AT 31 DECEMBER 20X4

	£
Intangible fixed assets (goodwill)	300
Other net assets	4,800
	5,100
Share capital	2,000
Profit and loss account (W5)	2,240
	4,240
Minority interest (W4)	860
	5,100

2   Gobbo TM

(W1)   No change

(W1A) Translation

	Sly Inc $	Rate	Sly Inc £
Tangible fixed assets	12,000	4	3,000
Stock	1,914	2.9	660
Other current assets	4,986	3	1,662
	18,900		5,322
Long-term loans	(6,000)	3	(2,000)
	12,900		3,322
Share capital	4,000	4	1,000
Pre-acquisition profits	2,000	4	500
Post-acquisition profits	6,900	Balance	1,822
	12,900		3,322

(W2)   Net assets

	At date of acquisition £	At balance sheet date £
Share capital	1,000	1,000
Pre-acquisition profit	500	500
Post-acquisition		1,822
	1,500	3,322

(W3)   Goodwill

Purchase consideration	1,500
For 80% of net assets acquired (£1,500)	(1,200)
Goodwill	300

(W4)   Minority interests

£3,322 × 20%	664

(W5)   Profit and loss account

100% Gobbo	Nil
80% of post-acquisition reserves of Sly (£1,822)	1,458
	1,458

CONSOLIDATED BALANCE SHEET AT 31 DECEMBER 20X4

	£
Fixed assets	
Intangible (W3)	300
Tangible	3,000
Current assets	
Stock	660
Other	2,162
	6,122
Long-term loan	(2,000)
	4,122
Capital and reserves	
Share capital	2,000
Profit and loss account (W5)	1,458
	3,458
Minority interest (W4)	664
	4,122

3   Grofine I

CONSOLIDATED BALANCE SHEET AT 31 DECEMBER 20X3

	£000
Goodwill (W3)	2,000
Tangible fixed assets (W2)	960
Net current assets (652 + (W2) 8,320)	8,972
	11,932
Share capital	5,000
Group reserves (W5)	4,612
	9,612
Minority interest (W4)	2,320
	11,932

CONSOLIDATED PROFIT AND LOSS ACCOUNT FOR THE YEAR ENDED 31 DECEMBER 20X3

	S Inc $000	Rate	S Inc £000	Consol £000
Turnover	22,000	2.3	9,565	9,565
Cost of sales	(11,490)		(4,995)	(4,995)
Gross profit	10,510		4,570	4,570
Distribution and admin expenses	(3,910)		(1,700)	(1,700)
Profit	6,600		2,870	2,870
Dividend paid during year	(2,000)		(870)	
	4,600		2,000	
Minority interest				(718)
Retained profit for the year				2,152

STATEMENT OF RESERVES FOR THE YEAR ENDED 31 DECEMBER 20X3

	£000
Reserves at 1 January 20X3	3,975
Retained profit for the year	2,152
Exchange differences (W6)	(1,515)
Reserves at 31 December 20X3	4,612

(**Tutorial note** The exchange differences will also appear in the statement of total recognised gains and losses.)

Workings

(W1)   **Group structure**

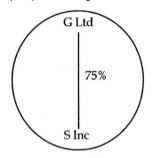

G Ltd
75%
S Inc

(W2)   **Translation**

	S Inc $000	Rate	S Inc £000
Fixed assets	2,400	2.5	960
Net current assets	20,800	2.5	8,320
	23,200		9,280
Share capital	4,000	3	1,333
Pre-acquisition reserves	8,000	3	2,667
Post-acquisition reserves	11,200	Balance	5,280
	23,200		9,280

(W3)   **Goodwill**

	£000
Purchase consideration	5,000
For 75% of net assets acquired (1,333 + 2,667) (W2)	(3,000)
Goodwill	2,000

(W4)   **Minority interests**

	£000
25% of net assets at balance sheet date (9,280) (W2)	2,320

(W5)   **Group reserves**

	£000
100% Grofine Ltd	652
S Inc 75% post-acquisition reserves (W2) 5,280	3,960
	4,612

(W6)   Exchange difference

	Opening net assets	+ Retained profit	= Closing net assets
$	18,600	+ 4,600	= 23,200
Rate of exchange	2	2.3	2.5
£	9,300	+ 2,000	≠ 9,280

The balancing figure required is the exchange difference (a loss) of 2,020, of which 75% (1,515) will be taken to reserves.

4   Grofine II

CONSOLIDATED BALANCE SHEET AS AT 31 DECEMBER 20X3

	£000
Goodwill (as before, W3)	2,000
Tangible fixed assets (W2)	800
Stocks (W2)	712
Other net current assets (652 + (W2) 7,636)	8,288
	11,800
Share capital	5,000
Group reserves (W5)	4,513
	9,513
Minority interest (W4)	2,287
	11,800

CONSOLIDATED PROFIT AND LOSS ACCOUNT FOR THE YEAR ENDED 31 DECEMBER 20X3

	S Inc $000	Rate	S Inc £000	Consol £000
Turnover	22,000	2.3	9,565	9,565
Opening stock	2,200	2.2	1,000	1,000
Purchases	11,000	2.3	4,783	4,783
	13,200		5,783	5,783
Closing stock	(1,710)	2.4	(712)	(712)
	11,490		5,071	5,071
Gross profit	10,510		4,494	4,494
Distribution and admin expenses	(3,610)	2.3	(1,569)	(1,569)
Depreciation	(300)	3	(100)	(100)
Exchange differences	–	W6	(1,557)	(1,557)
Profit	6,600		1,268	1,268
Dividend	(2,000)	2.3	(870)	
	4,600		398	
Minority interest				(317)
Retained profit for the year				951

Workings

(W1)   Group structure

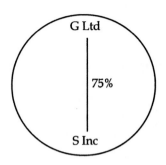

(W2)   Translation

	S Inc	Rate	S Inc
	$000		£000
Fixed assets	2,400	3	800
Stocks	1,710	2.4	712
Other net current assets	19,090	2.5	7,636
	23,200		9,148
Share capital	4,000	3	1,333
Pre-acquisition reserves	8,000	3	2,667
Post-acquisition reserves	11,200	Balance	5,148
	23,200		9,148

(W3)   Goodwill

	£000
Purchase consideration	5,000
For 75% of net assets acquired (1,333 + 2,667) (W2)	(3,000)
Goodwill	2,000

(W4)   Minority interests

	£000
25% (9,148) (W2)	2,287

(W5)   Group reserves

	£000
100% Grofine Ltd	652
75% S Inc post-acquisition (5,148, W2)	3,861
	4,513

(W6)   Exchange difference

Opening net monetary assets		+ Retained "money"	= Closing net monetary assets
		22,000 -	
		11,000 -	
		3,610 -	
		2,000 =	
$	13,700	+ 5,390	= 19,090
Rate of exchange	2	2.3	2.5
£	6,850	+ 2,343	≠ 7,636

The balancing figure required is the exchange difference (a loss) of £1,557, which is taken to the profit and loss account.

Multiple choice answers

1   C

The subsidiary is acting as a direct extension of the UK activities, so the temporal method is appropriate.

2   A

	Saint Ltd $	Exchange rate	£
Fixed assets	160,000	1.25	128,000
Net monetary assets	20,000	1.25	16,000
	180,000		144,000
Share capital	100,000	1.5	66,667
Pre-acquisition reserves	35,000	1.5	23,333
Post-acquisition reserves	45,000	Bal fig	54,000
	180,000		144,000

£

Goodwill
Cost $105,000/1.5	70,000
Net assets acquired $135,000/1.5 × 60%	54,000
Goodwill	16,000

Consolidated reserves
Hardy Ltd	440,000
Saint Ltd (54,000 × 60%)	32,400
Less goodwill (16,000/4 × 2)	(8,000)
	464,400

3   A

	Saint Ltd $	Exchange rate	£
Fixed assets	160,000	1.5	106,667
Net monetary assets	20,000	1.25	16,000
	180,000		122,667
Share capital	100,000	1.5	66,667
Pre-acquisition reserves	35,000	1.5	23,333
Post-acquisition reserves	45,000	Bal fig	32,667
	180,000		122,667

£

Goodwill
Cost $105,000/1.5	70,000
Net assets acquired $135,000/1.5 × 60%	54,000
Goodwill	16,000

Consolidated reserves
Hardy Ltd	440,000
Saint Ltd (32,667 × 60%)	19,600
Less goodwill (16,000/4 × 2)	(8,000)
	451,600

Chapter 11 solutions

1   Burrelli

CONSOLIDATED BALANCE SHEET AS AT 31 DECEMBER 20X5

	£000
Tangible fixed assets (1,740 + 840)	2,580
Net current assets (1,010 + 600 + 72)	1,682
	4,262
Called up share capital	2,400
Profit and loss account (W7)	1,502
	3,902
Minority interest (W6)	360
	4,262

 Note that the cancellation of the dividend creditor in Dawes Ltd accounts is effected by adding back the group's share.

Workings

(W1)   Group structure

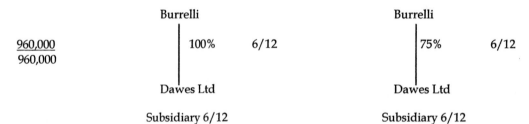

(W2)   Net assets

	At date of acquisition	At date of disposal 30.6.X5	At balance sheet date 31.12.X5
	£000	£000	£000
Share capital	960	960	960
Reserves	190	488 (W3)	480
	1,150	1,448	1,440

(W3)   Profit and loss reserve at the date of disposal

	£000		£000
Balance brought forward 1.1.X5			400
In year (480 – 400)	80		
Add back proposed dividend (960,000 × 10p)	96		
	176	× 6/12	88
			488

(W4)   Goodwill

	£000
Purchase consideration	1,200
For 100% of net assets acquired (1,150)	1,150
Goodwill	50

(W5)   Profit on disposal in group accounts

Disposal of subsidiary

	£			£
Net assets disposed of			Proceeds	400,000
1,448 × 25%	362,000			
Profit on disposal	38,000			
	400,000			400,000

(W6)   Minority interests

	£000
25% (1,440)	360

(W7)   Group profit and loss reserve

	£000
100% Burrelli	1,150
Add dividend receivable	72
Profit on disposal in Burrelli's books	100
(400 – (1,200 × 25/100))	
Less Goodwill (50 – (50 × 25/100))	(37.5)

Pre-acquisition 1,150

Dawes
1,440

Post-acquisition 290 × 75%	217.5
	1,502

Multiple choice answers

1   D

	£000
Sale proceeds	9,940
Less share of net assets (80% × 10,350)	(8,280)
Group gain	1,660

2   C

		£
Proceeds		250,000
Less	Net assets at disposal (100,000 × 40%)	(40,000)
	Unamortised goodwill (50,000 × $\frac{5}{10}$)	(25,000)
		185,000

3   **D**

		£
Proceeds		820,000
Less	Share of net assets at disposal (790,000 × 75%)	(592,500)
Less	Goodwill not written off through the consolidated profit and loss account (125,000 × $\frac{15}{20}$)	(93,750)
		133,750

4   **A**

Gill Group reserves   £230,000

Note: As the profit on disposal has been included within the remaining Gill Group reserves, no further adjustment is necessary.

Chapter 12 solutions

1   Field

GROUP CASH FLOW STATEMENT FOR THE YEAR ENDED 31 DECEMBER 20X6

	£000	£000
Net cash inflow from operating activities		710
Dividends from associate		50
Returns on investments and servicing of finance		
Interest paid	(110)	
Dividend to minority	(10)	(120)
Taxation		(110)
Capital expenditure		
Payments to acquire fixed assets		(1,070)
Equity dividends paid		(60)
Cash outflow before management of liquid resources and financing		(600)
Financing		
Share capital issue	600	
Loans taken out	150	750
Increase in cash		150

Note 1 Reconciliation of operating profit to net cash inflow from operating activities

	£000
Operating profit	640
Depreciation	70
Increase in stock	(300)
Increase in debtors	(200)
Increase in creditors	500
Net cash inflow from operating activities	710

Note 2 Reconciliation of net cash flow to movement in net debt

	£000	£000
Increase in cash in the period	150	
Increase in debt	(150)	
Change in net debt		NIL
Net debt at start of the period		(1,500)
Net debt at end of the period		(1,500)

Note 3 Analysis of changes in net debt

	At 1 January 20X6 £000	Cash flows £000	At 31 Dec 20X6 £000
Cash	100	(50)	50
Bank overdraft	(350)	200	(150)
	(250)	150	(100)
Debt due after one year	(1,250)	(150)	(1,400)
Net debt	(1,500)	NIL	(1,500)

2   Tender

CONSOLIDATED CASH FLOW STATEMENT FOR THE YEAR ENDED 30 JUNE 20X5

	£000	£000
Net cash inflow from operating activities (Note 1)		2,144
Returns on investments and servicing of finance		
Interest paid		(320)
Taxation (W1)		(596)
Capital expenditure		
Purchase of tangible fixed assets	(1,954)	
Proceeds from sale of tangible fixed assets (2,136 - 408 - 1,104)	624	
		(1,330)
Acquisitions and disposals		
Disposal of subsidiary undertaking (Note 4)	1,440	
Net cash disposed of with subsidiary	(134)	
		1,306
Equity dividends paid		(192)
Management of liquid resources		
Purchase of corporate bonds		(280)
Increase in cash		732

Notes to the cash flow statement

(1)   Reconciliation of operating profit to net cash inflow from operating activities

	£000
Operating profit	1,660
Depreciation charges	1,094
Increase in stocks (2,802 - 2,935 + 504)	(371)
Increase in debtors (2,203 - 1,924 + 346)	(625)
Increase in creditors (W2)	386
Net cash inflow from operating activities	2,144

(2)   Reconciliation of net cash flow to movement in net funds (Note 3)

	£000	£000
Increase in cash in the period	732	
Cash used to increase liquid resources	280	
Change in net funds		1,012
Net funds at 1 July 20X4		1,766
Net funds at 30 June 20X5		2,778

(3)   Analysis of changes in net funds

	At 1 July 20X4 £000	Cash flows £000	At 30 June 20X5 £000
Cash at bank and in hand	756	732	1,488
Current asset investments	1,010	280	1,290
Total	1,766	1,012	2,778

(4)   Sale of subsidiary undertaking

	£000
Net assets disposed of	
Fixed assets	1,104
Stocks	504
Debtors	346
Cash	134
Creditors	(576)
	1,512
Minority interests (1,512 × 25%)	(378)
	1,134
Profit on disposal	306
	1,440
Satisfied by cash	1,440

Workings

(1)   Taxation

	£000		£000
Cash paid (balance)	596	Brought forward	
Carried forward		Deferred tax	763
Deferred tax	517	Current tax	630
Current tax	750	Charge for year	470
	1,863		1,863

(2)   Increase in trade creditors

	£000
At 30 June 20X5 (1,910 - 750)	1,160
At 30 June 20X4 (1,980 - 630)	(1,350)
	(190)
Creditors of subsidiary sold	576
	386

Multiple choice answers

1   B

	Minority interest		
	£000		*£000*
Cash paid (bal fig)	40	Balance b/d	640
Balance c/d	700	Profit and loss	100
	740		740

2   A

Associated undertaking

	£000		£000
Balance b/d	360	Cash receipt (bal fig)	20
Profits of associate	80	Tax – associate	20
		Balance c/d	400
	——		——
	440		440
	——		——

3   A

Corporation tax

	£000		£000
Cash paid (bal fig)	50	Balance b/d	110
Balance c/d	120	Profit and loss group tax	60
	——		——
	170		170
	——		——

Chapter 13 solutions

1   Bethany

Balance sheet as at 1 July 20X1

	£000
Fixed assets	7,200
Net current assets	7,550
14% debentures 20Y8	(6,000)
	8,750
Capital and reserves	
15,000,000 25p ordinary shares	3,750
8% cumulative £1 preference shares	5,000
	8,750

The legal process would involve the following steps.

♦   Ensuring that the capital reduction is within s135 Companies Act 1985.

♦   Ordering a meeting of creditors and/or members if required by the court under ss425 and 426 Companies Act 1985; this will be essential where the reconstruction involves arrangements with creditors and/or members.

♦   Obtaining a 75% majority of the creditors and/or members voting, to agree to the arrangement and obtaining a sanction from the court so that it becomes binding on all the creditors and members of the class involved, and also the company.

♦   Filing a copy of the reconstruction scheme with the Registrar of Companies.

Workings

The proposed scheme would be accounted for using the following journals (references are to paragraphs in the question).

		Dr £000	Cr £000
(a)	£1 ordinary shares	20,000	
	Capital reconstruction account		20,000
(b)	11% debentures	7,000	
	14% debentures		6,000
	25p ordinary shares		1,000
(c)	Capital reconstruction account	1,000	
	25p ordinary shares		1,000
(d)	Capital reconstruction account	1,750	
	25p ordinary shares		1,750
	Capital reconstruction account	17,250	
	Profit and loss account		17,250

Reconstruction account

	£000		£000
25p Ordinary shares	1,000	£1 ordinary shares	20,000
25p Ordinary shares	1,750		
Profit and loss	17,250		
	20,000		20,000

(b)   Debentureholders

		£
Without reconstruction		
Interest 11% × £7,000,000		770,000
Less: Tax @ 31%		238,700
Reduction of after-tax profit		531,300
With reconstruction		
Interest 14% × £6,000,000		840,000
Less: Tax @ 31%		260,400
Reduction of after-tax profit		579,600

Therefore, £(3,000,000 – 579,600) = £2,420,400 is available for shareholders. (8% × £5,000,000) = £400,000 goes to preference shareholders, leaving £2,020,400 to the ordinary shareholders.

Old debentureholders' portion	=	$\dfrac{4,000,000 \text{ shares}}{15,000,000 \text{ shares}} \times £2,020,400$
	=	£538,773
Total share of after-tax profit	=	£(579,600 + 538,773)
	=	£1,118,373

Preference shareholders

Without reconstruction	With the current profit and loss account deficit no dividend is possible in the near future.	
With reconstruction		£
	Preference dividend	400,000
	Share of balance	
	$\dfrac{4,000,000 \text{ shares}}{15,000,000 \text{ shares}} \times £2,020,400$	538,773
		£938,773

Ordinary shareholders

Without reconstruction	Nil for the near future.	
With reconstruction		£
	$\dfrac{7,000,000 \text{ shares}}{15,000,000 \text{ shares}} \times £2,020,400$	942,854

(c)   Report

To: A Shareholder

From: AN Accountant

Date: X-X-20XX

Subject: **Company reconstruction of Bethany Ltd**

As a current ordinary shareholder you are being asked to participate in a capital reconstruction which the management considers necessary for the survival of the business. From our business correspondence I note that you feel the proposals are unfair. It is necessary for you to consider the following points.

In the event of the liquidation of the company the net realisable value of £13,200,000 would first be used to clear the £7,000,000 debentures, secondly to pay the cumulative preference dividend of £1,600,000, with the final balance of £4,600,000 being paid to the preference shareholders. These shareholders would therefore be 'losing' £400,000 and the ordinary shareholders would receive nil.

The ordinary shareholders are not being asked for finance and you will therefore not be putting any additional funds at risk.

There is a good chance that in the future your investment will give a return. At present no such return, in the form of dividends or capital, is likely.

The current ordinary shareholders have 100% control of the company. After the scheme they will only have a 46.7% holding and therefore relinquish control. This may be seen as unfair and a reduction in the number of new ordinary shares given to the preference shareholders could be made to 3,000,000, thus leaving the ordinary shareholders with a more equitable 50% stake.

If you require any advice on the above information, please do not hesitate to contact me.

Multiple choice answers

1   B

2   D

> £50,000 of the losses will be written off against the share premium account and the remaining £100,000 off the share capital leaving £200,000 of share capital which is made up of 800,000 25 pence ordinary shares.

3   D

Realisation account

	£		£
Fixed assets	284,000	Current liabilities	22,000
Stock	16,000	Consideration	304,000
Debtors	12,000		
Profit	14,000		
	326,000		326,000

Consideration is calculated as:

	£
Shares (400,000 × 50p × 1.2)	240,000
Debentures (£80,000 × 0.8)	64,000
	304,000

Chapter 14 solutions

Multiple choice answers

1   B

2   C

3   C

The company has changed its policy for accounting for freehold properties. FRS 3 gives the standard accounting for changes in accounting policy: they require a prior period adjustment. If the company has re-assessed the useful life from, say, 60 years to 50 years, this would have been a change of estimation technique.

Chapter 15 solutions

1   Sunshine

(When approaching a question on FRS 3 do make sure you consider whether the discontinuation or sale of an operation fulfils the strict definition of the standard. In this case it does, but do not assume it should. If you feel it does not then write down that it has been included in continuing operations and justify your classification. Even if you are incorrect and it should be treated as discontinued, you will gain some credit for having applied your knowledge.)

CONSOLIDATED PROFIT AND LOSS ACCOUNT FOR THE YEAR ENDED 31 DECEMBER 20X4

	Continuing operations	*Discontinued operations*	*Total*
	£m	*£m*	*£m*
Turnover	2,609.0	100	2,709.0
Net operating costs	2,252.2	51	2,303.2
Operating profit	356.8	49	405.8
Interest receivable			8.2
Profit on ordinary activities before taxation			414.0
Taxation			148.0
Profit on ordinary activities after taxation			266.0
Dividends			95.0
Retained profit			171.0

2   Claret

(a)   *STATEMENT OF TOTAL RECOGNISED GAINS AND LOSSES FOR THE YEAR ENDED 31 DECEMBER 20X8*

	£000
Profit for the financial year (1,825 + 250 - 62 + 55)	2,068
Unrealised surplus on revaluation (W1)	40
	2,108
Prior period adjustment (note 2)	(55)
Total gains and losses recognised since last annual report	2,053

(b)   Notes to the accounts

(1)   Reconciliation of shareholders' funds for the year

	£000
Profit for the financial year (as above)	2,068
Dividends	(250)
Surplus on revaluation	40
Shares issued (160 × £2.10)	336
Net addition to shareholders' funds	2,194
Opening shareholders' funds	21,741
Prior period adjustment	(55)
Closing shareholders' funds	23,880

(2)   Prior period adjustment

The prior period adjustment is in respect of a fundamental error in the valuation of stock. Closing stock and, hence, reserves at 31 December 20X7 were overstated by £55,000.

Workings

(1)   Unrealised surplus on revaluation

	£000	£000
Revalued amount		430
Original cost	650	
Accumulated depreciation to 31 December 20X8 650 × 8/20	(260)	
Net book value at revaluation		(390)
		40

(2)   Opening total shareholders' funds

	£000
Share capital (2,000 × 50p)	1,000
Profit and loss account	20,658
Revaluation reserve	83
	21,741

3   Meld

(a)   Profit and loss account for the year ended 30 June 20X4

	Continuing operations	Acquisitions	Total
	£	£	£
Turnover	468,000	4,800	472,800
Cost of sales and expenses (W)	(356,500)	(3,600)	(360,100)
Operating profit	111,500	1,200	112,700
Interest payable and similar charges			(15,000)
Profit on ordinary activities before taxation			97,700
Tax on profit on ordinary activities			(28,800)
Profit for the financial year			68,900
Dividends			(21,600)
Retained profit for the financial year			47,300

(b)   Statement of total recognised gains and losses

	£
Profit for the financial year	68,900
Unrealised surplus on revaluation of fixed assets (28,800 – (19,200 – 7,200))	16,800
Total recognised gains and losses relating to the year	85,700
Prior year adjustment (34,560 – 20,160)	(14,400)
Total gains and losses recognised since last annual report	71,300

(c)   Note of historical cost profits and losses

	£
Reported profit on ordinary activities before taxation	97,700
Difference between a historical cost depreciation charge and the actual	3,360
depreciation charge for the year calculated on the revalued amount	
Historical cost profit on ordinary activities before taxation	101,060
Historical cost profit for the year retained after taxation, minority interests, and dividends (47,300 + 3,360)	50,660

(d)   Reconciliation of movements in shareholders' funds

	£
Profit for the financial year	68,900
Dividends	(21,600)
	47,300
Other recognised gains and losses relating to the year	16,800
Net addition to shareholders' funds	64,100
Opening shareholders' funds (£456,000 before the prior-year adjustment of £14,400)	441,600
Closing shareholders' funds	505,700

(e)   Statement of reserves

	Revaluation reserve £	Profit and loss account £	Total £
At 1 July 20X3			
As previously stated	48,000	168,000	216,000
Prior year adjustment	-	(14,400)	(14,400)
As restated	48,000	153,600	201,600
Retained profit for the year	-	47,300	47,300
Surplus on property revaluations	16,800	-	16,800
Transfer of realised profits	(3,360)	3,360	-
At 30 June 20X4	61,440	204,260	265,700

Working

Cost of sales and expenses

	£
Per question	376,800
Interest	(15,000)
Acquisition element	(3,600)
Change of accounting policy regarding development costs	
Amortisation	(4,800)
Expenditure incurred	3,100
	365,500

4   Hill plc

Part (a)

(i)   *Problems of lack of guidance*

The ASB felt it was necessary to introduce a standard on provisions because the lack of guidance in this area had led to the following problems.

♦ *Inconsistency of treatment.* Where a diverse range of accounting treatments is possible this will lead to a lack of comparability between the financial statements of companies. Consistency and comparability are key principles to be applied if financial statements are to give a true and fair view.

♦ *Growth of creative accounting.* Provisions had been used more and more as a method of profit smoothing in an attempt to impress equity investors.

♦ *Risk.* Equity investors are in general perceived to be risk averse. They react unfavourably to large fluctuations in reported profit. A gently increasing pattern of profits over time gives the impression of quality earnings.

♦ *Big bath provisions.* This in turn has led companies to make large one-off provisions in years where a high level of underlying profits is generated. These general provisions, often known as 'big bath' provisions, smooth profits in future years as the provision is released, producing years of apparent good news.

♦ *Economic reality.* Financial statements should reflect the substance (commercial reality) and if profits fluctuate then the equity investors should be informed through the annual report.

(ii)   FRS 12 states that provisions should be recognised when, and only when:

1   an enterprise has a present legal or constructive obligation as a result of past events

2   it is probable that a transfer of economic benefits will be required to settle the obligation

3   a reliable estimate of the amount required to settle the obligation can be made. A reliable estimate can be made even if there is a range of possible outcomes.

An obligation exists when the entity has no realistic alternative to making a transfer of economic benefits. This is the case only where the obligation can be enforced by law or in the case of constructive obligation (see below). No provision is recognised for costs that need to be incurred to operate in the future. The only liabilities recognised are those that exist at the balance sheet date. The obligations must have arisen from past events and must exist independently from the company's future actions. If the company can avoid the expenditure by its future actions then no provision is recognised. These rules are designed to allow a provision to escape recognition only in rare cases. In these rare cases there is an obligation if, having taken into account all available evidence, it is more likely than not that a present obligation exists at the balance sheet date.

It is not necessary to know the identity of the party to whom the obligation is owed in order for an obligation to exist but in principle there must be another party. The mere intention or necessity to incur expenditure is not enough to create an obligation. Where there are a number of similar obligations the whole class of obligations must be considered when determining whether economic benefits will be transferred.

There is a need to provide for legal obligations although there is the important issue of timing and the identification of the past event which triggers the recognition. However FRS 12 also deals with the concept of 'constructive obligation', for example where a retail store gives refunds to dissatisfied customers even though there is no legal obligation to do so in order to preserve its reputation.

Therefore, an entity may be committed to certain expenditure because any alternative would be too onerous to contemplate. The determination of a constructive obligation is extremely difficult; it is a somewhat subjective concept.

Part (b)

(i)   *Factory closure*

The key issue is whether or not a provision should be made for the £79 million cost of restructuring. This will depend per FRS 12 on whether the group has an obligation to incur this expenditure.

There is clearly no legal obligation to close this factory but there may be a constructive obligation. FRS 12 states that a constructive obligation only exists if the group has created valid expectations in other parties such as customers, employees and suppliers, that the restructuring will be carried out.

As no formal plan exists and no announcements have been made to any of the affected parties, no constructive obligation exists. A board decision alone is not sufficient – no provision should be made.

(ii)   *Operating lease*

FRS 12 defines an onerous contract when:

'the unavoidable costs of meeting the obligations under it exceed the economic benefits expected to be received under it.'

The lease on the building seems to fall under this definition, ie it is an onerous contract.

The company has a legal obligation to pay the lease payments as they have signed a contract to do so.

The lease rentals will be paid, therefore a transfer of economic benefits will take place.

The amount involved can be estimated. The conditions are met and therefore a provision should be made for the remaining lease payments.

Full disclosure should also be made with regard to the nature, amount and timing of the obligations.

(iii)   *Legal proceedings*

It is unlikely the group has a present obligation to compensate the customer and therefore no provision should be recognised.

There may be a contingent liability but as the possibility of a transfer of economic benefit is remote we can ignore this in the accounts.

(iv)   *Environmental damage*

The company has no legal obligation to rectify this damage, but through its published policies it has created expectation on the part of those affected that it will take action to do so. There is therefore a constructive obligation to rectify the damage. It is probable that a transfer of economic benefits will take place and an estimate of the amount involved can be made.

A provision should be made of the best estimate of the cost involved, ie the full amount of £15 million should be provided for.

As the expenditure will not occur until the future the provision should be discounted to take account of the time value of money.

An environmental rectification asset will need to be set up for the same amount.

This asset so created will be depreciated over the next eight years via the profit and loss account.

The provision account will be recalculated each year and adjusted for changes in price levels and the unwinding of the discount.

Multiple choice answers

1   B

        FRS 3, para 14 analysis may be on the face of the profit and loss account or in the notes.

2   C

        Of the £7,025,000 'acquisitions' turnover in 20X6, £2,500,000 should be reallocated to 'discontinued' (7,950 + 2,500 = £10,450,000) and the remaining £4,525,000 reallocated to 'continuing' (25,750 + 4,525 = £30,275,000).

3   C

	£
Property 1	
Disposal proceeds	1,550,000
Less net book value $(1,900,000 \times \frac{8}{10})$	(1,520,000)
Profit on disposal	30,000
Property 2	
Revalued amount	2,000,000
Less historic NBV (1,000,000 – 350,000)	(650,000)
Unrealised gain	1,350,000

4   B

      (1)   A constructive obligation exists as the company has built up a valid expectation in customers.

      (2)   The signing of the lease is a past event and when the lease becomes onerous, a provision should be made.

Chapter 16 solutions

1   Appledore plc

(a)   *Trading account for 20X0*

	HC £	CC £
Sales (W1)	1,750	1,750
Cost of sales (W2)	960	1,100
Trading profit	790	650

COSA = 790 – 650 = £140

(b)   *Analysis of holding gains*

	£
Realised holding gains:	
Stock sold in March (50 × (13 – 12))	50
Stock sold in August (30 × (15 – 12))	90
	140
Unrealised holding gains:	
Stock held 31.12.X0 (20 × (20 – 12))	160
Total holding gains for 20X0	300

Workings

(1)   Sales

	£
50 @ £20	1,000
30 @ £25	750
	1,750

(2)   Cost of sales

HC

80 @ £12	960

CC

50 @ £13	650
30 @ £15	450
	1,100

Multiple choice answers

1   B

Holding gain	=	Replacement cost at time of sale – original cost
	=	£24,000 - £20,000 = £4,000

2   B

Recoverable amount	=	£15,000
Value to the business	=	Lower of replacement cost and recoverable amount
	=	£13,000

3   C

	Real financial capital maintenance £	Operating capital maintenance £
Net assets at 31 December	120,000	120,000
Real financial capital (£100,000 × 1.03)	(103,000)	
Operating capital (£100,000 × 1.05)		(105,000)
	17,000	15,000

Chapter 17 solutions

Multiple choice answers

1   C

	£
Balance b/f	1,000
20X1 to 20X3	(300)
	700
20X4	(140)
20X5	(140)
	420

The unamortised cost is written off over the revised remaining useful life, commencing with the period in which the change is made.

2   B

As at 1 January 20X4 NBV was £104,400 and remaining useful life was six years.

Depreciation charge for 20X4 should be £104,400 ÷ 6 = £17,400.

3   B

4   D

	Land £000	Buildings £000	Total £000
Cost on 1 July 20W3	80	300	
Ten years' depreciation (300 × 4% × 10)		(120)	
Net book value at 30 June 20X3	80	180	260
Revaluation surplus	120	420	540
	200	600	800
Depreciation $\dfrac{600-100}{20}$			(25)
			775

Chapter 18 solutions

Multiple choice answers

1   B

	£	
NBV	253,000	
Less historical cost NBV	(207,000)	
	46,000	Dr STRGL (via revaluation reserve)

	£	
Historical cost NBV	207,000	
Less market value	(180,000)	
	27,000	Dr P&L account

2   C

	£000
400,000 × 4%	16
Wages and salaries	2,355
60,000 × 50%	30
	2,401

3   C

Only FRS 10 allows an indefinite life. CA85 states that goodwill has a finite life. CA 85 would only permit an indefinite life if the true and fair view override were invoked.

4   D

	£
Consideration	100,000
Fair value of separable net assets other than goodwill	(80,000)
	20,000

Chapter 19 solutions

1   Rubislaw plc

**Profit and loss account (extract)
for the year ended 31 December 20X3**

	£
Dividends received	800
Debenture interest received £2,250 × 100/80	2,812
Interest payable (£200,000 × 10%)	(20,000)
Tax on ordinary activities (**Note 1**) (**W1**)	(40,000)

Balance sheet (extract) at 31 December 20X3

	£
Creditors: Amounts falling due within one year	
Other creditors including taxation and social security (**Note 2**)	45,938

Notes to the accounts	£

(1)	*Tax on ordinary activities*	
	Corporation tax on ordinary activities (W1)	45,000
	Overprovision for previous year (W1)	(5,000)
		40,000

(2)	*Taxation (balance sheet)*	£
	Income tax (W2)	938
	Corporation tax due on 1.10.X4 (W3)	45,000
		45,938

Workings

(1)   *CT for accounting period ended 31.12.X3*

	£
Profits	150,000
Corporation tax at 30%	45,000

Tax charge for the year	£
CT for year ended 31.12.X3	45,000
Overprovision for 31.12.X2 (£74,000 – £69,000)	(5,000)
	40,000

(2)

Income tax account

	£		£
Cash	5,000	Balance b/f	2,500
Debenture interest		Debenture interest paid	
received £2,250 × 20/80	562	£200,000 × 10% × 20%	4,000
Balance c/f	938		
	6,500		6,500

(3)

Corporation tax account

	£		£
Cash	69,000	Balance b/f	74,000
Profit and loss (overprovision on 20X2)	5,000	Profit and loss (liability 20X3)	45,000
Balance c/f	45,000		
	119,000		119,000

Multiple choice answers

1   C

CT

	£		£
Cash	194,300	B/d	187,500
		Profit and loss account	6,800
	194,300		194,300
C/d	137,600	Profit and loss account	137,600
	137,600		137,600

2   B

CT

	£		£
Transfer from IT a/c (23,000 × 20%)	4,600	Profit and loss account	189,000
C/d	184,400		
	189,000		189,000

3   D

Both items must be grossed up to include income tax.

4   C

Entertaining expenses are disallowable against tax.

Chapter 20 solutions

Multiple choice answers

1   C

2   D

Actuarial gains and losses are recognised in the STRGL.

Chapter 21 solutions

Multiple choice answers

1   C

Goods not yet accepted should appear as stock at cost   =   £54,000 × 10%

=   £5,400

Remaining goods sold cost £48,600 (£54,000 × 90%)

Profit on these sales = £48,600 × 20/80   =   £12,150

2   B

3   D

According to FRS 5 this transaction would be treated not as a sale of the land but as a loan secured on the land. The interest of £200,000, the difference between the sale value and the repurchase price, would be charged to the profit and loss account for the year as an expense.

Chapter 22 solutions

Multiple choice answers

1   B

Year	Amount b/f £	Interest @ 9.5% £	Interest paid £	Amount c/f £
20X0	394,408	37,469	(20,000)	411,877
20X1	411,877	39,128	(20,000)	431,005
20X2	431,005	40,946	(20,000)	451,951

2   D

Year	Amount b/f £	Interest @ 8% £	Interest paid 4% £	Amount c/f £
20X0	467,000	37,360	(20,000)	484,360
20X1	484,360	38,749	(20,000)	503,109
20X2	503,109	40,249	(20,000)	523,358

Redeemed	£523,358 × 30%	=	£157,007
Converted	£523,358 × 70% × 40/£100	=	146,540 £1 ordinary shares
Share premium	£523,358 × 70% - £146,540	=	£219,811

Chapter 23 solutions

1   Flash

Profit and loss account extract

	20X3 £
Operating profit (note 1)	X
Interest payable and similar charges (note 2)	1,171
Profit on ordinary activities before taxation	X

Balance sheet extracts

	20X3 £
Fixed assets	
Tangible assets (note 3)	X
	X
Creditors: amounts falling due within one year (note 4)	X
Creditors: amounts falling due after more than one year (note 5)	X

Notes

(1)   *Operating profit*

Operating profit is arrived at after charging:

	20X3 £
Depreciation of owned assets	X
Depreciation of assets held under finance leases (W1)	6,157
Hire of plant and machinery – operating leases	10,000

(2)   *Interest payable and similar charges*

	£
Finance charges payable – finance leases (W2)	1,171

(3)   *Tangible assets*

	£
Cost at 1 January 20X3	X
Additions	X
Cost at 31 December 20X3	X
Accumulated depreciation at 1 January 20X3	X
Charge for the year	X
Accumulated depreciation at 31 December 20X3	X
Net book value at 31 December 20X3	X
Net book value at 1 January 20X3	X

The net book value of fixed assets of £X includes an amount of £55,413 in respect of assets held under finance leases.

(4) *Creditors: amounts falling due within one year*

	£
Trade creditors	X
Obligations under finance leases (note 6)	8,708
	X

(5) *Creditors: amounts falling due after more than one year*

	£
Debenture loans	X
Obligations under finance leases (note 6)	51,033
	X

(6) *Obligations under finance leases*

The minimum lease payments to which the company was committed at 31 December 20X3 are as follows:

	£	£
Under one year		12,000
Over one year		
In the second to fifth years inclusive	48,000	
Over five years	15,000	
		63,000
		75,000
Less: Interest allocated to future periods		
(16,430 – 1,171) (W2)		15,259
		59,741
Due within one year (W3)		8,708
Due after more than one year (W3)		51,033
		59,741

(7) *Commitments under operating leases*

At 31 December 20X3 the company had an annual commitment of £10,000 under a non-cancellable operating lease in respect of plant and machinery which expires after more than five years from the balance sheet date.

Workings

(W1) **Depreciation charge for the year**

Cost of asset	£61,570
Useful life	10 years
Depreciation charge	£6,157

(W2)   Interest on finance lease

	£
Cash price	61,570
Instalment 1 October 20X3	(3,000)
	58,570
Interest October – December 20X3 (2%)	1,171
Balance 31 December 20X3	59,741
Instalment 1 January 20X4	(3,000)
	56,741
Interest January – March 20X4 (2%)	1,135
Balance 31 March 20X4	57,876
Instalment 1 April 20X4	(3,000)
	54,876
Interest April – June 20X4 (2%)	1,098
Balance 30 June 20X4	55,974
Instalment 1 July 20X4	(3,000)
	52,974
Interest July – September 20X4 (2%)	1,059
Balance 30 September 20X4	54,033
Instalment 1 October 20X4	(3,000)
	51,033
Total payments 26 × £3,000	78,000
Cash price	61,570
Total interest	16,430

(W3)   Obligations under finance leases

	£
Balance at 31 December 20X3 (W2)	59,741
Less: Current portion (12,000 – (1,135 + 1,098 + 1,059) interest for January – September 20X4)	8,708
Deferred portion	51,033

Multiple choice answers

1 B

Sum of the digits	=	$\dfrac{12 \times 13}{2}$
	=	78

	£
Total payments 12 × £1,800	21,600
Deposit	5,000
Less capital	(20,000)
Total interest	6,600

Fifth repayment – Interest $\dfrac{8}{78}$ × £6,600 = £676.92, ie approximately £677

2 B

Interest charge for 20X7	=	12% × 12,000
	=	£1,440

3 B

The information suggests that a transference of risks and rewards has taken place. Therefore the lease is a finance lease and should be capitalised at the present value of the minimum lease payments, ie £220,000.

Chapter 24 solutions

1   Orlando

(a)   .   Potential benefits of greater harmonisation include the following.

(i)   *A user's perspective*

Cross border investment is increasing and it is important that potential investors are not misled by the financial statements. For example, there could be an assumption that the liquidity position of a company that makes a full provision for deferred tax liabilities is worse than that of a company that is only required to provide an amount that is likely to crystallise as a liability.

(ii)   *A preparer's perspective*

There is an increase in the cost of preparing financial statements that need to be adjusted to comply with different national accounting standards.

Obstacles hindering greater harmonisation include the following.

(i)   *Different legal systems*

Countries vary in the amount of detailed legislation on accounting that has been enacted. In Europe for example this meant that prior to the issue of EC Directives accounting requirements in the UK differed substantially from those in France.

(ii)   *Different capital financing systems*

Types of business organisation and their financing differ internationally and it therefore follows that if financiers and owners differ then the primary users of accounting information will differ. The rule makers in the US and UK regard the existing and potential investors as the primary users. However, there are other ways of financing business and capital provided by banks may be very significant. In Germany and Japan the banks are important owners of companies as well as providers of debt finance. This enables them to appoint directors and they will therefore be able to obtain information other than that which is included in the published annual report.

Where there are fewer outsider shareholders external reporting has been largely for the purposes of government, as tax collectors or controllers of the economy.

(iii)   *Degree to which taxation regulations determine accounting measurements*

In some countries the tax rules are the accounting rules. For example, although depreciation in the UK differs from the capital allowance for tax purposes, in other countries the accounting depreciation is required to be the same as the equivalent of the capital allowance for tax purposes.

(iv)   *Differences in the size and competence of the accounting/auditing profession*

The lack of a substantial body of private investors and public companies in some countries means that the need for and status of the auditors is much smaller than in the US or UK. Also there is an impact on the type of accounting that is or could be practised. Without a strong profession there is a limit to the extent to which national accounting standards can be developed.

(v)   *Environmental/cultural factors*

These include educational standards which can be an important factor in developing countries; political factors where there is central control over the accounting and reporting system; and cultural factors where for example cultures that tend towards secrecy are unlikely to adopt full disclosure-based financial reporting practices.

(b)   (i)   *Capitalised interest*

There is no mandatory requirement in the UK in respect of the capitalisation of interest (FRS 15 gives a choice) so companies have a choice of writing off or capitalising and amortising. Orlando group appears to have written off interest costs. In the US the interest relating to this fixed asset would be capitalised and amortised with an amortisation charge of £5 million.

Merger accounting adjusted to acquisition accounting

There has been a merger during the year which has satisfied UK criteria for treatment as a merger. The adjustment indicates that this has not however satisfied the US criteria. Consequently pre-acquisition profits of £190 million are eliminated on reconciliation, together with additional depreciation and amortisation of goodwill of £200 million.

(ii)   *Capitalised interest*

The equity will be increased by any unamortised balance outstanding.

Merger accounting adjusted to acquisition accounting

The equity will be increased by any increase in net assets (most likely) and decreased by any decrease in net assets (unlikely) arising from fair value adjustments. The equity would also be increased by the unamortised amount of any consolidated goodwill that would arise under acquisition accounting.

(iii)   *Proposed dividend*

The shareholders' equity will be increased by the amount of the proposed dividend because in the UK dividends are accounted for in the accounting period to which they relate.

Multiple choice answers

1   B

	£
Original profit	143,000
Additional deferred tax – full provision	(12,000)
Amendment of profit on sale (40 – 22)	(18,000)
Research costs written off	(16,000)
Amended profit	97,000

2   C

Chapter 25 solutions

Multiple choice answers

1   C

There is no legal or constructive obligation for Ferndale to incur the factory costs, therefore no provision is required.

Fernbank has a constructive obligation, due to its past actions, to clear up the contamination so a provision is required.

Chapter 26 solutions

1   Witton

(a)

(i)   Profitability

	20X6	20X5
Gross profit: Sales		

$\dfrac{\text{Gross profit}}{\text{Sales}} \times 100$ $\dfrac{2{,}070}{11{,}500} \times 100 = 18.0\%$ $\dfrac{1{,}850}{7{,}650} \times 100 = 24.2\%$

Return on capital employed

$\dfrac{\text{Profit before tax} + \text{Long-term interest}}{\text{Share capital} + \text{Reserves} + \text{Loans and other borrowings}}$ $\dfrac{1{,}550 + 350}{5{,}900 + 5{,}700 + 3{,}350} \times 100 = 12.7\%$ $\dfrac{1{,}650 + 50}{5{,}900 + 5{,}000 + 350} \times 100 = 15.1\%$

(ii)   Solvency

Gearing

$\dfrac{\text{Long - term borrowings}}{\text{Share capital} + \text{Reserves} + \text{Long-term borrowings}}$ $\dfrac{3{,}350}{11{,}600 + 3{,}350} \times 100 = 22.4\%$ $\dfrac{350}{10{,}900 + 350} \times 100 = 3.1\%$

Acid test

$\dfrac{\text{Current assets} - \text{Stock}}{\text{Current liabilities}}$ $\dfrac{6{,}300 - 2{,}450}{2{,}700} = 1.4$ $\dfrac{3{,}600 - 1{,}500}{2{,}400} = 0.9$

(iii)   Working capital

Trade debtors collection period

$\dfrac{\text{Trade debtors}}{\text{Credit sales}} \times 365$ $\dfrac{3{,}800}{11{,}500} \times 365 = 121 \text{ days}$ $\dfrac{1{,}200}{7{,}650} \times 365 = 57 \text{ days}$

Stock turnover

$\dfrac{\text{Cost of sales}}{\text{Year–end stock}}$ $\dfrac{9{,}430}{2{,}450} = 3.8 \text{ times pa}$ $\dfrac{5{,}800}{1{,}500} = 3.9 \text{ times pa}$

(Tutorial note

There is a wide range of ratios that could be calculated. However, to assist comments requested in part (b), it is advisable to choose some ratios in each area of profitability, solvency and working capital efficiency.)

(b)   Commentary on results

(i)   Profitability

The profit margin to sales has significantly decreased from 24% to 18%. Profitability to capital employed has also decreased from 15% to 12.7%. The decline in the first ratio is not surprising given the reduction in selling prices. Sales have significantly increased — a growth of

$$50\% \text{ ie} \left(\dfrac{11{,}500 - 7{,}650}{7{,}650} \times 100 \right)$$

The overall effect is an actual increase in gross profitability from £1,850,000 to £2,070,000. However, loan interest has eliminated this favourable result. Presumably the additional finance was raised for the sales expansion. To date, therefore, the expansion policy has not been successful but the additional finance may not be invested efficiently as yet. A more favourable result may be forthcoming next year.

(ii)   Liquidity

Owing to the expansion, cash balances have disappeared by the year end. There has been a large increase in other elements of working capital however. Provided that the increase in debtors simply represents the extended credit terms being offered to customers rather than problem payers, liquidity is healthy. The acid test ratio in fact shows an increase from 20X5 to 20X6.

(iii)   Efficiency

There has been little change in the stock turnover ratio. This may be a sign of inefficiency as, if the company is selling the same range of goods as before, the stock turnover ratio should increase if sales volume has been increased because of lower prices. The debtor collection period however has been greatly extended from 57 days to 121 days. 57 days was a long period in the first place, and it may be that the more generous credit terms are being abused by the customers.

Creditors have not increased in line with the expansion of sales volume (and thus purchases volume) thus increasing the pressure on funding working capital.

(iv)   Shareholders' interests

Shareholders have had a maintained dividend and have not been required to invest any further funds.

The return on shareholders' capital employed is:

	20X5	20X6
$\dfrac{\text{Profit before tax}}{\text{Share capital} + \text{reserves}}$	$\dfrac{1,650}{10,900} \times 100 = 15.1\%$	$\dfrac{1,550}{11,600} \times 100 = 13.4\%$

This shows a slight decline, owing to the growth in the profits of the business being swallowed up by interest charges. The shareholders' capital position is still satisfactory. The new loans may have raised the gearing ratio from 3% to 22% but 22% is still low.

Much will depend on whether the additional finance was sufficient for this year's and future years' expansion.

(c)   Further information

(i)   Profitability

Reason for raising the additional finance

Likely timing of increased profitability resulting from additional finance

(ii)   Liquidity

Reasons for increase in debtors other than extended credit terms

Bad debt write-offs this year compared with last

(iii)   Efficiency

Any change in the range of goods sold

(iv)   Shareholders' interest

Sufficiency of the additional finance for long-term trading

2   Big Brother

Report

To   The Directors, Big Brother Group plc

From   AN Accountant

Date   20 July 20X9

Subject   Big Brother Group plc — Profitability, liquidity and solvency of the group

(a)   Terms of reference

This report examines the profitability, liquidity and solvency of Big Brother in 20X7 and 20X8, and recommends necessary action. It is based on financial statements and industry statistics provided. Ratios calculated from the statutory accounts are included in Appendix 1.

(b)   Executive summary

The group is under capitalised, highly geared, and approaching a liquidity crisis. It is, however, profitable and the ordinary dividend was covered 12 times in 20X8 (20X7 14 times).

A rights issue to raise around £10 million is recommended. This would reduce gearing to around 50%, and provide the liquid funds needed.

(c)   Profitability

The gross margin has exceeded the industry norm at the same time as the net margin remained at industry levels. This discrepancy is probably due to non-standard cost allocations between cost of sales and other categories. This would also explain the low stock turnover ratio.

It is possible that the gross margins are genuinely high, in which case overheads are also high, and savings may be available. A comparison of Big Brother's and the industry's usual cost allocation methods would allow more conclusive analysis.

Return on capital has improved in the year, and is well above industry levels. The apparent improvement is due mainly to the lack of extra long-term finance referred to below, and is not an underlying strength.

(d)   Liquidity

Liquidity has deteriorated in the period, and the company is exhibiting signs of overtrading, its expansion not being financed by long-term methods.

The company is financing its increased working capital requirements out of rentals in advance. The low industry quick ratio indicates that some reliance on short-term finance is usual, but Big Brother's is excessive.

Unless further long-term finance is raised soon, the company will have liquidity problems.

(e)   Solvency

The company is highly geared compared to the industry average, although a slight improvement occurred in the year. The gearing ratios referred to in the Appendix exclude any overdrafts and loans included within current liabilities, and it is likely that underlying gearing is substantially higher.

The high level of gearing, allied to poor liquidity, casts doubt over the company's continued stability.

Appendix 1: Ratios

	Big Brother Group plc		Industry average
	20X8	20X7	
Gross profit margin	58.2%	57.8%	50%
Net profit margin	25.4%	24.9%	25%
Current ratio (including rentals in advance)	0.93	1.05	1.20
Quick ratio (including rentals in advance)	0.58	0.63	0.90

Gearing

$$\frac{5,000+30,105}{22,360+30,105+8,095} = 58\% \qquad \frac{5,000+27,419}{17,669+27,419+7,217} = 62\% \qquad 50\%$$

Stock turnover

$$\frac{21,705}{8,159} = 2.66 \qquad \frac{18,221}{7,181} = 2.54 \qquad 3.5$$

ROCE

$$\frac{13,157}{22,360+30,105+8,095} = 21.7\% \qquad \frac{10,761}{17,669+27,419+7,217} = 20.6\% \qquad 17\%$$

Dividend cover

$$\frac{5,391-300}{400} = 12.73 \qquad \frac{4,493-300}{300} = 13.98$$

Appendix 2

Assuming that £10 million is raised from a rights issue

Gearing
$$\frac{5,000+30,105}{22,360+30,105+8,095+10,000} = 49.8\%$$

Quick ratio
$$\frac{10,021+3,609+10,000}{15,215+8,261} = 1.01$$

(including rentals in advance)

Multiple choice answers

1   B

Return on long-term funds	$=$	$\dfrac{\text{Operating profit (before debenture interest)}}{\text{Share capital} + \text{Reserves} + \text{Debentures}}$
	$=$	$\dfrac{795}{4,000}$
	$=$	19.9%

2   D

Credit sales	$=$	£200 × 80%
	$=$	£160
Average debtors	$=$	$\dfrac{£(16+24)}{2}$
	$=$	£20

			£160
Debtors' turnover	=		$\dfrac{£160}{£20}$
	=		8 times
Collection period	=		$\dfrac{365}{8}$
	=		46 days

	£000	%
Sales	200	100
Cost of sales (40 + 120 – 50)	(110)	55
Gross profit	90	45

3   A

$$\frac{\text{Profit}}{\text{Capital employed}} = \frac{\text{Profit}}{\text{Turnover}} \times \frac{\text{Turnover}}{\text{Capital employed}}$$

(Return on capital employed)   (Profit margin)   (Asset turnover)

$$0.80 = \frac{\text{Profit}}{\text{Turnover}} \times 1.10$$

$$\frac{\text{Profit}}{\text{Turnover}} = \frac{0.80}{1.10}$$

$$= 0.73$$

4   B

Dividend yield	=	$\dfrac{\text{Dividend}}{\text{Share price}} \times 100\%$
Price earnings ratio	=	$\dfrac{\text{Share price}}{\text{Earnings per share}}$
Dividend cover	=	$\dfrac{\text{Earnings per share}}{\text{Dividend per share}}$
Let earnings per share	=	£1
Share price	=	6 × £1
	=	£6
Dividend	=	£1 ÷ 3
	=	33p
Dividend yield	=	$\dfrac{33p}{£6} \times 100\%$
	=	5.5%

Chapter 27 solutions

Multiple choice answers

1   D

Theoretical ex-rights price

				£
6 shares	@	£1.50	=	9.00
1 share	@	£1.15	=	1.15
7 shares	@	£1.45		10.15

Current year EPS

Earnings	=	£77,540

Shares

$600,000 \times 3/12 \times 1.50/1.45$	=	155,172
$700,000 \times 9/12$	=	525,000
		680,172

EPS 30 June 20X2	=	$\dfrac{£77,540}{680,172}$
	=	11.4 pence

Comparative EPS

10.8 pence $\times 1.45/1.50$	=	10.4 pence

2   B

Basic EPS	=	$\dfrac{548,000 + 102,000}{1,600,000}$
	=	40.6 pence

	£	£
Diluted EPS		
Basic earnings		650,000
Add interest saved £200,000 × 5%	10,000	
Less tax	(3,000)	
		7,000
		657,000

Number of shares	=	$1,600,000 + £200,000 \times 120/£100$
	=	1,840,000

Diluted EPS	=	$\dfrac{£657,000}{1,840,000}$
	=	35.7 pence

3 B

Basic EPS

		£
Profit after tax		232,000
Less preference dividend		(24,000)
Earnings		208,000

Basic EPS	=	$\dfrac{£208,000}{1,000,000}$
	=	20.8 pence

Diluted EPS – number of shares

Options	=	200,000 × £1.50
	=	£300,000
At fair value	=	$\dfrac{£300,000}{£1.90}$
	=	157,895
Shares issued free	=	200,000 – 157,895
	=	42,105
Diluted EPS	=	$\dfrac{£208,000}{1,042,105}$
	=	20.0 pence

Chapter 28 solutions

Multiple choice answers

1   A

Common costs can be deducted from the total of segment results rather than allocated to segments.

Index

Abstract 4 202
Abstract 5 253
Abstract 9 138
Abstract 19 139
Abstract 21 139
Abstract 27 260
Abstract 29 253
Accounting policies 201
Acquisition of subsidiary mid-year 30, 57
Aggregation 199
Applied research 260
Articulation 199
ASC handbook 241
Asset valuation 237
Assets 197, 292
Associate 35, 50
Associate becoming subsidiary 105
Associate held by subsidiary 86

Capital reconstruction schemes 183
Cash flow risk 304
Cash flow statements 161
Classification 199
Closing rate method 123
Comparability 196
Conceptual framework 195
Consignment stock 294
Consolidated accounts 2
Consolidated balance sheet 3, 84
Consolidated Profit and Loss Account 45, 96
Contingencies 221
Contributions from owners 197
Convertible instruments 302
Credit risk 304
Credit sale 314
Currency risk 304
Current cost accounting 236
Current tax 273
Current value accounting 234

Deemed disposal 155
Deferred tax 277
Defined benefit scheme 284
Defined contribution scheme 283
Demergers 156
Depreciation 250
Derivative 304
Development costs 260
Diluted EPS 370
Discontinued operations 206
Discounting 336
Disposals 143
Distributions to owners 197
Dividends from subsidiary 28
Dividends out of pre-acquisition profit 31
D-shaped groups 92

Earnings per share 359, 367
Elements of financial statements 197
Environmental reporting 339
Equity instrument 304
Equity method of accounting 36, 50
Equity shares 299
European Eco-Management and Audit Scheme
   (EMAS) 339
Exclusion from consolidation 16
Exempt groups 14
Extended credit agreement 313
External reconstructions 189

Factoring of debts 295
Fair value 63
Fair value adjustments 64
Finance costs 248
Finance leases 314
Financial asset 304
Financial instrument 304
Financial liability 304
Financial Reporting Standard for Smaller
   Entities (FRSSE) 223
Financial review 224
Foreign currency 113, 123
FRED 8 333
FRED 22 219
FRED 23 309
FRED 24 140
FRED 25 333
FRED 26 373
FRED 27 334
FRED 28 335
FRED 29 252
FRED 30 310
FRED 31 225
FRS 1 162
FRS 2 .... 14, 108
FRS 3 205
FRS 4 299
FRS 5 292
FRS 6 71
FRS 7 63
FRS 8 333
FRS 9 .... 36, 61
FRS 10 .... 19, 257
FRS 11 264
FRS 12 219
FRS 13 303
FRS 14 367
FRS 15 247
FRS 16 273
FRS 17 283
FRS 18 201
FRS 19 280
Full provision basis 279
Funded scheme 284

Gains 197
Gearing ratios 357
Goodwill 19, 257
Goodwill on acquisition 3
Government grants 247
Gross equity accounting 41
Group structure 2

Hedging 118
Hedging in group accounts 139
Hicks and Fisher 232
Hire purchase 314
Historical cost v revaluation 216
Holding gains 242
Human resource accounting 345
Hyper-inflationary economies 137

Impairment 264
Increasing stake in subsidiary 102
Information needs 347
Inherent goodwill 258
Intangible assets 258
Interest rate risk 304
Internally generated intangible assets ... 259
International Accounting Standards Committee
     (IASC) 329
International harmonisation 327
International Standard ISO 14001 ... 339
Interpretation of a cash flow statement 172
Interpretation of accounts 347
Intra-group balances 11
Intra-group transactions 46, 51
Investment properties 252
Investments by subsidiary 82
Investors' ratios 358

Joint ventures 41, 60

Leases: implementation of a new approach ... 324
Leasing 313
Liabilities 197, 292
Linked presentation 293
Liquidation 189
Liquidity ratios 354
Liquidity risk 304
Loan transfers 295
Long-term contracts 297, 335
Losses 197

Market price risk 304
Materiality 196
Merger relief provisions 72
Mergers 69
Mid-year acquisition 30
Minority interest 3, 6
Mixed group 92

Negative purchased goodwill 258
Net investment in a lease 319
Net realisable value 264
Non-equity shares 299

Objective of financial statements ... 195
Off balance sheet gearing 315
Offset 293
Operating and Financial Review 339
Operating gains 242
Operating lease 315, 322
Ownership in group accounts 8
Ownership interest 197

Partial disposal 150, 151, 153
Partial provision 279
Pensions 283
Permanent differences 277
Piecemeal acquisitions 101
Positive purchased goodwill 258
Post balance sheet events 334
Post-acquisition reserves 10
Pre-acquisition reserves 8, 31
Preference shares in subsidiary 24, 54
Presentation of financial information ... 198
Price level accounting 231
Price-earnings ratio 359
Prior period adjustments 212
Private Finance Initiative 295
Profitability ratios 350
Proportional consolidation 41
Provisions 220
Purchased intangible assets 259
Pure (or basic) research 260

Qualitative characteristics of financial
     information 196
Quasi-subsidiaries 293

Ratio analysis 347
Recognition in financial statements ... 198
Reconciliation of movements in shareholders'
     funds 210
Reconstruction 186
Recoverable amount 264
Related parties 333
Reporting financial performance 205
Reporting financial performance: Proposals for
     change 218
Reporting the substance of transactions ... 291
Research costs 261
Residual value 251
Return on capital employed (ROCE) ... 350
Risk 304

Sale and repurchase agreements 294
Scrip dividend 302
Securitised assets 295
Segment net assets 377
Segment result 377
Segmental reporting 375
Share reduction 185
Share-based payment 225
Single entity concept 2, 11
Social reporting 344
SSAP 2 (withdrawn) 201

SSAP 4 253
SSAP 5 271
SSAP 9 335
SSAP 13 260
SSAP 17 334
SSAP 19 247
SSAP 19 252
SSAP 20 113
SSAP 21 313
SSAP 25 375
Statement of principles 195, 291
Statement of total recognised gains and losses
.... 210
Statements of financial performance 199
Subsidiary 14
Substance over form 291, 314
Summary financial statements 224
Supplementary information 200

Tangible fixed assets 247
Tax credit 274
Taxation in company accounts 271
Temporal method 128
Time apportionment 58
Timing differences 277

UK GAAP 332
Unfunded scheme 284
Unrealised profit 23, 92
US GAAP 332
Useful economic life 251

Valuation gains and losses 249
Value added tax 271
Value in use 264
Value to the business 237
Vertical groups 81
Voluntary liquidation 189

Warrants 302
Withholding tax 275

Year-end financial reports: improving
  communication 224

Exam Text Review Form

CIMA PAPER 7a TEXT – FINANCIAL REPORTING

We hope that you have found this Text stimulating and useful and that you now feel confident and well-prepared for your examinations.

We would be grateful if you could take a few moments to complete the questionnaire below, so we can assess how well our material meets your needs. There's a prize for four lucky students who fill in one of these forms from across the Syllabus range and are lucky enough to be selected!

	Excellent	*Adequate*	*Poor*
Depth and breadth of technical coverage			
Appropriateness of coverage to examination			
Presentation			
Level of accuracy			

Did you spot any errors or ambiguities? Please let us have the details below.

Page	Error

Thank you for your feedback.

Please return this form to:

The Financial Training Company Limited
Unit 2, Block 2, Wincombe Conference Centre
Wincombe Business Park
Shaftesbury
Dorset SP7 9QJ

Student's name: ....

Address: ....

....

....

CIMA Publications Student Order Form

THE
FINANCIAL TRAINING
COMPANY
PUBLICATIONS DIVISION

To order your books, please indicate quantity required in the relevant order box, calculate the amount(s) in the column provided, and add postage to determine the amount due. Please then clearly fill in your details plus method of payment in the boxes provided and return your completed form with payment attached to:

THE FINANCIAL TRAINING COMPANY, 22J WINCOMBE BUSINESS PARK, SHAFTESBURY, DORSET SP7 9QJ

OR FAX YOUR ORDER TO 01747 858821 OR TELEPHONE 01747 854302

For examinations in Nov 03 ❑ May 04 ❑ Nov 04 ❑ (please tick)

FOUNDATION

PAPER	TITLE	TEXT ORDER	PRICE £	EXAM KIT ORDER	PRICE £	FOCUS NOTES ORDER	PRICE £	AMOUNT £
1	Financial Accounting Fundamentals		21.00		11.00		6.00	
2	Management Accounting Fundamentals		21.00		11.00		6.00	
3a	Economics for Business		21.00		11.00		6.00	
3b	Business Law		21.00		11.00		6.00	
3c	Business Mathematics		21.00		11.00		6.00	

INTERMEDIATE

PAPER	TITLE	TEXT ORDER	PRICE £	EXAM KIT ORDER	PRICE £	FOCUS NOTES ORDER	PRICE £	AMOUNT £
4	Finance		21.00		11.00		6.00	
5	Business Taxation [FA 2002] (May & Nov 2003)		21.00		11.00		6.00	
	Business Taxation [FA 2003] (May & Nov 2004)		21.00	Available Feb 04	11.00	Available Feb 04	6.00	
6a	Financial Accounting (UK Standards)		21.00		11.00		6.00	
7a	Financial Reporting (UK Standards)		21.00		11.00		6.00	
8	Management Accounting - Performance Management		21.00		11.00		6.00	
9	Management Accounting - Decision Making		21.00		11.00		6.00	
10	Systems & Project Management		21.00		11.00		6.00	
11	Organisational Management		21.00		11.00		6.00	

FINAL

PAPER	TITLE	TEXT ORDER	PRICE £	EXAM KIT ORDER	PRICE £	FOCUS NOTES ORDER	PRICE £	AMOUNT £
12	Management Accounting - Business Strategy		21.00		11.00		6.00	
13	Management Accounting - Financial Strategy		21.00		11.00		6.00	
14	Management Accounting - Information Strategy		21.00		11.00		6.00	
15	Management Accounting - Case Study		21.00					

Sub Total	£	
Postage and packing – please note a signature is required on delivery *UK & NI* £5 for up to 10 books If only Focus Notes are ordered, £1 each (max £5) **First book** **Each additional book** *Europe* £25 £3 *Rest of World* £40 £4	£	
TOTAL PAYMENT	£	

The following section **must be filled in clearly** so that your order can be despatched without delay.

TO PAY FOR YOUR ORDER TICK AN OPTION BELOW

A. I WISH TO PAY BY   MASTERCARD ❑   VISA ❑   DELTA ❑   SWITCH ❑

CARD NO. ⌷⌷⌷⌷ ⌷⌷⌷⌷ ⌷⌷⌷⌷ ⌷⌷⌷⌷ (Some cards don't need all boxes)

EXPIRY DATE ⌷⌷⌷⌷   ISSUE No. ⌷⌷⌷ (Switch only)   All cards - last 3 digits on signature strip ⌷⌷⌷

Cardholder's Signature _____

Cardholder's Name & Address: _____

Cardholder's Tel. No. (Day):

B. I WISH TO PAY BY CHEQUE ❑ Cheques should be made payable to **_The Financial Training Company Ltd_** and must be attached to your order form. **Personal cheques cannot be accepted without a valid Banker's Card number written on the back of the cheque.**

STUDENT NAME:		
DELIVERY ADDRESS: (Must be the same as cardholder's address. Please contact us if you wish to discuss an alternative delivery address.)		
POST CODE:	TEL. NO. (Day):	

April 2003 (This order form replaces any previous order forms.)